THE FALL OF EGYPT AND
THE RISE OF ROME

Στη μνήμη της Α. και του Α.
για την ανθεκτικότητα, την ευεργεσίαν και τη προνοητικότητα τους

THE FALL OF EGYPT AND THE RISE OF ROME

A History of the Ptolemies

GUY DE LA BÉDOYÈRE

YALE UNIVERSITY PRESS
NEW HAVEN AND LONDON

For information about this and other Yale University Press publications, please contact:
U.S. Office: sales.press@yale.edu   yalebooks.com
Europe Office: sales@yaleup.co.uk   yalebooks.co.uk

Set in Adobe Garamond Pro by IDSUK (DataConnection) Ltd
Printed in Great Britain by Clays Ltd, Elcograf S.p.A

Library of Congress Control Number: 2024937311

ISBN 978-0-300-27552-0

A catalogue record for this book is available from the British Library.

10 9 8 7 6 5 4 3 2 1

CONTENTS

CONTENTS

PLATES AND MAPS

PLATES

All photographs are by the author unless otherwise stated.

1. Temple of Isis at Philae from the adjacent island of Bigeh, by David Roberts, 1838. Public domain.
2. Bust of Alexander the Great, Alexandria, and Alexander at the Temple of Luxor.
3. Tetradrachms of Alexander and Ptolemy I Soter, Memphis and Alexandria. Private collection.
4. Tomb of Petosiris, Tuna el-Gebel.
5. Limestone relief of Arsinoe II. Arthur M. Sackler Museum, Harvard University, Cambridge, Massachusetts. Photo: PP Daderot.
6. The Canopus Decree, copy found at Tanis. Photo: 𐤍𐤊𐤂𐤇.
7. Site of the Labyrinth, Hawara, stripped out by Ptolemy II.
8. Papyrus from the archive of Zenon during the reign of Ptolemy II (?), the Fayum.
9. The eastern Mediterranean from Lindos, Rhodes.
10. Coins of Ptolemy IV–X. 1 & 5: CNG; 2, 3 & 4: private collection.

11. Ptolemy VI Philometor and Cleopatra II, Kom Ombo.
12. Ptolemy VIII, Cleopatra II, and Cleopatra III, Kom Ombo. Photo: Rémih.
13. Ptolemy IX, gateway added to Medinet Habu, Thebes.
14. Ptolemy XII Neos Dionysos symbolically smites his enemies, Temple of Horus, Edfu.
15. Remains of the hypostyle hall, Temple of Sobek and Haroeris, Kom Ombo.
16. Tetradrachms of the period. Antony and Cleopatra: CNG; all others: private collection.
17. Ptolemaic-era Greek-style mosaic from a house in Alexandria. Cairo, Museum of Egyptian Civilization.
18. Ptolemaic-era burials: coffins of Harsinakht (Kharga Oasis), Nedjemankh (Heracleopolis Magna), and Hornedjitef (Thebes). Photo of Hornedjitef: geni.
19. Ptolemy XII enjoys the protection of Egypt's traditional gods, Temple of Sobek and Haroeris, Kom Ombo.
20. Statue of Pen-Menkh, governor of Dendera under Cleopatra VII. Cairo, Museum of Egyptian Civilization.
21. Thutmose III and Ptolemy XV Caesarion, Karnak.
22. Tomb relief showing a Roman trireme warship, Ostia, Italy, c. 25–20 BC.
23. Cleopatra VII and Caesarion at the Temple of Hathor, Dendera.
24. Relief of Augustus and obelisk from Heliopolis of Psammetichus I.

MAPS AND PLANS

FOREWORD

The story of the Ptolemaic rulers of Egypt is an allegory for all regimes including Rome, their nemesis. This book's title does not mean that the Ptolemaic pharaohs were doomed to destruction from self-inflicted wounds and the merciless brutality of an opportunistic Roman Empire. Instead, the earlier Ptolemies (which means both male and female rulers) met the challenge of state-building with aplomb, imagination, and accomplishment, but they and their successors ruled in febrile times. From the outset the new Egypt was at war with one or more of the other Hellenistic kingdoms which enervated them all. The ceaseless posturing and fighting, and the maintenance of an extravagant court, were ruinously expensive.

What matters in life is not what goes right, but what goes wrong and how one deals with that. Despite proving more resilient than their rivals, the Ptolemaic rulers were increasingly confronted by other challenges, including rebellions at home and the rising power of Rome, and their own descent into murderous family feuds and power games. They turned to Rome for help and to intercede in their affairs but became dependent on the Romans to stay in power. A dangerous combination of accumulating factors led to their fall, and finally the annexation of Egypt by Octavian in 30 BC.

By the late fourth century BC Classical Greece was giving way to the Hellenistic era. This term defines the politics, culture, and art of the Greek-speaking kingdoms and autonomous cities across territory now known to us as Greece, Macedonia, Bulgaria, Turkey, and Syria. They were clustered around the Aegean, the Black Sea, and the eastern Mediterranean.

Athens, once the shining star of intellectual and political development, was on the wane, shattered by the Peloponnesian War (431–404 BC) against Sparta. The dominant power in the area was Macedon, first under Philip II (ruled 359–336 BC), but far more importantly under his son Alexander III, the Great (ruled 336–323 BC). Carthage, a trading settlement founded by the Levantine Phoenicians in what is now modern Tunisia, was the major naval power in the western Mediterranean. The Persian Empire's greatest days were long past, knocked back by the Greeks in the fifth century BC. Under Artaxerxes III (359–338 BC) Persia looked briefly to be on the brink of a revival with his recapture of Egypt.

When Alexander crossed into Egypt in 332 BC the ancient dynastic land's history already stretched back almost three millennia. By *c.* 1600 BC Egypt had passed through the Old and Middle Kingdoms and the second of two intermediate periods when the country fragmented into petty fiefdoms and kingdoms. The Delta region was then ruled by Asiatic invaders called the Hyksos, expelled by Ahmose I (*c.* 1550–1525 BC). He regarded his grandmother Tetisheri as his key dynastic forebear, an important symbol of the role of women in Egypt.[1] During the 18th Dynasty (*c.* 1550–1295 BC), which he founded, Egypt's power was unmatched in the region with a succession of warrior pharaohs such as Thutmose III (1479–1425 BC) who fought wars of conquest into Nubia and Syria. During this time some of the earliest signs of Greek contact emerged, well over a millennium before Alexander.

In around 1069 BC the declining New Kingdom gave way to another period of anarchy. From *c.* 945 BC Egypt was taken over by Libyan kings who ruled as pharaohs and lost Nubia. In *c.* 747 BC the Nubians took control of Egypt (25th Dynasty) but they faced the rising power of the Assyrians. Under Assyrian influence and with their approval, the native 26th ('Saïte') Dynasty was established in 664 BC, named after its base at Saïs in the Delta. Psammetichus I (Psamtik I, 664–610 BC) oversaw the return of Egypt's prosperity briefly, along with a deliberate revival of its cultural traditions. Older monuments and relics provided inspiration, leading to works that are difficult to distinguish from earlier ones. Psammetichus also established a town in the Delta called Naucratis to act as port of entry for trade from the Greek world.

The Saïte era lasted only just over 130 years. In 525 BC Persia toppled Psammetichus III. Egypt was seized by the Persian king Cambyses II, becoming a province (satrapy). Although the Persians established military control of Egypt, they did not fundamentally change the country. However, with no resident king in Egypt there was no-one to protect and preserve Egyptian culture. According to Strabo, in a fit of 'madness and sacrilege' Cambyses wrecked both temples and obelisks at Heliopolis, with several of the latter still lying several centuries later where they had fallen. Even the standing ones still visibly bore fire damage.[2]

Unsurprisingly, none of this endeared the Persians to the Egyptians who transferred to the new invaders a long-established public contempt for foreigners. In practice, immigrants continued to be readily absorbed on an individual basis as they had been for centuries. Cambyses was persuaded by an Egyptian priest called Uzahorresneit to adopt the trappings and titles of a pharaoh when he came to Saïs. Cambyses did not live long enough to reform his character and find a long-lasting relationship with the Egyptians. In 522 BC he died and was briefly succeeded by his brother Bardiya before being overthrown by a noble who became king as Darius I (522–486 BC). Darius understood how to embrace Egyptian traditions and religion but those who came after his death were far less accommodating.

Taking advantage of the hatred for the Persians, an Egyptian rebel called Amyrtaeus from Saïs managed to restore Egyptian independence but failed to establish any stability. He was followed by the short-lived 29th Dynasty. It was not until 380 BC that Nectanebo (more accurately Nakhthorheb) I established the 30th Dynasty and began a programme of restoring Egyptian monuments and culture. Nectanebo I was briefly followed by his ambitious son Djedhor/Teos (362–360 BC) who was forced off the throne when he over-taxed Egypt to prosecute a war against Persia. He was replaced by his nephew Nectanebo II who followed his grandfather's policies. Nectanebo II fled after being defeated by the Persians at Pelusium in 343 BC and disappeared from history (see Chapter 10 for his sarcophagus).

The Persians moved in again, determined to crush Egyptian resistance, but folded in the face of the rise of Macedon under Philip II and then Alexander the Great. Alexander's victory over Darius III (336–330 BC) at the Battle of Issus in 333 BC shifted the balance of power in favour of the Hellenistic world and ended Persian ambitions. Mazaces, the last Persian satrap (governor) of Egypt, waved Alexander into Egypt in 332 BC to save himself and the country from a war of conquest. Alexander was received as a liberator.

Alexander's premature death in 323 BC led to the division of some of his vast empire into new Hellenistic states. Each was ruled by one of his chief followers, among them Ptolemy who took control of Egypt. Their struggle for primacy eventually made them easy prey for Rome which in just over a century became the most powerful state in the Mediterranean, North Africa, and the Near East.

To begin with, Rome was just background noise from the west. Founded in 753 BC, according to myth, Rome was ruled by kings until 509 BC when the last was expelled and the Roman Republic established. This unique institution was less susceptible to the vagaries of a dynastic monarchy but was instead prone to other abuses. By around the time Alexander took Egypt, Rome was still immersed in taking control of Italy. Within 120 years it had become a naval power and defeated Carthage, its greatest rival. Less than two centuries later Augustus, its first emperor, ruled much of the known world. During that time

Ptolemaic Egypt had moved from being the richest and most successful of the post-Alexander Hellenistic kingdoms to becoming a Roman province.

Today, apart from Cleopatra VII, the Ptolemaic story is little known in modern popular culture but contains many of the same dramatic ingredients of the history of the Roman Empire and other regimes. This was a world of war on land and sea, jealousy and greed, extravagance and excess, internecine feuds, murderous ambition, decline, and collapse. Ptolemaic Egypt included some of the most memorable characters of all ancient history, intellectual enlightenment in the legendary city of Alexandria, imaginative and effective state-building utilizing a highly developed bureaucracy, and a hybrid culture epitomized in their magnificent traditional temple architecture (plate 1).

N.B. The numbering of the various Ptolemies, Berenices, Arsinoes, and Cleopatras of the dynasty is a modern convention. Thanks to various complications and reconsiderations, some of this numbering has changed over the years, particularly with the later incumbents, meaning that cross-referencing with certain older books can be confusing. There are further complications with the titles and prerogatives of the Ptolemaic queens. These are discussed in the text and Appendix 3.

Hyperlinks have been provided for some source material in the Notes and in the Further Reading section. These were correct at the time of going to press, but hyperlinks are liable to change or disappear over time.

Guy de la Bédoyère
Lincolnshire, England, 2024

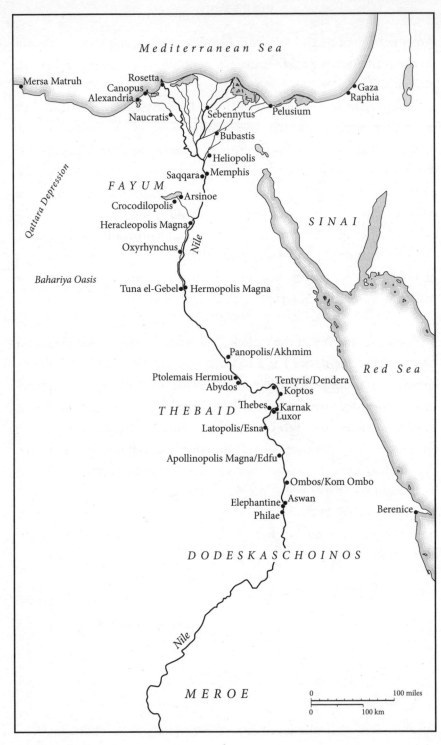

1. Egypt 332–330 BC.

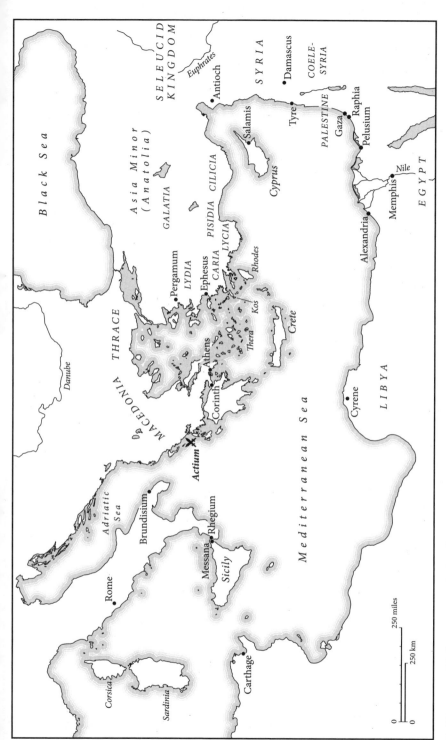

2. The eastern Mediterranean in the late first millennium BC.

INTRODUCTION

From 323–330 BC Egypt was ruled by the Macedonian Ptolemaic dynasty descended from Ptolemy I Soter (king from 305 BC), one of Alexander the Great's generals. It was one of the longest of Egypt's dynasties.[1] The old country was transformed into Egypt's Gilded Age under the Macedonian Raj of the Ptolemaic kings, though unlike the British in India, and the Persians in Egypt, the Ptolemies at least ruled in Egypt.[2] For some of that time Egypt's power was greater and more far-reaching than it had ever been in earlier ages. The Ptolemies introduced a dominant Macedonian-Greek ruling class while at the same time flattering and absorbing Egyptian royal and religious traditions.[3]

Ptolemy I and some of his successors had real ability as rulers. Others descended into venal mayhem. What began well ended badly. This is no less true of Rome, first in the fall of the Roman Republic and then under the emperors. Their stories are all those of the human condition and the corrosive effects of power.

For ancient historians, Ptolemaic Egypt's subsequent decline served as an enticing and gratifyingly familiar moral tale of rise followed by fall, precipitated by the corruption of Greek culture when exposed to oriental decadence and despotism. That narrative arc has proved resilient because there is some truth in it. Classical historians were no less interested in the parallel rise of Rome, often being Romans or philo-Romans themselves. Some, such as Livy, openly feared how the Roman people were succumbing to the effects of wealth bringing 'destruction to one and all through debauchery and extravagance'.[4]

Ptolemy I's rule was an accident of fate that came about only because of Alexander's unexpected death in 323 BC. Ptolemy did not plot, fight, or usurp his way to power. He was granted Egypt when Alexander's empire was divided up, establishing an absolute monarchy which derived its characteristics and legitimacy from both older Egyptian royal traditions and Hellenistic models.

Ptolemaic Egypt was stabler than any of the other Hellenistic monarchies that emerged after Alexander the Great's death and better able to combat threats from its rivals, at least to begin with. The Ptolemies established dynamic dynastic prestige, presented in a unique combination of Hellenistic and Egyptian idiom. Despite dissolving into family feuds and seeing Egypt's wealth and influence waning, the Ptolemies held on to power for a remarkable length of time. Part of the reason was an increasing reliance on Rome as it emerged onto the world stage.

Rome had started out as little more than a fortified collection of hilltop villages clustered along the banks of the Tiber, not far from the coast of the Tyrrhenian Sea. When Ptolemy I became king in Egypt, Rome was still midway through three wars in Italy against the Samnite peoples and trying to bring its recalcitrant Latin allies to heel. Rome differed from most other ancient civilizations, and particularly the Hellenistic kingdoms, because it had expelled its kings in 509 BC and established an elective republic based on a property qualification. While this brought new and dangerous tensions, the republican constitution was the bedrock on which Rome's resilience was built, even though it consisted only of principles and precedent rather than a formal written code.

INTRODUCTION

THE TURNING POINT

In 217 BC Ptolemy IV defeated Antiochus III of the Seleucid kingdom at Raphia (Gaza). The Ptolemaic regime was at the height of its powers. Ptolemy IV failed to pursue the victory for several reasons, some sensible and others negligent. The rest of his reign was compromised by serious outbreaks of domestic resistance which were to last well into the reign of his son and beyond. This opposition, which had first emerged in 245 BC, was provoked by the way the Ptolemies exploited Egypt. It was exacerbated by periods of famine and shortage, leading to the establishment of short-lived native-led regimes in Upper Egypt. These rebellions proved very difficult to suppress and damaged royal authority. Thereafter, Egypt's fortunes faded, but not without moments when it seemed recovery might be at hand, for example in 146 BC when Ptolemy VI was declared king of Egypt and Asia.

Soon after Raphia, as the Ptolemies fumbled their way into murderous dynastic infighting and opportunistic and more unnecessary wars, Rome emerged as the greatest political and military force in the Mediterranean world. This was thanks to its unexpected victories in the first two Punic Wars (264–241 BC and 218–201 BC) and the scratch creation of a navy. Nonetheless, in 217 BC Rome was catastrophically defeated by the Carthaginians under Hannibal on land at Lake Trasimene in Italy. This should have annihilated the Romans, especially as an even greater disaster followed at Cannae in 216 BC. However, the Roman response was to return to the fray with even greater determination which proved to be decisive. In 202 BC the Romans defeated Carthage in its homeland at Zama. With their navy, the Romans could now go where they pleased and strike where they pleased. Roman seapower was to play a fundamental role in ending the Ptolemaic dynasty in 31–30 BC.

The history of the Ptolemies is thereafter littered with increasing references to Rome. Roman interference in Egyptian affairs was inevitable because the weakened Ptolemies looked to Rome for help. In the century following the Second Punic War Rome defeated the Macedonians and the Seleucids, destroyed Carthage once and for all, seized Greece, advanced into Spain, and acquired Asia Minor by bequest. The Ptolemaic kingdom and its possessions steadily shrank in the face of a leviathan.

THE NATURE OF EGYPT

Egypt was known to the Ptolemies and subsequently the Romans as Aegyptos, though spelled in Greek Αἴγυπτος (*Aigyptos*), a Greek word with its origins in one of the ancient names of the country, *Hewet-ka-Ptah*. This means 'Mansion of the Soul of Ptah', the ancient name of the Temple of Ptah at Memphis.

Egypt is a country like no other. Without the Nile it could not be one at all. Most of the land is largely useless for human life. Thanks to the annual inundations, now curtailed by the construction of the Aswan High Dam, the result was a naturally fertile valley that snaked like a ribbon through the desert from south to north. The cultivatable land fanned out into the Delta, where the Nile reaches the Mediterranean. To the southwest of the Delta lies the Fayum depression surrounding Lake Moeris, itself supplied by a channel from the Nile. In antiquity, and especially the Graeco-Roman era when it was greatly enlarged by drainage and irrigation, the Fayum was one of the most important agricultural zones.

In earlier dynastic times, Asiatics to the north and Nubians to the south were routinely depicted as chaotic, cowardly, and hapless foes led by imbeciles, against whom the valiant semi-divine pharaoh defended his people. This was so familiar a trope that these traditional enemies became a mainstay of pharaonic art. The Egyptian king was shown locked in timeless combat, smiting or running them down in his chariot, his legitimacy enshrined in his unmatchable capacity to protect the country from the forces of chaos and preserve Maat (the Egyptian concept of harmony, cosmic order, and truth). Times were changing. The Saïte kings of the 26th Dynasty had established much stronger links to the Greek world, for example through the trading city of Naucratis in the Delta serving by *c.* 570 BC as the conduit of Greek trade.[5] The Ptolemies and their administrations were more in tune with the outside world; after all, these new kings were Macedonian Greeks. They were serious players in a more far-ranging and international environment.

ALEXANDER THE GREAT

Alexander III of Macedon was compassionate, brave, and charismatic. He was also impulsive, ruthless, and brutal. Alexander's titanic personality was as vulnerable to fate as anyone else's. By dying from a sudden illness in Babylon in 323 BC, shortly before his thirty-third birthday, Alexander the Great saved himself the trouble of planning for the succession but left the intractable problem to others to solve. The main obstacle was that none of them was Alexander, or anything like him.

Alexander also escaped taking responsibility for creating the administration and bureaucracy necessary to manage the paper empire he had won so quickly. His ill-timed death opened a Pandora's box. The only available heir of his Argead dynastic royal house of Macedon was Alexander's intellectually-disabled half-brother Philip Arrhidaeus. Alexander's widow Roxane was only a few months away from giving birth, but to whom or what remained to be seen. In the settlement that followed, Philip became king as Philip III. The real power was in the hands of Alexander's friends and generals known as the *Diadochi*, 'the Successors', except that they were uncertain what to do with it.

THE FIRST PTOLEMY

Alexander's death was followed initially by a civilized division of the spoils by the Diadochi. They took individual control of vast swathes of his territory. Ptolemy, son of Lagus, was granted Egypt, which he governed as satrap (from *khshathapavan*, the Persian term for a governor). He immediately set about expanding his territorial control and influence west across to Cyrene and throughout the region. If that sounds straightforward, it was anything but. The Wars of the Successors followed Alexander's death, during which time Philip III was murdered.

He was succeeded by Alexander IV, the son Roxane had given birth to, still only a small boy, who was assassinated too (see Chapter 2).

The Successors started turning themselves into kings, some forming alliances. Ptolemy arranged to have himself declared king in Egypt in 305 BC. All his male successors bore the name Ptolemy, which came from the Greek word πόλεμος/πτόλεμος (*polemos* or its older form *ptolemos*) for 'war' or 'battle', employing the prefix form πτ (pt), and was derived from Homer's Epic Greek poetry.[6] Ptolemy had taken power as a Hellenistic monarch, just as some of the other Successors had, but, unlike them, on public monuments within Egypt the Ptolemies would pose as pharaohs of old.

When they started out, the Ptolemaic kings would have cheered the soul of the conquering Ramesses II, the Great (*c.* 1279–1213 BC) of the 19th Dynasty, whose body had been quietly rotting in a lost cache of royal mummies at Thebes for eight centuries by then. In contrast, the body of Alexander the Great survived as the great religious and political relic of the Ptolemies in Alexandria, conferring legitimacy on their rule and available for visiting dignitaries to gaze upon in wonder. New hieroglyphic texts on temple walls and other monuments proclaimed the Ptolemies with all the old titles and slogans of the days when Egypt bestrode the region like a colossus. The continued use of hieroglyphs helped maintain traditional pharaonic identity.[7]

Compared to earlier Egyptian history, the three centuries of the Ptolemaic era can seem like little more than an interlude, no more than a 'tiny slice', of the whole before ancient Egypt came to an end.[8] This overlooks that for the people who lived in Ptolemaic times, their experience was as full and as real as any other, whether that involved complicity and acquiescence in Ptolemaic rule or resistance and rebellion.

AN ANTIQUE LAND

Under the Ptolemies, Egypt was still a place of visible and epic antiquity. Egyptian history was by then so magnificently long and idiosyncratic, what passed for facts had long blurred into eccentric myth.

When Herodotus explored the Nile Valley in the fifth century BC, he was treated to an enchanting and bewildering mix of fantasy and fact. His description forms 'the first phase' in the cultural relationship between Greece and Egypt, the arrival of Alexander and the Macedonians being the second.[9] When Herodotus wrote, the time had long since passed when anyone might have been able to unravel the truth, if indeed a truth had ever really existed. Egyptian perceptions of the past and present had always been coloured by what they imagined to be ideal or perfect, the truth forever blurred into lore, just as the Romans mythologized their own origins and qualities.

The Ptolemaic rulers created the most effective rebranding and restoration of Egyptian power in centuries since the Saïte kings of the 26th Dynasty, whose efforts inspired them. The Ptolemies went further and managed a unique synthesis of foreign and indigenous culture. The effect was both to preserve and modernize but the Ptolemaic state was always something of a veneer. Old Egypt continued timelessly in fields and villages beside the Nile and in the oases in spite, not because, of its new Macedonian rulers, as it had done under earlier invaders and would continue to do under the Romans and thereafter. Other forces were at work and other nations were on the rise. The absolutism of the Bronze Age despots was already an anachronism. Rome epitomized the new age, most obviously of all in the way the Roman state could withstand and endure the vagaries of its leaders, something Ptolemaic Egypt was less able to do.

SOURCES

The history of ancient Egypt remains precariously dependent on taking on trust statements contained within the flotsam and jetsam of ancient sources (whatever their origin or date). The historian Robin Lane Fox summed the general problem up in his *Alexander the Great*. 'The past', he said, 'like the present, is made up of seasons and faces, feelings, disappointments, and things seen . . . It is a naïve belief that the distant past can be recovered from written texts.'[10]

All historical narratives are therefore constructs, artefacts of historians' minds. They form an essential ingredient of every culture, creating meaning and a framework to contextualize the present, and provide a foundation for the future. But if one questioned everything there would be nothing left to say. To dismiss the classical sources outright for their shortcomings is to miss the point, even to misunderstand them completely. Their narratives served an allegorical purpose at the time that suited and reflected ancient society: in the Ptolemies the Roman-era historians saw the evils of despotic monarchy, and the hazards of wealth and power that threatened their own. Today's revisionist historians, who enthusiastically denigrate the prejudices and agendas of the Roman historians as if they had set out maliciously to deceive, only create their own pastiches and allegories of the past blurred with the concerns and obsessions of the present day.

Ancient (indeed, any historical) sources cannot be weighed in scales, but it is possible to understand the problems they present without implying they are useless. The history of the Roman Empire, parts of which are far better recorded than Egypt's, is replete with issues concerning understanding and interpretation as well as gaps in the ancient records. Egyptian history is, by comparison, obscure often to the point of non-existence, especially before 525 BC. Even a relative chronology is a struggle to assemble. In the absence of any surviving Ptolemaic chronicles, our reliance thereafter on Greek and Roman historians is both welcome and unavoidable, but obviously with caution. Most of these sources were written much later, are overtly pro-Roman, are inclined to disparage the Ptolemies in what are often only incidental references, and are sometimes confused. Despite these faults, they at least provide the basis for a narrative of sorts which is founded on absolute dates. The only alternatives might be an edict on a stela, or a scrappy phrase written on a fragment of pottery, as evidence for a major event or dynastic development, or more often nothing at all.[11]

Some ancient historians well understood the problems they faced when compiling their accounts. In his account of the Peloponnesian

War, written in the late fifth century BC, Thucydides explained that he had found it 'impossible' to gain precise knowledge even of the history immediately preceding his own time. He observed how details handed down by tradition were unreliable and far too readily accepted at face value, and that different eyewitnesses gave contradictory accounts of the same events thanks to their personal bias or unreliable memories. Arrian and Curtius Rufus, key Roman sources for Alexander, explained how they filtered variable and conflicting evidence. Diodorus Siculus (*fl.* first century BC) was concerned by the selectivity and narrowness of scope in earlier histories and the impact on a wider understanding.[12]

No contemporary historian of the Ptolemaic dynasty ever emerged or, if one did, his work has not survived. Ptolemy II commissioned the priest Manetho's history of Egypt, showing how important it was for the Ptolemies to position themselves. Whatever Manetho wrote survives now only in extracts and epitomes recorded by later writers such as Josephus. None makes proper sense. There are manifest contradictions with what we now know to have been the main sequence of kings. Manetho's sources are lost, but some clues survive of what he might have had access to. In the fifth century BC Herodotus was read to from a document that recorded the names of 330 kings.[13] Diodorus referred to the priestly 'sacred writings' and explained that 'the priests had records which were regularly handed down in their sacred books to each successive priest from early times, giving the stature of each of the former kings'.[14] Ptolemy III is recorded as having written a set of Commentaries, but these have vanished.[15]

Polybius was a contemporary of the middle Ptolemies and early Cleopatras, but his interest was the rise of Rome. Egypt appeared only as a player in that drama. Diodorus wrote a century later, but his focus was a 'universal history of all events'. There was even active suppression. Ptolemaic records were destroyed by the Romans. The future emperor Claudius (AD 41–54) was prevented from writing about the civil war period of the late first century BC by his mother Antonia Minor (Mark Antony's daughter by Octavia) and grandmother, Augustus' empress Livia.[16]

This attitude had a powerful impact. The Ptolemies were usually depicted by later sources as degenerate oriental despots and a source of anecdotes about excess and curiosities. Strabo described how 'all the kings after the third Ptolemy, being corrupted by luxurious living, have administered the affairs of government badly'. He added that Augustus had destroyed Antony and Cleopatra, thereby 'putting an end to Egypt's being ruled with drunken violence', and explained how well the place was run by the Romans as a province.[17] For a philo-Roman, Strabo's verdict was predictable enough. He ignored how the Romans maintained much of the Ptolemaic system of government. There are numerous other fleeting references to Ptolemaic Egypt in, for example, Appian, Justin, Pliny the Elder, Plutarch, or even the biblical commentaries by St Jerome, the works of Eusebius, and the proverbs collected by Zenobius, which preserve among others fragments of certain lost works such as Porphyry. We have not a hope of ever finding their long-vanished original sources, let alone reading them, or the archives that historians like Diodorus Siculus scoured in the vanished libraries of antiquity.

An unintended consequence of the zealous and exploitative enthusiasm of Ptolemaic rule, and the unmatched archaeological conditions in Egypt, was to leave a huge quantity of papyri and inscribed potsherds or stones (ostraca) written either in Greek or Egyptian demotic. That so many of these late records were written in Greek helps transport the papyrologist from the cryptic technicalities of Egyptian into a language that is far better understood. These contemporary written sources, however, are not a historical archive and only occasionally provide supplementary information for political or military history.[18] They are also often incomplete, damaged, or obscure. Nevertheless, the window to Ptolemaic times is flung open to reveal the workings of the government and the way its tentacles pervaded every household, farm, and business in the country, providing an exceptional record of a premodern state in action. Survival of that evidence is mainly due to the recycling habits of the cartonnage manufacturers in the funeral industry.[19]

There are contemporary inscriptions which record dedications, events, and edicts rather than providing us with a chronicle. It is important to recognize that distinction and, as with the papyri and ostraca, not to treat them as substitutes for the gaps in, or absence of, historical sources. The inscriptions are formulaic statements of officialdom, one-sided and replete with hyperbole, as all state inscriptions are, and often cryptic or damaged and incomplete.[20] But they do provide essential detail, for example the Egyptian titles held by Ptolemaic female rulers (see Appendix 3).

As a result, some books on the period, however worthy, can seem impenetrably arcane when labouring through cryptic evidence. The Ptolemies, therefore, generally exist otherwise today swiftly passed over in chapters sitting at the end of books about the whole of Egyptian history or, equally often, as a preamble to a biography of Cleopatra VII. Some Egyptologists visibly wince when pressed by publishers to include a section on the Ptolemies. This has denied the Ptolemies the place in modern culture they deserve. This is odd given the similarity between their machinations and stories in modern popular fantasy novels. If anything, the Ptolemies frequently turn out to have been more lurid and dramatic. The author George R. Martin has said with reference to his fictional Targaryen family: 'The Targaryens have heavily interbred, like the Ptolemies of Egypt . . . interbreeding accentuates both flaws and virtues, and pushes a lineage toward the extremes.'[21]

In general, the more familiar Latinized forms of names are used even where those differ from the original Greek. Sometimes the latter is a useful distinction from better known individuals with the same name. The reader will therefore find Serapis but not Sarapis, Arrhidaeus instead of Arridaios (or Arridhaios), and so on, reflecting common usage in modern translations and most other books on the period.

The present book owes a great debt to the works of many scholars, such as Günther Hölbl's *A History of the Ptolemaic Empire* (2001). This important study succeeded in pulling together a vast amount of ancient evidence and modern scholarship to give Ptolemaic history a more comprehensive and coherent structure.

Ptolemaic scholarship has moved on apace in the last two decades. Wherever possible, more recent works have been prioritized here, including links to electronic resources that have made the ancient papyri texts much more accessible. A book of this length has necessarily meant avoiding some of the arid plains of the more obscure issues, for which some readers will be grateful and others not. There are many intractable problems in the study of Ptolemaic Egypt. Hopefully, readers who want more detail will find within the notes the tools with which to take the subject further.

Part I

RISE

Ptolemaic Egypt rose to become the dominant Hellenistic kingdom under Ptolemy I–III. By Ptolemy IV's reign signs of the problems that presaged its decline and fall were emerging.

1

THE ROAD TO SIWA
Alexander's Egyptian Adventure (332 BC)

For thousands of years, it had been a given that the king of Egypt claimed to have been chosen and sired by Amun. Such myths were enduring tropes throughout antiquity for any ruler keen to claim unimpeachable credentials. It was inconceivable anyone could have tried to rule the country without adding himself to the god's line of descent. It suited Alexander's purpose to depict himself as a ruler backed by the gods of his own ancestry, as well as the most ancient of all, now known in the Greek world as Ammon.

'In setting out to visit Ammon, Alexander's intention was to acquire more information about himself – or at least to say that he had acquired it', said Arrian, a Roman senator and one of our principal sources for Alexander, particularly his journey into Egypt.[1] Although he wrote more than four hundred years after Alexander's death, Arrian is indispensable because he used books now lost. The most important were those by Aristobulus and Ptolemy, son of Lagus. They were only two of at least twenty contemporaries of Alexander who wrote about him but whose works have vanished. Ptolemy was Alexander's boyhood friend and became one of his generals. Aristobulus, the military engineer who accompanied Alexander's campaigns, is better known as Aristobulus of Kassandreia (*c.* 375–301 BC). Both men were close to

Alexander and witnessed some of his great achievements. Their accounts did not always tally. Arrian found he had to use whichever seemed the most plausible. It is also obvious that Ptolemy might have been self-serving in his version of events.

Much of what Diodorus wrote is lost but the section dealing with the immediate aftermath of Alexander's rule has survived. Other extant sources include Plutarch's Life of Alexander. They too share the shortcoming of having been written down long after the events they describe by using original sources that cannot be verified. Each claimed to be reliable. All were infected in some way by Alexander's bequest of his fearsome glamour and afflicted by the selectivity and judgement they applied to the now-vanished sources they used.

ADVANCE TO EGYPT

After defeating Darius III at Issus on 5 November 333 BC, Alexander, then aged just twenty-three, avoided chasing his Persian enemy into the east. Instead, he first secured his rear with risky sieges of Tyre and Gaza which kept him busy until the late summer of 332. The people of Tyre chose to resist rather than capitulate. That was a mistake, at least for them. Both sides resorted to ever more ingenious weaponry such as the spinning marble wheels that the Tyrians hurled at the Macedonian catapults.[2] Eventually, Alexander's men prevailed. He dealt with Tyre ruthlessly, the women and children being sold into slavery. Many thousands of Tyrian men had been killed during the fighting but two thousand remained, whom Alexander crucified.[3] The possibility of similar treatment played a part in Egypt's easy capitulation shortly afterwards.

Alexander's cruelty and barbarity took on various forms. When his beloved friend Hephaestion subsequently died unexpectedly in 324 BC he ordered the execution of the hapless doctor in charge. He followed this up with a campaign against the Cossaean mountain tribe and had all the youths and adult males killed; this was passed off as a sacrifice in honour of Hephaestion.[4]

Alexander next besieged the Persian garrison at Gaza, which took two months. He raised more troops in Macedon. Only then did he set out by land for Egypt, determined to make himself the latest member of the most ancient of absolute monarchies in the known world and integrate that with his identity and achievements. Nothing less would do.

To say Alexander merely posed as a liberator of Egypt would be unfair. He might have been primarily pursuing his interests, but it was a legitimate claim. His arrival freed the Egyptians from the hated Persian occupation. Being a foreigner ought to have counted against him in Egypt, but the convincing way his rule was presented in an Egyptian idiom appears to have encouraged his acceptance.

Alexander crossed unopposed into Egypt at the border outpost called Peremoun by the Egyptians (and Pelusium by the Romans, the name by which it is now normally known) at the north-east corner of the Nile Delta.[5] Landlocked today, the site was an important port town during Alexander's time. Alexander made the six-day journey overland from Gaza. It was only at Pelusium that he was able to catch up with his naval forces that had gone ahead and waited for him. Pelusium was the gateway to Egypt from the Near East because it overlooked the main easterly (Pelusiac) branch of the Nile into the Mediterranean. By Alexander's time its location was rapidly turning into an island because the Pelusiac branch had divided, leaving its fortress and the accompanying settlement between the two waterways.

Alexander also met Mazaces, the satrap of Egypt, at Pelusium. Mazaces had the wit to see that the game was up before it began. Alexander's reputation had preceded him. Mazaces had no intention of dying a pointlessly heroic death in an unwinnable battle. He had been left in charge of only the rump of the Persian garrison of Egypt. Darius had fled. Most of the Persian army had already been seized by Alexander. Mazaces handed Egypt over without a murmur.[6]

Alexander had more important priorities than casual tourism. He installed a garrison at Pelusium then travelled south to Heliopolis and then to Memphis, Egypt's ancient administrative capital and its necropolis at Saqqara. Memphis was a place to celebrate his new acquisition and be crowned according to Egyptian ancient ritual. Alexander had a very important purpose in mind.

However impressed Alexander might have been by Heliopolis, all but nothing is left of the city today apart from the standing obelisk of the 12th-Dynasty pharaoh Senwosret I (1971–1926 BC). By Alexander's time, the obelisk had stood for around sixteen centuries. Now only disheartening fragments remain of the massive temple complex in which it stood. The Memphis that Alexander visited has also long gone. The city was at the mercy of the Nile. Almost all of Memphis has been washed away or buried. Lonely fragments of buildings, such as the Ramesside Temple of Ptah, protrude above the reeds and swamps among the palm trees, though it was once probably among the largest temples in the ancient world.

Alexander paid his respects to the Egyptian gods, especially Apis, a bull manifestation of Ptah to whom he sacrificed. He respected the power of existing cults and especially the exceptionally long traditions in Egypt. The Apis cult took place at the Serapeum in Saqqara which had been in use since the New Kingdom to bury the Apis bulls (see Chapter 9). Alexander held games here.[7]

Memphis was as far up the Nile as Alexander ever reached, at least so far as we know. He had a more pressing engagement in mind. Instead, he turned north and headed into the Delta, this time by water, the most efficient way of crossing the region. He brought an elaborate escort of guards, archers, Agrianian light infantry (raised in what is now part of Bulgaria), and the royal cavalry. This cavalcade of Macedonian military might marched into Canopus, the city that lay on the Mediterranean coast where the western branch of the Nile met the sea. From here Alexander set out to explore Lake Mareotis.[8]

On the coast nearby, 16 miles (25 km) south-west from Canopus, Alexander disembarked and announced that the strip of land between the sea and Lake Mareotis was the perfect location for a new city.[9] A fishing village called Rhakotis stood there, but Alexander spotted that the place had enormous potential, though exactly what for at that stage is not clear.[10] The name Rhakotis was probably linked to the Greek word ρακος (rakos), one of the meanings of which is 'a strip of cloth', surely a reference to the location.

The site was an ingenious choice. Alexandria evolved into one of the most important cities of antiquity and the showcase of Ptolemaic power (see Chapter 7). Alexander became temporarily absorbed by the Alexandria project, wanting it to be a conflation of Greek and Egyptian culture. The gods of both would be worshipped there in temples built across the plan which he laid out in person. Arrian recounted a story which he decided was probably true: lacking any other material to hand, Alexander laid out his plan with the soldiers' barley-meal (what they thought of having their food requisitioned this way goes unrecorded). This was interpreted by his priests as a sign that the city would prosper. The story is more likely to have been dreamed up in later years as 'proof' of Alexander's brilliant foresight since the city, which was named Alexandria, turned out to be such a commercial, political, and cultural triumph.

Alexandria commemorated its anniversary on 7 April, probably the day that Alexander chose the site.[11] The Roman historian Livy believed Alexandria's foundation (*Alexandream conditam*) was in 326 BC, using the word *proditum* which means it was a tradition (i.e. handed down).[12] The date is close enough to 332 BC to be plausible but with enough years elapsing between for it to be possible that it was not until 326 BC that the city was advanced enough for its formal incorporation to be announced. Alexander had left the whole project to be taken care of by others. He never returned to admire their work. In any case, there was no indication he imagined it would be anything other than a coastal Greek colony in Egypt, albeit an extravagant and conspicuous one. He did not move the Egyptian capital from Memphis to Alexandria. The triumphant development of Alexandria would be the work of the Ptolemies, though like other aspects of their rule it suited them to depict their actions as following Alexander's cue.

Alexander left any further planning to Dinocrates, the Macedonian architect who had accompanied Alexander into Egypt.[13] Alexandria was so well placed that it developed a life force of its own, sharing its eponymous founder's glamour and exhilaration. The city, which was ineradicably Greek, remained resiliently independent-minded, its communities, customs, and privileges setting it apart from the rest of Egypt, and was regarded by officialdom and foreigners as a separate entity.

Alexander claimed that he was descended from Perseus and Heracles, the sons of Zeus, and that his ancestors included Ammon (the Greek version of Amun, conflated with Zeus). Whether he believed this or not does not matter. By making the claim he was demonstrating how he wanted to validate his entitlement to rule. He wished to consult the god's oracle at Siwa in the remote western desert, close to the modern border between Egypt and Libya, to secure the god's endorsement in person. Since the pharaohs had claimed Amun as their father, Alexander's plans were logical. This would legitimise his status in Egypt and consolidate a wider claim to entitlement across his empire. Zeus-Ammon was already venerated throughout the Greek world. Perseus and Heracles were said to have visited the oracle at Siwa, so Alexander's whim to cross the desert was inevitable. He set out for Siwa in late 332 or early 331 BC.

The *Alexander Romance*, now attributed to Pseudo-Callisthenes (an umbrella term for works of unknown authorship once believed to have been written by Callisthenes), circulated widely in antiquity in many different versions. Its origins are unknown, but the story reflected the ideology Alexander was constructing for himself. In most respects the *Romance* bears more resemblance to an Arthurian-style myth, making most or even all its contents of dubious merit, even if it was borne out of some of Alexander's personal fancies. Nonetheless, it is treated by some scholars as if it was written at first hand by a reliable witness, which is almost as much of a curiosity as some of the curiosities it contains. Obviously, this shortcoming afflicts virtually all our ancient sources, regardless of their origins or when they were written. The *Alexander Romance* has the air of a self-serving contrivance, even a fancy.

In one early passage, sometimes known as the *Deceit of Nectanebo*, the *Romance* described how Alexander's mother Olympias sought a meeting with Nectanebo II while her husband Philip II was away at war. She had heard a rumour that on his return he planned to divorce her and take another wife. Nectanebo was entranced by Olympias and at her request foretold her future, which included the revelation that Ammon of Libya 'with horns upon his head' would soon sleep with her and she would bear a son who would avenge Philip's death (assassinated in 336 BC). Nectanebo, reimagined here as a magician, then darted off to prepare potions to help Olympias dream that she was sleeping with the god. Olympias was terrified by the dream and sought Nectanebo's reassurance while also expressing her desire to sleep with the god. Nectanebo then told her about the different manifestations of Ammon, with the inevitable consequence that he ended up sleeping with her in the guise of the god.[14]

The point of the story was obvious: Alexander had been sired by Ammon and Nectanebo II combined in one person, buying into routine Egyptian royal tradition that the queen was impregnated by Amun disguised as the king. It also created a myth of continuity, bridging the intermediate Persian episode. Alexander was thus able to pose as the restorer of Maat and therefore the predestined and legitimate king of Egypt.

The discovery of Nectanebo II's sarcophagus in a mosque in Alexandria has always defied easy explanation.[15] Since the king had fled Egypt in the face of the Persians it is unlikely it was ever used for his burial, though obviously it had been created for that purpose. Nectanebo was in Memphis when he gave up the kingship.[16] Ptolemy I perhaps took it to Alexandria, perhaps incorporating it into the tomb of Alexander as part of a web of associations that directly linked him to Alexander (see below).

ADVENTURES IN THE DESERT

The only realistic way of reaching Siwa, which at the time was regarded as being in Libya (now within Egypt's borders), was to travel along the coast and take advantage of available fresh water as far as Paraetonium (modern Mersa Matruh). Only then could Alexander and his entourage turn south and make for Siwa, benefiting from chance and very unusual rain. This was automatically interpreted as propitious. However, the track was obscured by wind-blown sand. Alexander and his men became lost but followed either crows or snakes said to have led the way (the accounts vary). Such yarns are typical of ancient sources, but since the route was almost due south-west and marked for some of the way by a dried-up riverbed it is more likely that they were able to navigate by the sun and stars. Heading in the correct direction could hardly have taxed even the most amateur explorer, or they may also have sourced a local guide. If Ptolemy was involved in this adventure, and he may well have been, he went unmentioned in any of the extant sources.

In antiquity the Siwa oasis was about 4.5 miles (7.2 km) wide and was isolated by the surrounding desert. The oracular temple that Alexander visited survives and had been built by Amasis II of the 26th Dynasty on the nearby hill of Aghurmi. The structure is an asymmetrical complex of chambers quite unlike a conventional Egyptian temple. There were no pylons, courts, great columned hypostyle halls, or obelisks. Instead, it was designed to accommodate priests and provide a special room into which royal pilgrims could be admitted to the oracular presence. Here Alexander met the oracle and received answers to his questions, witnessing the oracular procession that passed between the Aghurmi temple and the nearby temple of Ammon at Umm 'Ubayda. The oracle spoke exclusively to kings and much of what Alexander was told has remained a secret. Diodorus provides a description of the procession and Alexander's visit, but his source is unknown. It is unlikely he ever visited Siwa himself. Alexander allegedly asked the senior prophet (priest):

'Tell me if you give me the rule of the whole earth.' The priest now entered the sacred enclosure and as the bearers now lifted the god and were moved according to certain prescribed sounds of the voice, the prophet cried that of a certainty the god had granted him his request, and Alexander spoke again: 'The last, O spirit, of my questions now answer; have I punished all those who were the murderers of my father or have some escaped me?' The prophet shouted: 'Silence! There is no mortal who can plot against the one who begot him. All the murderers of Philip, however, have been punished. The proof of his divine birth will reside in the greatness of his deeds; as formerly he has been undefeated, so now he will be unconquerable for all time.' Alexander was delighted with these responses. He honoured the god with rich gifts and returned to Egypt.[17]

Plutarch provides a similar account but adds that Alexander had tried first to find out if the death of his father had been avenged, and that no guarantee of the length of Alexander's reign had been forthcoming.[18]

Today the Siwa temple is battered and surrounded by mud-brick buildings, with the lush oasis vegetation and lakes visible beyond and further off the ominous and forbidding desert. It is possible to walk through the chambers but the huge blocks of the walls with repaired patches, the weathered and empty recesses, and the doorway lintels and jambs make the experience resemble exploring a ruined medieval castle keep. There are no reliefs, paintings, or statues.

Alexander was impressed and pleased by the experience, as well he might have been. His rule had been endorsed. He headed back to Memphis, where the careful choreography of the whole exercise became clear. There he was greeted by representatives from Miletus (in Ionia, Anatolia) who told him how among others the oracle of the shrine of Apollo at Didyma had confirmed Alexander was the son of Zeus, and that the Sibyl of Erythrae (another Ionian city) had also affirmed his high birth.[19] These were referred to by Arrian only as embassies from Greece.[20] More celebrations and sacrifices were held honouring Zeus Basileus ('Zeus the King'), the Greek version of Ammon as king of the gods. A parade of Alexander's army provided the muscle in case anyone doubted his ideological claim to supremacy.

CORONATION?

The climactic moment was allegedly Alexander's coronation at Memphis where, according to the *Alexander Romance*, 'they seated him upon the throne of Hephaestus [equivalent to Ptah in Egypt] and clothed him after the manner of Egyptians'. If this really happened, Alexander thereby established an identity followed by the Ptolemaic kings which they assumed as part of legitimizing their rule in Egypt. The funeral stela of the high priest of Ptah, Pasherenptah, who crowned Ptolemy XII in 76 BC, is one of the most important records.

Alexander followed this up by grasping a black stone which the priests told him was a statue of Nectanebo II.[21] Arrian mentions no such ceremony but does say that Alexander made sacrifices to the gods 'specifically including Apis', and then held games. These were kingly prerogatives and showed that he was *de facto* pharaoh but may not have had the time or inclination to wait around for a full-scale coronation to be organized.[22] Plutarch jumps straight on from the visit to Siwa to Alexander leaving Egypt.[23] Diodorus says only that once Alexander had dealt with Alexandria he saw 'to the reorganization of Egypt' and left.[24] Arrian provides more detail, but no colourful description of a coronation in the Egyptian style. No Egyptian primary source record of the event has survived.

Some sort of occasion ought to have taken place in Memphis that confirmed Alexander's rule over Egypt and at which he took his Egyptian royal names.[25] A formal crowning ceremony would have served Alexander very well in drawing a line between his rule and that of the absentee Persians and formed an essential component of legitimizing his rule. Plato stated that no king in Egypt could rule without being a priest.[26] Pharaonic titles were applied to Egyptian reliefs of Alexander, for example in the barque shrine at the Temple of Luxor where the cult of Alexander's royal *ka* (spirit) was practised, and which he claimed to have built (plate 2). This was inserted into a part of the structure built by Amenhotep III (*c.* 1390–1352 BC) of the 18th Dynasty. They feature

Alexander as a pharaoh, making offerings to Amun, complete with his personal name transliterated into hieroglyphs and his Egyptian throne name Setepen-Re-mery-Amun, 'Chosen by Re, beloved of Amun'.[27] His titles include the traditional 'Lord of the Two Lands' and 'Lord of Horizons'. This supports the idea of a formal occasion that would have emphatically presented him as the lawful incumbent and heir.[28]

The small possibility exists that perhaps no such coronation ever took place. Alexander was not depicted at Luxor as a deceased pharaoh, but in the years soon after his death it was probably convenient to create retrospective monuments purporting to be from his lifetime. Alexander's pharaonic guise may have been, at least in part, retrospectively contrived by Ptolemy I. Ptolemy needed to position himself as Alexander's successor in Egypt. That would legitimize his own rule of Egypt and link his dynasty back through Alexander to Nectanebo II, underpinned by a dynastic cult transmitted through Alexander as a divinity. Ptolemy I Egyptianized his public image as a king for the sake of domestic consumption though he and his successors never adopted Egyptian royal birth names. Nor did any of them, apart from Cleopatra VII, trouble themselves to learn to speak Egyptian (or so we are told). In other ways their image as rulers was unequivocally Egyptian within Egypt. It would have made sense for Ptolemy to interpose a pharaonic Alexander between Nectanebo II and himself, allowing the line of descent to glide seamlessly from one to the other. In antiquity, especially Egypt, the symbolic always obscured the truth. What really happened was of secondary importance, or even irrelevant.

Conveniently, the Macedonians also allowed themselves to believe that Ptolemy (who through his mother was distantly related to Alexander) was Philip II's son, his mother having been 'given' to Lagus by Philip when she was already pregnant.[29] This then would be the context for the Romance's fanciful account of a coronation.

Nothing altered the fact that Alexander was in total control of Egypt. Armed with his gold standard portfolio of oracular validation, Alexander was justifiably buoyant. Not everyone was impressed. Some of his

Macedonian troops regarded Alexander's claim to be descended from Zeus-Ammon as ridiculous.[30] The idea was much more likely to have been widely accepted in Egypt where descent from Amun was an integral component of the ideology of kingship.

Alexander installed his men in Egyptian administration and military commands which continued to be governed as if it was a Persian satrapy, but under Macedonian management. Civil administration was split between two men, Doloaspis and Petisis.[31] This was nothing radical. The length and size of the country made the task overwhelming. However, Petisis declined to serve, and the task was left after all in the hands of Doloaspis. Eventually, Egypt ended up being governed by Cleomenes who had started out in charge of tribute.

Alexander divided up military control, placing the navy under a separate commander. One man in sole charge of the Egyptian garrison could seize power for himself in a country that would have been extremely difficult to recapture. Next, the conquering hero set off back to Tyre and to confront his destiny.

Alexander was later said to have been visited about this time by an embassy from Rome. The precocious Italian city state was just starting to flex its muscles, but Arrian thought the story implausible. He had found it in two (now largely lost) accounts of Alexander. Arrian pointed out that no Roman source mentioned the occasion and Rome was too far away and too obscure for such a diplomatic mission to have had any value at that time. Alexander was, according to the tale, impressed by the Romans and speculated on the potential for their future greatness; this sounds conveniently like an elaboration, even if a meeting had taken place.[32]

UNTIMELY TO HIS DEATH

There matters might have rested, had Alexander enjoyed a long life and established a dynasty to rule his domains. On 10 or 11 June in 323 BC he died in Babylon after contracting a fever. Not yet thirty-three, he already had packed in enough for several lifetimes. His unexpected death had repercussions that echoed down through the centuries that followed.

According to Plutarch, a curiosity was that while Alexander's followers argued over what to do for several days, his body showed no signs of decay and 'remained pure and fresh'.[33] This is self-evidently impossible unless Alexander was still alive and in a state of torpor caused by a now unidentifiable infection that meant he appeared to have ceased to be. If so, he was not dead – yet.

Curtius Rufus thought the claims about the lack of decay were implausible, saying *traditum magis quam creditum refero*, 'I am reporting what has been handed down in tradition more than in belief'. He added how the Egyptians and Chaldeans were then told to see to the corpse 'in the traditional way'. They were scared to do so because Alexander seemed so alive. After praying to be allowed to touch a god, they proceeded with the work and cleaned Alexander's body before installing it in an *aureum solium*, 'golden sarcophagus', filled with perfumes. If he had not been dead to begin with, he was now. *Solium* can also mean a throne or chair of state. This illustrates the significance of the term; it was clearly much more than a coffin.[34] Diodorus supplies a similar description but places it misleadingly two years later when preparations were being made to move the body from Babylon to its final resting place. He says it was immersed in preservative aromatics, using the word ἄρωμα (*aroma*) which can mean any spice or sweet herb, suggesting he had no idea what these were, in an anthropoid gold coffin.[35] The *Alexander Romance* says that Alexander asked that his body be placed in 'white honey that has not melted'.[36]

Mummification was a break with Macedonian tradition. Arrian is unlikely to have known much about the procedure except that it was an Egyptian phenomenon. It was certainly available to discerning customers in Rome under the emperors.[37] The evidence of surviving mummies from the latter part of Egyptian history is that practitioners were much less skilled than those of earlier dates. Conversely, Alexander's body is unlikely to have been processed by incompetents, assuming anyone could make the judgement. Nonetheless, what goes unexplained is how suitably equipped embalmers were on hand in Babylon in the aftermath of Alexander's death. The story about what happened to Alexander's body is therefore unsatisfactory in several different ways. What we do know is that Alexander's corpse was subsequently available for inspection by later rulers, most notably Augustus, whatever state it was in (Chapter 10).

Alexander left comparatively few monuments to commemorate his projection of Macedonian royal power onto Egypt. A small temple of Alexander was erected at Qasr Allam near the oasis at Bahariya in the western desert. An insignificant small rectangular building, it was dedicated to Alexander and supplies the earliest evidence for his full Egyptian pharaonic titles. There are some badly preserved and barely legible reliefs, now patchily restored in what remains of the structure at the edge of a sprawling Graeco-Roman cemetery. Disarticulated skeletal human remains still erupt alarmingly from the sand here like the vanguard of a grisly but interrupted day of judgement. Coin finds in the vicinity show that the temple compound was still being visited at least as late as the mid-fourth century AD.[38]

2

LEFT TO THE WORTHIEST
The Satrap's Tale (332–305 BC)

After Alexander the Great's unexpected death in 323 BC his empire's territories were divided up among his 'Successors' (Diadochi). Alexander's friend Ptolemy, son of Lagus, was made satrap of Egypt, the richest of all Alexander's domains. Although Ptolemy governed Egypt first in the name of Alexander's half-brother Philip III Arrhidaeus and then Alexander's son, Alexander IV, there was no question who was really in charge. Ptolemy turned out to be master of the hand fate dealt him and immediately embarked on turning Egypt into a fully fledged Hellenistic nation. He seized Alexander's body and made it a showcase symbol of his regime in Alexandria.

ALEXANDER'S RIGHT-HAND MAN

Ptolemy, son of Lagus, was born around 367 BC. In 331 BC he was made one of Alexander's seven Bodyguards, an eighth being added in 325 BC.[1] In the winter of 331/330 BC at the Battle of the Persian Gates Pass, en route to Persepolis, the redoubtable Ptolemy was left with 3,000 infantry at the rear so that if the Persians fled there would be Macedonian troops waiting to cut them down. However, the story was probably derived from Ptolemy's own account and may have exaggerated his importance at the time.[2]

In 329 BC a message arrived from a Bactrian warlord called Spitamenes and a turncoat Persian called Dataphernes. They said that with the help of a small force they could arrest the Persian commander Bessus and hand him over to Alexander. Ptolemy was picked for this mission impossible, which he chose to accept, racing ahead to cover a ten-day march in four. Ptolemy naturally captured Bessus and handed him over to Alexander, naked and tied up as Alexander had instructed. Again, the story reads like one contrived to show Ptolemy's special qualities and his favourable honouring of Alexander's directions at feverish speed.[3]

By 328 BC one of Alexander's commanders, Cleitus, had become increasingly frustrated by Alexander's orientalizing inclinations and his obsequious hangers-on. Not everyone was susceptible to Alexander's glamour. One day, fuelled by drink at a party, Cleitus laid into Alexander. Drinking to excess was common at Alexander's court. The gathering quickly spilled out of control. An equally blurred Alexander, now tired and emotional, attacked Cleitus in a rage. Ptolemy hustled Cleitus outside only for Cleitus to return and resume the taunting. Alexander killed him with a pike. The drama exposed Alexander's weakness for alcohol and how easily he could be moved to anger (his own death followed a bout of excessive drinking).[4] The story is ostensibly about Alexander and Cleitus. Ptolemy's contribution to the occasion conveniently depicts him as the one man capable of taking the initiative even if Cleitus was bent on self-destruction. According to Arrian, most of his sources described how a contrite Alexander 'took to his bed and lay there grieving', which sounds like a euphemism for nursing a hangover. Ptolemy's involvement in the Cleitus affair was fleeting and ultimately futile, but he came out of the story best, no doubt deliberately.[5] Ptolemy frequently appeared alongside Alexander, allegedly making subtle and well-timed interventions to Alexander's advantage.

In 327 BC a plot among Alexander's Macedonian pages provided Ptolemy with another opportunity to be the man of the moment. When an informant told Ptolemy, he went to Alexander who had the culprits arrested and tortured. One of the gang's associates was the historian

Callisthenes. Arrian reported that while Aristobulus said Callisthenes was arrested and carted off with Alexander's army until he died of disease, Ptolemy said he had taken it upon himself to torture Callisthenes and then crucify him. Arrian's point was that even eyewitnesses to the events did not agree on what had happened. Ptolemy appears once again as a proactive player loyally defending or pursuing Alexander's interests.[6] This general theme continued unabated. Shortly afterwards, when a spring of water and one of oil suddenly popped up, the sensational news was taken to Ptolemy who passed it on to Alexander.[7]

Around that time the ever-vigilant Ptolemy was placed in charge of one-fifth of the army Alexander was currently leading in Sogdiana, equivalent to parts of modern Uzbekistan and Turkmenistan.[8] In the winter of 327/326 BC in India, Alexander was wounded in the shoulder by an arrow, a *simpatico* Ptolemy being conveniently and honourably wounded at the same time.[9] Ptolemy was by chance not badly hurt enough to prevent him riding out and spotting the Indian leader, even dismounting when the terrain became too steep and single-handedly chasing him on foot and killing him. The reliable Ptolemy clung to centre stage by taking 'his own initiative' to track down where the 'local barbarians' were camped and estimate their numbers from their campfires. In the ensuing engagement, with Ptolemy commanding one-third of the greatly outnumbered Macedonian force, Ptolemy naturally managed to help pull off a resounding victory, though his contribution was the only one recounted in any detail.[10]

Shortly afterwards, at the Rock of Aornus in the Indus Valley, local quislings provided Alexander with intelligence about the weakest part of the rock. Ptolemy was sent to take it, a manoeuvre he accomplished with his usual effortless aplomb, reinforced its defences, and lit a beacon to guide Alexander. The next day went badly, Alexander being held back by 'the barbarians', and Ptolemy struggling to hold his position. A day later, Alexander sneaked up and joined Ptolemy, a tactic that of course made it look like Ptolemy was the linchpin of the engagement. The barbarians pretended to sue for peace as a time-buying ruse to return to their bases, but Alexander realized what was happening and attacked them. The enemy fled and Alexander seized and garrisoned the rock.[11]

In 326 BC Alexander's force besieged a Brahmin city called Harmatelia during his Indian campaign. Some of his soldiers were struck by poisoned weapons and died extremely unpleasant deaths. Ptolemy was allegedly one of the victims. Alexander is said to have been devastated by his friend's illness and the prospect of his death. The story went that Alexander had a dream in which a snake showed him an antidote plant. Alexander awoke, went to find the plant, and prepared it so that he could apply it to Ptolemy. Ptolemy survived. Diodorus probably took it from Ptolemy's lost history of Alexander. Ptolemy could have included or invented the story which portrayed him as one of Alexander's principal favourites, and his generosity to others.[12]

The other possibility is that Ptolemy and others were largely telling the truth about his star appearances. After all, given his later successful career, Ptolemy had to have been a man of considerable abilities. By then he had nothing to prove. At the Battle of Arbela in 325 BC in India Alexander was badly wounded by an arrow. Arrian discovered that some of his sources claimed Ptolemy had played a key role in saving the fallen Alexander by protecting him. The occasion was said by some to be the basis of Ptolemy's later title Soter (see next chapter). Conversely, Ptolemy had explained in his own account of Alexander's life that he was not involved but was fighting somewhere else.[13] This might make the other occasions when his presence was decisive seem more plausible.

In 324 BC at Susa, Alexander organized a multi-marriage ceremony for himself and his Companions. Ptolemy was given Artakama, a daughter of Artabazus, one of Darius' loyalists.[14] Within a year Alexander was dead, an epic and unexpected event that changed the course of history in an instant.

AFTER ALEXANDER

Before Alexander's demise Ptolemy must have assumed he would spend the rest of his life in Alexander's service or that of Alexander's descendants. He cannot have expected that he would necessarily live much longer himself, since he was now in his sixties. Ptolemy was not appointed king of Egypt during Alexander's lifetime or in the immediate aftermath of Alexander's death. Instead, the Successors submerged themselves in a curious interlude of sundry feuds, wars, and alliances. Ptolemy cannot at this stage have imagined that he would one day be king of Egypt, or king of anywhere else, or indeed the progenitor of a dynasty that would last several centuries.

THE SHADOW OF A DREAM

Alexander did nothing to give his vast empire, stretching from eastern Europe to India, any enduring substance. His domains were no more than the shadow of a dream. To be fair to Alexander, fate and his own imperfections denied him the opportunity to rectify that glaring shortcoming, but it would never have been possible in antiquity to hold together an empire which covered such a vast land mass.

By the time the Roman Empire came under the control of Octavian, who became Augustus, three hundred years after Alexander's death, it was already managed by a complex system of provincial government overseen by the Roman Senate. The Romans had seized their empire over several centuries, gradually infusing its possessions with Roman culture and enticing local elites into Roman power structures. This had proved largely effective and created, in ancient world terms, relative stability. Augustus developed the system, as well as establishing a standing army that owed its fealty first to him and then to his dynastic successors. They were able to inherit his unique suite of offices and magistracies that collectively formed (and occluded) the basis of his monarchical power. That same army served in carefully placed frontier garrisons.

Equally importantly, and perhaps more decisively, the Roman world came to surround the Mediterranean and its subsidiary seas. This meant travelling from one end to the other was a feat accomplished with comparative ease. The Roman Empire experienced episodes of extreme instability, but usually overcame those problems without disrupting its cohesiveness, coherence, and integrity as a political unit until the third century AD when military insurrection and civil war became endemic. Reforms and adaptation recovered some imperial authority in the fourth century.

In contrast, Alexander's empire was spread across vast tracts of the Middle East and Asia that required laborious communications and movement over land. It had been won in short order and pivoted about his person. He only ever saw the territory he conquered as personal property that could serve as the source of the resources necessary to conquer more. Alexander was uninterested in consolidating his victories or installing provincial government to manage his possessions beyond his version of the Persian system of satrapies, though he was quick to punish any abuses of power.

Alexander was also unconcerned about the future of his empire beyond his death; it was almost as if he was unable to envisage such a time. There was no foundation myth that underpinned a sense of destiny apart from his own, and no cultural coherence or desire to conflate local identity with being simultaneously a subject of Alexander's. This did nothing to improve his system of rule, especially when Alexander's inclination to orientalize his appearance and style of rule began to alienate some of his supporters. This led him to hire a 30,000-strong force of highly trained Persians as a defence against some of the Macedonians who started questioning Alexander's leadership and claims to divine descent.[15]

SUCCESSION

> The crown will find an heir: great Alexander
> Left his to the worthiest; so his successor
> Was like to be the best.[16]

Shakespeare's lines imply that Alexander had clear intentions for the succession. The surviving evidence suggests the opposite. Like most autocrats and narcissists, Alexander only understood power with himself in charge. He did nothing to ensure a succession except for fathering an as-yet unborn child by his wife (since 327 BC, Roxane). His so-called illegitimate son Heracles, allegedly born to his mistress Barsine, is unmentioned by most ancient historians and was irrelevant in 323 BC.[17] Dying when Alexander did was a catastrophic error of political judgement and a monumental inconvenience to all concerned, though it did resolve the question of what Alexander himself could possibly have done next. His early death, while leaving everyone around him disoriented and frightened, rapidly turned into his apotheosis. He had wanted to be a god and now he was one.

The crisis demanded quick thinking. Alexander had been so remarkable it was obvious no single individual could replace him. Alexander's bodyguards frantically convened his friends and senior military officers in Alexander's tent at Babylon to find a solution.[18] Panic simmered in the ranks. Others gathered around waiting for developments, ignoring orders to keep back and thereby preventing some of those who had been summoned from getting through. Any lamenting soon gave way to the deafening silence of apprehension and fear.

Perdiccas, one of Alexander's most senior generals, was impresario. Appropriately enough, he deployed an ingenious theatrical gesture. He had Alexander's vacant throne brought out along with his crown, robe, and arms, as well as the ring Alexander had given Perdiccas before he expired. Perdiccas then delivered a motivational speech. He flagged up Roxane's pregnancy and proposed they all hoped a son would be born who could grow up to become king in his father's stead.

There was a great deal of talk and no decisive action. Perdiccas persisted with his vision in the face of some opposition from those who thought the plan was insane. There was no guarantee that the child would be born alive, be a boy, or survive to adulthood. Scrabbling about for a more constructive suggestion, Ptolemy proposed that Alexander's associates should meet in the presence of the throne and make decisions based on majority verdicts. It was a radical proposition that did nothing to resolve what had immediately become dangerously contentious. The risk was that the fragile edifice of Alexander's empire would swiftly disperse like vapour in a gale of misadventures.

In the event, Alexander's half-brother, the obliging Philip Arrhidaeus, was crowned king as Philip III. If Roxane delivered a son, he would be named Alexander and reign as joint king with Philip III until he came of age; Philip would then stand aside. Roxane conveniently produced a boy, temporarily calming everyone's nerves. Meanwhile, three of the most senior Macedonians took joint control of the empire: Craterus served as the crown's representative, Antipater took control of Europe, and Perdiccas assumed supreme control of the royal army. The provincial government satrapies were divided up among Alexander's most important followers on the Persian model. Among them was Egypt and its associated territories in Cyrenaica and the Levant, which were handed to Ptolemy.

The arrangement was pragmatic but was bound to end in tears, and it did. It depended on all the participants accepting the limits placed on their individual autonomy and sacrificing their personal ambitions. The plan also relied on them acceding to the centralized control of the empire but without that power being clearly defined either in precedent and practice or in any written constitution. It is going too far to suggest that the scheme was doomed because the Successors were individually bent on replacing Alexander from the outset. Alexander's death had been wholly unexpected. To begin with they were floundering, uncertain initially even of their own ambitions in a scenario they could not have imagined. Nevertheless, in fits and starts, new plans were made. 'It was difficult to remain satisfied with what the opportunity of the moment had brought them', said Curtius Rufus.[19] Their aura of patriotism gradually vaporized and exposed their clamours of self-interest and faction.

War broke out when those who wanted to hold Alexander's empire together with the help of obliging lieutenants faced the others who wanted their own kingdoms instead. These were Ptolemy, Lysimachus, and Seleucus. Once Alexander's empire had disintegrated, the new kingdoms could only assert and increase their power at the expense of the others. One of the first causes of tension was that while Craterus was in

Cilicia (south-eastern Turkey), Perdiccas took over his role as a temporary solution. Power-sharing fell apart when the expedient arrangement became permanent, leaving Perdiccas effectively with supreme power.

THE CYRENE AFFAIR

Ptolemy moved fast once he was made satrap of Egypt. The ousted satrap, Cleomenes, had already made himself unpopular with excessive taxation during Alexander's lifetime. Cleomenes was also loyal to Perdiccas. Ptolemy could see problems ahead, so he had Cleomenes killed.[20] That earned him local support and cut off a means of Perdiccas' government exerting influence.

Ptolemy's first territorial move was to take advantage of a power struggle in the wealthy free city of Cyrene in Cyrenaica (now eastern Libya) to the west of Egypt. It was inspired lateral thought. Egypt's famously linear geography had made it a north–south nation. Ptolemy thought outside the Egyptian box from the beginning. In Cyrene, the local leaders had been expelled. They asked Ptolemy to restore them.[21] Ptolemy agreed, recognizing like the Romans after him the advantages of having local power in his gift. Ptolemy sent out an army that put the local leaders back in place and turned Cyrenaica into a Ptolemaic client state and military protectorate. Ptolemy created a political settlement by 320 BC leaving the restored Cyrene elite in position but only at his pleasure. It was the first stage in expanding Ptolemaic imperial power.

NOW THE GAME'S AFOOT – ALEXANDER'S BODY

Early in his time as satrap, Ptolemy pulled off a remarkable coup. The claim was made by various later historians, among them Diodorus Siculus and Curtius Rufus, that Alexander wanted to be buried at Siwa. Whether he expressed any wishes at all is doubtful. A senior officer, called Arrhidaeus and not to be confused with Alexander's half-brother (Philip III Arrhidaeus), was given the job by Perdiccas of preparing the extravagant catafalque that would take Alexander's mummified body from Babylon to its place of burial.[22]

The alternative plan, dreamed up by Perdiccas, to inter Alexander in a suitable Macedonian tomb, came to nothing. The work on the catafalque took two years, after which the body was conveyed in all its pomp to Syria. This was the shortest route to the sea, telling us nothing about what the plan was at that stage since from the Syrian coast it could obviously have been taken to any one of several places. Whatever the conflicting plans and agendas were does not really matter, because we do not know what they were. What does matter is what happened.

Ptolemy made his way to Syria with an army to intercept the cortège. Whether he did so with Arrhidaeus' connivance or not, we are not told, but Ptolemy clearly knew where to go and when. He was also prepared to use force, or at least make a convincing display of muscle. Given the distances and time involved, Ptolemy cannot have been leaving anything to chance. Ptolemy's scheme was to take over the catafalque and divert it to Egypt. Strabo said Ptolemy was 'moved by greed and a desire to make that country his own'.[23] In another version, Ptolemy arranged for an imitation body of Alexander, lavishly clothed and in a luxurious bier carried in a Persian chariot, to be fashioned in order to fool Perdiccas while he made off with the real corpse, disguised as that of an ordinary person.[24] It was a calculated and fabulously provocative moment. Ptolemy must have known his stunt would trigger a violent response from Perdiccas and lead him into a trap.

Ptolemy took Alexander's remains first to Memphis where he buried the body 'in the Macedonian style'.[25] Subsequently, the body was moved to Alexandria, supposedly under the supervision of Argaeus, thought to have been a son of Ptolemy but clearly named as an homage to Alexander the Great's Argaed dynasty.[26] Whatever the truth, the body ended up at Alexandria eventually and became one of the foundations of Ptolemaic legitimacy in the nerve centre of Ptolemaic power. 'There', said Diodorus, 'he [Ptolemy I] prepared a precinct worthy of the glory of Alexander in size and construction to house the body in its golden coffin. Entombing him in this and honouring him with sacrifices such as are paid to demigods and with magnificent games, he won fair requital not only from men but also from the gods' (see Chapter 10 for Alexander's body and tomb in later history).[27]

In the meantime, Ptolemy became frustrated with the way Perdiccas was flaunting his power and influence. The distrust was mutual. Perdiccas did not believe Ptolemy would acquiesce in his plans to rule Alexander's world.[28] Perdiccas was correct. Ptolemy had joined a loose confederation with some of the other Successors, including Lysimachus, Craterus, and Antipater. The taking of Alexander's body was the last straw for Perdiccas who recklessly invaded Egypt. Going to war before he had subdued Ptolemy ensured his defeat. It also exposed his regime to two fronts.[29]

In his haste Perdiccas overlooked the possibility that Ptolemy might have strengthened his defences, which he had. Perdiccas invaded at Pelusium, but his siege works were destroyed by a river bursting its banks when an attempt was made to dredge a canal. Nonetheless, Perdiccas persuaded his men all was well and took them off to attack another fort. Ptolemy personally led the defence, so well that Perdiccas had to call off the assault. A follow-up effort to cross the Nile at Memphis went wrong after his forces churned up the riverbed, leaving it impossible for most of the army to follow. Thousands lost their lives and the army turned against Perdiccas. It was a river crossing too far. Everything about the mission had been wrong, from the planning to the execution. He was assassinated by his officers. This provided Ptolemy with another opportunity. Instead of wreaking revenge on Perdiccas' army, he treated the soldiers well and provided rations.[30]

This campaign against Perdiccas included Ptolemy's only exploit to earn a mention in Frontinus' *Stratagems*, unlike some of the Successors. Ptolemy ordered his cavalry to drive pack animals along with brushes tied to their tails, throwing up so much dust that Perdiccas' army was terrified at the prospect of a vast Egyptian army approaching and was defeated.[31]

Perdiccas' death ended any serious attempt to keep Alexander's empire intact. In 320 BC at Triparadeisos (now in modern Lebanon), the Successors bit their lips and confirmed each in his territories.[32]

Ptolemy's exploits in Cyrene were made legal, and so would be any other territorial expansion to the west along the north African coast. Ptolemy, ever ready to cash in on unexpected good fortune, moved swiftly when Antipater died by 318 BC. He helped himself to Syria and Phoenicia but installed selected garrisons only, thereby creating a buffer zone to strengthen Egypt's defences.

THE POST-PERDICCAS POWER VACUUM

In 317 BC Alexander the Great's mother Olympias, who had been allowed to help govern the empire, moved decisively to end the ambitions of Philip III's wife Adea Eurydice II of Macedon. The problem had been triggered by Adea Eurydice's shameless favouring of Cassander, son of Antipater. She forced her hapless husband to issue a decree that made Cassander regent.

Olympias, equally ambitious, and who had withdrawn to Epirus (north-west Greece) with Roxane and Alexander IV, could not stomach this. With another of the Successors, called Polyperchon, she led an army into Macedon and captured both Adea Eurydice and Philip. Philip was assassinated and Adea was told to commit suicide, an instruction she was in no position to refuse.[33] Olympias had miscalculated. Cassander arrived quickly, subjecting Olympias to a trial at which she was sentenced to death in 315 BC.[34] One by one, Alexander's family was being eliminated. The nominal king now was the boy Alexander IV who, as it turned out, had only a few years to live himself.

Thus, under the rule of Alexander IV, who became pharaoh, Ptolemy continued as satrap of Egypt. With Perdiccas gone, a power vacuum emerged, at least in the eyes of those with ambition to fill it. Antigonus Monophthalmus ('the One-Eyed'), commander of the European part of Alexander's empire, was first up. He had allegedly lost an eye in 340 BC to a catapult bolt at the siege of Perinthus under Philip II of Macedon, reputedly refusing to have it removed until the day was won.[35] Having only one eye seems to have sharpened his focus. In 315 BC Antigonus went to Babylon to intimidate Seleucus, the satrap there. To begin with, Seleucus welcomed Antigonus and feasted his army. Antigonus then turned on Seleucus and insisted on seeing the accounts for the satrapy revenues. Seleucus was furious and said that he was under no obligation to provide any such explanation for the management of territory he had been placed in charge of by Alexander. The tension mounted and Seleucus realized there was a good chance Antigonus meant to kill him. Seleucus took fifty cavalry and beat a hasty escape to Egypt and Ptolemy, whom he had heard would be accommodating.[36]

Ptolemy lived up to his reputation. He was charming and hospitable. Seleucus repaid Ptolemy by warning him about Antigonus' strength and ambition and encouraged him to go to war against Antigonus. The latter had anticipated this development and sent out his envoys to Ptolemy, Lysimachus, and Cassander to encourage them to stick to the existing arrangements. This backfired when all three made impossible demands about the division of the spoils which Antigonus refused. They formed an alliance against, rather than for, him. Antigonus rounded up some other allies in Cyprus and a new war broke out.[37]

WAR WITH ANTIGONUS

To begin with, Antigonus did well, first in Syria and Anatolia, though it took a siege lasting fifteen months to defeat the Ptolemaic garrison in Tyre.[38] That had entailed building a new navy with the help of local leaders in Phoenicia and Syria because Ptolemy had detained all the Phoenician ships and crews in Egypt. Antigonus pointedly did this in Alexander IV's name in the nominal capacity of one of the young king's officials (an epimeletes). Like Lysimachus, Seleucus, and Ptolemy, and his son Demetrius, he continued to issue silver Heracles tetradrachm coins in Alexander's name, perpetuating the fiction that somehow his empire still existed (plate 16).

Antigonus followed up his achievements by declaring that the Greek cities were autonomous, or rather that their freedom was his to give. Not to be outdone, Ptolemy issued a similar declaration.[39] Gaining the goodwill of the Greeks was a major priority.

Ptolemy avoided falling into the trap of starting a major land campaign against Antigonus. He commissioned his brother Menelaus to take one hundred ships and 10,000 men to coerce the Cypriot kings into abandoning their support for Antigonus. Seleucus obligingly joined forces with Menelaus.

By 312 BC the wily Cyrenaeans had spotted their chance to escape Ptolemy's control while his back was turned. They attacked the citadel and were on the point of wiping out the Ptolemaic garrison when envoys arrived from Alexandria. Diplomatic privileges were ignored. The Cyrenaeans killed them. When the news reached an enraged Ptolemy, he sent over an army and a fleet to seize the city. The renegades were trussed up and sent to Alexandria for trial.[40]

Ptolemy then led another army into Cyprus to mop up the operation there and tackle any of the local kings still flirting with Antigonus. Cyprus had been under Ptolemy's control since 313 BC. Nicocreon, king of Salamis, had been made his strategos over the island, effectively its puppet ruler. Ptolemy and Seleucus then embarked on a joint strategy to start pushing Antigonus into retreat. Seleucus wanted Babylon back, and Ptolemy wanted to restore lost territory.

By the late summer of 311 BC Seleucus was back in control of his satrapy. He rapidly took over all Alexander's former eastern possessions which then became the Seleucid kingdom, though whether it or indeed any of the Successor kingdoms including Ptolemaic Egypt can really be called empires is a point of some contention.[41] Before that, in 312 BC Ptolemy and Seleucus faced an army commanded by Antigonus' son Demetrius at Gaza. Demetrius cut quite a figure, celebrated for his physical beauty and size, compared to his ageing father. He was inexperienced but that also meant his men, at least so far, had nothing to hold against him. Moreover, he had a charisma that endeared him to them. He later earned himself the additional name Poliorcetes ('besieger of cities').[42]

The battle of Gaza went badly for Demetrius. Ptolemy used spikes to neutralize Demetrius' Indian elephants. Their mahouts were killed, and the animals captured.[43] Elephants were the Hellenistic equivalent of the tank. They had their vulnerabilities, but no Hellenistic king could afford to be without them. The Ptolemaic kings ended up sending expeditions into Africa to build up their phalanxes of war elephants (see Chapter 4). Gone was the Bronze Age image of the pharaoh racing along in his wood and leather horse-drawn war chariot, wheels spinning as he mowed down his foes with a bow and arrow. Now the Ptolemaic Egyptian king trundled along to war or in parades in a vehicle pulled by four elephants, the Hellenistic heavyweight version of the old motif for a new age.[44]

Demetrius fled but asked to have his dead collected.[45] Ptolemy and Seleucus were magnanimous in victory, as usual. They returned the royal baggage. Ptolemy sent the captured soldiers to Egypt, dispersed them among the administrative districts (nomes), and then set about the cities of Phoenicia. He won over Sidon and told Andronicus, then in charge of the garrison at Tyre, to capitulate. Andronicus refused to turn on Antigonus and instead hurled insults at Ptolemy. Ptolemy reacted in his customary fashion. He sent Andronicus gifts and declared him to be one of his friends. 'It was this very thing that most increased his power and made many men desire to share his friendship', said Diodorus.[46]

Demetrius, meanwhile, turned to his father for support and returned to Syria where Ptolemy still was. Ptolemy gave one of his friends, a Macedonian called Cilles, an army and instructed him to push Demetrius out of Syria or corner him and destroy him. This was a marvellous opportunity to shine but Cilles blew it. He camped with his army and failed to keep his plans secret. Somehow, the information reached Demetrius who raced ahead with a forced march, made a surprise dawn attack, and captured Cilles. Delighted by his son's remarkable recovery and success, Antigonus joined Demetrius. Assembled in anxious expectation, Ptolemy discussed the situation with his friends and generals. They advised him that it was pointless trying to risk a battle against such a huge army.[47]

THE END OF ALEXANDER IV

Ptolemy's pragmatism, bolstered by his experience and maturity, won the day. He returned to Egypt but sacked most of the cities he had captured along the way. In 312 or 311 BC (Diodorus' dating references are slightly contradictory) Ptolemy, Cassander, and Lysimachus made a peace treaty with Antigonus.[48] Cassander was confirmed as strategos in Europe but only until Alexander IV came of age, leaving a time bomb in place since, when that happened, Cassander would be finished.

Alexander IV was effectively under house arrest. Rumours emerged of a conspiracy to spring the boy and place him in proper charge of his kingdom. That obviously threatened drastic consequences for Cassander, and all the other Successors. In 310 BC Cassander ordered his commander of the guard to murder Alexander and Roxane and dispose of the bodies. News of their deaths was suppressed. An extraordinary subterfuge followed. For the next five years, the pretence was maintained that Alexander was still king. Diodorus observed, though, that 'henceforth, there being no longer anyone to inherit the realm, each of those who had rule over nations or cities entertained hopes of royal power and held the territory that had been placed under his authority as if it were a kingdom won by the spear'.[49] With Alexander IV eliminated, the secret of the Successors had been revealed: any of them who would be king could be. It would take a few years for them all to realize this.

In 309 BC Alexander's illegitimate son Heracles was seventeen and now a focus of a dangerous plot to make him king. Polyperchon had been at war with Cassander for a decade. His alliance with Antigonus had broken down, though Antigonus had supplied Heracles as a chip Polyperchon could use to bargain with Cassander. In return for his estates in Macedon and an army, Polyperchon killed Heracles. Alexander's direct line was now eradicated.[50]

THE SATRAP STELA

In the dead Alexander IV's phantom 7th regnal year as king of Egypt, Ptolemy erected the so-called Satrap Stela after the victory over

Demetrius. The stone commemorated the restoration of the rights of a temple at Buto in Lower Egypt. The text belonged firmly to an ancient tradition of bombast more usually applied to the king, whose full Egyptian titles start the text.

> So there was a great Viceroy in Egypt, Ptolemaeus was he called. A person, of youthful energy was he, strong in both arms, prudent of mind, powerful amidst men, of firm courage, steady foot, repelling the raging, not turning his back, striking the face of his foes amidst their combat. When he had seized the bow not a shot is from the opponent, a flourish of his sword in the fight no one could stand his ground, of mighty hand, nor was his hand repulsed, nor repented he of what his mouth utters, none is like him in the stranger's world.[51]

Ptolemy was celebrated on the stela as a great leader and military commander, but then he was bound to be. There was no question that he was *de facto* pharaoh and paying only superficial lip service to Alexander IV's honours as the legitimate king. The text proceeds to describe Ptolemy performing in a religious role that would normally have been the king's prerogative. Although the main text features Alexander's names as king, the name cartouches accompanying the figure of the king presenting to the gods of Buto are blank. This was either intentionally ambiguous or served as possible evidence that Ptolemy was already preparing the ground for backdating certain monuments when he became king, a promotion he was almost certainly already lining up for himself. This, however, does not explain why they were never completed.[52]

The peace of 311 BC settled nothing permanently. The freedom of the Greek cities was supposedly guaranteed but Ptolemy accused Antigonus of installing garrisons in some of them. It was a pretext to resume the war between the Successors, but also a miscalculation. Antigonus sent his sons to retaliate against Ptolemy's army, an endeavour in which they were successful, Demetrius leading the campaign.[53]

Ptolemy refused to back down. By 309 BC he had sent another army to western Anatolia. His forces managed to recover several cities but faltered at Halicarnassus when Demetrius, Ptolemy's new nemesis, pushed them back. Ptolemy established a foothold at a few cities in Greece such as Corinth. This proved to be only temporary, lasting no later than 303 BC when Demetrius and Cassander resumed control.

DEFEAT AT SALAMIS

Ptolemy suffered a catastrophic setback in 306 BC. Demetrius led a campaign against Ptolemy's control of Cyprus. He captured almost half the Egyptian fleet, wrecking some of the rest, and at Salamis routed a force led by Ptolemy's brother Menelaus who had to surrender his troops and cavalry. Ptolemy lost equipment, including 'engines of war, armaments, and money'.[54]

Demetrius tried to hang on to his prisoners and keep them in his own army. They insisted on absconding back to Menelaus because all their baggage was still in Egypt with Ptolemy. The attractions must also have included the cleruch colonist land grants which Ptolemy had introduced, providing inactive soldiers with a home and a reason to stay in Egypt on preferential terms.[55]

The victory at Salamis prompted Antigonus' military assembly to declare him king, and for him to make Demetrius his co-regent. The gesture ended the farce of pretending that Alexander IV was still ruling. Antigonus had repositioned himself as the monarchical heir of Alexander, but with his own new dynasty and claiming rule over all of Alexander's dominions.

Cleopatra of Macedon, Alexander the Great's only full sibling, represented an enticing prospect for the Successors. Her name, which recurred throughout the Ptolemaic dynasty, meant either 'the glory of her father' or more allegorically 'the fame of the paternal bloodline'. Either way, the sense is clear enough; the name suggested a female who was the product of a celebrated line of descent. Several, including

Antigonus and Lysimachus, had tried to secure her in marriage for obvious reasons. She refused them all but ended up in a form of house arrest in Sardis under Antigonus' control. Machinations followed which culminated in her accepting Ptolemy's offer of marriage. Antigonus knew that might prove a dramatic turning point in Ptolemy's ambitions and end his own. Antigonus had her assassinated in 308 BC before the marriage could take place.[56] With Cleopatra gone, Alexander's family had been almost entirely obliterated. Only his half-sister Thessalonike (d. 295 BC) and her sons Philip IV, Antipater I, and Alexander V of Macedon remained.

The other Successors were not to be outdone by Antigonus, but they adopted a more egalitarian approach. In a gesture unusual for their era, they recognized each other as rulers. One by one each was declared to be a king in his own right, including Ptolemy who publicly assumed the title in 305 BC. The tireless contrarians Antigonus and Demetrius obtusely recognized none but themselves as kings. One of the most conspicuous developments was the modification of the coinage. Seleucus and Lysimachus, for example, removed Alexander's name from the Heracles tetradrachms and substituted their own.

ANTIGONUS ATTACKS EGYPT

Obviously, given Antigonus' and Demetrius' claims, the emergence of the new kings was intolerable. Antigonus and Demetrius put together an army of 80,000 infantry, 8,000 cavalry, and dozens of transport ships. Next, they advanced down the coast from Syria towards Egypt bent on a punitive land grab.[57] Emboldened by their recent successes, they acted in haste.

Storms and a lack of suitable harbours damaged the fleet but arrival at the Nile Delta only made things worse. A lack of preparation and reconnaissance were bad enough, but the impenetrable nature of the Delta helped Ptolemy cripple the Antigonid force.[58] Ptolemy had positioned troops at all the suitable landing places, including Pelusium, the Delta waterways were too narrow for the invading ships, and supplies were running low. Ptolemy had also enticed some of the soldiers to switch sides and join him, despite Antigonus' desperate efforts to fight back and torture any recaptured deserters. The special military operation was supposed to be over quickly, but soon started to drag on, making it increasingly difficult to feed the soldiers and the animals.

Antigonus called a council of war, the upshot of which was that a face-saving plan to come back better prepared and when the Nile was low was tabled. The invasion was abandoned, supposedly for the moment. Antigonus and Demetrius beat as hasty a retreat as they could manage.

Just as Ptolemy had discovered that his own ambitions for power in Asia and Europe had proved unrealistic, now Antigonus had discovered he was no more able to move south than Ptolemy had been able to move north. Ptolemy was secure, at least for the moment. He was at liberty to set about managing his identity and image as pharaoh of that most ancient of kingdoms.

3

FOUNDATION
Ptolemy I Soter (305–282 BC)

When Ptolemy became king of Egypt by 305 BC, the western ancient world's centre of gravity was still in the eastern Mediterranean. The struggle for power among the Successors and their descendants was unresolved. Alliances had come and gone, only to be replaced by others and new tensions. Ptolemy's focus was on the men who ruled the fragmented dominions of Alexander's empire and consolidating his grip on Egypt and adjacent territories by creating an ideology and image for his new role as a pharaoh.

Ptolemy I's achievements as king of Egypt earned him an enduring reputation. It was not one many of his successors could match. Three centuries later, the Roman historian Tacitus said he was 'the first Macedonian [king] to strengthen the power of Egypt'.[1] Ptolemy had already acquired the additional name 'Soter', the Greek for 'Saviour' or 'Preserver', possibly thanks to his role in saving Alexander (see Chapter 2). Alternatively, it may not have emerged until 306 BC, perhaps because he saved Egypt from invasion by Perdiccas, Antigonus, and Demetrius.[2] Other such distinguishing epithets, followed in various forms by the later Ptolemies, gave them a quasi-divine status that set them apart from ordinary mortals.

Ptolemy had to legitimate his rule in Egypt and the Hellenistic world. He also had to be convincing. That meant being a pharaoh of Egypt for domestic consumption, while simultaneously imposing and developing the machinery of Hellenistic-Macedonian kingship. This would facilitate the exploitation of his Egyptian subject population and allow him to take his place on the Hellenistic world stage with the prestige and resources appropriate to, and necessary for, an absolute monarch.[3] Ptolemy did not work alone. He had the help of trusted advisers, among them the ousted ruler of Athens, Demetrius of Phalerum, who assisted him with laws and possibly the inception of the library in Alexandria (see Chapter 4 for more about Demetrius).

Ptolemy's name, and that of all his successors, appeared in hieroglyphs adapted from the Greek *Ptolemaios* to the Egyptian PTUALMYS (or variants on) with Cleopatra as KLAUAPADRAT. The recumbent lion hieroglyph for the 'l' was used in earlier times for 'rw' and 'r'. Written Egyptian had no sign for 'l', probably because the sound was not distinguished from the other sonorants, in this case 'r' (a similar issue affected 'd' and 't' which were sometimes used interchangeably).[4] This suggests that, when pronounced by some native Egyptians, Ptolemaios might have sounded more like *Ptuarmys* (with similar implications for Cleopatra and Alexander), possibly accentuating the difference between the native population and their Macedonian rulers (see Chapter 8 for more on the languages). However, the open mouth hieroglyph, which also represented 'r', was used for that letter in the latter part of Cleopatra's and Alexander's names, probably to try and make a phonetic distinction for the Greek 'l'. The name of Ptah, whose cult was of such importance to Ptolemaic legitimacy (see Chapter 9), also conveniently started with the same two letters, and therefore hieroglyphic signs, as Ptolemy. This helped associate the new king and his successors with ancient tradition through an alliterative resonance.

Ptolemy's reign and the beginning of the reign of his son Ptolemy II were dominated by the protracted so-called Wars of the Successors. Although these are enumerated today to distinguish them, the confusing array of dates obscures how they were each only phases in a conflict that lasted almost four decades after Alexander's death. The conflicts would see a gradual whittling away of some of the cast, and result in three major Hellenistic kingdoms presiding over the region thereafter until the Roman Republic became a significant international player a century later.

A NEW TYPE OF PHARAOH

Ptolemy was now emphatically a Macedonian *basileus* ('king'). This equated him with the other Successors and was how he was described in Greek (ΒΑΣΙΛΕΩΣ ΠΤΟΛΕΜΑΙΟΥ, 'King Ptolemy') on his coins, struck now at Alexandria, to where he had moved the mint from Memphis (see Appendix 4). In Egypt he adopted the image and titles of a traditional pharaoh. Whether now or under the later Ptolemies these pharaonic titles amounted to an 'Egyptianizing' of Ptolemaic kingship or just paid lip-service is a moot point.[5] Since that was what Alexander had done, and how Alexander's half-brother and son had been portrayed too, Ptolemy was positioning himself as the legitimate pharaonic heir of Alexander, just as Alexander had presented himself as the heir of Nectanebo II.

Pharaohs routinely identified themselves as the offspring of Amun who had appeared in the guise of their fathers to impregnate their mothers. They thereby also absorbed some of their predecessors' achievements, often by usurping their monuments and statues. Ptolemy had to be careful. Alexander had experienced hostility from some of his own men when he went too far with his notions of grandeur. Curtius Rufus noted that although the Macedonians were used to monarchy, they were also more accustomed to liberty than most people. They had therefore 'rejected Alexander's pretensions to immortality with greater obstinacy than was good either for them or Alexander'.[6] For some of the later Ptolemies that would change, but for the moment the new king needed to tread carefully.

In 304 BC Ptolemy I celebrated his coronation feast on the anniversary of Alexander's death, the preceding twelve months being counted as his 1st regnal year. Alexander the Great's Egyptian throne name was Setepen-Re-mery-Amun, 'Chosen by Re, beloved of Amun' (or sentiments to that effect, see p. 25).[7] As an easy way of further asserting his legitimacy, Ptolemy chose the same throne name as Alexander though in practice all such throne names were subject to technical modifications and variant forms.

One of the earliest versions of Alexander the Great's and Ptolemy's shared throne name is at Tuna el-Gebel in Middle Egypt in two cartouches on the façade of the subterranean temple of Thoth. The carving is crude, and the cartouches blundered, but there is no question about what they were meant to say.[8] The absence of the birth name may well be deliberate, serving to blur Ptolemy's identity with the deceased Macedonian king, or the result of uncertainty on the part of the mason.

Ptolemy also adopted a full suite of the three additional formal names (Horus, Nebty, and Golden Horus names) in the extensive Egyptian formulaic royal titulary that accompanied every pharaoh through his reign. To a modern eye these names are cryptic and almost impossible to remember.[9] They need not concern us here, but they formed an important part of the panoply of a true pharaoh, such as the Nebty name associated with the goddesses Nekhbet and Wadjet, the protector divinities of Upper and Lower Egypt, respectively. These names were thus integral to Ptolemy's new identity and that of his dynastic successors.

Ptolemy maintained Egypt's existing administrative arrangements, such as the nomes. The most conspicuous difference was the introduction of Greek as the day-to-day administrative language of Egypt, while Egyptian was increasingly limited to religious and ceremonial purposes. Official documents were sometimes compiled in Greek and Egyptian, the latter being written in both hieroglyphs and the simplified form of demotic. Demotic was also used alongside Greek in more local contexts. Official documents and packages bore lead seals with Hellenistic-style portraits, as did the coinage.[10] On temples, Ptolemy and his successors were depicted in traditional pharaonic poses, typically smiting their foes, or in choreographed scenes with Egyptian gods, all copying established Egyptian formats and styles.

PTOLEMY AND APELLES

Apelles was a celebrated painter from Kos (an Aegean island close to Rhodes) in the later fourth century BC. Ptolemy disliked him, perhaps because Apelles had found an ingenious way of painting Antigonus from a particular angle so that his missing eye was hidden, thereby improving his appearance. During Ptolemy's reign, or so the story went, Apelles was forced to take refuge in Alexandria during a storm. Rival painters spotted their chance to humiliate Apelles. They bribed one of Ptolemy's household staff to invite Apelles to dinner. Ptolemy was enraged when he saw the unwanted guest. He demanded an explanation from his stewards, who had to parade in line so that Apelles could pick out the culprit. Apelles used a scrap piece of charcoal off the floor to sketch an instant likeness of the guilty man. It was so accurate that Ptolemy recognized him immediately. Unfortunately, what happened next is unknown, but the anecdote is an interesting vignette of Ptolemy I's character.[11]

A GOD IN RHODES

War broke out between Rhodes and Antigonus in 305 BC, around the time Ptolemy was crowned king of Egypt. Rhodes was well governed and had a first-class navy. It had skilfully avoided taking sides during the various regional conflicts, thereby benefiting from a constant stream of gifts and overtures from other nations desperate to be friends (plate 9). The Egyptian trade routes were the most important financially. As a result, the Rhodians tended to favour Egypt, if anywhere at all.

The wily Antigonus saw instantly that Ptolemy could make Egypt richer, stronger, and dangerous. Rhodes turned down Antigonus' offer of an alliance. He resorted to intimidation, sending a fleet to intercept any freighters heading from Rhodes to Egypt and requisition their cargoes. The Rhodians used their own muscle to repel the Macedonian fleet, exactly as Antigonus had hoped: he treated that as a declaration of war. The Rhodians changed tack. They tried to flatter Antigonus and offered him honours.

Antigonus rejected the gesture and sent his son Demetrius with an army equipped for a siege.[12] The terrified Rhodians decided they had no choice but to offer to help Antigonus in his war with Ptolemy. They passed this on to Demetrius. His demands of hostages and access to Rhodian ports were so onerous, they gave up and prepared for war. Demetrius had brought too much firepower with him to back down. The Rhodians turned to Ptolemy, Lysimachus, and Cassander for help, pointing out that Rhodes was fighting Antigonus and Demetrius on their behalf.

The plucky Rhodians prepared defences and attacked Demetrius' supply ships. With Demetrius focusing his attention on the harbour, the Rhodians made it their priority.[13] Several weeks of major fighting left Demetrius on the back foot. Rough seas wrecked some of his ships on boulders. His position worsened and he was defeated. Ptolemy was among those who reinforced Rhodes at that point.[14]

The following year (304 BC), Demetrius was still bogged down in Rhodes but kept calm and carried on. He was so devastatingly good-looking and heroic in appearance that men followed him regardless.[15] He ordered the construction of even larger and more ingenious siege engines, earning himself the nickname Poliorcetes ('besieger of cities'). Rhodes remained resilient and resourceful, building a new inner wall in case Demetrius breached the outer one.

Athenagorus had been sent to Rhodes by Ptolemy as the commander of a unit of mercenaries. Some of Demetrius' men tried to buy him in the hope he would let them into the city.[16] Athenagorus led them on but told the Rhodians about Demetrius' plans and they were able to catch the enemy sneaking in.

Demetrius continued with his heavy engineering siege, toppling the strongest tower in the Rhodian defences, and compromising a whole section of the curtain wall. Ever with an eye for the moment, Ptolemy sent a consignment of Egyptian grain and other food to the beleaguered island, supplemented with more sent over by Lysimachus and Cassander.[17] Demetrius tried to divert the Egyptian transports but was foxed by a wind that favoured the Rhodians. They were inspired to mount a counterattack and then use the aftermath to improve their defences further. Additional supplies, and 1,500 troops as well this time, arrived from Ptolemy. Efforts to broker a peace collapsed.[18]

Demetrius began an all-out assault, but two of his most senior officers died from their wounds and he lost other soldiers too. Antigonus decided enough was enough: he told Demetrius to sue for peace on the best terms possible. Ptolemy had also written to Rhodes, promising more supplies and men, but added that he wanted peace. They made a deal. Rhodes would hand over one hundred hostages and would also fight for Antigonus unless he went to war against Ptolemy; in other words, Rhodes would remain neutral in any war with Ptolemy. In return, the city would be self-governing, ungarrisoned, and keep its revenues.[19] Demetrius packed up and sailed home.

The siege had lasted a year. The exhausted Rhodians honoured their war heroes and set up statues of Lysimachus and Cassander. They also erected the celebrated statue of Helios and one of the seven wonders of the ancient world known as the Colossus of Rhodes over the entrance to the harbour. They sent a deputation to Siwa to ask the oracle to make Ptolemy a god. In the city of Rhodes, a square precinct surrounded by a 607 ft (185 m)-long stoa on each side was erected and named the Ptolemaeum, one of the first to be created for the ruler cult of the Ptolemies. The complex does not survive among the ruins of the Acropolis of Rhodes today.[20]

ALLIANCES AND EXPANSION

Ptolemy had done well out of the siege of Rhodes without personally taking part. For all his skill, Demetrius had failed to push the siege to a convincing victory. Bad luck had not helped, but he never factored in the Rhodian Blitz spirit. Ptolemy had helped arm and feed the Rhodians, gaining popularity as a result and all for a trivial outlay. Ptolemy had also avoided direct conflict with Antigonus and Demetrius and ended up being declared a god for good measure. He could not have asked for more.

By 302 BC Ptolemy and Seleucus had agreed to a cooperative effort with Cassander and Lysimachus: they would act as allies in the war against the intractable Antigonus.[21] Being part of this alliance had an unintended consequence. Later that year Ptolemy was on campaign in Coele-Syria (also known as Koile-Syria or Syria-Phoenicia, the Syrian corridor), successfully reducing the cities there into submission. The fighting meant Ptolemy could actively contribute to the war against Antigonus while acquiring the territory he coveted. While he was besieging Sidon, Ptolemy fell for some false intelligence. The story was that Antigonus had defeated Lysimachus and Seleucus and was marching with all haste towards Syria. Ptolemy was uncharacteristically spooked. He made a truce with Sidon, garrisoned his new conquests, and withdrew to Egypt.[22]

In 301 BC Antigonus was defeated at Ipsus in Phrygia by an alliance between Lysimachus, Cassander, Seleucus, and Ptolemy. Even more decisively, and conveniently for the Successors, he was killed, 'his body having been pierced by many missiles'. Demetrius scuttled off to Cyprus. With Antigonus gone for good, the victors helped themselves to his glittering possessions like magpies. After a tense period which nearly saw them fall out, Ptolemy and Seleucus came to a gentlemen's agreement about Syria. Those parts already under Ptolemy's control were left as they were, even though Seleucus had rights over them.[23] In later years the view was that this deal amounted to Seleucus taking control of Asia but leaving Coele-Syria and Phoenicia to Ptolemy, even though under an earlier arrangement Cassander and Lysimachus had agreed that Seleucus was entitled to Syria.[24] Unfortunately, with no formal resolution the matter was left to simmer and would lead to war breaking out between the kingdoms later.

Ptolemy had the riches of the Nile Valley at his disposal, together with Cyrenaica and much of Syria. This left him in control of the whole region and the trade routes followed by valuable caravans making their way from the east, with Egypt's deficiencies (such as a lack of timber) made good by the produce of the area, which included Lebanese cedar trees. Ptolemy was starting to make some of Egypt's earlier warrior pharaohs look like pipsqueaks.

In the aftermath of Ipsus, Ptolemy made peace with Demetrius, brokered by Seleucus. This involved various marital alliances which included Ptolemy's daughter Ptolemaïs being married to Demetrius (this did not happen until 288 BC, see below), and Demetrius' daughter Stratonice marrying Seleucus.[25]

Part of the deal was that Pyrrhus of Epirus, a member of Demetrius' entourage, was sent to Egypt as a hostage. Pyrrhus' mother was Alexander's sister, Cleopatra of Macedon. His father Aeacides had ruled Epirus as joint king with a grandson of Philip II and Olympias called Neoptolemus. Aeacides was wounded and died in a battle during a complex series of disputes. By 307 BC Pyrrhus had been placed on the throne of Epirus but six years later was away at a wedding when he was toppled in a rebellion and Neoptolemus was made king again. That was when Pyrrhus fled to Demetrius, his brother-in-law.

In Egypt, Pyrrhus impressed Ptolemy and his queen Berenice with his hunting skills. He came across as a young man of sterling character. For this he was rewarded by Ptolemy with marriage to Antigone, one of Berenice's daughters by her previous husband (a little-known man called Philip and of no historical importance apart from his position in the genealogy). The relationship with Ptolemy was so successful that in 297 BC he subsidized and armed Pyrrhus. That meant Pyrrhus could retake his kingdom which he did as a joint king with Neoptolemus.[26]

DEALING WITH DEMETRIUS

Ptolemy skilfully cultivated men like Seleucus and Pyrrhus. Demetrius, however, remained volatile and untameable. By 297 BC he had managed to have himself made king in Macedon in the turmoil that followed the death of Cassander. There was a real danger he would become a new Antigonus while actively pursuing his interests. Unfortunately, his friendship with Seleucus had fallen apart when the latter insisted Demetrius sell him Cilicia. After Demetrius refused, Seleucus had demanded Tyre and Sidon instead. This enraged Demetrius who 'declared that not even if he should lose ten thousand battles like that at Ipsus would he consent to pay for the privilege of having Seleucus as a son-in-law' (Demetrius' daughter Stratonice having just become Seleucus' queen).[27]

Demetrius strengthened the garrisons in cities he controlled and, spotting how factional disputes at Athens made it easy prey, set out to take it. Initially, he was thwarted by a storm, but he tried again. This time the Athenians thought they were about to be saved by 150 ships sent over by Ptolemy. In a spectacular piece of good timing, ships arrived from cities in the Peloponnese and Cyprus to reinforce Demetrius in his hour of need. Ptolemy's ships made themselves scarce and Athens fell to Demetrius. It was a rare bonus, given the difficult times he had had.[28]

Ptolemy, Lysimachus, and Seleucus moved swiftly to seize control of many of Demetrius' more remote territories closer to their own. Ptolemy acquired Cyprus (apart from Salamis), another vital link in trade routes but also of enormous value because of its copper ore deposits. He also took Tyre and Sidon, and Lycia in Anatolia.[29] Together with Syrian territory, these acted as powerful buffer zones for the Ptolemaic domain.

In 288 BC Ptolemy, Lysimachus, Seleucus, and Pyrrhus formed a gang of four against Demetrius. Pyrrhus agreed to attack Macedon from Epirus with Lysimachus joining in from Thrace. Ptolemy sailed to Greece, using a base on the island of Andros, and encouraged the cities there to rebel against Demetrius, provoking a rebellion in Athens in

287 BC. Callias of Sphettos, Ptolemy's commander on Andros, arrived with 1,000 soldiers to support the rebellion 'acting in accordance with the goodwill of King Ptolemy towards the people [of Athens]', a key event recorded on a detailed inscription found in Athens.[30] A peace was negotiated and Callias continued to support Athens' interests at the court of Ptolemy II after his father's death. Athens' port of Piraeus was still garrisoned by Demetrius' men, but Athens was supplied from Egypt. By then, though, Ptolemy had even taken control of the Island League founded by Antigonus.[31]

Demetrius lost control by trying to fight on too many fronts. Pyrrhus and Lysimachus seized Macedon. Demetrius fled and tried to regroup. Only then did the marriage to Ptolemy's daughter Ptolemaïs go ahead. Demetrius began trying to recover Anatolia but was to end up capitulating to Seleucus. He was imprisoned in Syria, where he died in 283 BC.[32] Ptolemy followed him in the winter of 282 BC. The era of the Successors was coming to an end.

PTOLEMY'S WIVES

Ptolemy had at least four female partners, some of whom he certainly married, and by whom he had at least a dozen children. All his military ventures must have been accompanied by frequently tucking his tunic in, as he bid farewell to his latest female companion. Ptolemy was a genial man who could charm other men, so perhaps it is unsurprising that he could also charm women.

Ptolemy's known wives and partners:

1. Artakama (married by 324 BC). Persian, great-granddaughter of Artaxerxes II. Disappeared after Alexander's death. No known children.[33]
2. Thais, a courtesan. Three children. Fate unknown.[34]
3. Eurydice, daughter of Antipater (regent of Alexander's empire 320–319 BC) and niece of his brother Cassander. Eurydice and

Ptolemy were the parents of Ptolemy Ceraunus. She and her children were set aside in favour of:

4. Berenice I, daughter of Cassander and thus niece of Eurydice. Her children by Ptolemy I included his successor Ptolemy II and his sister-wife Arsinoe II (see next chapter).[35]

A VERDICT

Ptolemy was about eighty-four when he died in 282 BC during the 124th Olympiad (284–280 BC). Lysimachus and Seleucus I expired during the same Olympiad.[36] Ptolemy's longevity was unusual for the time. It was especially so given his career which had propelled him from being a figure of secondary importance in Alexander's entourage to rule over the region's oldest kingdom. It was an astonishing achievement, but not as astonishing as the luck that had brought him there.

Ptolemy emerges from the scattered source material as a dynamic and vivid personality. Ptolemy was an amiable and engaging man whose natural charm proved to be a great asset. His generosity of spirit earned him friends and disoriented his enemies. 'It is better to enrich others than be rich ourselves', he is alleged to have said.[37] He was also ruthless, as Josephus' tale about the Jews of Jerusalem illustrates (see Chapter 7) but, among the more successful monarchs, this combination of characteristics is not unusual.

Ptolemy pursued his and Egypt's interests overseas but withdrew when it was sensible to do so. His strategic and tactical judgement was usually sound. When he made mistakes, he reacted with pragmatism, applied lateral thought, and usually recovered. He left Egypt stronger than it had been for centuries, protected by buffer zones in the Near East, the eastern Mediterranean (Cyprus), and along the North African coast to Cyrenaica. Although Egypt's greatest conquering pharaoh is usually said to have been Thutmose III of the 18th Dynasty over 1,100 years earlier, Ptolemy had exceeded Thutmose's territorial acquisitions. Nevertheless, Ptolemy's was not much less of a paper empire than Alexander's. It was held together by a gossamer network of alliances and affiliations vested in the prestige and presence of personalities and fleets, rather than anything more substantive.

There is no evidence that Ptolemy had ever planned to become king of anywhere. That he managed to live to such an advanced age and died in his bed is a testimony to the esteem with which he was held and his abilities. By adopting Alexander's pharaonic throne name, he merged himself with Alexander and thus with Alexander's spurious divine and Egyptian lineage. Few would have 'believed' this, but that did not matter. Ptolemy was only playing a symbolic game integral to Egyptian culture.

Ptolemy engineered the beginning of a transition to a Greek-style administration and bureaucracy, developed and refined by his son. He shifted everyday government from Memphis, the traditional pharaonic administrative capital, to Alexandria when the city was ready (plate 3). From there he could send out assets across the Mediterranean to where they were needed to pursue his interests. In Alexandria he could receive foreigners and representatives of his allies. Alexandria served as a port of entry in every possible way, for literature, art, and philosophy, as well as trade (see Chapter 7). Ptolemy was determined to make sure that his rule extended throughout Egypt. To the south he had founded the city of Ptolemais Hermiou in the Thebaid (the region around Thebes, now Luxor) soon after 312 BC to serve as the capital of Upper Egypt. It grew to rival Memphis in size and had a Greek-style government.[38]

Although Ptolemy both initiated and participated in wars, the fighting took place outside Egypt, and he saved the Nile Valley from the direct impact of battles. Ptolemaic Egypt was established on a firm foundation which dragged it into the Hellenistic world as a powerful, secure, and resilient state with a new hybrid identity. The only question now was whether his successors would be able to live up to, or even exceed, his achievements and hold the edifice together. For a while it must have seemed to those who lived in Egypt in those days that they would.

4

MARRIAGE COMES BY DESTINY

Ptolemy II Philadelphus (285/284–246 BC) and
Arsinoe II (273–270/268 BC)

Ptolemy II Philadelphus ('Sibling-lover') was named co-regent before his father's death. A series of events ensued which included disputing his right to rule. The deaths of Lysimachus and Seleucus ended the long-running saga of the Wars of the Successors, but a new series of conflicts erupted between Egypt and the Seleucids. There were also the machinations involving Ptolemy II's sister Arsinoe II and his elder half-brother Ptolemy Ceraunus. Arsinoe II, despite her very short reign, proved an enduring phenomenon. After her death, following their brief and controversial marriage, Ptolemy II established a posthumous cult in her name that proliferated throughout the Ptolemaic world. Ptolemy II was also responsible for some of the principal embellishments to Alexandria, especially the celebrated Pharos lighthouse and the development of the library.

The Macedonian, Egyptian, and Seleucid kingdoms were locked in a relentless struggle. None was strong enough to overwhelm the others, even when two became allied against a third. Instead, power, or rather its display, was a matter of prestige showcased in war-posturing rather than anything conclusive. They were arranged around the Aegean and the eastern Mediterranean, amid a febrile jumble of other lesser petty states and autonomous cities. Any attempt to extend Egyptian power beyond the Nile Valley meant entering the traditional flashpoint of Palestine, Phoenicia, and the Syrian corridor (Coele-Syria) between Arabia and the sea, across the Mediterranean to Cyprus, Rhodes, and what is now central and southern Turkey into which the Seleucid power stretched from the east.

Polybius described how possession of Coele-Syria and Cyprus made it possible for the earlier Ptolemies to maintain pressure on the rulers of Syria 'both by sea and land'. The implication is that pressure was all it ever came to. Polybius also explained that the use of client states made the Ptolemies feel secure in their rule in Egypt, leaving them little concerned about foreign affairs. Egyptian momentum looked to be in the ascendant. The Ptolemies controlled the coastline right round and up the eastern seaboard of the Aegean to the Hellespont, including cities and harbours. Egypt used client kings as buffer zones and to keep an eye out further afield, especially on Thrace and Macedon.[1] The Ptolemies could never have seized and ruled large tracts of Seleucid territory. The colossal resources and systems necessary to achieve such extended control did not exist. There was no vision to create them, and nor was there a grand strategy to conquer such territory.

The result was a long period of intermittent recreational warfare. The rulers gesticulated at one another, flexed their muscles, displayed their armies, and formed and broke alliances. These tentacles and manifestations of power and influence were tenuous. Maintaining that pressure depended on the friends and allies of the moment, bribes and gifts, and the parading of Egyptian might. This weakness was first most graphically exposed under Ptolemy IV. For the moment, under Ptolemy II and III, the fragile flaunting of success continued.

National prestige was vested in the armed forces as the 'foundation of the state's claim to a monopoly on violence'.[2] Military and naval power achieved legitimacy for the crown at home and abroad through the successful pursuit of foreign campaigns which diminished Egypt's enemies and rivals. They were also how the Ptolemaic regime's power was imposed across Egypt, thereby securing the state through the symbolism of protection, coercion, and cultural affiliation of their presence.

SUCCESSION AND DISPOSING OF RIVALS

The unintended consequences of Ptolemy I's extended family came to their bloody and complicated climax during the reign of Ptolemy II. There was a considerable age gap. Ptolemy I was into his eighties when he made Ptolemy II, son of Berenice I, co-regent in 285/284 BC at the age of twenty-three. There was an obvious reason. Ptolemy I had so many children by different women that the decision was intended to guarantee a peaceful transfer of the crown when he died.

The sole reign of Ptolemy II from 282 BC confirmed the Ptolemaic monarchy as hereditary, regardless of the complex symbolism in the way the crown was transmitted in Egyptian tradition. He went much further than his father in the quest to establish Ptolemaic dynastic ideology.

Ptolemy II had had no rival dynastic claimants to the throne of Egypt and took nothing for granted. Like any self-respecting despot, he targeted members of his family or anyone who questioned his right to rule. As Berenice I's son, he was technically junior to the older children by Eurydice, and those of Thais. In 307 BC the philosopher and orator Demetrius of Phalerum (c. 350–280 BC), fearing Antigonus, fled from Athens where he had ruled since 317 BC to Ptolemy I for sanctuary. There he became 'first among the friends' of the king and advised him on laws (as well as probably helping instigate the library at Alexandria, see below).[3] Demetrius encouraged Ptolemy to treat his children by Eurydice as the ones worthy of sovereign power. Ptolemy insisted that his successor would be the son of Berenice. After Ptolemy I's death, Berenice forced Demetrius into rural exile where he 'somehow received an asp bite on the hand which proved fatal'.[4] This mishap doubtless helped discourage anyone else from speaking up for Eurydice's children, one of whom – Ptolemy Ceraunus ('Thunderbolt'), who was Ptolemy I's eldest legitimate son – was to take matters into his own hands.

Ptolemy II did away with his half-brother Argaeus, who had been given the job of moving Alexander's body from Memphis to Alexandria during their father's reign. The charge was conspiracy. Either he was trying to challenge Ptolemy II's accession, or the charge was trumped up. Another half-brother called Leontiscus vanished from the record. He was captured by Demetrius Poliorcetes during the siege of Salamis in 306 BC and returned to Egypt where he joined the ranks of the disappeared. There may have been another brother.[5]

TRADITION

Ptolemy II was dedicated to investigating Egypt's past and thus, by implication, his own dynasty's position in Egypt's history. He commissioned a priest called Manetho of Sebennytus (in the Delta) to research the archives, which are of course long lost. This resulted in Manetho's *Aegyptiaca*, a history of Egypt back to earliest times. Surviving now only in fragments, the work created the structure of Egyptian chronology by dynasties which is still used today.

Ptolemy II's interests were much wider. His father's adviser, Demetrius of Phalerum, had been bent on buying up as many books as possible and in every language which probably formed the basis of the library at Alexandria. Thanks to his fate (see above, this chapter), his contribution was never formally acknowledged, whatever it really amounted to; the source for this information is of uncertain authorship and date.[6] Vitruvius, who makes no mention of Demetrius in this context, attributed the main development of the project to Ptolemy II's jealousy of the great library of the Attalid kings at Pergamum. Vitruvius also claimed that Ptolemy had the Greek grammarian Zoilus executed for daring to criticize Homer in a presentation given in Alexandria.[7]

Promising Ptolemy II that the book total would eventually reach half a million, now Demetrius supposedly suggested that, since the Jews had numerous books, they ought to be translated and added to the burgeoning archive. Ptolemy was excited by the idea and wrote to the high priest Eleazar in Jerusalem asking to translate the Torah, promising to free 100,000 Jews. He also sent 100 talents for spending on sacrifices in the Temple. Seventy-two elders, six from each tribe, were dispatched to Alexandria to do the work. The upshot was that eventually the Greek version of the Septuagint was created and installed in Alexandria.[8] The Torah story is now regarded as 'largely fiction', not least because Demetrius' alleged role in this episode is impossible to reconcile with the accounts of his fall from favour and subsequent death at Berenice's inception (see previous section). The point was not to mislead but rather to create 'plausible circumstances' that symbolized the role of Hellenistic patronage in Jewish learning.[9] A similar intention probably explains the story that Ptolemy paid the philosopher Strato 80 talents for teaching him.[10]

Ptolemy II also devoted himself to Egyptian religion. Money and gifts, some raised from taxation, were poured into the temples and ancient cults such as those of the Apis and Mnevis bulls.[11] In 264 BC he visited the shrine of the ram god Banebdjedet at Mendes and ordered its rebuilding, thereafter conveniently associating the worship of Arsinoe with the ram.[12] Among other religious projects, he initiated the construction of the shrine of Isis at Philae (see Chapter 9).

PTOLEMY CERAUNUS AND MARITAL MATTERS

Ptolemy II was helped to secure his throne by his half-brother Ptolemy Ceraunus ('Thunderbolt'). Once Ceraunus had been made king of Macedon in Seleucus' place in 281 BC, he thoughtfully abandoned any claim he might have had to rule Egypt.[13]

Meanwhile, Ptolemy II's first queen was a woman known to history (confusingly) as Arsinoe I. Her parents were Lysimachus I and his first wife Nicaea (daughter of Antipater). The union therefore obviously represented an important tie between Lysimachus and Egypt. Lysimachus was thus Ptolemy II's father-in-law. He would become Ptolemy's brother-in-law too, though by then he was dead (281 BC), which saved him from any further confusion. Arsinoe I dutifully supplied Ptolemy II with several children, including the future Ptolemy III. If she thought that guaranteed her place in the Ptolemaic sun, she was soon disappointed.

Had Arsinoe I been the only Arsinoe, marital matters might have proceeded relatively seamlessly. Ptolemy II's full sister was also called Arsinoe, Ptolemy I's daughter by Berenice I. In addition, this Arsinoe was Ptolemy Ceraunus' half-sister. Today she is known as Arsinoe II, who was thus Arsinoe I's sister-in-law. In 300/299 BC, and in her mid-teens, Arsinoe II had been married to Lysimachus I as his third wife and bore him three sons. This made Arsinoe II also Arsinoe I's stepmother. Lysimachus' son Agathocles (by Nicaea and thus Arsinoe I's brother) was executed for treason at some point between 284 and 281 BC, the story circulating thereafter that Arsinoe II had fitted him up so that her own sons were more likely to succeed their father.[14]

Agathocles' death left a bereaved wife. She was Lysandra, Ptolemy I's daughter by Eurydice, and thus another half-sibling of Ptolemy II and Arsinoe II. Lysandra sought sanctuary with Seleucus I, together with her children, several other family members, and associates of Agathocles. Bolstered by Seleucus' support, they triggered a war against the hapless Lysimachus, now in his mid-seventies. Lysimachus was killed at the Battle of Korupedion against Seleucus I in Lydia in 281 BC.

Like most battles of the era, Korupedion settled nothing except to provide a pretext to have another one. Seleucus decided the time was right to invade Europe. He marched straight to his death (also 281 BC). Lysandra's full brother, Ptolemy Ceraunus, who had fled to Seleucus with his sister, murdered Seleucus and moved immediately to ensure after this brazen treachery that he was crowned king of Macedon as Seleucus' successor there. This also meant the Seleucid forces there went over to him.[15]

The assassination of Seleucus also ended the Wars of the Successors but Ptolemy Ceraunus had a problem. His half-sister Arsinoe II's sons by the dead Lysimachus had a potential claim on his Macedonian crown. Ceraunus needed to make sure his half-nephews were under his control and preferably eliminated. Arsinoe II had fled with the children to Kassandreia (Chalkidiki, northern Greece). In her vulnerable state she was easy prey for Ceraunus, who cornered her. She married him in 281 BC and became a queen for the second time, this time of Macedon.[16] Not long afterwards, Ceraunus took control of Kassandreia, where Arsinoe II's sons were in residence, and had the boys assassinated. Arsinoe II fled to Egypt and the protection of her brother Ptolemy II in 279 BC.[17] We will return to her story below.

In early 279 BC Ceraunus was faced by an invasion of Galatian Gauls. Ceraunus attacked the Gauls before he had gathered a sufficiently large force. He was defeated, captured, and killed.[18] By 277 BC Macedon had fallen under the control of Antigonus II Gonatas, the son of Demetrius I Poliorcetes.[19]

In 273 BC a treaty of friendship was signed between Ptolemy II and Rome, according to tantalizing fragments. Ptolemy's gifts were handed back by the Senate to the Roman envoys to take home out of admiration for their achievements.[20] The emerging force of Rome had yet to make any serious impact in the eastern Mediterranean.

THE APOTHEOSIS OF ARSINOE II

Once established at Ptolemy II's court, the resourceful Arsinoe II set about becoming a ruler for the third time. This involved pushing out her brother's wife, the hapless Arsinoe I, by c. 273 BC. She was sent away from court to live in Koptos (modern Qift, 27 miles (43 km) north of Luxor). She was the first of a line of powerful Ptolemaic female rulers.

Officially, Arsinoe II was known as 'great of praise, a lady of loveliness, sweet of love, king's wife, Mistress of the Two Lands, Arsinoe, daughter of the king of Upper Egypt, Lord of the Two Lands, Ptolemy, the divine Philadelphus'.[21] Arsinoe's cartouche on a magnificent relief provides us with her Greek birth name converted into Egyptian with suitable titles. It reads *Sit-Amun Irs'n wr* together with the determinative for a queen, thus 'Daughter of Amun, Arsinoe, Great Queen' (plate 5). To the side, an additional series of titles calls her 'Daughter of Amun, Mother of the Apis bull'. Arsinoe wears the red crown of Lower Egypt, sporting a solar disc and Hathor's horns.[22] She also acquired the kingly title *nswt-bitj*, which translates as 'female king of Upper and Lower Egypt', and others such as 'lord/lady of the horizons', confirming her a ruler in her own right, and appearing alongside her brother-husband in reliefs participating in cult activities.[23]

Since the concept of a queen regnant did not exist in Egyptian royal tradition, the mechanism involved awarding Arsinoe the ruling titles that would normally have been used only by a king. Earlier Egyptian royal women who made themselves into kings had done the same, most notably Hatshepsut of the 18th Dynasty. Sharing her brother's titles confirmed them as joint rulers, obliterating the idea that gender had any bearing on entitlement to rule. This was a dramatic development for the Hellenistic world. However, there was some uncertainty about how to present this to a wider public. Egyptian titles did not appear on Ptolemaic regnal coinage or in Greek texts because there were no Greek equivalents (see Appendix 3). When Arsinoe II appeared on coins she was named ΑΡΣΙΝΟΗΣ ΦΙΛΑΔΕΛΦΟΥ ('Arsinoe *of* Philadelphus').[24]

Associating his sister with himself in this important symbolic way provided Ptolemy II with useful religious and ideological credibility. He and Arsinoe could pose as the living manifestation of divine sibling spouses, and thus develop the cult of the dynasty's divine right. This precedent was followed by some of his successors, some royal marriages being presented as sibling unions when the two were not related (for example, Ptolemy III and Berenice II, who were cousins through their grandmother, Berenice I).[25]

Arsinoe II played a high-profile role until, and even more so after, her death in 270 or 268 BC. According to the poet Theocritus, Arsinoe arranged for a palace performance of a play that depicted the affair between Aphrodite and her mortal lover Adonis.[26] The occasion was designed to help associate her with Aphrodite who was herself associated with Isis in Greek culture.

Sibling marriages had occurred in earlier dynastic times in Egypt, serving the useful but unhealthy purpose of helping to keep power within the family. The marriage of Ptolemy II and Arsinoe II appalled some within the Greek and Macedonian world, while others professed to welcome the union. Pausanias erroneously said the marriage was in direct contravention of Macedonian tradition (Alexander's sister Cleopatra had married her uncle) but was 'agreeable' to the Egyptians.[27]

Sotades the poet, who notoriously never held back, according to Athenaus, 'had said many bitter things against Ptolemy the king, and especially this, after he had married his sister Arsinoe. He pierced deadly fruit with a bitter sting.' Realizing that he had gone too far, Sotades and his scathing pen fled from Alexandria to the island of Kaunos, just off the south-western corner of Turkey close to Rhodes, where he mistakenly believed he was safe. Ptolemy was incensed at the monstrous allegations that marrying his sister might have been in poor taste. His general Patroclus ran Sotades down on the island, arrested the errant poet, and sealed him alive in a lead jar which was then hurled into the sea.[28] The story is gratifyingly colourful but belongs too easily to the canon of stock tyrannical brutality to be accepted without question.

Theocritus spotted that the easiest way to come up with obsequious praise was to point out that Zeus and Hera had been siblings. He trilled, 'he [Ptolemy] and his fine noble spouse, who makes him a better wife than ever clasped bridegroom under any roof, seeing that she loves with her whole heart brother and husband in one. So too in heaven was the holy wedlock accomplished of those whom august Rhea bore to be rulers of Olympus, so too the myrrh-cleansed hands of the ever-maiden Iris lay but one couch for the slumbering Zeus and Hera.'[29]

This was exactly what Ptolemy II, whom Theocritus tactfully called a demi-god, and Arsinoe II wanted to hear. It also bought into the Egyptian religious tradition of the marriage between the siblings Osiris and Isis. Ptolemy and Arsinoe were known in Greek as *Theoi Adelphoi* ('the Sibling Gods'), adapting the Philadelphus part of the king's name in a device that conveniently associated the pair with Osiris and Isis. This dynastic cult evolved in subsequent reigns so that their successors could be incorporated, for example as *Theoi Euergetoi* (for Ptolemy III and Berenice II).[30]

Since Arsinoe had been previously married to her deceased half-brother Ceraunus, marrying her full brother cannot have seemed (to her at least) particularly radical. There was also the custom, found in many papyri texts, of Egyptian married couples referring to each other as brothers and sisters, even though they were not related.[31] The most likely explanation is that the union helped fulfil Arsinoe's ambitions, bringing her the absolute power she wanted but would otherwise have missed out on.

There were no known children from the marriage (though Pausanias claimed that Ptolemy had been in love with Arsinoe).[32] Arsinoe II may have already been past easy childbearing. She was probably already in her early forties. Having had three children successfully, her past fertility was not in doubt (and nor was her brother's). With no gynaecological history available, which is hardly surprising, either she (or he) was unable to have children by the time of the marriage to her brother or it was a mainly political arrangement. The convenient consequence was that Ptolemy's existing son and heir by Arsinoe I, the future Ptolemy III, was not displaced.

The real prominence of Arsinoe II came after her death in 268 BC at the latest.[33] It was a remarkable testimony to the struggle she had endured to come so far and her wholly focused determination to pursue her dynastic interests by whatever means necessary.[34] Ptolemy II made her the focus of a major posthumous cult, adding her to the already vast pantheon of Egyptian deities. She was deified as the 'Divine Lady Philadelphus, Arsinoe', repositioning her outside the dynastic state cult as a goddess in her own right with a college of priests. She was identified with Isis, Hathor, and Aphrodite, but could be shown alongside these deities as another in their class. On the Stela of Mendes, carved in 264 BC, it was recorded that during her lifetime Ptolemy II had awarded her the titles 'the friend of the Holy Ram and of Uta-Ba [the name of his Priestess], sister of the King and wife of the King, who loves him, the

Princess of the Nation, Arsinoe'. The text proceeds to describe her post-humous apotheosis 'after she received life a second time'. She was 'crowned . . . and she received the name of "The Beloved of the Holy Ram, Goddess, The Beloved of her Royal Brother, Arsinoe"'.[35]

Arsinoe was honoured in similar ways, and statues dedicated to her, in temples of various cults across Egypt. Among her worshippers was Ptolemy II himself, for example at Philae where she appears next to Isis while he sacrifices. Festivals and cities were named after her, for example Arsinoe in north-western Cyprus, which replaced the old city of Marion, destroyed by Ptolemy I in 312 BC for supporting Antigonus I. There were several other cities in Cyprus called Arsinoe, as well as in Greece and Cilicia. Ephesus was also for a time known as Arsinoeia.

The name Arsinoe became institutionalized as part of everyday government. The administrative district (nome) in the Fayum was named after her as the Arsinoite nome. Its Lake Moeris was drained to expand farmland for settlers and the area became prosperous during the later part of the reign and thereafter. The celebrated Labyrinth by the pyramid of the Middle Kingdom 12th Dynasty pharaoh Amenemhet III (1855–1808 BC) at Hawara in the Fayum, and which had so amazed Herodotus, was dismantled on Ptolemy II's orders to provide the materials to build a new city called Arsinoe in honour of his sister.

Arsinoe's association with other major female deities meant her worship blurred into a well-established and wider enthusiasm for protective mother-goddesses. Some of the cities named after Arsinoe also issued posthumous coins in her name. At Ephesus, local magistrates struck coins with her veiled portrait. They bear the image of a stag on the reverse, serving as a play on her name with the Greek for male, αρσεν (arsen), applied as an adjective to a male deer.[36]

The worship of Arsinoe II fell neatly into a well-established Egyptian tradition. Ahmes-Nefertari, the great matriarch of the 18th Dynasty, was deified after her death along with her son Amenhotep I. The two became the centrepieces of an enduring and popular joint cult for centuries. Arsinoe in death managed something more radical by becoming a Greek deity too. The poet Callimachus recorded how she became a goddess in his *Deification of Arsinoe*.[37] This took on a remarkable form in Alexandria where she had a temple (the Arsinoeum). If Pliny the Elder is to be believed, lodestone was to be used in the roof so that an iron statue of Arsinoe could be suspended in mid-air by harnessing magnetism. The project was abandoned when Ptolemy II died.[38] The temple precinct also featured a full-size obelisk (apparently from the time of Nectanebo I or II) which was installed by Ptolemy II 'as a tribute to his affection' to his sister, contributing an Egyptian tone to what was probably a Greek-style shrine.[39] Obelisks, potent solar symbols of rebirth, were often set up in miniature form in pairs outside private tombs in a tradition dating back to the Old Kingdom and still in use during late Egyptian history.

NUBIA

By Ptolemaic times northern Nubia had become known as the Meroitic kingdom. No longer a vassal territory of Egypt, it was an independent territory between the Nile's Fifth and Sixth Cataracts. In or around 275 BC Ptolemy organized a military expedition there. It may have been a punitive operation, designed to tackle border incursions, but it was probably also a pretext for more opportunistic purposes. Pharaonic Egypt had always looked to Nubia as a source of slaves and mineral wealth. Ptolemy was said to be the first to lead an army of Greeks into the area, utilizing 500 cavalrymen to do so.[40]

On the Red Sea coast, in what is now Sudan, Ptolemy II created a new city through which he honoured his mother. Berenice Panchrysos, which means 'All-Gold Berenice', was an allusion to the nearby gold mines of Jebel Allaki, an important source of Egyptian gold, though the name is only known in this form from Pliny. It was one of three cities named after Ptolemy's mother, the others being a Berenice linked to Koptos on the Nile by a road, and 'Berenice on the Neck' located on an isthmus stretching out across the Red Sea towards Arabia. Not far off was Ptolemais Theron ('Ptolemy's Hunting Lodge') built by Ptolemy for the pursuit of elephants which he liked to have captured alive. The Stone of Pithom announced that 'elephants in great number for the king' had been caught, brought next as 'marvels to the king' and taken by sea and then canal into Egypt near Heliopolis, adding that 'no such thing had ever been done by any of the kings of the whole earth'. As such, they could be used as war elephants, a vital ingredient if Egypt was to be able to stand up to the Seleucid army and its Indian elephants. This became a major and regular operation under the early Ptolemies.[41]

THE SYRIAN AND CHREMONIDEAN WARS OF PTOLEMY II

The three dominant rulers in the region were Ptolemy II in Egypt, Antiochus I (281–261 BC) in the Seleucid kingdom, and Antigonus II Gonatas (277–274, and 272–239 BC) in Macedon. A series of wars followed as an extension of the Wars of the Successors. The evidence is scattered and often obscure, leading to much unsubstantiated speculation. More importantly, the wars were largely inconclusive. No king achieved a decisive expansion in power.

In 281 BC Antiochus I controlled Anatolia and east to India, but the capital Seleucia-in-Pieria in northern Syria was threatened by local disturbances. The undated Ilion Decree, found in the Troad (part of north-western Anatolia), says that soon after succeeding Seleucus, Antiochus set out to restore cities in Seleucid territory which had suffered 'difficult circumstances' caused by 'a rebellion . . . against the kingdom'. The rebels go unidentified, but the situation was serious enough to compromise his rule. Antiochus turned up and claimed to have settled matters, bringing the Seleucid state 'to a greater and more brilliant condition'.[42]

Regardless of Antiochus' spin, the rebellion made him more vulnerable, compounded by the takeover of his father Seleucus I's army in Macedon by Ceraunus (assuming the text has been correctly attributed). This did not go unnoticed by Ptolemy II and led to the so-called Syrian War of Succession (280–279 BC), or so at least some believe.[43] Ptolemy, 'then at the height of prosperity', was actively pursuing his interests in Anatolia. Memnon of Heraclea (probably Heraclea Pontus on the Black Sea coast) says Ptolemy gave his city a new temple of Heracles and a gift of corn, as well as presents to other cities.[44] Ptolemy went to Palestine (or Persia) in 280/279 BC where he found Egyptian gods and brought them, presumably in statue form, back to Egypt.[45]

The evidence for Ptolemy expanding his influence includes a decree from Athens which names Callias of Sphettos as commander of troops at Halicarnassus under Ptolemy II.[46] Inscriptions from Lycia that supposedly show 'Ptolemaic territorial expansion' there do nothing more than cite 'Pttole' (sic) in their incomplete and damaged texts.[47] At best, these suggest a nebulous assertion of influence in various places over a very wide range of territory by whoever was able to at any given moment.

By 279 BC Ptolemaic–Seleucid hostilities had temporarily abated. Ptolemy II's half-brother Magas (see Family Tree 1) had no viable claim on the Egyptian throne. His mother Berenice I had arranged for him to govern Cyrene to keep him out of the way. Predictably dissatisfied, Magas organized a revolt and foolishly invaded Egypt in *c.* 275 BC. Ptolemy II prepared his defences and waited for the Cyrenaean army to arrive. It did not because a Libyan rebellion had conveniently forced Magas to fall back on Cyrene.

Ptolemy II seized the initiative and marched to Cyrene but discovered the mercenaries he had hired included 4,000 treacherous Galatian Gauls plotting to take Egypt. Ptolemy relocated them to an island in the Nile or the Delta where they dissolved into squabbling and killing each other or dying from hunger.[48] He commemorated his treatment of them with a Galatian shield beside the Ptolemaic eagle on a special-issue gold multiple coin called a trichryson.[49] Meanwhile, Magas married Apama, daughter of Antiochus I, and the pair were also in league with Antigonus II, presenting a threat to Egypt.

Ptolemy II, who clearly had informers on the ground, dispatched commando units into Seleucid territory to attack targets of opportunity. The First Syrian War (274–271 BC) had broken out. Ptolemy's army was immediately confronted with a counterattack by Antiochus and withdrew. In 273 BC Ptolemy II and Arsinoe II set out for the eastern Delta not far to the north of Heliopolis to the eastern Harpoon nome where the king 'discussed with his sister, the wife and sister of the king, [how] to protect Egypt against enemies'.[50] However, Ptolemy and Antiochus soon discovered that neither was really in control of events. A plague supposedly hit Babylon and an economic crisis hit Antiochus' army.[51] Antiochus withdrew, leaving Ptolemy able to pose as the victor. From the minimal evidence available, that Ptolemy II was still in control of Damascus over a decade later, in 259 BC, suggests, even if the Seleucids had made any sort of advance, those gains had been temporary.[52]

Magas clung on to independent control of Cyrene until his death in *c.* 250 BC. Before then, he arranged for the marriage of his daughter Berenice II to the future Ptolemy III Euergetes, son and successor of Ptolemy II.

In 267 BC the Chremonidean War began, named after Chremonides, an Athenian statesman who in 268 BC had brokered an alliance between Ptolemy, Athens, and Sparta. Ptolemy II wanted to use his naval power to assert Egypt's interests in Greece and the Aegean to keep Macedon in check. Antigonus II had defeated Pyrrhus and taken control of much of Greece either directly or through local tyrants he had installed. Ptolemy sent an expeditionary force commanded by Patroclus to support Athens.[53] An attempt to trap Antigonus' army between the Egyptians and Athenian allies evaporated when Areus, the king of Sparta, withdrew, his supplies running short. Patroclus was unwilling to risk unilateral action. Athens held out long enough for Antigonus to back down anyway, but he installed a garrison as a condition.[54]

Ptolemy II used his navy to show his strength in the Aegean and on the Ionian coast, without any intention to conquer new territory. His ships used the islands of the Aegean as bases along the way, Thera and Crete being among them. By the end of the Chremonidean War, which Ptolemy effectively lost, he had still enhanced Egypt's influence in the Aegean.

The Second Syrian War lasted from 260 to 253 BC. An Aetolian called Timarchus killed a Ptolemaic general in Samos, called Charmades, and established himself as tyrant in Miletus and over Samos. This information only survives in the works of the Roman senator Sextus Julius Frontinus, written over 350 years later. Frontinus illustrates very well just how patchy the record is for the Ptolemaic kings and their affairs; he only mentioned it in passing because he was interested in how Timarchus had disguised himself in Macedonian dress as Charmades to be allowed into the harbour.[55] If this is an accurate description of what happened, that also tells us something about how Ptolemaic generals presented themselves as Macedonians, not Egyptians.

A naval battle took place near Ephesus between the Rhodians and a Ptolemaic fleet. The Ptolemaic fleet put to sea to force the Rhodians to fight. The Rhodians pretended to retreat, causing the Ptolemaic crews to burst into cheering and return to port. The Rhodians reappeared, catching the Egyptian fleet by surprise and defeating it.[56] When this occurred is unclear. It is no less mysterious why the Rhodians would have wanted to attack a Ptolemaic fleet, unless it was one that belonged to 'Ptolemy the Son'. The possible product of Ptolemy II's marriage to Arsinoe I, 'the Son' had by 267 BC been placed in command in Ephesus on his father's behalf but had gone rogue, probably in league with Timarchus. This would have piled further pressure on Ptolemy II in the region.

Whatever happened, and whoever he really was, 'Ptolemy the Son' disappears from the records thereafter.[57]

Timarchus' seizure of Samos did not look good for Ptolemy II. The situation deteriorated further when the Seleucids weighed in on the action. Antiochus II (261–246 BC) killed Timarchus (how, we do not know). This delighted the Milesians who named Antiochus 'Theos' ('the Divine').[58] They do not seem to have wanted Ptolemy back.

Around 255 BC Antigonus II defeated Ptolemy II's navy in a battle near Kos. The sources for the occasion are incidental references. Athenaeus was only interested in explaining why he had not mentioned Antigonus' trireme in his more discursive discussion on large ships.[59] By the late 250s BC, one island, either Hydreia or Andros (the text is corrupt), was under Antigonus' control.[60]

In the meantime, Ptolemy II possibly undertook a campaign in Syria in 257 BC.[61] A demotic ostracon from Karnak records the classification of land in a census for fiscal purposes under Ptolemy II in his 28th regnal year (see Chapter 8). The text's preamble says, 'the pharaoh who won a victory over the pro-Persian king when [he] went to the land of Syria'. Strictly speaking, neither king is named but Ptolemy II and Antiochus II are assumed. Even Syria is not specifically mentioned, since the Egyptian words used were *t3 Hr* which mean 'distant land'. While this might be, and could well be, a synonym for Syria, then again it might be somewhere else, though Syria is a reasonable stab. As so often in Egyptology, going back to the primary source leaves one with the dispiriting sense of the promised evidence slipping through one's hands like sand.

The outcome of the Second Syrian War was unlucky for Antiochus II. The accommodation he came to with Ptolemy II involved divorcing his determined wife Laodice and marrying Ptolemy's daughter Berenice Phernophorus (see next chapter) and refuting Laodice's children as potential heirs. Laodice moved to Ephesus.

PRESTIGE

According to Athenaeus, Ptolemy II used his wealth also to invest a navy that outnumbered those of other rulers. He had 'two [ships] with thirty banks of oars, one with twenty, four with thirteen, two with twelve, fourteen with eleven, thirty with nine, thirty-seven with seven, five with six, and seventeen with five. But there were twice as many ships with four to one and a half banks of rowers. The ships dispatched to the islands and the other states over which he ruled, as well as to Libya, numbered more than 4,000.'[62] The purpose of course was posturing. In the Ptolemaic world, banks of oars were bells and whistles. Theocritus trumpeted Ptolemy's achievements in one of his Idylls:

> He rules, the prince of heroes, Ptolemy.
> Claims half Phoenicia, and half Araby,
> Syria and Libya, and the Æthiops murk;
> Sways the Pamphylian and Cilician braves,
> The Lycian and the Carian trained to war,
> And all the isles: for never fleet like his
> Rode upon ocean: land and sea alike
> And sounding rivers hail king Ptolemy.
> Many are his horsemen, many his targeteers,
> Whose burdened breast is bright with clashing steel.[63]

Theocritus was a court sycophant. He started out here with Ptolemy's claims on overseas lands. The most reliable interpretation is that Egypt was currently enjoying, or posed as having, considerable international prestige. Ptolemy had the freedom to exert influence and control when he needed to and well into what ought to have been Seleucid territory. At a time when huge tracts of territory were involved and the power of the states concerned was so limited, this influence was probably intermittent rather than evidence of wholesale authority being exerted. One thing is certain: Ptolemy II failed to eliminate his opponents just as they failed to eliminate him. Nor did he expand the Egyptian Empire to such an extent that his dominance was uncontested and sustained.

PTOLEMY II'S GRAND PARADE

The works of Callixeinus of Rhodes, a contemporary of Ptolemy II, III, and IV, are lost but some extracts survive.[64] They include his account of a grand parade laid on by Ptolemy II in Alexandria. This formed part of the Ptolemaieia festival celebrations and, more importantly, the *performance* of power.[65] These represented the pinnacle of Ptolemaic Egypt's wealth and influence. The parade probably took place early in the reign, perhaps after Magas' ambitions were curtailed.[66] Whatever the context, its purpose was clear. Callixeinus might have obtained his information from another source, but he could have been an eyewitness.

The centrepiece was a lavishly decorated pavilion that accommodated 130 members of the elite on couches, at some distance from where the 'soldiers, artisans, and tourists' were to be entertained. The pavilion was covered with flowers, statuary, paintings, and displays of cloaks and shields. Three-dimensional figures drawn from myth had been used to create tableaux of drinking parties, with furnishings such as tapestries, Persian carpets, gold tables and tableware, and silver basins. The estimated value was 10,000 talents, a huge sum but still less than the annual cash revenue the Ptolemies raised from Egypt.[67] The crowd was also treated to a march past by 57,600 infantry and 23,200 cavalry.

The parade had discrete sections, beginning with the 'Morning Star' contingent. The last part of the parade was called the 'Evening Star' because the procession lasted all day and into the evening on an occasion when Venus was visible in the early morning and Mercury in the evening (or vice versa). This occurred in midwinter in Ptolemy II's reign in 279/278 BC and 247/246 BC. The Morning Star part was followed by one named after Ptolemy and Arsinoe's parents, and then more sections for 'all the gods', each indicated by appropriate attributes.

A detailed account of the various other displays and floats followed, described as the Dionysiac procession. This climaxed in an array of exotic animals, an 18 ft (5 m)-long statue of Dionysus riding on an elephant, twenty-four elephant chariots, eight teams of ostriches, Ethiopian birds, and a rhinoceros.

The parade included an important dynastic statement. A statue of Ptolemy and another of Alexander the Great were featured. The late Ptolemy I, and Berenice I, who was possibly still alive, were honoured with three gold statues each, as was Ptolemy II with two. All these statues were displayed on gold columns. No explicit mention, however, is made of Arsinoe II (or Arsinoe I) other than referring to the 'king and queen', rather complicating how to position the event in the narrative of the reign and to understand why exactly it had taken place and who was behind it. Berenice is the only queen mentioned, making it more likely that the parade happened early in Ptolemy II's joint reign with his father in or soon after 285 BC, but without any certainty.

Such accounts belong to a long rhetorical tradition in antiquity.[68] They were designed to create an image in the reader's mind. The result is therefore as much a product of the reader's imagination as anything else. They also amplified the perceived significance of the writer for having a privileged ringside seat to witness the action, or at least appearing to do so. Callixeinus calls Ptolemy 'the most excellent king'. He was in the business of eulogizing the leader with an eye to his own benefit. A possibility, and a likely one, is that, even if Callixeinus was present, he wrote down his account later, perhaps referring to an uncredited third party. The meticulously enumerated detail suggests he used archival sources that he researched subsequently.

The king's intent to overwhelm guests with unlimited extravagance is probably broadly accurate. The indulgence and ostentation were wasteful but at the time made sense to a monarch bent on advertising his legitimacy and the prestige of the state over which he ruled. Ptolemy II was also said to have had some of the 'finest houses' to accommodate his mistresses. According to Polybius, he decorated them with portraits of one of them, Cleino, 'dressed only in a chiton [shoulder-fastened tunic] and carrying a rhyton [drinking cup]'.[69]

Ptolemy II died in 246 BC. He had made a significant contribution to consolidating the Ptolemaic regime in Egypt. Among his innovations from 263 BC was the system of tax farmers, taxation having previously been paid into temples (see Chapter 8).[70] The administration of Ptolemaic Egypt had been enhanced to help the regime harvest the country's wealth to fund its international prestige, war, and court extravagance. His work in Alexandria had done much to realize Alexander's ambitions for the city. For the moment, Egypt under the Ptolemies was becoming wealthier but their assiduous attention to exploiting the country was sowing the seeds of resistance.

5

GREAT BENEFACTORS
Ptolemy III Euergetes I (246–222 BC) and Berenice II (246–222 BC)

Ptolemy III Euergetes was Ptolemy II's son by Arsinoe I. He was around thirty when he became king in 246 BC, just as Rome's First Punic War was in its final stages. He ruled alongside his cousin Berenice II as the Benefactor Gods. His reign of around twenty-four years saw the Ptolemaic kingdom reach its greatest geographical extent. Ptolemaic power was far from secure at home. Some native Egyptians had come to resent bitterly being ruled by Macedonians and other Greeks. A series of popular risings erupted over several decades.

Ptolemy III Euergetes became sole king on 28 January 246 BC when 'he received his exalted rank from his father', recorded on the Canopus Decree (plate 6). He may already have been made joint monarch.[1] He took care to assert his legitimacy by describing himself as the son of Ptolemy II and Arsinoe II, 'the two Sibling-Gods'. His real mother Arsinoe I was quietly forgotten. Soon after his accession, the new king was married to his cousin Berenice II, whose mother Apama was Antiochus I's daughter. Berenice's father was Ptolemy Magas.

Ptolemy III and Berenice II shared descent from Berenice I, Ptolemy III being her grandson from her marriage to Ptolemy I, and Berenice II being her granddaughter from her marriage to the little-known Philip. There was a strategic advantage. Berenice II brought her father Magas' Cyrene at no additional cost (Magas had died *c.* 250 BC). Given how much time and trouble the wars of Ptolemy II's reign had involved, the recovery of Cyrene must have seemed an easy bonus. The acquisition contributed to Ptolemy III eventually presiding over Ptolemaic Egypt at the height of its power and territorial control. The success of the Ptolemaic dynasty to date had been paid for by exploiting Egypt and the native population as much as possible. Rebellions broke out, with the bitterness being directed at the Greek and Macedonian administrators. The resistance lasted well into the reign of Ptolemy IV (222–205 BC) and beyond.

Soon after Ptolemy II died in early 246 BC, the Seleucid king Antiochus II abandoned his wife Berenice Phernophorus ('the Dowry Bearer', a sister of Ptolemy III) and returned to Laodice. It was a breach of the agreement made with Ptolemy II who had provided his daughter Phernophorus six years earlier in 252 BC, supposedly sending her water from the Nile so that she need only drink that.[2] The express condition was that Antiochus give up Laodice, and her children were prohibited from succeeding him. Ptolemy II accompanied Phernophorus to Pelusium, from where Ptolemy's chief minister Apollonius the dioiketes (in charge of finance) and Artemidorus the physician escorted her to the Syrian border.[3] There was thus no doubt about Ptolemy II and his daughter's expectations concerning the match, part of the price of ending the Second Syrian War in 253 BC.

Antiochus II had no intention of honouring the deal once Ptolemy II was dead but an aggrieved Laodice, whom Antiochus had married as a 'love match', had her own agenda. Soon after she returned, Antiochus II died in suspicious circumstances in Ephesus, almost certainly assassinated on her orders. He was succeeded by their son as Seleucus II Callinicus ('the Gloriously Victorious'), Laodice insisting that Antiochus had named her son as heir just before he expired. Conveniently, she was the only witness to the dying king's last words.

THE THIRD SYRIAN WAR (246–241 BC)

Laodice next turned her attention to Berenice Phernophorus and her baby son, then resident in Antioch. She feared him growing up to be a rival and more legitimate claimant to the throne. Phernophorus stood her ground and declared her son (another Antiochus) king. She sought help from her brother Ptolemy III and took refuge at the shrine of Apollo at Daphne near Antioch. The Seleucid kingdom was fragmenting into factions gathering around the rival claimants and their spirited and ambitious mothers. Before Ptolemy reached her, by the end of 246 BC, Phernophorus and her son, possibly on the orders of Seleucus II egged on by Laodice, were murdered. Ptolemy III reacted by organizing the assassination of Laodice, invading Syria, and reaching Babylon in what is now known as the Third Syrian War. Avenging his sister was a handy pretext.[4]

Ptolemy III's three-year war started well. He was helped by the cities, appalled at the death of Phernophorus and the boy, coming on side out of sympathy. He left Berenice II at home to govern in his absence. She took the opportunity to strike coins in her own name and with her portrait.[5]

A legend arose that Berenice II, in honour of her husband's war, had dedicated a lock of her hair to Aphrodite, only for it to disappear and be later found among the heavenly constellations as the *Coma Berenices* by an astronomer called Conon. The story was known in Roman times, the poet Catullus reworking it in Latin and recalling how the king, 'blessed in his new marriage, had gone to waste the Assyrian borders'. He had based it on the original, composed by Callimachus of Cyrene in around 245 BC.[6] In his *Aetia*, Callimachus trumpeted Berenice's chariot team's victory at the Nemean Games in Greece, though he was either ignorant of her origins or chose to upgrade her pedigree, calling her 'nymph, holy blood of the sibling gods'. She was not the daughter of Ptolemy II and Arsinoe II.[7] The fact that Callimachus had created his poems in the first place was a testament to the esteem in which Berenice was held in intellectual and literary circles, though her reputation has suffered through a desire in her own time to depict her as the embodiment of contemporary Greek ideas about ideal womanhood. Part of the problem is trying to unravel political realities from the text of courtly poetry.[8] One modern view is that Berenice II was set on presenting herself as Hathor to her husband's Horus.[9] At a more prosaic level she appeared on some demotic documents in dating formulae with the feminized form of the Egyptian word *pr3t* ('pharaoh' – the final *t* feminized the term), placing her on a par with Ptolemy III.[10] On coinage she was ΒΑΣΙΛΙΣΣΗΣ, 'queen', matching her husband's ΒΑΣΙΛΕΩΣ, 'king'.

Ptolemy III swiftly reached Antioch with land and sea forces and was received unopposed. From here he headed to Babylon rather than pursue Seleucus II, and extravagantly claimed to have conquered Mesopotamia, Babylonia, Susiana, and 'all the rest as far as Bactria'. A text to this effect appeared on a throne made for Ptolemy III at Adulis on the Red Sea and is backed up by some of the countries also appearing in a list on a now-lost shrine at Esna.[11] These were obviously largely symbolic rather than literal claims, designed to help Ptolemy pose as a new Alexander. Merely having strutted past with an army was enough.

According to St Jerome in his commentary on the Book of Daniel (using the lost works of Porphyry), Ptolemy:

carried off as booty 40,000 talents of silver, and also precious vessels and images of the gods to the amount of 2,500. Among them were the same images which Cambyses had brought to Persia at the time when he conquered Egypt. The Egyptian people were indeed devoted to idolatry, for when he had brought back their gods to them after so many years, they called him Euergetes (Benefactor). And he himself retained possession of Syria, but he handed over Cilicia to his friend, Antiochus, that he might govern it, and the provinces beyond the Euphrates he handed over to Xanthippus, another general [probably the same man hired by Carthage, see p. 171].[12]

After his campaign, Ptolemy III was able to turn his attention to Egypt. His success was something of a mirage. 'If [Ptolemy] had not been recalled to Egypt by disturbances at home, he would have made himself master of all Seleucus' dominions', said Justin cryptically.[13] Ptolemy had no choice but to withdraw in 245 BC. He had left Egypt to go on campaign because he believed his throne was secure. That was a mistake.

The rising did not last long on this occasion, but it was an ominous portent. Holding Egypt together had just become briefly the main priority for the crown and the army. One recent hypothesis is that volcanic eruptions compounded deep existing tensions in Ptolemaic Egypt by suppressing Nile floods and may have acted as the trigger for rebellions and withdrawing from campaigns. The theory is plausible but depends to some extent on modelling. Demonstrating cause and effect is likely to be impossible since of course contemporary documentation made no link between the river and remote volcanic events.[14]

The Seleucid kingdom remained intact. Any advantage Ptolemy had gained had only come about because of the self-inflicted problems caused by Antiochus II and Laodice. With Ptolemy gone, Seleucus II organized a fleet to attack Egypt, but it was wrecked in a storm. He only just survived. The cities that had at one moment gone over to Ptolemy were dismayed by Seleucus' misfortune and supported him once more. Seleucus assembled an army but was defeated in battle by the Egyptians. Battered but unbowed, Seleucus offered his younger teenage brother Antiochus Hierax a share in ruling the Seleucid kingdom. That spurred Ptolemy into making a ten-year truce with Seleucus, who was tripped up by his brother: Hierax wanted total power and thereby undid himself. The brothers descended into civil war, emasculating the Seleucid kingdom for two decades.[15] Hierax invaded his brother's territory but was defeated, later being murdered by Galatian Gauls in 227 BC. Seleucus II died the following year after a fall from his horse.

The peace of 241 BC left Ptolemy with some of his conquests, including Ephesus and the vital port of Antioch at Seleucia-in-Pieria, where Seleucus I was buried. Egypt now had control of the coast from the west to Libya and round the Levant and along Anatolia and up through the Aegean to Thrace.

The year 241 BC was also when Rome won the First Punic War against Carthage (see Chapter 11). Carthage was reduced from having been the most important naval power in the western Mediterranean to paying reparations and ceding control of Sicily to Rome. Rome had abruptly become an international power just as Ptolemaic Egypt reached the peak of its success.

GREEK AFFAIRS

The brilliant Greek general Aratus (271–213 BC) became strategos of the Achaean League, a confederation of cities in the central and north Peloponnese in 245 BC, renewed every two years until his death. The League's allies included the Roman Republic, and its principal enemies were Macedon, then ruled by Antigonus II Gonatas (died 239 BC), and its ally, the Aetolian League in central Greece. Tension with Macedon, not surprisingly, made an alliance with Egypt an attractive prospect. In 243 BC Aratus made Ptolemy an ally and commander on land and sea. In return, Ptolemy paid 6 talents annually to Aratus, giving him a foothold in Greek affairs from where he could check Macedonian power.[16]

The relationship was doomed. During the rule of Demetrius II of Macedon (239–229 BC) the Aetolians went over to the Achaean League. They were promptly attacked by Demetrius. By 229 BC his son Antigonus III Doson (died 221 BC) was king of Macedon. He went to war against the Aetolians, blockaded them and then offered them safe passage, only to double-cross them as they retreated and annihilate them.[17] By 229 BC Aratus and the Achaean League had gone to war against a newly strengthened and dangerous Sparta under Cleomenes.

The Achaeans wanted to stay friends with Ptolemy III, partly as a debt of honour for his past assistance, but they had to run with whomever could help them best. This led Ptolemy to abandon his support for the Achaean League, thereby forcing Aratus' hand. He replaced Ptolemy as commander on land and sea with Antigonus Doson.[18] Ptolemy therefore found himself being courted in turn by the Aetolians and Athens. He was awarded a new tribe in his name in Athens called Ptolemais, following a tradition of using hero names for tribes. As such, he was worshipped in his own hero cult, a privilege granted out of Athenian 'goodwill'.[19]

Egypt's importance to Greece's chaotic power games continued. Cleomenes begged Ptolemy for help and was obliged to send his mother and children to Egypt as hostages. His mother discovered in Egypt that Ptolemy was also being contacted by Antigonus Doson and that the Achaeans were offering peace terms to Cleomenes. Cleomenes did not dare end the war without Ptolemy's permission. His mother told Cleomenes to stand up for himself.[20] In 222 BC 'an envoy from Ptolemy reached Cleomenes informing him that he withdrew his subsidy and requested him to come to terms with Antigonus'.[21] Cleomenes toyed with the idea of paying his men from his own resources and forged ahead but in the summer of 222 BC Antigonus Doson invaded Laconia and defeated Cleomenes who fled to Alexandria.[22]

Ptolemy III was taken with Cleomenes' charm, regretting siding with Antigonus. Ptolemy 'kept encouraging Cleomenes with assurances that he would send him back to Greece with ships and treasure and restore him to his kingdom' with an annual pension of 24 talents. Cleomenes spent the money on a modest life and on helping any other refugees from Greece who had made it to Egypt.[23] Ptolemy never followed through with his promises. He died later that year and his son, Ptolemy IV, did nothing to fulfil his father's undertakings.

Ptolemy III's interventions in Greece, and the general turmoil there, epitomized so much of Hellenistic politics in the third century BC. The perennial pugilistic posturing for primacy, fragile friendships, subsidies offered and then abruptly withdrawn, weakened every one of the protagonists, regardless of the position they started from. Distracted by their endless squabbles, they were oblivious to what Rome had pulled off over two decades earlier to the west and the imminence of the Second Punic War (218–201 BC).

There was a much more immediate threat. The Seleucid kingdom was emerging from the past few decades of chaos. Antiochus III, the Great, had become king in 223 BC after the short and disastrous reign of his older brother Seleucus III Ceraunus (226–223 BC). Seleucus III had confronted the growing ambitions of Attalus I of Pergamum; his invasion of Attalus' kingdom was a catastrophe, and he was murdered by his officers. Not yet twenty years old, Antiochus III ruled until 187 BC. He took control of a fractured state. His ambitions took time to bear fruit, but they also drew Rome into the region in an unprecedented way, sowing the seeds that would turn the Hellenistic world upside down.

THE BENEFACTORS AT HOME

Ptolemy III became interested in Egyptian religion, either out of a personal enthusiasm or because he had sensed the political advantages of doing so. From the beginning of Ptolemy I's rule, preserving the integrity of Egyptian traditions, especially when it came to cults, had been treated as a priority.

Given the domestic disturbances which had called Ptolemy III back home, respectful patronage of Egypt's oldest institutions was sensible. The Serapis cult was fully developed by the Ptolemies. Ptolemy III performed 'many great and benevolent deeds for the temples of the Egyptians' and with a special focus on the Apis and Mnevis bull cults. The recovery of Egyptian cult statues from Persia during the expedition was an inspiring moment for the king, reinforcing the sense that his military achievements had made Egypt secure.[24] The works included starting the remarkable Temple of Horus at Edfu (not completed until around 57 BC). He also continued the shrine building at Philae started by his father.

FOUNDATION DEPOSITS

A curiosity of the reigns of Ptolemy III and IV, lasting from 246 to 204 BC, was the bilingual (Greek and Egyptian) dedicatory foundation plaques for temples, shrines, and connected structures.

They were buried under the corners of the new buildings and made in the name of the royal couple to local gods including Serapis, Isis, and their son Harpocrates (a Greek adaptation of 'Horus the Child'), Bastet, Heracles, Osiris, and Aphrodite/ Hathor. Most are known from Alexandria and the general area under Ptolemy III but they have also been found elsewhere in Egypt dated to Ptolemy IV's reign.

Foundation deposits were nothing new in Egypt. These Ptolemaic examples were unprecedented in being bilingual, designed to show commitment to the indigenous community and their gods. Each deposit seems to have been made up of sets of ten plaqn fixed combinations of certain materials, such as five of glass, one of faience, one of mud brick, and the remainder in gold, silver, and copper.[25] They bore the names of the royal couple together or individually as in the case of Berenice II at the Alexandrian Bubasteum, where the focus on childbearing made it more likely to be a woman's preserve), and their children. They were discontinued after Ptolemy IV's reign.[26]

Although Egypt's climate and geographical state is relatively stable, the country is not immune to natural disasters. An unusually low Nile flood occurred prior to Ptolemy III's 9th regnal year (238 BC), recorded on the Canopus Decree that year: 'During their reign there came a year with a very low Nile (water), and the hearts of all men and women in Egypt were smitten with grief.'[27]

Ptolemy III and Berenice II remitted taxes and arranged for shipments of expensive grain from Syria, Phoenicia, and Cyprus to alleviate starvation. Ptolemy was formally given his new honorary title Euergetes (Benefactor). The royal couple shared the title, being known as the Benefactor Gods, and were honoured in a five-day festival.[28] Priests were obliged to wear rings bearing the title, linking them more closely to the state as its servants and loyalists. Through priestly decrees and motifs, the Macedonian Ptolemaic pharaohs were 'indigenized' as protectors. This also involved risk, should they be seen to fail in those duties. In the Canopus Decree Ptolemy III and Berenice II are portrayed as rulers of such powerful beneficence that they could serve as saviours of the Egyptian people and as guarantors of the Nile flood.[29]

A correction was made to Egypt's defective calendar, also mentioned on the Canopus Decree. For well over 2,000 years the calendar in operation contained twelve months of thirty days each (360 days) plus five intercalary days to make a 365-day calendar. This overlooked the fact that the solar year lasts 365¼ days and meant that the civil and solar calendars moved out of synchronization by one more day every four years, taking 1,461 years to come back into alignment before drifting apart again four years later. A new festival in honour of Ptolemy III and Berenice was added every four years to introduce an additional day, so that 'the rules which exist as to the laws of the science of the ways of heaven have now been set right'. The couple had lost a daughter, also called Berenice, as an infant, from unknown causes. She was made queen of the virgins to reflect her own status as a virgin as well as being deified and honoured in all of Egypt's temples. She was also commemorated in a festival, and the 'bread of Berenice' given to the wives of priests.[30]

Stelae recording the Canopus Decree were set up in temples throughout Egypt. The text was therefore inevitably rhetorical to some degree. All the credit for the achievements is given to the royal personages. The modified calendar is a rare instance of admitting that part of the structure of Egyptian life had been awry.

THE OCTADRACHMS OF PTOLEMY III

Ptolemy III continued the tradition of largely depicting his grandfather, Ptolemy I, on his coins, for example the gold octadrachm (8-drachm) piece he issued with the portraits of his father and Arsinoe II and his grandparents. But a unique series of gold octadrachms honouring Ptolemy III was produced, probably by

Ptolemy IV.[31] These show the king with several divine symbols: Helios' radiate crown, the aegis of Zeus, and the trident of Poseidon. The question is whether Ptolemy III was being portrayed as a syncretic version of all three and thus a divinity in his own right, or whether the intention was only to associate him with divine-type attributes so he would be 'godlike' but not an authentic god. The legend ΒΑΣΙΛΕΩΣ ΠΤΟΛΕΜΑΙΟΥ is the standard Greek one that names him as 'King Ptolemy' (see Appendix 4). This makes more sense with how it was only during the reign of Ptolemy V that claims of royal divinity started to be used in official documents and inscriptions, even though they had been commonly used in unofficial documents before then.[32]

Ptolemy III's generosity to the Egyptians and their cults was not just self-interest. In *c.* 226 BC Rhodes was badly damaged by a catastrophic earthquake that also caused the celebrated Colossus to collapse. He was among those who stepped in promptly, though the island's strategic and economic importance meant that it was obviously beneficial to do so. Polybius misplaced the Rhodian disaster to around or just before the Battle of Raphia in 217 BC, implying that Ptolemy IV was the source of aid. The earthquake had occurred almost a decade earlier, during the reign of Ptolemy III, so it was he who promised the Rhodians 300 talents in silver, as well as corn, timber for ships, sail cloth, bronze coins and more bronze to repair the Colossus, skilled labour, and food.[33]

The cost was met from Egyptian coffers, currently filled with war spoils or what was left after Ptolemy III's gifts to the temples. The rebellions had been swiftly crushed, but they were a sign of how carefully the Ptolemaic dynasty would have to be with over-zealous taxation.

It was probably under Ptolemy III and Berenice II that hundreds of older statues of gods and pharaohs were cleared from the Temple of Amun at Karnak and buried in the so-called 'cachette' in front of the Seventh Pylon. The purpose was likely to have been to make way for new statues and monuments of the Ptolemaic regime, reflecting the support shown to established native cults by Ptolemy and Berenice. This also helped to reinforce the depiction of traditional Egyptian religion in a Ptolemaic idiom.

Polybius praised the Rhodians for how they dealt with the earthquake in 226 BC. 'So great is the difference both to individuals and to states between carefulness and wisdom on the one hand, and folly with negligence on the other, that in the latter case good fortune actually inflicts damage, while in the former disaster is the cause of profit.'[34] Polybius might as well have said this about how Rome dealt with the catastrophic defeats at Hannibal's hands at Trasimene (217 BC) and Cannae (216 BC) in ways that led ultimately to their victory in the Second Punic War. The accession of Ptolemy IV could not have come at a worse time.

6

THE SHAPE OF THINGS TO COME
Ptolemy IV Philopator (222–204 BC) and Arsinoe III (220–204 BC)

Ptolemy IV Philopator and Egypt were both the victims of his shortcomings, but also of the machinations of Sosibius, an ambitious and manipulative court official. Although Ptolemy IV won a brilliant victory at Raphia in 217 BC against Antiochus III, his reign was distinguished only by his inability to rule as his predecessors had done. Ptolemy IV's rule coincided with the Second Punic War (218–201 BC) between Rome and Carthage. The emergence of Antiochus III on the scene and then a newly empowered Rome at the beginning of the second century BC changed everything.

THE ACCESSION OF PTOLEMY IV PHILOPATOR – 222 BC

A common phenomenon in a weak ruler's court is a charismatic individual who controls the monarch. In Ptolemy IV's case that was Sosibius, a brilliant sportsman who had risen to prominence under Ptolemy III. His blaze across the Ptolemaic firmament marked the point at which the crown began to lose control of the court to favourites, chancers, and ambitious members of the very aristocracy the regime had created and favoured.

Ptolemy IV's reign also marked the beginning of sixty years in which the rivalry and warfare between the Ptolemaic and Seleucid kingdoms dramatically intensified. Within two decades, success in the Second Punic War gave Rome the power and influence that encouraged the later Ptolemies to decide that Roman support and guarantees would be decisive in holding on to their crowns.

The poet Callimachus composed the *Soeibiou Nike*, 'the Victory of Sosibius', celebrating the hero's success in a chariot race.[1] Somehow, Sosibius found his way to court after serving as a priest in the cult of Alexander, and became the 'head of affairs'.[2] His closest associate was a minister called Agathocles, a distant relative of the Ptolemaic ruling house through his great-grandmother Theoxena, a daughter of Berenice I by her earlier marriage to the nonentity Philip and thus a half-sister of Ptolemy I. The two were aided and abetted by parasites and hangers-on, among them Philammon, whose crimes included murdering Berenice II.[3]

Ptolemy IV slid easily into the clutches of Sosibius. Cleomenes was still in Alexandria, frustrated that Ptolemy III had never made good his promise to help him recover his throne and lands. Cleomenes appealed to Ptolemy IV, but the otiose king was unable to locate his interest in Cleomenes' problem and ignored his requests to leave. Sosibius and his henchmen wondered what to do about Cleomenes. Spending money on helping Cleomenes was regarded as a waste. There was also the worry that, with Antigonus gone, Cleomenes might recover his kingdom and then easily make himself master of all Greece.[4]

Sosibius plotted to kill Berenice II, and the new king's younger brother Magas (not to be confused with his maternal grandfather Ptolemy Magas of Cyrene who died in *c.* 250 BC).[5] Either there was some doubt about Ptolemy IV's entitlement to succeed his father or there was already a court faction of malcontents gathering around young Magas. If Ptolemy's defective personality was already in evidence, that would not be surprising. He was about twenty when he became king, old enough for his inclinations to be known. The killing of Magas and his supporters left Ptolemy IV confident he was safe at home. Accidents of fate had left Macedon and the Seleucid kingdom being ruled by two very young kings (Philip V and Antiochus III), who were thus of no concern to Egypt for the moment.

Ptolemy IV instead enjoyed the pomp and circumstance of being king, ignoring both domestic and foreign affairs.[6]

Sosibius was concerned that Berenice II's 'courage' might ruin his plot to kill her. It was essential for Sosibius that as many people in the court circle be brought onside first with the promise of favours, thereby guaranteeing that his scheme to take control would be unopposed. Sosibius decided that Cleomenes ought to be in on the plot. Cleomenes was so desperate for resources from Ptolemy IV that he would surely be a useful ally. Cleomenes obliged, enthusiastically promising support from his 4,000 mercenaries.

That was when Sosibius realized he might be walking into his own trap. In a context where the king was so apathetic, Cleomenes' popularity with his mercenaries might prove very dangerous. Sosibius put it about that Cleomenes was plotting to overthrow the king and had him arrested. Ptolemy IV was persuaded to agree to Cleomenes being locked up. However, Cleomenes escaped while the king was in Canopus by getting his guards drunk, and tried with his friends to take control of Alexandria but failed. He and his men committed suicide, conveniently solving Sosibius' problem.[7] Sosibius and Agathocles ended up being responsible for the deaths of Ptolemy III's brother Lysimachus, Ptolemy IV's brother Magas, and their mother Berenice II, and later even the king's sister-wife Arsinoe III (killed by Philammon on their orders), the mother of his son and successor Ptolemy V Epiphanes.[8] In a proverb compiled by Zenobius, Magas' death was blamed on Ptolemy IV and their mother's death on suicide by poison after he locked Berenice up.[9]

Polybius, who lived and wrote close enough to the time for Ptolemy IV's nature to be widely remembered (or at least how Polybius' sources *chose* to remember him), added that the king's 'shameful amours and senseless and constant drunkenness' led him to have no interest in foreign policy or Egypt's security. His predecessors had been able to threaten the kings of Syria thanks to their control of Coele-Syria, Cyprus, and numerous cities around the coast and in Anatolia. Ptolemy

IV, though, took to 'a life of dissipation' after the Fourth Syrian War. He 'never took any thought for the future' and was defined by folly.[10]

Although in *c.* 212 BC he had married his sister Arsinoe III, by whom he had a son who succeeded him as Ptolemy V Epiphanes, Ptolemy IV took as his mistress Agathocleia, sister of Agathocles.[11] Arsinoe III was the last Egyptian queen known to have used the title *ḥmt-nsw-wrt*, 'King's Great Wife', which dated back at least as far as the 12th to early 13th Dynasties in the Middle Kingdom, sixteen centuries earlier.[12]

The Greek polymath scholar Eratosthenes of Cyrene was sufficiently taken with Arsinoe III to write a memoir of her, now lost apart from quotes in the works of others. He described how she had looked on with disapproval at her brother-husband's behaviour. Athenaeus recorded how, according to Eratosthenes, the king had been interested in a variety of festivals and sacrifices, especially those associated with the cult of Dionysus. On one such occasion, Arsinoe asked the man who was carrying the olive branches what festival it was. She was told that it was the Flagon-Bearing celebration when the participants drank from flagons they had brought. Arsinoe turned to her companions, including Eratosthenes, saying 'that must indeed be a dirty get-together. For the assembly can only be that of a miscellaneous mob who have themselves served with a stale and utterly unseemly feast.'[13]

THE *TESSARAKONTERES* (THE 'FORTY-ROWED')

Ptolemy IV's celebrated 'Forty-Rowed', a vast catamaran galley, was an excellent example of the vacuous flaunting of showcase Hellenistic military equipment. The ship had 4,000 rowers in 40 banks of oars, 400 sailors, and 3,000 marines, but was so large it was effectively immobile and unusable. The given size was 280 cubits in length, equivalent to 420 feet or 130 metres. HMS *Victory* (1765), still the flagship of the British Royal Navy's First Sea Lord, is 227 ft (69 m) long, just over half the length of the *Tessarakorontes*. The gigantic white elephant was purely for show, a pointless conceit designed solely for Ptolemaic prestige.[14]

THE FOURTH SYRIAN WAR (219–217 BC)

Antiochus III wanted to restore the Seleucid kingdom to its original prestige. The accession of Ptolemy IV ought to have been a gift to the Seleucids and it was, but not just yet. Antiochus' first target was Antioch's port of Seleucia-in-Pieria. In 219 BC he brought up a naval squadron, based himself five stades (0.5 miles) away, and sent a force to Coele-Syria to prevent the Egyptians stationed there from coming to help. He offered the city authorities various incentives to surrender but they refused, so he attacked by land and sea. The decisive moment came when some of the officers in the city (who had been secretly persuaded to join Antiochus) begged their commander to sue for peace. He gave in and the city fell to Antiochus.[15]

The fall of Seleucia-in-Pieria challenged Egyptian control of the eastern Mediterranean. Disgusted by Ptolemy IV's behaviour, Theodotus, governor of Coele-Syria, became a turncoat. He offered to discuss terms with Antiochus and hand the territory over to the Seleucids. He had good reason for his treachery. In 221 BC Theodotus had fought off an earlier attack on Coele-Syria by Antiochus. For this reward he was summoned to Alexandria where he 'barely escaped with his life'.[16] Antiochus seized the moment and ignored the Egyptian–Seleucid treaty. He took Tyre and Ptolemais (Acre), helping himself to armaments and at least forty ships. Antiochus learned that Ptolemy IV had reached Memphis while an Egyptian army was in Pelusium and taking measures to obstruct an invasion by blocking off any sources of drinking water. Antiochus' solution was to avoid a battle. Instead, he used his muscle to start coercing individual cities to go over to him one by one.[17]

While Antiochus did as he pleased, the Egyptian king sat on his hands. Defending Pelusium was all very well, but the indolent Ptolemy had made no preparations for war. Sosibius and Agathocles stepped in, giving orders to ready the army. They also tried to convince Antiochus that Ptolemy would prefer to negotiate terms via arbitrators such as Rhodes and the Aetolian League, rather than come to blows. Agathocles and Sosibius established themselves in Memphis to receive the diplomatic missions.

Alexandria became the assembly point for existing mercenaries on the Egyptian payroll and any others who could be bought in. It made sense to keep the two separate. The diplomats had no idea what was going on in Alexandria. For all their skulduggery and other unedifying characteristics, Agathocles and Sosibius were equal to the moment, unlike their king. They recruited highly experienced military commanders from various locations in the region to train and prepare the armed forces, though it is possible, even probable, that the reforms had begun earlier.[18]

The decision to buy in these men, such as Echecrates of Thessaly and Eurylochus of Magnesia, proved to be decisive. The soldiers were supposedly formed into ethnic-based units, suitably equipped, drilled, and taught to handle weapons, according to Polybius. This does not correspond with documentary evidence from the time for ethnically mixed units. Polybius was probably trying to amplify the superiority of the Greeks hired.[19] They attended motivational lectures on skills and techniques used in Greek warfare. Polybius lists units of mercenaries amounting to just under 50,000 men, to which 20,000 Egyptians under Sosibius himself were added, along with a 4,000-strong contingent of Thracians and Galatian Gauls and another 2,000 new recruits.[20] The reported size of the army reflected the resources available to Egypt, but it also illustrated the dependence on hired muscle.

Antiochus bought time by playing along with the diplomatic negotiations. A four-month truce was organized. Antiochus went home for the winter of 221/220 BC, confident that Ptolemy IV would agree to terms, just as Agathocles and Sosibius planned, even though they were secretly determined to go to war. Antiochus even sent his army to disperse back to their homes. He argued to the Egyptian diplomatic mission that arrived in Seleucia how in Coele-Syria he had only been taking back what was rightly his; and that had been the intention of the agreement made after the Battle of Ipsus in 301 BC between Seleucus I, Cassander, and Lysimachus. The Egyptian mission argued the exact opposite, insisting that Ptolemy I had helped Seleucus I on the understanding that Coele-Syria would remain under Egyptian control.[21]

With negotiations at a stalemate and the winter giving way to spring, both sides prepared to fight. During 220 BC Antiochus advanced. He was elated when one of the most senior Egyptian officers, Ceraeas, changed sides, followed soon after by Hippolochus of Thessaly who brought 400 cavalry.[22]

RAPHIA

It was not until early 217 BC, when Rome suffered its first great catastrophe of the Second Punic War at Lake Trasimene (21 June) in Italy, that the Ptolemaic and Seleucid armies were ready to fight. Perhaps Sosibius and Agathocles were occupied in ensuring that Egypt's war elephants were in good condition. A papyrus records a special order 'to deliver hay to the elephants in Memphis', dated 2 December 218 BC, and necessitating the requisitioning of a large galley-type ship (*lembos*) then conveniently moored at Ptolemais Hormou in the Fayum.[23]

Learning that Ptolemy IV was on his way via Pelusium, Antiochus prepared his army of 62,000 infantry, 6,000 cavalry, and the vital 102 war elephants, and advanced south. The armies camped about ten stades (1.1 miles) apart until Antiochus closed in to five stades, with the result that men sent out to fetch water and food bumped into one another and became involved in minor skirmishes.

Theodotus and two companions brazenly sneaked into the Egyptian camp before dawn and made it into Ptolemy's pavilion unnoticed. The plan was to murder him, but Theodotus was unaware the king was sleeping elsewhere in a private tent, presumably with Arsinoe who had accompanied him. This slip-up was a decisive turn of events. Although Theodotus killed the king's doctor, had he been able to assassinate Ptolemy IV the history of Ptolemaic Egypt might have ended then and there.[24] Another five days dragged past before Ptolemy and Antiochus started to position their forces on the battlefield. Lacking any achievements of their own, they boasted to their men about their glorious predecessors and promised rewards for fighting that day.[25]

THE GRIEVANCE OF PISTOS

On a papyrus dating from 217 BC, Pistos described himself as a 'Persian of the Epigone', which theoretically means he was a non-active, unpaid soldier. It might also have become the equivalent of a rank which was only used with 'Persian'. The term Persian (*perses*) was a pseudo-ethnicity, probably used as a taxation category, though it might reflect remoter parental ancestry. Pistos is Greek for 'trusted one'.[26]

The new campaign gave Pistos an opportunity to earn some money. Pistos had been hired by a Thracian cavalryman called Aristocrates who lived in the Fayum at the village of Autodice where he held 100 arourae (about 28 hectares) of land, around three to six times as much as the estates of those who could be regarded as 'modestly well off'. Pistos signed a contract in which he agreed to accompany Aristocrates on the campaign and bring him home in return for a monthly wage which the men had agreed. Pistos fulfilled his side of the deal, or so he claimed, but Aristocrates refused to hand over an outstanding amount of 10 drachmae in a bid to trick him. Pistos had to make an appeal to Ptolemy IV via Diaphenes, the local strategos (chief administrator of the nome), who would in turn have to go to Pythiades, the epistates (local police financial superintendent). A docket on the appeal indicates that an instruction was given to ensure that Pistos received justice.[27]

Unlike Trasimene the same year, where Rome's Republican citizen army was cut to pieces by Hannibal, the violence at Raphia (near modern Rafah, Gaza) began with the elephants of both sides advancing against each other. Ptolemy had a disadvantage. His African elephants were frightened by the smell and noise of Antiochus' Indian elephants.[28] The Egyptian elephants fell back. Antiochus' army launched a two-pronged assault on the Ptolemaic cavalry and the peltast (armed with a javelin and light shield) infantry. The Egyptian left wing was visibly crumbling until Echecrates of Thessaly led a counterattack from the right wing which involved one unit of mercenaries attacking the enemy in front of them while he took his cavalry around the back of the elephants and bore down on the Seleucid cavalry.

Abruptly, Ptolemy emerged into open view to urge his men on. The faltering army recovered their spirits and began a fightback. The inexperienced Antiochus assumed that, because one part of the Egyptian army had started to retreat, the whole Ptolemaic force was falling apart. Only when an officer pointed out that a dust cloud showed the Seleucid camp was threatened did he realize the day had been lost. Antiochus blamed everyone else's cowardice for the defeat, insisting that he had done everything to ensure victory.[29]

Antiochus fell back on Raphia, and then to Gaza, from where he asked Ptolemy for permission to recover the remaining bodies of the dead. The figures reported by Polybius are effectively meaningless except that Antiochus had lost about seven times as many men as Ptolemy but held on to most of his elephants and captured most of the Egyptian ones.[30]

More to the point, Antiochus might easily have won at Raphia. But the Egyptian victory was indisputable. Ptolemy kept Coele-Syria, and the cities that had been so swift to side with Antiochus were equally speedy in changing back to Egypt. Polybius called it 'opportunistic ingratiation'. His scathing observation overlooked the basic desire to survive. In such an endlessly contested area it made sense to go with the flow. Within little more than a decade, though, rebellion at home had changed the picture completely for Egypt.

AFTERMATH OF RAPHIA

At home the jubilant priests of Memphis took the opportunity to celebrate the victory as if Ptolemy IV was a new Thutmose III. They exulted in the booty, the offerings, and the restoration of the temples that

Antiochus had taken control of and desecrated. The priests heaped more honours on the king, including a festival and a procession, and commissioned a statue of him, 'Ptolemy, the avenger of his father, him whose victory is beautiful'.[31]

Antiochus III had a more three-dimensional mind than his enemy. He could see Ptolemy IV might follow up the victory by invading Syria. Instead, Ptolemy IV was overjoyed to have Coele-Syria back. He was even more delighted by the prospect of peace. He agreed to a truce in a trice (some sources say a year, but the Raphia Decree says two years and two months) and, after settling matters, withdrew to Egypt and decided to sit back.[32] That, at least, was how Polybius put it, but he may have been unfair. Ptolemy III had prosecuted a war deep into Seleucid territory and had to withdraw when rebellions occurred at home. His son might have been lazy, but he was not a complete fool. Although, to a modern eye, the region may look relatively limited in size, at the time the distances were substantial and dangerous. Diplomatic correspondence might take several months to pass between Asia and Egypt. It would also take time to get the measure of Antiochus III.

Ptolemy's withdrawal meant Antiochus could start recovering Seleucid prestige. One by one, the eastern satrapies in Parthia and Bactria returned to the fold. By the 190s BC Antiochus was able to turn his attention westwards to Macedon, and next to face a newly invigorated and confident Rome.

In 216 BC Capua in Campania surrendered to Hannibal, then roaming at will in southern Italy. The leader of the pro-Roman party there, Decius Magius, was sent to Carthage by sea. During a storm his ship was driven to Cyrene where he sought sanctuary. He was taken to Alexandria and Ptolemy IV set him free to return to Rome or Capua, but Magius chose to stay in Egypt where the king was a 'giver and defender of freedom', rather than be what amounted to a deserter in Rome.[33]

Sosibius, unlike Ptolemy, recognized the risk that Antiochus posed. He avoided becoming embroiled in wars elsewhere, which suited Ptolemy. An Egyptian mission joined forces with Chios, Rhodes, and Byzantium to broker a peace between the Hellenistic and Aetolian Leagues in 217 BC.[34] In Sicily the teenage Hieronymus (215–214 BC), ruler of Syracuse, had supported Carthage during the Second Punic War. He exploited a long-standing tradition of friendship with the Ptolemies to ask that Egypt support the Carthaginian cause. Hieronymus sent an embassy to Italy to treat with the Carthaginians and simultaneously sent his brothers to Alexandria.[35] The scheme fell apart when Hieronymus was murdered after ruling for only thirteen months.

At the same time as fighting the Second Punic War, the Romans had gone to war with the Aetolian League against Philip V of Macedon (221–179 BC) in the First Macedonian War (214–205 BC).[36] They needed to stop Philip from helping the Carthaginians. Egyptian missions tried three times to end the war. One reported speech by an ambassador, obviously a retrospective invention, warned the Aetolians that once the Romans had defeated Hannibal, they could turn their full strength to fighting in Greece. Their purpose would be, he warned, only to pretend to be helping when the real intention would be to conquer all Greece.[37] The Romans knew they needed Egypt onside, the only country in the entire region free from the ravages of war.[38] In 211 BC or thereabouts, Ptolemy IV was approached for help by a desperate Rome, on the brink of defeat and starvation (see Chapter 11). In 210 BC Marcus Atilius and Manius Acilius arrived from Rome as ambassadors to the Alexandrian court. They brought a purple toga and tunic for Ptolemy IV, and an ivory chair, as well as an embroidered mantle (*palla*) and purple cloak for Arsinoe III so that the two could dress as wealthy Romans.[39] At the time Rome was fighting for survival. Within a few decades Ptolemy IV's descendants would be looking to Rome to guarantee their thrones.

THE LEARNED PTOLEMY IV

Despite his shortcomings, Ptolemy IV had inherited his predecessors' interest in learning and intellectual pursuits. He invited the philosopher Sphaerus to Alexandria. In one discussion Sphaerus argued that it was impossible for a wise man to hold an opinion. Ptolemy tricked him with some fake pomegranates which Sphaerus accepted as real. Triumphant, Ptolemy burst out with 'you have given your assent to a presentation which is false'. Sphaerus retorted that he had not accepted the proposition they were pomegranates, merely that there were good grounds for believing them to be, which was an important distinction.[40] Ptolemy also built a temple dedicated to Homer, probably in Alexandria, and decorated it with images of the various cities that claimed to be where Homer was from. He commissioned a painter called Galaton to produce a portrait of Homer with the peculiar metaphor of Homer throwing up and other poets collecting his vomit.[41]

DISCONTENT

By 207–206 BC disturbances erupted again in Egypt. This time they were much more serious, lasting into the 180s BC and the reign of Ptolemy V, and marked a turning point for the regime. No longer could securing Egypt be guaranteed. Dissatisfaction with pharaonic rule was nothing new. At the end of the 18th Dynasty, Horemheb (*c.* 1323–1295 BC) introduced reforms to correct abuses of pharaonic privilege. In the 20th Dynasty, industrial action broke out in the tomb-workers' village at Deir el-Medina in Western Thebes after this state-sponsored community was left short of supplies during the reign of Ramesses III (*c.* 1186–1153 BC).[42]

Under the Ptolemies exactions increased with the enhanced use of surveillance, fines, and punishments to keep farmers and workers tied to the land. They were obliged to deliver predetermined amounts of produce or other goods, set by the state, on due dates, and were personally liable for any shortfalls and were pursued by administrators on behalf of the state. The 'disturbances' of Ptolemy III's time had probably been sparked by the impositions made to pay for the Third Syrian War. The underlying problems had not disappeared. The Ptolemaic kings depended on paying for large numbers of mercenaries, as had been evident at Raphia. More specifically, by the 220s BC, or soon after, the proceeds from the harvest tax were shifted from the cult of Amun to the crown, along with state officials meddling with temple management, ostensibly to set right abuses.

The so-called 'Demotic Chronicle' (late third century BC) is a palimpsest that celebrated a prophecy about 'a man of Heracleopolis who will rule after the foreigners (and) the Greeks . . . the priest of Aseph will be happy after the Greeks have left'. The text is jumbled. It criticizes not only the Persians but also the native rulers such as Nectanebo I and II, and the Greeks. The sentiment was a hope that a native king would emerge to rid the ordinary people of their troubles.[43]

Just as had been the case in earlier pharaonic times, Ptolemaic absolutism ensured there was no means of expressing political opposition to the state, no popular assembly, and no system of representation. Grievances had to be directed personally to the king through a hierarchy of intermediaries with no guarantee of satisfaction or even that the matter would be considered.

THE SERAPIS–ISIS TETRADRACHMS OF PTOLEMY IV

Ptolemy IV produced a unique series of tetradrachms, continued by Ptolemy V, depicting the jugate busts of the sibling deities Serapis and Isis instead of royal portraits, probably an allusion to Ptolemy IV and his sister-wife Arsinoe III (plate 10.1).[44] It was perhaps an effort at propaganda during a time of domestic disturbances to associate the crown more overtly with Egyptian gods.

The type was minted in large quantities, presumably also to try and meet a pressing need for sound bullion coinage and help shore up confidence in the state.[45] By the first few years of his reign, silver coinage was in such short supply it had virtually ceased to be mentioned in financial documents.[46]

Polybius described how the Egyptian troops were jubilant about the Raphia victory. They had become convinced that they now deserved a suitable leader under whom they could serve as an independent power and were disinclined to obey any orders from their current commanders.[47] This of course was an implicit sideswipe at Ptolemy by Polybius who was suggesting that his own men had no respect for him.

Elsewhere, Polybius explained how, late in his reign, Ptolemy became embroiled in 'a war which, apart from the mutual savagery and lawlessness of the combatants, contained nothing worthy of note, no pitched battle, no sea-fight, no siege'.[48] The description is that of an unedifying and vicious guerrilla war with no set-piece battle scenes and thus unworthy of a Hellenistic war leader. The war might have been against those soldiers who had returned from Raphia determined to be led by someone more capable. A papyrus of about this date uses the term 'the Egyptians' for the first time to refer to the attackers of a fortified village. One interpretation of that passage is that it refers to a more general phenomenon of persons living on the margins of society, who had been pushed out because of the exploitation of rural people. They engaged in opportunistic banditry against organized social centres of villages and temples.[49]

The Rosetta Stone of 196 BC provides some explanation with a clause stating that Ptolemy V had 'ordained that those [soldiers] who return of the warrior class, and of others who were unfavourably disposed in the days of the disturbances, should on their return be allowed to occupy their old possessions'. It also mentions a 'long-standing disaffection' which had led to rebels occupying the city of Lycopolis in the Busirite nome in the Delta causing 'much damage to the temples and all the inhabitants of Egypt' before it was taken 'by storm' by Ptolemy V, who destroyed the 'impious men'. He also punished in Memphis the leaders of the rebels during his father's reign 'who had disturbed the land and damaged the temples', thereby avenging him.[50]

The humiliating chaos in the Delta under Ptolemy IV carried on into his son's reign. Raphia had been a triumph but Ptolemaic authority was rattled by these long-running grievances. That a Hellenistic monarch could be so brazenly challenged worried Antiochus III and Philip V enough to set any other tensions aside and to offer help to Ptolemy IV.[51]

Ptolemy IV's unwholesome reign ended abruptly, or so it seems, in 204 BC during the period of disruption when he was about forty. If he was murdered, we know nothing about it. Sosibius and Agathocles might have found the prospect of ridding themselves of an unreliable king attractive, especially if they could also do away with Arsinoe (and that is exactly what seems to have happened) and then rule through Ptolemy V Epiphanes. The boy, born in 210 BC and co-regent since infancy, was only five or six years old. That this was all planned is a plausible hypothesis but cannot be tested. The passing of Ptolemy IV and the accession of a small child delighted Antiochus III and Philip V. Any help they had offered the boy's father was instantly forgotten with the prospect of dividing up Ptolemaic territory between them.[52] At the same time, the Second Punic War in the west was grinding towards a bloody Roman victory at Zama in 202 BC. Rome's tumultuous journey to that point now made it inevitable it would play a major part in Ptolemaic affairs.

Part II

ASPECTS OF LIFE IN PTOLEMAIC EGYPT

In these four chapters some important aspects of life in Ptolemaic Egypt are explored, looking back over the first century or so of the regime, and forward to the end.

7

A TOWN LIKE ALEX

Alexandria was the international showcase of Ptolemaic legitimacy. The greatest centre of art and learning in the region, Alexandria was celebrated throughout antiquity. It was a febrile place, always teetering on the point of erupting into violence, especially during times of political instability, and had a large and important Jewish population.

The most obvious problem for any student of Alexandrian history and archaeology is that the principal ancient written accounts, by Diodorus and Strabo, are by Greeks and belong to late in Ptolemaic history or just after. There are no comparable Ptolemaic-era descriptions. Few scraps of ancient Alexandria survive to be studied in situ. Today, Alexandria is a sprawling Egyptian coastal city and port and far larger than its ancient counterpart. The features that made Ptolemaic Alexandria so famous, the Pharos lighthouse, the Hippodrome, the Library-Museum complex, and the tombs of Alexander and the Ptolemies, are long gone, along with other monuments like the temple of the cult of Arsinoe II.

Earthquakes have ravaged the site since antiquity. Only in modern times has underwater archaeology started to uncover the extent of submerged areas, like the royal quarter.[1] Inscriptions occasionally turn up but are rarely found in their original locations. Alexandria's environmental conditions have resulted in very few documents in the form of papyri and ostraca surviving unless they were written and sent elsewhere, such as the Fayum. Alexandria was never the greatest city that ever was or ever would be, but its story is unique and its prominence in antiquity and popular lore exceptional. It was always regarded as a separate entity from Egypt.

By 311 BC Ptolemy as satrap had completed the process of transferring his government from Memphis to Alexandria. Now his regime could far more effectively exert influence over the wider region and simultaneously control Egypt. Among the innovations that asserted Alexandria's primacy was an order that the priests assemble annually there, an obligation we know about because it was remitted by Ptolemy V in 196 BC, recorded on the Rosetta Stone.[2] Alexandria was also the pivotal force in the complex Ptolemaic governance of the nation. This is where the censuses, the reports and records of production, taxation, court cases, land disputes, arrears, the mint, and movement of money into the state coffers were all managed.

Lake Mareotis was fed by canals from the Nile, on which vast quantities of goods and produce were brought by boat and barge to Alexandria and sold on to markets across the Hellenistic world. The north side of the city faced the Mediterranean with two harbours, the Great (east) and the Eunostus (west), divided by the peninsula which led out to the island of Pharos (see Chapter 8 for a consignment of barley in 252 BC destined for Alexandria). Here it was transferred to ocean-going vessels for export. Several faience vessels of early Ptolemaic date, probably made in Alexandria, subjected to modern analysis show stylistic adaptations from foreign influence. One, for example, is a rhyton (drinking cup) of Near Eastern style with decorative features from there and Greece (such as rosettes and a gryphon), as well as the technical innovation of lead added to the glaze.[3] Excavations in Alexandria have yielded Greek-style geometric mosaics that belonged to elite houses (plate 17).[4] Both symbolize the vast commercial interests involved in catering to an immigrant and cosmopolitan community.

As well as the Greek trading city of Naucratis, to the east of Alexandria in Abukir Bay were the long-established major trading port cities of Canopus and Thonis-Heracleion. These have only recently started to give up their secrets thanks to underwater archaeology.[5] Alexander and the Ptolemies developed the Greek *polis* (city), which first arrived in Egypt under the Saïte kings, with new semi-autonomous foundations. Public buildings housed administrative institutions and served the population with facilities like gymnasia, baths, theatres, and sports arenas such as hippodromes.

Among these new cities was Ptolemais Hermiou, founded around 22 miles (about 36 km) south of Thebes. By Strabo's time it was larger than Memphis.[6] A proliferation of smaller towns and settlements, some resembling major cities, serviced the wider community in the hinterland, all linked together through the Ptolemaic administrative and taxation structure. Many included Ptolemy, Arsinoe, or Berenice as part of their names, thus serving as a visible and everyday reminder of the ruling house's dominance.[7]

THE PEOPLE OF ALEXANDRIA

The Alexandrian population consisted of the royal household, the palace guard, elite troops, and a seething mass made up of Greeks, Egyptians, Jews, and countless numbers of others drawn from all around the region, including Roman visitors, traders, and diplomats. Alexandria's Greek population was the largest of all the Greek colonial cities. They enjoyed their own privileges and administrative organization, known as the *politeuma*, also permitted to the Jews of Alexandria. However, Greeks who lived in Alexandria avoided calling themselves Alexandrians, remaining wedded to their Greek ethnic identities.[8]

Alexandria has been called the 'first "urban giant" in the Mediterranean' but, even at its greatest extent, the population is not thought to have exceeded 320,000, around a third of Rome's at its height. Diodorus Siculus was told, when he visited Egypt between 60 and 56 BC, that 'not including slaves' there were 300,000 people living in Alexandria.[9] While

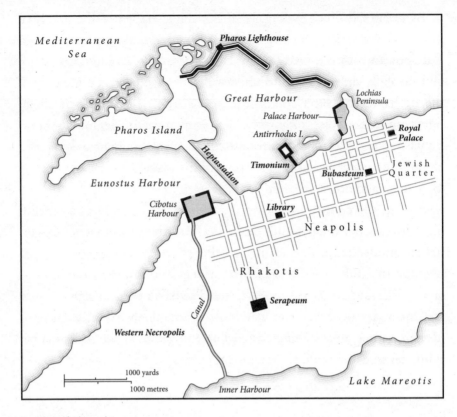

3. Plan of Alexandria.

it might occasionally have been necessary for someone living further south, whether of Egyptian or Greek origin, to visit Alexandria for business, most probably never came near the place.[10] Only about 15 per cent of the cleruch class lived in Alexandria, the majority generally living and working in villages or towns close to their holdings.[11] This does not mean they all worked their grants. Papyri record the common practice of subletting the land to Egyptians.[12] Although Strabo described the beneficial effects of the Nile's inundation flushing away the fetid marshy banks of Lake Mareotis, he ignored what must have happened when the Nile receded. By the sixteenth century AD, 'fevers', presumably malaria, were reported there, as was typhus.[13]

By *c*. 300 BC Euclid, the principal mathematician of the era, had moved to Alexandria. Euclid's *Elements* was the summation of all Greek mathematics and the bedrock of scientific reasoning in antiquity and ever since. By the early third century BC another resident was Ctesibius, the mechanical engineer responsible for a pump and water clock, among other inventions. Herophilus of Chalcedon came to Alexandria about the same time. He and Erasistratus led the study of applied medicine, Herophilus with dissection, Erasistratus with physiology and anatomy.[14] These men and others inspired later generations throughout the ancient world. They owed their opportunities to the early Ptolemaic kings who provided the patronage and enlightenment that such learning and investigation should be integral parts of the nation's future. Alexandria was not the only important centre for learning. Archimedes (killed during the Roman invasion of 212 BC) lived and worked at Syracuse. But for a city that had only come into existence a few years earlier, Alexandria had quickly earned itself a reputation for being home to giants on whose shoulders so many others would stand.

THE LIBRARY AND MUSEUM

The library was the most famous part of the Museum (Mouseion) of Alexandria which acted as a centre for the study of science (including medicine, anatomy, mathematics, and astronomy) and literature to create a 'Ptolemaic world order'.[15] One scholar has observed that the disparity between what has been *said* about the library and 'our near total ignorance of it, has been unbearable'. He proceeds to point out that the numbers of books claimed for the library fall well short of any modern research library. Even so, the quantity would still have over-whelmed any cataloguing system at a time when the card index method was still unknown. Moreover, Alexandria's climate would have prevented papyrus books from surviving (papyri are scarcely known from the city), even if the library had escaped burning in war (see below).[16] Nonetheless, Alexandria's reputation as the 'capital of Hellenistic schol-arship' remains largely unchallenged in the modern world.[17]

The library may have been founded by Ptolemy I, based on the *Letter of Aristeas* which refers to Demetrius of Phalerum as the 'keeper of the king's library' who had been instructed to obtain a copy of every book in the world.[18] Demetrius lived from approximately 350 to 280 BC, but was banished by Ptolemy II when he fell out of favour (see Chapter 4). It is more likely that Ptolemy II was responsible for really establishing the library, even if Demetrius had made a start. Aulus Gellius (AD 123–170) claimed that almost 700,000 volumes were acquired by the Ptolemaic kings, but that 'these were all burned during the sack of the city' in 48 BC as a result of an accident caused by Roman auxiliary troops.[19] Although the library may have been burned by Caesar that year, there is no reference to its destruction in his *Civil Wars*, which only mentions general street fighting.[20] Cassius Dio, writing over two centuries later, described how the library, 'whose volumes, it is said, were of the greatest number and excellence', was burned.[21] Even if the library was damaged, Mark Antony seems to have replenished at least some of the stock with 200,000 volumes brought from Pergamum which he gave to Cleopatra.[22] The emperor Claudius (AD 41–54) enlarged the museum to house his works on Etruscan and Carthaginian history, which probably gathered dust until they turned to dust themselves.[23]

Whatever the truth about the Alexandrian library's destruction, for almost the entire Ptolemaic era, this facility was available to readers from around the known world. That was the case even if we know frustratingly little about exactly what it contained, how it was designed and used, or what scholarship it generated. Perhaps then its greatest contribution to the history of scholarship is that it existed at all, inspiring countless imitations of all sizes from civic libraries in country towns in Australia to the modern library in Alexandria itself. Alexandria's library, despite its loss, therefore deserves to be recognized as the greatest gift of Ptolemies to the ancient world. It serves as proof that their regime was capable on occasion of being both enlightened and inspiring.

A TOWN LIKE ALEX

THE JEWS OF ALEXANDRIA

There are a great many synagogues in every section of the city.

Philo[24]

One of the most important communities in Ptolemaic Alexandria was the Jewish one which came into being during the third century BC. The Jewish Roman historian Josephus, who wrote around 350 years later, claimed that Ptolemy I had entered Jerusalem deceitfully on the Sabbath, posing as if he was about to make a sacrifice. Since it was a day of rest, the Jews assumed he was being respectful and did nothing to oppose his arrival. Ptolemy thus seized the city effortlessly, proceeding to collect captives from surrounding areas and then forcibly settling them in Egypt, relying on their traditional loyalty to oaths and agreements, and where they were given equal rights to Macedonians. However, Josephus went on to explain that other Jews went voluntarily to Egypt, attracted by its fertility and 'by the liberality of Ptolemy'.[25]

There is obviously something contradictory about this version of events. It seems incongruous that the enforced resettlement of Jews in Egypt would have served to attract others. Strabo described the privileges the Jews in Egypt enjoyed:

> The Jews have places assigned them in Egypt, which they inhabit, besides what is peculiarly allotted to this nation at Alexandria, which is a large part of that city. There is also an ethnarch allowed them, who governs the nation, distributes justice to them, and takes care of their contracts and of their laws, as if he were the ruler of a free republic. In Egypt therefore this [Jewish] nation is powerful because the Jews were originally Egyptians and because the land they inhabit, since they went thence, is near to Egypt.[26]

The later Ptolemies continued to encourage Jewish immigration, awarding them privileged status and protection in response to the persecution of Jews in the Seleucid kingdom, especially during the Hellenization enforced by Seleucus IV in 167 BC.[27] The numbers of Jews in Egypt increased markedly under Ptolemy VI, part of the reason being the loss of Coele-Syria. As Ptolemaic power contracted, so the Jews withdrew further into Egypt into settlements ranging from Alexandria and the Delta in the north and as far south as Thebes. The Jews never used the terms 'god' or 'gods' when making dedications to the Ptolemaic ruling house. since Yahweh was the only divinity, there could be no others.[28]

THE PHAROS

The Pharos at Alexandria was built around 280–247 BC under Ptolemy II and supposedly cost 800 talents.[29] Pharos (Φάρος; its etymology is uncertain) was the name of the island on which the lighthouse stood at the easternmost point overlooking Alexandria's Great Harbour to the south and the Mediterranean to the north. The building was designed by an architect called Sostratus of Cnidus, whom Ptolemy allowed to have his name inscribed on the building. The inscription read (as given with Latin name spellings by Lucan), 'Sostratus, son of Dexiphanes, of Cnidus, on behalf of all Mariners to the Saviour Gods'. Sostratus was obviously a nickname or pseudonym since in Greek it means a deliverance or a reward for saving life. It was as if he was called in English 'Lifesaver', which is hardly likely to have been a serendipitous birthname for a man who grew up to build a celebrated lighthouse.[30] Lucan called the structure 'incomparable', whether for beauty or functionality. He likened it to a mountain, the only commentator to make this comparison.[31] He added that Sostratus had concealed the inscription with his name under plaster, knowing that one day it would be revealed. Josephus claimed the Pharos was visible from 300 stades out to sea (about 38 miles or 60 km).[32] The lighthouse survived until the fourteenth century AD when it was brought down by earthquakes.

THE CULT OF SERAPIS AND THE SERAPEUM

Serapis was created out of the syncretic cult of Osiris and the Apis bull but with other associations (plate 10.1). Serapis appeared in Egypt as a bearded Hellenistic figure with Egyptian attributes. He was worshipped as a solar deity but was also associated with healing and fertility.

Exactly where and how the identity of Serapis originally developed is far from clear and was not much clearer in antiquity. A temple of Serapis is attested in (apparently) Babylon just before Alexander's death in 323 BC, but the cult had probably been introduced there from Egypt at some earlier date.[33] Egypt appears to have had its own Serapis cult already which, according to Plutarch, was the Egyptian name for Dis (Pluto). However, the story went that, after a dream, Ptolemy I brought the cult of a deity from Sinope, a city in the middle of the southern shore of the Black Sea, to Egypt, and it was then associated with Serapis and adopted the appearance of the Sinope god.[34]

One of the most important religious complexes in Alexandria was the Serapeum, the epicentre of the Alexandrine Divine Triad of Serapis, Isis, and Harpocrates, 'the most famous in Egypt'.[35] Many other deities were worshipped there too, such as the Greek god Asklepios and Egyptian gods. The cult was a central part of the Ptolemaic state's relationship with religion and the priesthood.

Serapis worship was actively promoted by the Ptolemies, beginning with Ptolemy I, as a means of encouraging the merging of Greek and Egyptian cultures and became immensely popular. The principal cult centre was the Serapeum in Alexandria's Rhakotis district, the original fishing settlement on the site when Alexander chose it for his new city. It was begun at least as early as the reign of Ptolemy II but building continued throughout the third century BC under Ptolemy III and IV, by which time Serapis and Isis were seen as explicitly saviour deities.

Although once a very prominent building (parts of some of the walls remain), the Serapeum goes unmentioned by Strabo. The building was broadly Greek in design and quite unlike an Egyptian temple, as a modern attempt to reconstruct the precinct has shown.[36] A large rectangular precinct, with a complicated and bewildering maze of underground passages, was surrounded by a colonnaded and covered ambulatory. The tetrastyle temple stood at the northern end on the east side, paired by a stoa-like building on the west side. By Ptolemy III's reign, the complex had become elaborated with Egyptian statues, while new shrines added to the temple received bilingual foundation deposit plaques in Greek and Egyptian (see Chapter 5). It was also equipped with a Nilometer to measure the inundation.[37]

By Roman times the temple and precinct were described as being filled with numerous 'almost breathing statues' and dedications, both public and private, to Serapis, Isis, and Harpocrates, any other deity with syncretic links to the core triad, and to dignitaries. There were the sound, sight, and smells of the priests going about their business with incantations and sacrifices, together with worshippers and supplicants, as well as commercial activities operated by, or on behalf of, the priests, which included manufacturing and dream interpretation. There were also 'a great number of other works of art' on display.[38]

The worship of the Serapis triad proliferated across the city. Surviving inscriptions are usually unprovenanced, brief, and do not name the dedicants.[39] One exception is Archagathus, governor of Libya, and his wife Stratonice, whose inscription was recovered from a canal. It probably originated in a subsidiary shrine.[40]

Serapis worship remained popular and spread into the Roman world along trade routes by the late second century BC. An inscription from Puteoli in Italy records the building of a wall 'which is in front of the Temple of Serapis', here being simply used as means of locating the plot.[41]

The Serapeum complex burned down in AD 181 but was rebuilt afterwards, the cult temple on a much larger scale.[42] Caracalla (AD 211–217) was an enthusiastic follower of Serapis, and ordered a major public sacrifice to the god when he visited Alexandria and the temple.[43] Destruction by Christian iconoclasts followed in AD 391, though it had survived longer than most of Alexandria's temples.[44]

Alexandria also had a Bubasteum dedicated to the cat deity Bastet. It goes unmentioned in written sources and was discovered only recently, highlighting the dangers of generalizations about cult practices and their history in a city so difficult to explore archaeologically. The site has yielded large numbers of votive dedications reflecting the cult's protection of women in childbirth, helping to explain its importance.[45] The Bubasteum at Saqqara has long been known, with its vast necropolis of cat burials and serving as a focal point for elite New Kingdom burials.

Above all else, Alexandria was the hub and showcase of Ptolemaic government of Egypt. This was its most important function. The king's officials stood at the apex of a vast hierarchy of bureaucrats whose reach stretched as far as the humblest village and farm. Paperwork was transmitted in epic quantities back and forth, carrying directives, proclamations, appeals, reports, and accounts. The palace archives might be lost but throughout the rest of the country – which specialists in the period like to refer to as the *chora*, without defining the term (see Glossary) – the finds of papyri and ostraca form the bedrock of our understanding of how Ptolemaic Egypt functioned.

8

THE YOKE OF GOVERNMENT

Ptolemaic government's premise was to take as much advantage as possible of Egypt's exceptional wealth to support the Ptolemies in their mission to be the most successful, prestigious, and conspicuous of the Successor kingdoms. To achieve and pay for that they developed a hybrid ideology and image of kingship, and a bureaucracy that managed the remarkable feat of being both efficient and rapacious as well as corrupt and ramshackle.

STATE-BUILDING, IDEOLOGY, AND IMAGERY

By Ptolemy II's reign, the way the Ptolemies governed Egypt and their other territories was well established though there were changes over time, especially in divine status and authority. Rule was personal and in person, helped by confidants and friends (with an obvious vulnerability when some of these overstepped their remit) drawn from a Macedonian immigrant upper class that openly identified itself as such.[1] There was a court bodyguard of Macedonians.[2] Ancient land tenure rules were maintained, and the vanities of local elites flattered.[3]

The Ptolemies fashioned a hybrid image of Egyptian historical and cultural tradition to provide their authority.[4] Within Egypt, the kings and queens appeared on temples as fully fledged but impassive and rigid pharaonic figures ingratiating themselves with traditional gods who bestowed on them the honours and protection Egyptian rulers needed, or energetically smiting their real and imaginary foes with maces. This way they aped the Thutmosid and Ramesside kings of a thousand years earlier and in their art fashioned a synthetic order more alluring than the reality of their times.

The Bronze Age royal motif of the dynamic chariot-driving pharaoh loosing off arrows at his enemies was forgotten. The Ptolemies occasionally used the ponderous four-elephant chariot, but not in an Egyptian context because it was a Hellenistic image (see Chapters 2 and 4). Although rearing horses were known in Egyptian art as far back as the New Kingdom, depicting a king riding one was very unusual and remained so under the Ptolemies.[5] On the Raphia Decree of 217 BC, Ptolemy IV rides a rearing horse into the battle against Antiochus III, the dual white and red crown of Upper and Lower Egypt teetering precariously on his head. In 145 BC Ptolemy VI died after falling from a horse in battle (see Chapter 13). The mounted ruler motif can, for example, also be found on the coinage of Philip II of Macedon.[6] It is likely, therefore, that the Ptolemies who went to war did so on horseback, but this was not an image normally made use of in state propaganda.

The Ptolemies presented themselves to the world as Hellenistic monarchs and maintained a Macedonian royal court in Alexandria. They posed in a different way as 'serene and distant' rulers in their Hellenistic portraiture. This evolved rapidly from the florid and individualized dynamism of Alexander and the Diadochi into the idealized and symbolic, and largely ceased to be a medium for representing true physical likenesses. This is most obvious with the perpetuation of Ptolemy I's portrait on the tetradrachm coinage (Appendix 4). It also appears in the way incumbent rulers were shown as florid, wide-eyed, and full-faced, deliberately evoking notions of luxury and wealth (τρυφή = *tryphe*) suffused with peaceful detachment.[7]

Egypt was a rare instance of a country with the natural resources necessary to support extravagant ambitions, but only so far. Success in war would provide the convincing prestige to enable the Ptolemies to tap Egypt for everything they needed and to intimidate their enemies. Paying for the army was essential. The crown had to have control over as much of Egypt's production above the basic subsistence level as possible. To begin with, the Ptolemaic regime was broadly successful in establishing a powerful and far-reaching bureaucracy and surveillance system, the full introduction and control of money, and tax farming. Bureaucracies can suffocate a society, and the effect was also to inhibit innovation and development by preventing a 'private property regime' from developing alongside.[8]

The Ptolemies asserted their sovereignty through decrees. Officials made determinations in the crown's name which therefore carried royal authority. These were founded in Egyptian and Greek law, but a new Ptolemaic codex that combined both was never created. By Ptolemy II's time, justice was carried out through a court system divided into those hearing cases involving Greeks, and others involving Egyptians or ethnically mixed cases, and royal courts which dealt with cases on a non-specific but as-needed basis.[9]

The crown's prerogative was to have the final determination. A story recorded by Aelian (c. AD 175–235) probably refers to Ptolemy III and Berenice II. Ptolemy was playing dice while an official read out the names of the condemned for the king to decide who should live or die. Berenice was furious at the casual disdain shown for such important matters, believing that the position of royalty had its corresponding duties. The king was impressed by her impassioned objections and never played dice on such occasions again.[10] The anecdote, even if only partly true, is an interesting vignette of Ptolemaic absolutism's vulnerability to the idiosyncrasies and failings of individuals, and the influence wielded by female rulers of the dynasty. Ptolemaic rulers who were unable or unwilling to shoulder the burden of kingship undermined the whole system of royal authority.

THE YOKE OF GOVERNMENT

THE REALITY OF PTOLEMAIC POWER

The Ptolemaic rulers faced existential threats from kings such as Philip V and Antiochus III which created increased pressures and provided opportunities for humiliating debacles. Efforts to exclude outsiders by resorting to consanguineous marriages within the Ptolemaic dynasty for a variety of symbolic, religious, and self-serving reasons may have contributed to the emergence of behaviour that was sometimes only at best sociopathic and at worst psychopathic (see Chapters 14 and 15). Of course, these phenomena could just as easily have been the product of unlimited absolute power, the relative youth of some of the incumbents, and the high stakes. One of the few, but perverse, methods open to the Ptolemies for changing the course of events was to murder or execute rival family members, a phenomenon found in countless other ruling houses, most notably the Julio-Claudians who ruled Rome from Augustus to Nero (27 BC–AD 14).

By the late third century BC, the system was beginning to falter. Some, such as Ptolemy VIII and Cleopatra III, engaged in enervating, futile, and self-serving murderous dynastic feuds and civil war. There was an increasing need for money to fund an extravagant court, sometimes even rival courts, and armies. Driven by the costly wars, the consequent pressure placed on the population led to a rising tide of rural discontent which manifested itself in serious rebellions. The desire to cling on to power led the Ptolemaic regime to seek and become dependent on Roman support.

THE POPULATION

There were around 200,000 people of Greek origin in Ptolemaic Egypt, drawn from the whole region as far apart as Cyrenaica and Macedon and almost anywhere in between and across Anatolia. These Greeks – of whom around half were probably soldiers, based on the known make-up of the Egyptian army at Raphia in 217 BC – represented about 5 per cent of the total population of about 4 million, based in part on estimates of 3.8–4.5 million in the nineteenth century.[11] The imbalance is obvious. The ruling class of Ptolemaic Egypt was restricted to a relatively small group who were Greek but were 'neither homogeneous nor completely Greek'.[12] Over time, more and more Egyptians were drawn into that ruling class, even if that was usually at lower levels, but in general resilient cultural traditions kept the communities largely separate.[13] The population was not spread evenly across space or time. Disease and famine also caused significant fluctuations.

The population included an unknown number of slaves, but slavery was not on the industrial scale of the Roman Empire. Ordinary Egyptians did most of the work. Slaves included those acquired in war or purchased in the slave trade in Palestine and Syria, debtors who were enslaved, and the children of slaves. Many came originally from Syria and were owned by those of Greek origin. The average household had only one or two slaves. Naturally, the state benefited through import duties and taxes levied on the individual sales. Slaves could be bequeathed or freed by the owner's will.[14]

A SOLDIER'S WILL

In 126 BC Dryton of Pathyris (Gebelein) in the Thebaid, a soldier who called himself a Cretan, wrote his will. He had had children by two wives, the first presumably having died, and possessed cattle, a warhorse, armour, and various pieces of land, buildings, and equipment. He owned several household slaves, including a woman called Myrsine with three children, and two other females of unspecified age. These slaves were to go to his current wife Apollonia, who appears to have been Egyptian, since she was also known as Semmonthis, and her 'sisters' (meaning their four daughters). The five women were to inherit the two female slaves and a cow in equal shares across their households. Although Dryton owned several slaves, three were adult females or were old enough to work, and three were children, their father (or fathers) unnamed. Myrsine had business interests of her own which Dryton recognized in the will.[15]

THE FAYUM

Much of Ptolemaic and Roman Egypt's produce came from the Fayum. Ptolemy II, or at least those who advised him, realized that the Fayum's potential had barely been touched. This fertile depression in the western desert to the south-west of Memphis was close enough to the Nile Valley to be relatively easily developed. The hydraulic works used canalization to control Lake Moeris' level, allowing land reclamation with managed irrigation, much of which was handed to cleruchs (soldiers not on active service and who were preferred for state land grants, among whom Thracians seem to have benefited particularly) to farm.[16] The potential to build a livelihood in the Fayum was also attractive to people of both Jewish and Arab origin from Palestine who decamped in whole village communities to move there, especially in the later third century BC.[17]

However, despite the potential productivity, salinization in the Fayum (and the Delta) caused by poorly maintained drainage (especially in times of disorder), and malaria-carrying insects living in the artificial waterways and lakes, created problems. Both regions had a significantly lower population density than elsewhere in Egypt and right up to modern times.[18]

THE BUREAUCRACY

The Ptolemies ruled through a coordinated and substantial hierarchical bureaucracy dedicated to enriching the crown, mainly through taxation. Under Ptolemy II the annual amount raised ran to 14,800 talents in cash alone. It was still running at 12,500 under Ptolemy XII, 'the last and most indolent of the Ptolemies'.[19] More money was raised by selling overseas produce from taxes paid in kind.

Ptolemaic bureaucracy meticulously managed farming with comprehensive assessments of potential yields. The focus was on agricultural productivity, but the state also tightly controlled industry, especially oil and papyrus.[20] Control was divided between state factories and concessions. The latter meant independent ownership and operation of a facility under the surveillance of the state which imposed whatever conditions were necessary to maximize the yield to the crown. Imported olive oil was bought up by the state at a fixed price to be sold alongside domestically produced oil at the same artificial high price. Fishermen were liable for submitting 25 per cent of their catch to the state. The Ptolemaic crown possessed all the land, which was largely distributed in the form of land grants to tenants who paid rent, for example the cleruchs. State-owned livestock was rented out.[21]

Surviving documents show that the system was supposed to work with rapacious efficiency. They also reveal countless problems. Most importantly of all, the state could not control the annual inundation of the Nile. A bad year could prevent a peasant farming family from producing enough to feed itself, let alone cover their tax liability. Several bad years could lead to starvation, abandonment of land, and rebellion.

The Ptolemies believed they could tax anything and everything with impunity. State agents were even exempt from lawsuits being brought against them.[22] Taxation and a litany of fees for positions, concessions, and rents were easily perceived as oppressive. Excessive tax demands and over-zealous enforcement could (and did) lead to resistance on an individual, community, or regional level. This included anything from people going 'off grid' by abandoning land and disappearing out of the state's control to breakaway regimes. A widespread black market existed. Any attempt to stamp that out at a village level could find a tax farmer coming up against bitter and violent locals. One benefit of these subversive activities was that they mitigated to some extent the effect of the oppressive nature of the regime.

Civil administration was managed by the dioiketes (sometimes more than one) through whom the king maintained total economic control. The dioiketes' authority was reinforced by garrisons. Under Ptolemy II the most important was Apollonius, known from an archive of papyri. One of these (259 BC) recorded how his office dealt with the management of the royal oil monopoly by setting the prices at which produce would be sold to those authorized to buy it, limiting imports only to approved concessionaries and imposing a tariff on imported oil, specifying the penalties for any infractions.[23] In 247 BC Apollonius received a petition from an aggrieved Theopropos, an official at Calynda in Caria in western Anatolia, who wanted payment of an outstanding balance on wine he had provided for a festival in a village called Kypranda. The document is a useful piece of evidence for the extent of Ptolemaic interests at the time.[24] State monopolies covered many commodities, among them perfume.[25] Apollonius could exercise discretion on his own estates. On one occasion he told his own officials not to bother the farmers in a place called Tapteia for the salt tax (see below).[26]

By 246–240 BC, for unknown reasons, Apollonius had fallen from favour, losing all his privileges, which included a 'gift' estate, and business interests, for example the cultivation of olives, presumably for oil, recorded in a papyrus from the archive of his secretary, Zenon (plate 8).[27] Ptolemaic Egypt was dependent on loyal officials. Gift estates were an essential part of Ptolemaic royal patronage used by the king to encourage his loyalists to develop land by transferring revenue rights from the crown to them.[28] There was, though, always the danger of an overmighty subject whose dominant control and private wealth accrued from office could elicit jealousy and suspicion, leading perhaps either to exile, assassination, or execution. In Apollonius' case, his official duties and private affairs were messily intertwined, his staff dealing with both as needed.[29]

The dioiketes presided over the traditional division of Egypt into regional zones, known by then in Greek as *nomoi* (nomes, 'districts', in Egyptian *sp3t*). There were thirty-six of these originally, but three more were added by Ptolemy II, including the Arsinoite nome for the Fayum, named after his sister. Each nome was locally managed by the nomarch at the apex of a hierarchy of lesser officials and bureaucratic staff. The strategoi (technically a military term) had started out as managers of the cleruchs but evolved into a post with civilian administrative responsibilities. The job included dealing with local disputes and grievances in the manner of a French investigating magistrate. An oikonomos assisted the dioiketes by overseeing local taxation matters.

A scribe in each settlement dealt with the copious amounts of paperwork generated by the system. Letters, accounts, edicts, and petitions entered a postal service covering the country. Each postal office served as a relay station where a team of couriers was based. They carried documents between their station and the nearest ones, where other couriers took them on further. Incoming and outgoing mail was entered in a ledger daily, identifying the senders and addressees, the nature of each document, the name of the courier, and the time.[30]

TAXES

Tax farmers, liable for any shortfall in the amounts they were due to submit, were essential for maximum exploitation of the nation's productive capacity. The right to collect taxes, such as the so-called salt tax, was auctioned off.[31] The system had some checks and protection. Taxation receipts were issued, usually on pottery or stone ostraca. These provided the taxpayer with a written record of what had been paid, which ought to have prevented them from being charged twice. They could also potentially be used to expose tax farmers who had overcharged.[32]

Ptolemy II created the 'salt tax' (poll tax), levied on professions from at least as early as 263 BC and down to the reign of Ptolemy IV, and probably for several generations after that. Exemptions were awarded to those who had excelled in Greek cultural achievements. These included teachers, actors, and sportsmen. Although the Greek elite were favoured, priests and others who worked with cults were exempt too. This helped to balance out the overt favouritism showed towards Greeks, but those of lesser social status were still more likely to bear the burden.[33]

A papyrus from the late third century BC records a series of standard instructions from a dioiketes to a lesser official in charge of inspections of farming in villages. The advice was to 'try . . . to cheer everybody up and put them in better heart'. The official was also instructed to address complaints made by villagers about the actions of the local scribes concerning agriculture and to stop any abuses. The scribes were supposed to report on the local output twice a year. However, the lesser official was still expected to keep his eyes open for bad farming, or anyone who had filched seed to use for some other purpose.[34]

Just how probing and inventive the system was can be seen from the taxation of pigeon breeding (the birds' droppings were valued as fertilizer). There were two levies: a one-third revenue tax for the number of breeding nests levied on large installations of up to around a thousand nests, and a property tax for the physical area of small dovecotes which were operated for the owners' benefit on small farms rather than as commercial enterprises. Since the latter did not generate an income, it made more sense to tax them just for existing. A couple of demotic receipts written on wooden tablets record the meticulous measurements of a vineyard in Pathyris (Gebelein) and the consequent tax liability.[35] No wonder some of the Egyptians felt they were overburdened.

The system depended on the cooperation of local officials, informants, the moral pressure of the royal oath, and compliance, but there was probably constant low-level corruption and intimidation. The holding of office was an easy route to private profiteering.[36] It could, and did, get out of control sometimes. When discontent emerged, part of the reason is bound to have been frustration with a system that felt onerous and intimidating.[37]

The reality of enforcement was very different when officials tried to avoid asserting their authority, fearing resistance. In 225 BC three brother priests had fallen behind with their payments on land they had mortgaged to pay the tax levied on cloth made at temples. An investigation was begun. Land and property, including a shrine at Dendera put up as security, were auctioned off. The investigation was run by a special commissioner (*praktor*) called Milon who is known from other documents to have accepted low bids on seized property, claiming, when he was investigated himself, that he had been beaten up and had to flee south to Elephantine. There he hid his archive, which was found in 1906.[38]

THE GRIEVANCE OF APOLLODORUS

Over a century later, in 114 BC, Menches, scribe in the Fayum village of Kerkeosiris, received a petition from Apollodorus, a local contractor for oil sales and oil taxes. Apollodorus had heard gossip about another villager called Sisois who was hiding a consignment of contraband oil in his house, which Apollodorus had also reported to the local epistates (police financial superintendent), Polemon. The house was part of the temple of the Egyptian hippopotamus goddess Thoeris, which adds more colour to the part temples played in local lives (see Chapter 9). Menches and other officials refused to help apprehend Sisois (they were probably scared of him, or were on the take themselves). Apollodorus had cut round to Sisois' residence with an agent of the local oikonomos who had been sent to collect the tax due.

A bad situation immediately became worse. Sisois and his wife Tausiris allegedly beat the pair up, threw them out, and locked the doors to the temple and their house. Not long afterwards Apollodorus (who was with his wife), the agent, and a sword-bearer associate tried to arrest Sisois beside the Temple of Zeus. Several others, including Sisois' brother, appeared and knocked them about using weapons. The assailants may have been fiddling taxes themselves. Whether or not Apollodorus was exaggerating (and he naturally does not admit using any violence himself), the upshot was that he was down 10 talents' worth of copper on the tax he was due to pay on his contract, which he wanted exacted 'from them' (presumably Sisois and his wife).[39] One possible reason for the tension is that Apollodorus, like many officials, might have been creaming off his own percentage, which he obviously omitted to mention, and bitterly resented Sisois trying to have a slice of the action too.[40]

This picaresque incident shows how in a small community a variety of officials in different capacities were either working for the state or trying to dodge legal obligations, in this case evading tax. That Apollodorus had to be his own muscle suggests that anyone supposedly working in the state's interests could easily find themselves on their own. The papyrus is cut short so what happened next is lost.

Having the audacity to beat up a tax contractor and his wife (allegedly) is an indication of the sort of tensions that could arise in a village. Among these were the jeopardy Apollodorus felt about being liable for the money himself if he could not recover it. Similarly, Sisois and his wife probably resented impositions of the type that had led to so much strife and rebellion for over a century. They are unlikely to have been unusual. However efficient and managed the Ptolemaic taxation system was supposed to be, the reality was a constant struggle against corruption and evasion, while risking violent resistance.

JAILBREAK

At some point in the second century BC, Dexilaus was strategos in Memphis. News reached him and the local epistates that a couple of convicted tax farmers from Sebennytus called Isidorus and Heracleides, then doing time, had pulled off a jailbreak and disappeared. We do not know why they had been sentenced, but the possibilities include failing to deliver the tax they were liable for or siphoning off more than their commission.[41] Presumably the plan was to put together a posse and set out after them. Their case is another example of how the Ptolemaic bureaucratic system was sometimes much shakier than it was supposed to be.

DIOPHANES THE STRATEGOS

Diophanes was strategos of the Arsinoite nome in the Fayum between 222 and 218 BC. More than 125 documents from his archive survive in full or in part, preserved only because an office clear-out had led the papyri to be reused as mummy cartonnage (see Chapter 10). The result is that the civilian work of Diophanes, a man of Greek or Macedonian origins, is better known than that of any other strategos. He received a fusillade of petitions, each of which required an office copy to be made. It was these that ended up at a coffin manufacturer. Every petition was addressed to the king, but at a local level it was Diophanes who had to process each one, preferring in his case to tone down the adversarial nature of the grievances and find some sort of amicable resolution.

The cases that came before Diophanes, who then passed on instructions to the police, involved Egyptians complaining about Greeks, Greeks about Egyptians, Egyptians about Egyptians, and Greeks about Greeks. Care needs to be taken with such ethnic labelling, such as 'Greek born in Egypt', or geographic association, like 'man of Philae born in Egypt' and 'Persian of the Epigone'. Some individuals, particularly those associated with the military, can be seen to 'change' their ethnicity during their lives, ethnicity turning out to be an 'occupational status designation' linked to the fiscal category a person belonged to at any one time.[42]

TETOSIRIS AND HER LAWSUIT

Tetosiris, probably an Egyptian, was pursuing a lawsuit against a Greek called Apollodorus over a house in Berenice Thesmophorou in the Fayum. She alleged that he had rustled up a gang to terrorize her witnesses, all Egyptians, so that they bolted before giving evidence. Apollodorus resented an Egyptian trying to use the legal system for redress. Conversely, Heracleides of Crocodilopolis (Medinet el-Fayum) went to Pysa on a personal matter but had a chamber pot thrown over his head by a local Egyptian woman called Psenobastis. Heracleides protested so she tore his robe off and spat in his face. He begged the king not to ignore how he had been 'manhandled by an Egyptian woman', allegedly 'for no reason'. Psenobastis was probably expressing a more general grievance about Greeks. Many other cases involve overdue payments on debts.[43]

CROOKED POLICE

Sometimes, the authorities turned out to be the problem. In 109 BC Petermouthis, a handicapped cobbler in the village of Oxyryncha in the Arsinoite nome, was mugged by the local chief of police (ἀρχιφυλακίτης, archiphylakitês), Dionysius, and his accomplices, and robbed of money and his clothing. The gang also forced a third party to deposit a promissory note at the bank in Petermouthis' name in an attempt, it seems, to pay off a debt owed by Dionysius. This story paints a gloomy picture of the sort of abuse of authority that was possible. The outcome is unknown (as usual), but Dionysius and his cronies could only have acted as they did if they thought it likely they would get away with the crime.[44]

There are many similar instances involving gratuitous violence, arbitrary seizures, and requisitions but this is not necessarily evidence for institutionalized corruption in the Ptolemaic police. Ptolemaeus was a general dogsbody of a policeman, charged with various random duties such as rent collection and transport. His superiors were constantly on at him to get on top of his duties, improve his behaviour and efficiency, and not harass taxpayers. Whether this was just a case of excessive supervision or a genuine instance of a lazy, ineffectual, and poor-performing member of staff is unclear, but the bombardment of admonitions is indicative of expectations that the police ought to be doing a good job.[45]

STRIKE

In 252 BC in the Memphite nome, peasants who worked the land which had been apportioned to the cleruchs downed tools and hid out at a temple of Isis. The reason could have been a general dissatisfaction at their lot, or it could have been provoked by an over-zealous official throwing his weight about. Maimachus, nomarch in the town of Crocodilopolis, was instructed to set off and chase them out, and presumably back to work.[46] If an incident like this was not calmed down it could easily trigger copy-cat action and rapidly develop into serious resistance.

THE MUNDANE DUTIES OF MENCHES

When the system worked, it did so almost invisibly, with no need to start firing off angry letters and petitions, which inevitably make for good copy when writing about the period. The letter Apollodorus sent to Menches (see above) must have livened up his day. Menches spent most of his time on the tedious task of writing up his laborious surveys of the land around the village of Kerkeosiris. One, for example, itemizes the crops being grown on crown land in 117–116 BC and the rents due. Another provides a register of unusable crown land and the rents lost as a result: 'I undertake to provide the artaba-tax upon them for the said year or to measure it out from my private means', he wrote.[47] Most days must have felt like counting grains of sand.

NUMBERS

The Ptolemies inherited a long-standing Egyptian tradition of counting people, animals, and goods. Coinage appeared in Egypt just before the Ptolemies but only became an integral part of the economy during their rule, and made it easier for payments to be made. That in turn encouraged the Ptolemies to use the census enthusiastically.

In 261/260 BC Ptolemy II issued two orders concerned with, respectively, the registration with the local oikonomos of cattle and slaves. Failure to comply was to be dealt with by confiscations and fines in a manifestation of 'strong statehood' that could even be beneficial. The registration of slaves ought to have acted as a safeguard against illegal enslavement (slaves acquired through war were exempt).[48]

In 258 BC a census was ordered by Ptolemy II 'from Elephantine to the sea (Mediterranean)'. This demanded from each of the nomes a comprehensive breakdown of what land was held and by whom, the land's productive capacity and what was grown, even 'tree by tree', together with full details of water systems including irrigation, and details of tools, and the payment of priests and 'servants of the crown'. The order is only known from a demotic ostracon translated into Egyptian from an original Greek document (now lost) produced in Alexandria, probably created so that local officials of indigenous origin would have a handy set of instructions to follow.[49]

The records that resulted from such an all-encompassing directive did not conform to any standard formats. These seem not to have existed, as if the census officers were left to devise their own way of recording. The result was a jumble of old and new information which meant that, despite written corrections, the records were bound to be wrong in some way. However, the census of the army appears to have been a separate operation.[50]

Royal and private cattle were measured separately. There were special instructions about registering the animals during the inundation; the water forced the herders to move the animals to higher ground where they would be more easily counted. The settlements were also operated as factories. The looms in operation were supposed to be the maximum possible, producing the amount the nome was expected to supply. There was no prospect of the weavers reducing standards to speed up the work: 'take especial care, too, that the linen is good and has the prescribed number of weft-threads.' There was a tight sowing schedule, and corn was to be delivered to Alexandria.[51] The system resembled the Soviet system of collectivization and quotas, which notoriously disincentivized agricultural workers to be efficient.

Those appointed to cultivate land were told how much produce was to be paid in rent. Any shortfall had to be made up from 'private means'.[52] In 222 BC Ptolemaeus was a soldier growing sesame on his landholding to be harvested the following year. A bank in Crocodilopolis in the Fayum loaned him the money for labour. After the harvest, the whole crop was due to be delivered to the crown and the bank loan repaid. Ptolemaeus was given a contract that meant, if he defaulted, he would be liable for 150 per cent of the original sum and could lose all his property to the toparchos, the local official.[53]

In 252 BC, a boat captain called Dionysius collected 4,800 artabae of barley for transportation to Alexandria. The consignment was under the supervision of an agent of the royal scribes called Nechthembes who had come upriver from Alexandria armed with a 'measure and smoothing rod' to make sure the quantity was correct.[54]

In an era without identity cards, individuals were distinguished by their appearance, meticulously described in documents, along with any visible ailments like limps. When three sisters sold a parcel of land in

107 BC their features, skin colour, and scars were all included, as were those of the buyer. One of the sellers, Taous, daughter of Harpos was 'about 48, fair-skinned, round-faced, straight-nosed, and with a scar on her forehead'. She and her sisters are called Persians, probably a pseudo-ethnicity referring to their taxation class.[55]

ETHNIC IDENTITY AND LANGUAGE

Paniskos, son of Sarapion, is recorded in Greek in a dedication he made to Serapis found at Thebes. The dedication was trilingual, including hieroglyphs and demotic Egyptian. The demotic version is to Coptite Osiris in the name of Pamin, son of Psenosire. Paniskos/Pamin emerges therefore as an Egyptian with an Egyptian name and a Greek identity he had acquired or adopted perhaps as a matter of convenience, using Egyptian or Greek as circumstances required. All such examples involve Egyptians who had acquired Greek identities. A related phenomenon was the way some Egyptian families alternated Greek and Egyptian names across generations.[56]

Those of Greek origin did not adopt Egyptian names. No Egyptian loan words crept into the Greek used in Egypt.[57] Cultural separation led to the Egyptian language being dismissed as inferior by the Greek ruling class even though it continued to be deployed on state and religious monuments. Even knucklebones, which had sometimes been used since the Second Intermediate Period in the traditional Egyptian game of senet, were only played with in Ptolemaic Egypt with Greek rules or used in ritual.[58]

The state encouraged the use of Greek and provided teachers of Greek. Egyptians, especially those already literate, who became proficient in Greek had enhanced employment opportunities. Relatively few Egyptians under the Ptolemies were literate in their own language (one estimate is about 7 per cent having some ability to read and write demotic by the fourth century BC); it had always been a skill limited to a privileged few. Greek's use only of alphabetic characters meant more people were probably able to read and write Greek, regardless of their individual origins, adding to the native Greek speakers who had come to Egypt.[59]

Ptolemaic bureaucracy depended on specialized scribes. Low-level local jobs were filled by Egyptians, who continued to use demotic. Those involved in tax collection and in charge of administering nomes and higher up the chain had Greek names. Some, perhaps many, of these people were Egyptians who adopted Greek names and had enough proficiency in Greek to be able to perform the necessary tasks.[60]

A sharp operator called Dionysius, son of Kephalas, lived in Crocodilopolis in Middle Egypt and left an archive dated to 117–103 BC. He had begun his working life as a tenant of the crown, and then performed military service, as well as holding a priesthood in the local ibis cult in the Hermopolite nome. He was competent in Greek and demotic. He was also an astute and ruthless operator. His documents (thirty-three in Greek and seven in demotic) show that, among other activities, he borrowed grain and money to lend at very high interest rates to those desperate enough to get themselves into debt, while at the same time deliberately withholding his own repayments for as long as possible. He was also known by an Egyptian name, Plenis, which suggests that he was an Egyptian who had been given a leg up by being educated and bilingual.[61] He was thus able to move freely between the native population and the Greek administrative world.

Ptolemaic governance adapted some features of pharaonic Egypt, but it was primarily a Hellenistic imposition designed to maximize the country's yield. With religion, the Ptolemies were aware that their legitimacy depended more on visibly supporting traditional cults and posing as being under their protection. Spending much of their revenue on the priests and temples was therefore a major priority.

9

TEMPLES OF THE PTOLEMIES

Some of the most prominent surviving Egyptian temples are Ptolemaic. Religion showcased the Ptolemaic dynasty's dedication to traditional gods and customs through royal endowments. The priesthood served the state by operating temples as administrative hubs and offering up honorific endorsements of the monarchy. Temples also acted as important cultural centres in which religious life merged with other aspects of community life.

PTAH AT MEMPHIS

One of the largest and most important pre-Ptolemaic temple complexes was that of Ptah at Memphis. It had already played an important role when its treasury was used to guarantee the silver standard under the Persians, evolving into a notional term for an amount of Ptolemaic silver coins.[1] This was where a new king passed through initiation ceremonies that included leading the Apis bull around Memphis before taking the animal into a temple where the king swore an oath to protect Egypt's land and water. When the Apis bull died it was renamed Osorapis and mummified on site where the 26th-Dynasty embalming table still survives, and a new bull chosen. The body was transferred to the underground vaulted burial chamber galleries of the Serapeum at Saqqara. These chambers were built in the 26th Dynasty but continued a burial tradition that went back to the 18th Dynasty under Amenhotep III (*c.* 1390–1352 BC). By Alexander's time the deceased bulls were being interred in 70-tonne granite sarcophagi in an underground complex of tunnels. The practice ceased under the Romans.

The cult of Ptah made the loyalty and support of its priests vital to the Ptolemaic state, as the funeral stela of the high priest of Ptah, Pasherenptah, who crowned Ptolemy XII in 76 BC in an ancient tradition, demonstrates (see Chapter 16). The king was known as 'ever-living, beloved of Ptah'. Ptah's temple at Memphis, which started life under Ramesses II, is today barely explored, and most of the structural remains appear to have long since been dismantled for stone.

TEMPLES IN THE PTOLEMAIC STATE

There are few surviving traces of Ptolemaic temple building in Middle and Lower Egypt, some having been destroyed by flooding in early modern times, such as the temple to an unknown god at Antaiopolis (Qaw el-Kebir), or the stone was stolen. Further south, Ptolemaic temples are among the most impressive extant monuments in the country.

Temples were the focus of far more complex activities than just the pursuance of ritual and serving as backdrops to festivals. In earlier, pharaonic times they were administrative centres and businesses that managed lands, livestock, and factories owned by the cults, while storing and distributing the produce. They were the beneficiaries of endowments by the crown, usually in the form of booty and tribute transferred to them. Temples had their own bureaucracies, requiring small armies of officials and scribes, presided over by the priests who often held their positions through their own dynastic descent, as in Pasherenptah's case. The temples resembled states within a state, especially the larger ones, but were also the bedrock of the state. The Ptolemies both courted and controlled the priesthood, for example by allocating the tax on vineyards and orchards to the new cult of Arsinoe II in 263 BC but via the new system of tax farmers.[2] Obviously, this risked temple income disappearing en route into secular use. Promises had to be made in 196 and 118 BC to guarantee temple income.[3]

The Ptolemies supported the physical temples, actively rebuilding some and constructing new ones in projects that lasted for generations. At the same time, they transferred responsibility to the state for at least some of what the temples had once taken care of. Cleopatra VII's distribution of grain from crown granaries in Alexandria during the famines of the 40s BC is a case in point (see Chapter 17).

The power of the priests in Egypt's remoter past, particularly at the end of the New Kingdom during the eleventh century BC, had exposed the way they could operate like an overmighty medieval aristocracy with the resources of vast estates at their disposal. The priesthood had the potential to threaten the state. In some instances when the crown was weakened, certain priests could become regional rulers. Pinudjem I, sometime high priest of Amun at Thebes, effectively ruled Upper Egypt between 1054 and 1032 BC. The Ptolemies still needed the priests but gradually subordinated the temples to royal authority and its bureaucratic institutions, a process that accelerated during the second century BC.[4] Harwennefer and Ankhwennefer, who led the rebellion in the Thebaid under Ptolemy IV and V (see Chapter 12), are likely to have been disaffected priests.

Temples, cults, priests, and others who made their lives at the temples make frequent appearances in inscriptions and papyri, but the record is very patchy. At Theadelphia in the Fayum three temples are known from Ptolemaic inscriptions but are unmentioned in the hundreds of papyri, which are almost all Roman in date, known from there.[5] Conversely, two papyri are known that record the involvement of local contributions to the building of the Temple of Horus at Edfu.[6]

A temple precinct was dedicated by a priest called Chares to an otherwise unknown variant of the Greek god Poseidon, named here Poseidon Hippios and depicting on one of the reliefs a pair of seahorses (Poseidon's association with horses is well known), during the reign of Ptolemy V. Poseidon is virtually unknown in Ptolemaic Egypt, making the pieces even more remarkable. The stones are unprovenanced but are probably from Alexandria, so they serve as a good example of the randomness of the record and the likelihood that during the period shrines of all sorts and sizes were to be found everywhere.[7]

The recent discovery of the hitherto unknown Bubasteum in Alexandria also shows how haphazard our knowledge of Ptolemaic buildings in the city is (see Chapter 7 for Alexandria's Serapeum). Similar problems afflict most other sites in the Delta and Lower Egypt, even though discoveries of inscribed blocks show that Ptolemaic building activity occurred at many places, whether as new builds or repair work. One example is Terenuthis (Kom Abu Billo) in the western Delta where a temple begun by Ptolemy I was finished by his son.[8]

PRIESTS AND PATRONS

Priests were privileged, salaried, and literate. Their roles were usually classified according to their personal specialisms, including prophesying or serving as scribes. They supervised rituals, such as purification through bathing and managing temple records, and presided over the dozens of annual festivals. The shrines were supported by those who voluntarily placed themselves for life in the service of the temple, performing menial duties. They included the katochoi (see Glossary), of whom the best known is the dream interpreter and porridge seller Ptolemaeus at the Serapeum at Saqqara (see Chapter 13). Priests also had to receive supplicants seeking a cure or resolution of a grievance.

In one papyrus of *c.* 152 BC, a passing comment mentions that 'the strategos is coming up tomorrow to the Serapeum [at Saqqara] and will spend two days in the Anubeum drinking'.[9] The Anubeum was a temple of Anubis that formed part of the extensive complex, serving also as a social club. Among the industrial and commercial interests operated by temples and their priests was beer production, run as a concession within the Ptolemaic state monopoly system.[10]

The Serapeum at Oxyrhynchus in the Fayum was surrounded by, and closely associated with, a market and shops, as well as having a podium for a public speaker.[11] The documents that attest to these activities are Roman, forming part of the huge Roman documentary archive for which Oxyrhynchus is famous, but it is likely circumstances were the same at temples under the Ptolemies.

Soldiers were responsible for many surviving religious dedications in Ptolemaic Egypt, either as individuals (generally officers) or groups. One possible explanation is a higher level of literacy than the general population. They also had an understandable need to express and prove their loyalty to the crown. They could do this with a dedication to a god and had a vested interest in doing so within a military community.

Soldiers also faced jeopardy from war or arduous assignments on state business, for example elephant hunts under Ptolemy IV. Lichas (a soldier from Acharnia in western Greece) combined a dedication to Ptolemy IV and Arsinoe III with one to Serapis and Isis. Temple precincts made conveniently defensible compounds. The precinct of Philae's Temple of Isis was home to a garrison. The soldiers were responsible for over a dozen dedications found at Philae. Having troops on site could lead to vandalism and disruption. In the late second century BC Philae's dynastic cult had to be suspended because of state officials making ruinous demands on temple resources. Priests sent petitions to the crown to have the unwanted guests turfed out.[12]

Soldiers also built local temples, either where they were based or when they settled in villages as landowners and farmed or rented out their land. Cavalrymen and infantrymen clubbed together in the Ombite nome in Upper Egypt to dedicate a shrine to Haroeris (Greek for Great Horus), Apollo, and other deities under Ptolemy VI and Cleopatra II. In another instance, the revenue from land owned by a group of Egyptian infantrymen was ceded to a temple in Apollinopolis Magna.[13]

This belongs to a wider phenomenon of soldiers building and dedicating temples only from the reign of Ptolemy IV onwards, at a time when rebellions necessitated the wider distribution of troops, mainly in the Fayum and the Thebaid.[14] A peak was reached between c. 180 and 107 BC, continuing thereafter but declining slowly.

The crown remained the main contributor to temple wealth along with revenue from temple estates, but private investment gradually rose. The state encouraged this, probably because its own income was beginning to decline as the costs of international wars and domestic resistance mounted. The military dedications are matched by the appearance in late Ptolemaic Egypt of increasing numbers of civilian Egyptian dedications and statues in temple precincts. They include those at Dendera and Edfu made by individuals who identified themselves as 'kinsmen' of the royal family who had been admitted to court circles, part of a policy of integration which helped prevent the escalation of ethnic violence.[15] Such individuals aped the Ptolemaic kings in posing either as Egyptian priests or as members of the Greek elite, depending on whom their monuments were targeted at, such as the statue of Pen-Menkh, governor of Dendera, royal deputy and priest of Hathor and Horus during the reign of Cleopatra VII.[16] The benefactor contagion of competitive munificence, when one or two prominent locals made donations to a temple, encouraged others feel obliged to match or exceed the gifts, for fear of losing face.

Some benefactors, usually of lower status, belonged to local associations (synods), for example the gooseherds of Theadelphia (Fayum). The so-called *topos* inscriptions, which include graffiti, show that such organizations frequently used temples as meeting places, recording their activities in Greek texts which were often accompanied by dedication scenes or depictions of gods carved in relief in Egyptian style.[17]

THE ROYAL WORKS

Ptolemaic temples copied older designs, but they were often better planned and more technically accomplished. Unlike earlier temples, they usually featured a carefully chosen range of brightly painted florid column capital designs. Even if construction ran across centuries, the buildings were executed according to an overall cohesive design planned from the outset. They did not accumulate haphazard and eccentric additions in the way some much earlier temples had over time. The

Temple of Luxor is an accretion of several distinct phases belonging mainly to the 18th and 19th Dynasties but with additions dating down to the Roman period. It occupies a skewed footprint, having been modified so that it could face an avenue leading to Karnak. The Temple of Amun at Karnak is famously chaotic, with haphazard and straggling additions of obelisks, hypostyle halls, pylons, and other components. Ptolemaic statues were set up among Karnak's clutter, emulating those of Egypt's past heroic pharaohs but injecting a new hybridized Hellenism to traditional forms (see p. 93 and plate 21).

Many Ptolemaic temples were built on existing shrine sites. They were political statements that allied the Ptolemies with the traditional maintenance of order and truth (Maat) and the patronage of indigenous cults. Others were additions and embellishments to existing buildings or were new foundations. These Ptolemaic projects also belonged to a broader process of renewal that had been under way since the 26th Dynasty. Survivors range from the magnificent Temple of Horus at Edfu to a small rock-cut shrine of Alexander IV at Beni Hasan in Middle Egypt. The latter is a few metres from another rock-cut shrine called the Speos Artemidos, created by Hatshepsut and Seti I of the 18th and 19th Dynasties, respectively, dedicated to the lion goddess Pakhet.

In some cases, Ptolemaic work was minor, such as the small Temple of Hathor at Deir el-Medina which has survived almost intact. In Ptolemaic times it was the sole shrine dedicated to Hathor in Western Thebes, super-seding the Hathor shrine in the 18th Dynasty memorial-mortuary temple of Hatshepsut.[18] The Ptolemies added to existing temples. Ptolemy IV installed a gateway at Seti I's Temple of Osiris at Abydos, but this was only one of several modifications and reconstructions during his reign.[19] One of the final features at the 18th Dynasty 'Small Temple' at Medinet Habu in the precinct of the memorial-mortuary temple of Ramesses III (c. 1186–1153 BC) was an imposing gateway constructed under Ptolemy IX (plate 13). This gateway, which still bears some of its original colour, helped position the Ptolemaic rulers as integral and honourable guardians of traditional Egyptian monumental architecture.

Where Ptolemaic work was more significant, it still often replaced older work or continued existing projects. A short distance from the Medinet Habu temple is the Temple of Amun Djeser-set and Thoth at Qasr el-Aguz. The work embellished and rebuilt a New Kingdom structure in Ptolemy VIII's and Cleopatra II's names in honour of the eight primordial deities of the Ogdoad worshipped at Hermopolis.[20] These obscure gods represented opaque notions of light and dark, sky and water, and even invisibility. The surviving Temple of Hathor at Dendera, between Abydos and Thebes, was begun under the Ptolemies to replace an earlier complex dating back to the Old Kingdom but was never completed, even though the work continued well into the Roman period. At the Temple of Ptah within the precinct of the Temple of Amun at Karnak, the Ptolemies restored the 18th Dynasty structure but did not substitute their own names for those of earlier kings. The Ptolemaic work can be recognized by style. By far and away the most important extant Ptolemaic temple is that of Horus at Edfu (see below).

The major new temples served as canvases on which the Ptolemaic rulers could be shown in traditional costume with Egypt's ancient gods along with rambling hieroglyphic texts that itemized their elaborate pharaonic titles. This was quite different from how they appeared on their coinage or in other Hellenistic-style art and is particularly important for the Ptolemaic queens regnant. Temple texts were the most likely locations for the women's true status as Egyptian rulers to be recorded (plate 12) (see also Chapter 12 for Cleopatra I at Edfu). Around 80 per cent of the reliefs on Ptolemaic temple walls show the rulers actively engaged in the process of presenting sacrifices or gifts to the old deities in return for their royal power and the prospect of long lives. Others show male rulers smiting their enemies in compositions copied from earlier temples (plate 14). Female rulers or consorts are usually companions holding a sistrum (rattle used in ritual) or flowers, a format similarly copied from the past (plates 11, 24). The figures and faces are generic and impassive, a late manifestation of a style that developed in the 18th Dynasty and which was transmitted to Ptolemaic times through the 19th and 26th Dynasties via surviving monuments.[21] However, Ptolemaic figures are stylistically distinctive with their podgy faces, heavy limbs, wooden postures, and the women's protuberant breasts.

Subtle differences in design reflected power games in the increasingly turbulent court, either the result of official directives or the local sponsors and builders of the temples ensuring their loyalties were appropriately targeted. During the joint rule of Ptolemy VI and VIII with Cleopatra II, she is shown behind her brothers on the walls of the Temple of Hathor at Deir el-Medina.[22] However, as the dynastic complexities increased, in a unique instance at Philae, Cleopatra II was shown ahead of Cleopatra III and making an offering while her daughter remains passive. Subsequently, Cleopatra III does appear sacrificing at Kom Ombo in a deliberate showcasing of her enhanced power.[23]

PHILAE

Lake Nasser has drowned the island of Philae beneath the waters of the Nile, but reconstruction of its monuments on the nearby island of Agilkia has replicated Philae to brilliant effect. Philae's role as a religious centre belonged largely to the Ptolemaic era and the Roman period though development had begun back in the 25th Dynasty and included features constructed under Nectanebo I. The centrepiece was the Temple of Isis, which has survived substantially intact. It was a small building but the courtyard between the first and second pylons was trapezoidal in plan with a covered colonnade forming one side and a chapel the other. Several smaller temples and other structures of varying dates clustered around, leaving the complex today looking rather different to how it must have appeared under the later Ptolemies. The attractive setting drew pilgrims and visitors from all over the Mediterranean world, including some Roman tourists in 116 BC (see Chapter 15).

Philae's remoteness allowed it to endure for centuries. The worship of Isis seems to have staggered on until well into the sixth century AD, while elsewhere her cult had been subsumed into the Christian cult of

Mary. Thereafter, as various carved features and inscriptions attest, Philae was used as a Christian place of worship.

EDFU, DENDERA, AND KOM OMBO

No-one today can fail to be stunned by the cathedral-sized scale and symmetrical layout of the Temple of Horus at Edfu with its towering pylon gateway, the open court beyond, and the hypostyle halls leading to the inner sanctums. This realized in stone the culmination of the primeval 'tent shrine'. The building has lost most of its paint and its contents but is otherwise substantially and magnificently intact, making it the best preserved major Egyptian temple. It formed part of a much larger, but little explored, town settlement called Behdet founded during the Old Kingdom. Part of the original settlement was cleared away to make room for the new temple.

Unlike most earlier temples, Edfu is a disciplined and symmetrical structure, 450 ft long and 259 ft wide (137 x 79 m). Edfu was intended to showcase the Egyptian temple at the pinnacle of its technical development. It strictly adhered to the traditional form, but with refinements. The integrity of the design included the subtle and respectful incorporation of a small 13 ft (4 m)-high granite shrine (naos) of Nectanebo II at the north end which conveniently linked the new building to the site's origins. The new building replaced an east–west New Kingdom temple built on the sacred site nearby where in myth the brothers Horus and Seth had fought it out.[24]

The modern visitor passes through a precinct past the mammisi ('birth house') – which commemorated Harsomptus, the child of Horus and Hathor, and thus the birth of the king – to enter from the south through the imposing pylon which leads to an open court (plate 14). The effect is diminished by the loss of colour and the absence of flagpoles, though their recesses are conspicuous features in the pylons. The pair of obelisks and the avenue of sphinxes which once stood in front of the pylon are long gone. Beyond the pylon are two consecutive hypostyle halls and behind them two antechambers, followed by the

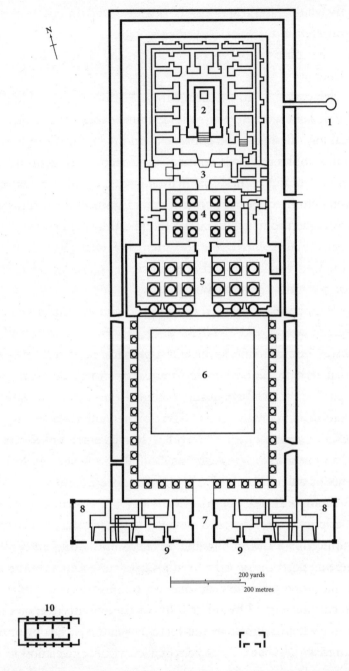

4. The Temple of Horus at Edfu: (1) Nilometer, (2) Sanctuary, (3) Hall of Offerings, (4) Inner Hypostyle Hall, (5) Outer Hypostyle Hall, (6) Courtyard, (7) Entrance, (8) Pylon, (9) Obelisks (lost), (10) Birth House.

sanctuary where the cult statue of Horus resided, surrounded by a range of chambers on three sides. The temple was home to a series of annual festivals, the most important of which was the annual visit of Hathor from Dendera.

The decoration featured scenes from Horus myths, including his battle with Seth and meeting with Hathor, and panels depicting the king making offerings. The content of the scenes at Edfu and other Ptolemaic temples was a self-conscious and meticulous effort to consolidate and celebrate centuries of mythology and ritual in a comprehensive, even definitive, form to protect the traditions for the future.[25]

Edfu's Ptolemaic temple took 180 years to build, using income from land which the cult owned in the Apollonopolite, Pathyrite, Latopolite, and Ombite nomes.[26] An inscription from the site records in detail the progress of the project, which began when the site was laid out in 237 BC under Ptolemy III up to 90 BC. Other texts from the building record its dedication in 70 BC and completion supposedly in 57 BC under Ptolemy XII (at the time ousted from his throne, making this date uncertain).[27] The use of traditional religious idioms to legitimize Ptolemaic authority, and the compliance of the priesthood and the local elite in that mission, were particularly important in Upper Egypt where the state was struggling to maintain its authority by the end of the third century BC. Building work was suspended between 202 and 186 BC due to the rebellion in the region (see Chapter 12).

Edfu's temple is now isolated within a modern town, giving no hint of the peripheral structures and estates it once controlled. The accumulation of occupation debris in the centuries after antiquity led to the temple being partially buried beneath rubbish and sand. This preserved the complex, now fully cleared, to an exceptional degree.

One curious feature found at Edfu was the priests' use of selective alliteration when composing the hieroglyphic texts, favouring words that started with ḥ (hard h), ḫ (ch as in loch, usually given now in transliteration as kh), s, š (sh), and w. The reason was probably practical. The incantations were likely to have been oral in origin; alliteration would have acted as a memory aid, useful for priests trying to hang on to older traditions. It becomes possible to imagine the rhythmic tone of the chants as the priests repeated them during rituals in the halls and chambers of the temple. One of these chants starts *kh'wewet.k khwed m kh'w nw kht kh'm.k im.sen khepery kh'wew m-khet.sen knenem.k.* . . . The transliteration is only a loose approximation but shows the repetition of sounds.[28]

DENDERA AND KOM OMBO

The extant Temple of Hathor at Dendera (Tentyris) provides an instructive example of how temple projects progressed and were not always finished. It replaced an older building but only the hypostyle hall, sanctuary, and associated chambers were completed. The outer court and pylon were not executed, and even the hypostyle hall was only built during the reign of Tiberius (AD 14–37). The cult was closely linked to that of Horus at Edfu, whom the goddess was taken to 'visit' in an annual festival. The outer back wall of the temple features a well-known relief depicting Cleopatra VII and her son Ptolemy XV Caesarion (plate 23). The work demonstrates exceptional technical competence, retaining some of the internal colour which was later damaged by Christian iconoclasts.

The unusual double Temple of Sobek and Haroeris at Kom Ombo belonged mostly to the period between Ptolemy VI and XII, with Roman additions. The building was partially robbed in later times, leaving it in a ruinous state so that the construction features can be studied along with the methods used to carve reliefs (plate 15). These include a variety of scenes and a calendar of festivals. The figures were carved first. Some of these are still accompanied by blank panels which would, if finished, have been cut back as the hieroglyphic texts were added. This, of course, made it possible to delay committing to the identity of the rulers involved. One relief depicts what look like surgical instruments. This may be a clue to the temple serving as a healing cult centre. These were well established elsewhere in the Graeco-Roman world so this would be an unsurprising function.

ANIMAL CULTS

The Alexandrian Bubasteum has already been mentioned, as have the cults of the Apis and Mnevis bulls (see Chapters 4, 5, and 7). The necropolis at Tuna el-Gebel in Middle Egypt is one of the best-known repositories of animal burials on an industrial scale. It lies close to the temple-tomb of Petosiris, a priest in the cult of the ibis god Thoth (plate 4). Thousands of mummified ibises, other birds, and baboons are known from the site. Elsewhere, mummified cats were used as votive deposits in the cult of Bastet at, among other places, Bubastis, Saqqara, and Speos Artemidos. Although these practices had much longer histories, they continued throughout the Ptolemaic era. Cleopatra VII and Ptolemy XIII, for example, donated 412 silver coins, food, drink, and oil in 50/49 BC to the Apis bull funerary rites, recorded on a demotic stela.[29]

Temples and shrines with their attendant offerings, statues, and dedications were only one part of the traditional observance of cult in Ptolemaic Egypt. The vast cemeteries of the Graeco-Roman period have produced huge quantities of human remains, preserving evidence both for mummification in Ptolemaic times and resilient traditional beliefs combined with foreign influence.

10

MUMMIES, GRAVES, AND GRIEVING

The evidence for death and burial in Ptolemaic Egypt is abundant but ironically not for Alexander and the Ptolemaic royal family, whose remains are without exception lost. Even bespoke tombs of the elite are little known. Instead, mummies and human remains have turned up in abundance, preserving some of the ancient traditions alongside new ones, but most are anonymous.

Unlike during earlier Egyptian dynastic history, royal and elite burials do not form a significant part of the study of the Ptolemaic era and therefore play almost no role in histories of the period. High-status tombs are largely unknown (see Petosiris below). If the Ptolemies still rest in unvisited tombs, it is because they were interred in the lost (or more likely destroyed) royal necropolis of Alexandria. Consequently, little is known about Ptolemaic royal funerary architecture and practices apart from the Roman-period descriptions of Alexander's and Cleopatra's tombs. Some sarcophagi from Alexandria, for example, belonged unsurprisingly to Greek and Hellenistic traditions and were un-Egyptian in nature. Cremation was also used.

The so-called 'Alabaster Tomb' in eastern Alexandria has been proposed as that of Alexander or one of the first three Ptolemies. With no evidence for the occupant, the matter is as good as closed. Lucan refers to 'the shades of the Ptolemies and their shameful dynasty, shut away in undeserved pyramids and mausolea'. This is about the only clue we have to the tombs' original appearance but may be a purely meta-phorical description.[1] Cleopatra had a separate 'lofty and beautiful' tomb for herself in the royal compound, 'beside the temple of Isis', and fitted with elaborate drop doors.[2] The temple of Isis is unspecified, and the tomb has never been found anyway.

ALEXANDER DIED, ALEXANDER WAS BURIED, ALEXANDER RETURNETH INTO DUST[3]

Despite endless searches, the tomb of Alexander the Great in Alexandria has evaded discovery.[4] There is no doubt that it was there, though he was originally buried in Memphis.[5] Strabo said the body was in an enclosure called the Sema ('Tomb') or Soma ('Body'), unless the Soma formed part of the Sema, part of the royal palaces district in Alexandria, set back about 550 yards (500 m) from the coast. The exact site is lost, along with all the bodies of all the other members of the Argaed and Ptolemaic dynasties.[6] According to sources used by Zenobius, the burial arrangements had been created by Ptolemy IV, supposedly out of guilt at his mother Berenice II's suicide (see Chapter 6). Exactly when Alexander's body arrived in Alexandria and where it was buried in the interim are unclear, including whether he built a new Sema.[7] Either way, Strabo says that Alexandria was where the body was in his time ('where it still now lies') but had been transferred from its original sarcophagus (meaning coffin) of gold into one made of glass (or depending on the reading, alabaster) by Ptolemy X.[8]

The survival of Nectanebo II's conglomerate sarcophagus (c. 345 BC) shows that some of the necessary skills had survived at least to his time. The sarcophagus, first noted in the Atterine Mosque in Alexandria in AD 1550, was traditionally associated with Alexander until it became possible to read the hieroglyphs and identify it as Nectanebo's. Since, so far as we know, he never used it, there is a slim possibility that it was pressed into service by those interring Alexander, perhaps attracted to the evolving myth that Nectanebo had been his father. It bears no amended inscription or other hint that it had ever been used for Alexander.[9]

Wherever it was or whatever it looked like, Alexander's tomb was a celebrated sight of Alexandria, attracting luminaries and particularly prominent Romans. Julius Caesar paid a visit.[10] Not many years later, Octavian, in control of Egypt after the Battle of Actium in 31 BC, visited too. He had the body brought out for his inspection and laid on it a gold crown and flowers. If Cassius Dio can be believed, Octavian was unable to resist touching Alexander's face but accidentally broke off his nose. The body was probably by then in a desiccated and malodorous state of decay.[11] Octavian's great-grandson Caligula liked to dress as a general, supplementing his costume with Alexander's breastplate which had been acquired from the tomb.[12] Caracalla visited in AD 215, donating his cloak, belts, and precious stones.[13]

The tomb's fate is as respectable a mystery as any other in Egypt. That it was wholly forgotten seems unlikely but it was probably subsumed into the city in succeeding centuries. After all, by the third century AD the large streetside tomb of the celebrated Scipio family (see Chapters 11 and 12), which had died out by then, by the Appian Way in Rome had been incorporated into the substructure of a house, where it was discovered in 1614. It is likely that the tsunami following an earthquake on 21 July AD 365 washed that part of Alexandria away, having 'levelled innumerable buildings in the cities'.[14] The tomb of Alexander remains, for the moment, well and truly lost. Perhaps it is just as well. It is very unlikely that any surviving remnants could now possibly match its occupant's reputation.[15]

When Octavian visited the tomb of Alexander (see box) he was also offered the opportunity to see the dead Ptolemies. He famously declined, saying 'my wish was to see a king, not corpses'.[16] The implication then is that he was also being invited to look at their bodies, probably in open coffins. Mummification was still practised in Egypt, but technical competence had declined. None of the royal bodies survive today and there are no specific descriptions apart from a reference to Ptolemy IV and Arsinoe III being cremated (see Chapter 12).

The lack of extant or accessible physical remains is, of course, normal for rulers of the ancient and medieval worlds. The remarkable survival of many of the royal mummies of Egypt's New Kingdom has been a major obsession of Egyptology ever since they were discovered in ancient caches in the late nineteenth and early twentieth centuries. The result has been a fixation with the idea that these bodies contain answers to pressing questions of identity and family relationships and therefore to the many historical problems of the period, despite numerous contradictory and inconclusive studies. The Ptolemaic period is largely denied (or perhaps spared would be a better word) such pursuits, though the tomb and body of Cleopatra are still sought with assiduous zeal by the hopeful.[17] Conversely, vast quantities of Ptolemaic and Roman mummified and naturally desiccated human remains have been discovered at cemeteries at various locations, especially in the Fayum.[18]

The Saïte Period revived many ancient traditions. These included the reappearance of stone sarcophagi. Much older tombs were being explored for inspiration and this continued into the Late Period. Among them was the Valley of the Kings tomb of Thutmose III (KV34) where his sarcophagus remains. An official called Hapmen had the long-dead king's sarcophagus copied for his own. He was probably also responsible for helping himself to the king's missing canopic chest for good measure.[19]

Stone sarcophagi were used into Ptolemaic times, but only just. It is not always possible to distinguish Ptolemaic burials from those of the Late Period. Like most of the techniques involved in processing and burying the dead at this time, the quality deteriorated. The numbers of sarcophagi also declined rapidly and eventually disappeared altogether.

MUMMIES

The mummy was known in Greek as a *soma eilismenon* (σῶμα εἰλισμέγον), 'body wrapped around'. A papyrus from the late second century AD in the Roman period uses this term in a receipt for a mummy (and the necessary fees and dues) which was being added to a consignment of corpses to be taken to a funeral undertaker in the Memphite nome.[20] Mummy labels were attached to ensure they were not mixed up. The arrangements had not changed much from Ptolemaic times. Burial was big business, and many livelihoods were made from providing the necessary services, including those who supplied papyri for recycling into cartonnage and the priests (including the choachytes: see below) and embalmers who carried out the work according to the grading of embalming that had been paid for. They used instruction manuals that guided the practitioners through the procedures and specified the magical significance of each.[21] That some mummies were left in their coffins on display in private homes for extended periods of time suggests that many years might elapse between mummification and burial.

Wooden anthropoid coffins continued from the Saïte and Late Periods into Ptolemaic times. They often had gilded faces, and some were fully gilded like that of the priest Nedjemankh. The head and upper body became disproportionately large, such as the coffin of Harsinakht (for both, see plate 18).[22] Increasingly, though, the deceased made do with gilded cartonnage mummy masks (the 'helmet-mask') and other components which were fitted onto the mummy once it had been embalmed and wrapped in bandages, replacing coffins. This papier-mâché equipage usually included suitable scenes of Osiris, Anubis, and the Four Sons of Horus. Although some featured hieroglyphic texts, which were often badly copied and full of mistakes (or gibberish), many did not. Simpler versions did away with the mummy masks and used only bandages.

Over time, the portraiture, if present, became less Egyptian and more 'Greek', but very stylized. Some of course may have been bought 'off the shelf' rather than trying to source a realistic portrait. They are notoriously difficult to date with any precision and are usually attributed to the Roman period when the painted mummy portraits also appeared.[23] The real value of the cartonnage to us was the habit of reusing discarded papyri as a raw material and thereby the accidental preservation of many documents. This practice was by no means universal.

When it came to the funeral, the ancient *Book of the Dead* was still available, but new texts had been written, such as the *Book of Traversing Eternity*. These documents served as manuals for the deceased as they made their way through the underworld and included the Opening of the Mouth ceremony when the senses of the deceased were symbolically restored to the newly mummified body.[24]

Bodies were usually buried in vast cemeteries linked to the settlements from where the deceased came. These sometimes clustered around earlier monuments, for example the small Temple of Alexander in the Bahariya Oasis or near pyramids. In some instances, rock-cut tombs were dug out to provide better protection. These were used for individual burials or contained communal burials of mummies that had been cleared out from households. Some had been stored in the home, usually contained in a cupboard resembling a small wardrobe with opening doors so that the deceased could 'participate' in family events. There are examples of Ptolemaic-era coffins or mummies being found in Roman-period cupboards, showing that the ancestor could have remained a familiar part of the household for many years before being deposited in a permanent tomb.

TOMBS

Those of higher status could invest in elaborate monuments. One of the best known is the temple-tomb of Petosiris, a high priest of Thoth at Hermopolis (near el Ashmunein), at Tuna el-Gebel, though it cannot be dated any more precisely than 30th Dynasty (Nectanebo I–II) to early Ptolemaic (plate 4). This delightful structure, which has survived intact, was designed as a miniature temple. Today, it most obviously resembles the façade of the Temple of Hathor at Dendera or the Temple of Khnum at Esna. The walls of the pronaos (vestibule) are covered with painted reliefs of agricultural scenes derived from both Egyptian and Greek styles. This leads to the chapel where the decoration was inspired by New Kingdom mythological scenes, with the burial chamber below accessed by a shaft.[25]

The temple-tomb of Petosiris is among the last of its kind known today, though nearby was the tomb of his priest brother, and that of another priest, both also in temple style.[26] The early Ptolemaic (?) tomb of an official called Tutu and his wife at Sohag (ancient Tmoupaei), about 100 miles (150 km) north-west of Thebes, discovered by chance in 2019, was clearly derived from Saïte examples. The chambers were decorated with traditional-style funerary paintings and hieroglyphic texts, Tutu's sistrum-playing Hathor priestess wife Ta-Shirit-Ast ('the Daughter of Isis') being accompanied by painted passages from the *Book of the Dead*. However, the granite sarcophagi were empty and only the anonymous mummies of a woman and a teenage boy, and several dozen animals, mainly falcons and rodents which were probably secondary burials, were recovered.[27]

For the most part, when they existed, Ptolemaic tombs were subterranean and simple. A triple-vaulted structure known as Hypogeum 1 (a subterranean chamber) at Abydos contained in the central vault the remains of limestone sarcophagi and wooden coffins, together with the physical remains of around five members of a family of priests from early Ptolemaic times. They were found with various grave goods such as shabti (or ushabti) statues, traditional funerary figurines intended to act as servants for the deceased in the afterlife. In one of the other vaults nineteen further individuals had been deposited.[28]

In earlier dynastic times the prodigy tomb chapels of the elite, for example that of the vizier Ramose in the middle of the 18th Dynasty at Thebes, were used to showcase the status of the deceased to mourners.

Extensive wall paintings of the great man showed him presiding over underlings, receiving tribute on behalf of the crown, and accepting gifts and honours from an admiring and grateful pharaoh.[29] This was supposed to enhance the standing of the deceased's descendants, except that Ramose appears to have fallen from grace. Such private funerary monuments did not apparently exist in the Ptolemaic period, royal patronage and elite status being exhibited in different ways and involving a governing class dominated by those of Greek origin. Priestly burials, more often involving native Egyptians, clung on to older customs but these were restricted to mummification and the use of traditional coffins.

THE TOMB OF HORNEDJITEF

Hornedjitef was a priest of Amun at Karnak in Thebes under Ptolemy II and III. His is an exceptional example of the burial (c. 240 BC) of a senior dignitary in Ptolemaic Egypt. Hornedjitef held several prestigious positions linking him to a long tradition of elite office holders back to the Old Kingdom. His body was placed in two anthropoid wooden coffins covered with traditional funerary motifs and scenes. The inner one was gilded (plate 18). They were based on archetypes dating back to the New Kingdom (c. 1550–1069 BC). The outer coffin was characteristic of the Late Period and early Ptolemaic times with very heavy features and an exaggerated head. His body was encased in cartonnage including a gilded mask depicting him as a young man. Although he had no apparent injuries, Hornedjitef had arthritis. He was buried with a copy of the *Book of the Dead*. In a Ptolemaic-era variant of custom, a box was provided for his internal organs, but they had been replaced in the body. Hornedjitef was accompanied by a statue of Ptah-Sokar-Osiris, a composite god who would ensure his resurrection.[30] Hornedjitef's burial was largely traditional but was modified by some features from his own time.

Ptolemaic-era graves are also known from huge numbers of intrusive burials in earlier tombs, including the temple-tomb of Petosiris, and others at Saqqara. Indeed, any available tomb of any date was treated as fair game. Some were stuffed with as many bodies as possible.[31]

Priests known as *choachytai* (from χοαχύτης, 'keeper of mummies', or in Egyptian a *w3ḥ-mw*, 'pourer of water/libations') recycled local tombs for reuse, which was obviously both labour-saving and cheaper than excavating new ones, as well as managing burials. Osoroeris was a member of a Theban choachyte family which included most of his brothers and their father Horos II (who died in 111 BC). Relatives of the deceased subcontracted the maintenance of burials and observation of rituals to such firms on a long-term basis. Choachytes owned liturgies and exclusive rights to their use but bought and sold these too. They operated under the protection of local associations, divided up zones in cemeteries between them, and could operate at more than one location. Gravediggers were a different profession altogether and were quick to protest if the choachytes overstepped their prerogatives.[32]

Theban Tomb 32 (TT32) in Western Thebes was originally created for a 19th Dynasty official called Djehutymes who served Ramesses II (*c.* 1279–1213 BC). By Ptolemy I's reign the tomb had been taken over by the Nesmin family. Side-chambers from the original burial shaft were cut out and used for family members until the time of Ptolemy III or IV. Later, the old tomb's hall was pressed into service as a communal burial place for low-status individual graves, probably because the Nesmin family had died out. A Third Intermediate Period (*c.* 1070–664 BC) hypogeum outside under the forecourt area was also reused for burials. The tomb was still used in the Roman period.[33]

TT32 was not unusual in serving as a second- or even third-hand tomb throughout the Graeco-Roman era. Next door is TT400 which contained the remains of forty-nine late burials, dated by the dominant presence of Ptolemaic-date objects. The main feature, as with Hornedjitef (see above), was the restoration of the internal organs to the body before the wrapped body was equipped with cartonnage fittings. In TT414, originally a 26th Dynasty tomb, the borrowing of the premises, which lasted from the 30th Dynasty into early Ptolemaic times, included reusing a 26th Dynasty coffin, by then around three centuries old. The new occupants were a prophet of Amun called Wah-ib-Re and his descendants.[34]

In Alexandria, Hellenistic-type tombs appeared. Their most obvious feature was a courtyard dug down into the rock from which doors led off to burial chambers, for example at the Necropolis of Al-Shatby which featured classical-style columns and funerary urns as well as inhumations. They lasted, with modifications, until Christianity transformed burial practices and phased out traditions that smacked of paganism.

Most Ptolemaic-era bodies found in general cemeteries are anonymous or at best provide us with a name, and nothing about cause of death or any other personal detail. They were buried in pits and are usually in a very poor state, often broken apart and with little soft tissue remaining. Expensive scientific investigations of the better-preserved can identify broken or damaged limbs and arthritis as well as infections such as bilharzia and malaria, and parasitic infections including tapeworm and threadworm. Many people in Egypt of all periods lived with an extensive array of debilitating ailments beyond the ability of contemporary medicine to deal with.

Funerals included processions of mourners, some professional if funds allowed.[35] There were also written lamentations for recitation. Aphrodisia, daughter of Evagaros, was the subject of a piece by an otherwise unknown Greek poet of Ptolemaic Egypt called Herodes. He wrote metrical funerary epigrams that eulogized the deceased. These had been individually commissioned but utilized stock themes and sentiments in a classical, rather than an Egyptian, rhetorical tradition. From the poem, which is addressed to the anonymous passer-by, we learn that Aphrodisia was married to a soldier called Ptolemaeus with whom she had had several children. She has left them at the pinnacle of their success and fled to Hades with her charms while her husband coped with the desolation of bereavement in the way he buried her. She sends the strangers who read her words on their way, wishing them good fortune and 'a happy heart'.[36]

Part III

RUIN

*We return to the narrative history of the Ptolemaic dynasty and the
circumstances that brought it to an end. First, however, we must consider
how the emergent power of Rome began to have an ever-increasing impact
on the destiny of the Ptolemaic kingdom.*

11

WAR OF THE WORLDS
Rome and Carthage: The First and Second Punic Wars
(264–241 and 218–201 BC)

In 264 BC, when Ptolemy II was developing Egypt into a showcase Hellenistic kingdom, the First Punic War broke out between Rome and Carthage. The conflict was to last a generation, only ending in 241 BC, and was followed by the Second Punic War just over two decades later. These conflicts took the story of Rome outside peninsular Italy with dramatic implications for Ptolemaic Egypt.

THE FIRST PUNIC WAR

In 264 BC western Sicily was controlled by Carthage, but this was only a minor part of an empire that also covered the coast of North Africa (modern-day Libya, Tunisia, Algeria, and Morocco), a large part of southern and central Spain, Sardinia, and Corsica. Carthaginian ships, manned by experienced and highly trained crews, dominated trade in the western Mediterranean and even up the Atlantic coast to Britain. This commerce was far more important to the Carthaginian empire than farming. The Carthaginian state was ruled by a mercantile aristocracy whose families controlled the Carthaginian assembly and associated magistracies. It employed an army made up of conscripts serving in units raised from North African states, and mercenaries.

Carthage did not challenge Rome for control of coastal Italy, but the Romans established colonies down the west side of Italy as a precaution. The war only started because of curious and unpredictable circumstances, following which some of Rome's elite decided that pursuing ambitions in Sicily might be profitable. In 288 BC a group of brutal Italian mercenaries, the Mamertines, seized Messana (Messina) in Sicily. Meanwhile, a band of Roman troops from Campania had rebelled and taken Rhegium (Reggio) in Italy, just across the Straits of Sicily from Messana. In 270 BC Roman forces crushed the rebellion and recaptured Rhegium. Meanwhile, the Mamertines ran riot in Messana until Hiero II, tyrant of Syracuse, defeated them. At this point the audacious Mamertines brazenly asked both the Romans and Carthaginians for protection against Hiero. The Romans were reluctant and held back. Spotting an opportunity, the Carthaginians stepped up and sent in a fleet. The Mamertines were annoyed to discover that the Carthaginians then refused to withdraw and they turned to the Romans, pointing out that, as Italians, they should help each other out, offering to become Roman allies in return. Faced with the unbearable prospect of the Carthaginians controlling all of Sicily, an ambivalent Senate, weary of recent wars in Italy, eventually agreed to send a force to recover Messana in 264 BC.[1] The Carthaginian fleet promptly pulled out, handing the Romans an easy victory. Carthage sent a new fleet and drew Hiero back into the fray. A new Roman army reinforced the troops in Messana. The Carthaginians resented losing control of the Straits. The Romans became enticed by the prospect of adding Sicily and its vast agricultural resources to its dominions. War loomed.

Messana also seems to have been the source of bronze coins struck c. 264 BC with the legend ROMANO(RUM), '[coinage] of the Romans', beside a head of Minerva and a reverse depicting a Ptolemaic-type eagle standing on a thunderbolt. These were probably struck for the Roman invading force and may be connected to the Carthaginian habit of using Ptolemaic coins.[2]

The Carthaginians' maritime economy depended on their naval skills. War at sea was unavoidable if the Carthaginians were to be challenged.

The Romans had to build a fleet from scratch, yet until now it had never occurred to them that they might need to become a naval power. Nor even had they considered invading Sicily. To begin with, the Romans borrowed ships to carry their troops over to Sicily. When they captured a Carthaginian vessel, they copied it. Armed with a fleet of one hundred quinqueremes and twenty triremes based on their prize, the Romans were able to set about training crews.[3] They also developed the remarkable 'raven', which used a pole, ropes, and a pulley to drop a gangplank with an iron spike from the Roman ship into the deck of an enemy vessel. Roman troops could then dash across and fight the enemy crews and troops.[4] Astonishingly, in 260 BC at Mylae the Romans won their first naval battle against incredulous Carthaginians. Further Carthaginian defeats came at Sulci (259 BC) and Cape Ecnomus (256 BC).

Almost twenty years of fighting followed, often at sea, costing Rome several fleets and thousands of men, despite the victories. The investment was enormous. If Polybius was correct, by 258 BC the Roman forces destined to make a landing in North Africa numbered 140,000, with each ship carrying 300 oarsmen and 120 marines. He estimated the Carthaginian forces at 150,000. At best these are approximations, and at worst pure invention.[5] The bulk of the fleet was withdrawn on orders from Rome after successful looting and the capture of 20,000 slaves, leaving the consul Marcus Atilius Regulus with 15,000 infantry and 500 cavalry.[6] The campaign went well to begin with, but a catastrophe followed that showed how draining the war was becoming. In 255 BC Regulus was defeated by the Carthaginian general Xanthippus near Utica, around 20 miles (32 km) north-west of Carthage. Xanthippus, a Spartan, had been hired by the Carthaginians for his skills in leadership, discipline, and training.[7] Using elephants, backed up by heavy infantry, Xanthippus annihilated Regulus' army, leaving only 2,000 alive plus another 500 who fled with Regulus before being captured.

Rome's experience in the First Punic War was an object lesson in not relying on luck, especially when things were going well. There were only two ways for men to reform themselves, Polybius said: 'either to learn from their own mistakes or those of others'.[8] This lesson was the single most important cause of Roman success. Their response to adversity was a remorseless resilience, even if the original attraction of having a war had been temporarily forgotten. After the defeat of Regulus, the Romans built another fleet, defeated a Carthaginian one, and rescued what remained of their army. The new fleet was wrecked off Sicily in a storm on its way home, destroying 284 ships out of 364, thanks to the commanding officers ignoring advice from pilots. Fighting back from disaster became the guiding principle for Roman policy during this war and most of the later ones.[9]

Carthage's naval power naturally brought it into contact with Egypt. Ptolemy II's admiral Timosthenes of Rhodes made two major journeys, one of which was to the western Mediterranean and thus right through the Carthaginians' sphere of control, which, it seems likely, must have taken place before the First Punic War broke out. The result of his voyages was a gazetteer of harbours, called *On Ports*, from Ethiopia to the western end of the Mediterranean.[10]

By 252 BC Carthage and Rome were exhausted and short of funds. The Carthaginians sent an embassy to Ptolemy II. They wanted to borrow the enormous sum of 2,000 talents for their war effort. According to Appian, who wrote around four hundred years later, Ptolemy preferred to try and act as a mediator but his attempts to broker a peace failed. Ptolemy kept hold of his money, saying it was not appropriate to help one friend against another.[11] He also had other calls on his resources.

In 242 BC, after further victories and defeats, the Romans assembled another fleet, commanded by Gaius Lutatius Catulus. The Carthaginians were stunned. After over two decades of fighting, the Roman treasury had no money left to finance the new ships. Instead, the richest senators formed themselves into syndicates of two or three, each paying for a new quinquereme.[12] It was an astonishingly resourceful cooperative venture. Lutatius Catulus focused on training, ending up with men better at the job of naval warfare than the Carthaginians, who had had to construct another fleet quickly. At the Aegates (Aeguas) Islands in 241 BC, off the western tip of Sicily, the fleets met. The Carthaginian defeat was total, forcing them to sue for peace. Rome was now pre-eminent in the western Mediterranean, overturning the balance of power within one generation.

The victory was remarkable because it had not come about from sustained success or because the Romans had magically found new allies or resources to outclass the Carthaginians. It was down to persistence, preparation, and self-belief. The prize was Sicily, any islands between Sicily and Italy, and 2,200 Euboean talents of silver to be paid by Carthage to Rome over twenty years (a Euboean talent weighed about 66 lbs (30 kg), an Attic talent 57 lbs (26 kg)).[13]

ROME EMBOLDENED

Grain fleets from Sicily would thereafter help feed the Roman population. The new province was managed directly by the Senate, appointing governors from their own number. With Rome now capable of moving into the eastern Mediterranean by sea, the process had begun in which Egypt's commercial and diplomatic contacts with Rome increased.

Energized, the Romans sent an embassy offering help to Ptolemy II in the Second Syrian War against Antiochus II. It was an important gesture, though Ptolemy turned them down because the war had ended. The offer to Ptolemy suggested that the Romans saw Egypt as a potentially vital source of help. Ptolemy had declined to get involved in the First Punic War but, crucially, he had not sided with Carthage. For this, Rome had much to be grateful.[14]

THE SECOND PUNIC WAR (218–201 BC)

By the late first century BC Livy thought the Second Punic War was 'the most memorable war in history' because Rome's and Carthage's resources were unprecedented.[15] Carthage still controlled an area of North Africa equivalent to Morocco, Algeria, Tunisia, and part of Libya. It also controlled most of the central and eastern part of the Iberian peninsula

(Spain). The catalyst for the war was believed at the time to be, or at any rate explained as, the Carthaginian seizure in 219 BC of the city of Saguntum (Sagunto) in Spain, in violation of an earlier treaty between Rome and Carthage. The Carthaginians were outraged by how the Romans had treated them. The Romans declared war on Carthage in 218 BC, enraged that the defeated Carthaginians had challenged them. According to Livy there were in 234–233 BC over 270,000 registered citizens in Rome but, in a war against the Insubrian Gauls in 222 BC, the Romans were able to field an army of 800,000.[16] The acquisition of Italian allies had dramatically enhanced Rome's ability to fight international wars.

Victories won by the Carthaginian general Hannibal's invading army in Italy began with the devastating defeat of Rome at Lake Trasimene in 217 BC which led to the Battle of Cannae in south-eastern Italy the following year. At Cannae Rome lost the vast majority of approximately 85,000 troops made up of Romans and allies while Hannibal held most of southern Italy. The fighting had destroyed much of the crops in Italy. At some point between 215 and 210 BC the Romans were forced to send envoys to Ptolemy IV to ask for corn, Egypt being the only nation unaffected by war and armies on campaign (see Chapter 6), but whether he obliged is unknown.[17] What Ptolemy may have supplied instead was hard bullion which found its way into a special batch of gold coins struck in Rome with an eagle astride a thunderbolt reverse, clearly copied from Ptolemaic types, followed quickly by the new silver denarius coinage in 212–211 BC. The coins helped bankroll the war, the denarius enduring for around 450 years as the staple Roman bullion coin and accounting unit.[18]

It was not until 209 BC that Rome began to recover. When the general Publius Cornelius Scipio invaded North Africa in 205 BC, his fleet included 50 men-of-war and 400 transports to carry not only the men and their equipment, but also cattle, food, and water for forty-five days.[19] This gives an idea of just how complex a Roman waterborne military operation could be. Their soldiers were effective, but the relatively cumbersome nature of their ships continued to be a potential liability.[20] The Carthaginian defeat on land at Zama (now in modern Tunisia) in 202 BC at Scipio's hands was total though it resulted as much from luck as Roman judgement.

Rome's Treaty of Versailles-type settlement with Carthage in 201 BC reflected uncertainty about what power and dominion over others would involve. Carthage was to remain in control of its homeland territory, cities, and property, and even escape the humiliation of a Roman garrison. Conversely, the Carthaginians lost their Iberian possessions, had to pay war reparations as well as 10,000 talents over the next fifty years, accept a gigantic reduction in the size of their armed forces and a ban on waging war outside Africa, as well as handing over any prisoners of war and a hundred hostages. Versailles was seen by Germany in 1919 as a devastating humiliation. In the ancient world, Rome's treatment of Carthage was regarded as astonishingly lenient. Hannibal told the Carthaginian assembly it was not even worth discussing the matter further.[21] Rome's acquisition of Carthage's Iberian territory was a decisive factor. Its colossal mineral resources, especially silver, were to have a major impact on Rome's ability to finance further military operations.

Scipio personally did extremely well out of the war, and was named Africanus in recognition of his victory but, considering he had brought the Romans freedom from the greatest threat they believed they had ever faced, that probably seemed reasonable. More importantly, the war had not been prosecuted for the purposes of his personal gain. In 205 BC the Senate decreed that the games Scipio had vowed to lay on would be paid for out of the bullion he had supplied to the treasury. After his return from Africa at the end of the war, games and festivals continued to be held in Rome at Scipio's expense.[22] It was said that he brought 123,000 pounds of silver into the Roman treasury.[23]

The destabilization of the eastern Mediterranean became an important problem at the same time as Rome was fighting the Second Punic War. Ptolemaic Egypt was in decline under Ptolemy IV with diminished international prestige and domestic instability. The Macedonian kingdom of Philip V and the Seleucid kingdom of Antiochus III began to fill the power vacuum, the Macedonians allying themselves with the Carthaginians. Several wars were eventually to be fought with Macedon, the effect of which was to draw Rome further into the complex and febrile territorial politics of the whole region. The question is whether Rome inevitably entered the Greek East in pursuit of its ambitions, or whether it was because the arrival of various embassies from Egypt, Rhodes, and other places that were alarmed by the threat posed by Philip V and Antiochus III served as the catalyst and enticement to opportunistic intervention.[24]

After 201 BC, by seeking to become more embroiled in foreign affairs, Rome was engaging in a determined effort to create a wider safety zone that surrounded the Italian homeland with nations and city states whose own ambitions were suppressed and contained. An essential part of that policy was to corral, destroy, or break up aggressive kingdoms like Macedon and the Seleucids, and to draw the more compliant and manageable ones like Egypt into the Roman sphere of influence.

1. Temple of Isis at Philae from the adjacent island of Bigeh, painting by David Roberts, 1838. Works like this and travellers' tales of journeys in Egypt thrilled the world. Although the shrine dates back at least to the 25th and 26th Dynasties, the extant structures mostly belong to the Ptolemaic period, mainly Ptolemy II, V, and VI, but with Roman additions. All the structures were relocated to the nearby island of Agilkia between 1977–80 before Philae was submerged by the rising waters of Lake Nasser.

2. Images of Alexander. *Left*: a Hellenistic posthumous and idealized marble bust of Alexander from Alexandria, *c.* 200–1 BC. *Right*: Alexander the Great, as a pharaoh on the walls of the central barque shrine at the Temple of Luxor, greeting Amun from whom he claimed descent. He is shown with cartouches for his name Alexander, and his Egyptian throne name 'Chosen by Re, beloved of Amun'. Probably posthumous under Ptolemy I.

3. Alexander and Ptolemy. *Above*: tetradrachm (silver) of Alexander the Great struck at Memphis (thunderbolt mintmark), *c.* 323–305 BC, by Ptolemy, son of Lagus, as satrap of Egypt during the reign of Philip III Arridhaeus or Alexander IV (29 mm, 17.2 gm). *Below*: tetradrachm (silver) of Ptolemy I (*c.* 305–282 BC), at the reduced Egyptian standard introduced by him. His portrait was continued on similar coins issued by his dynastic successors. The Greek ΑΧΡ monogram for Alexandria appears next to the eagle. The coin bears bankers' test marks (25 mm, 14.2 gm).

4. The temple-tomb of Petosiris, high priest of Thoth at Hermopolis (Tuna el-Gebel), Middle Egypt, late fourth century BC. The reliefs inside show a conflation of Egyptian and Greek-Hellenistic styles.

5. Section of unprovenanced limestone relief from a temple depicting Arsinoe II as 'Daughter of Amun, Arsinoe, Great Queen', *c.* 273–270 BC. She wears the vulture headdress of a queen, the red crown of Lower Egypt, a solar disc, and horns.

6. The Canopus Decree, found at Tanis (*left*: complete; *right*: detail of the top). The text, written in hieroglyphs, demotic, and Greek, is dated to 7 March 238 BC in honour of Ptolemy III, Berenice II, and their daughter Berenice, and celebrates various royal achievements in war, relief for the famine which followed an unusually low Nile flood, support for religion, and the reform of the calendar. Copies were set up in other cities. Height 204 cm.

7. Remains of the memorial-mortuary temple of the Middle Kingdom pharaoh Amenemhet III (*c.* 1860–1814 BC), named thirteen centuries later by Herodotus as the 'Labyrinth'. Ptolemy II dismantled the complex to provide the stone for a new city, named Arsinoe for his sister-wife Arsinoe II.

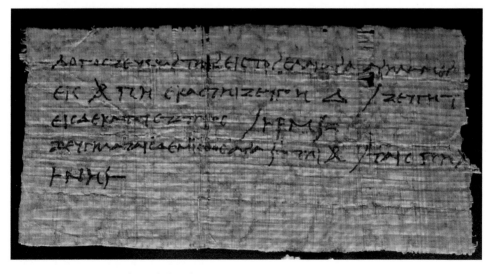

8. Ptolemaic bureaucracy depended on documents written in Greek and demotic Egyptian. This papyrus in Greek from Philadelphia in the Fayum concerns oxen used to cultivate an olive grove on an estate probably owned by Ptolemy II's dioiketes, Apollonius. From the archive of Zenon, Apollonius' secretary.

9. Lindos, Rhodes, looking north-east across where the Aegean meets the Mediterranean towards the coast of Asia Minor (Turkey), which was controlled by Ptolemaic Egypt for much of the earlier part of the period. Rhodes was a pivotal transit point for Ptolemaic Egypt's commercial links with Europe.

10. Coins of Ptolemy IV–X. *Top row (left to right)*: 1. Tetradrachm of Ptolemy IV and Arsinoe III (Alexandria, *c.* 220–206/5 BC). Obv: jugate busts of Serapis and Isis. Rev: ΒΑΣΙΛΕΩΣ ΠΤΟΛΕΜΑΙΟΥ (King Ptolemy) and Ptolemaic eagle (26 mm, 14.1 gm). 2. Obv (only): bronze diobol Cleopatra I or II as Isis. Rev (not shown): Ptolemaic eagle similar to previous (27 mm, Paphos, Cyprus?). 3. Rev (only): bronze obol(?) of Ptolemy IV with standard Ptolemaic eagle plus ΕΥΛ abbreviation for Eulaeus or a local magistrate. Obv (not shown): bears the standard Zeus-Ammon portrait as (4) below (21 mm, Paphos?). *Bottom row (left to right)*: 4. Bronze diobol(?) possibly of Ptolemy VI and VIII (*c.* 170–163 BC), indicated by the paired eagles on the reverse with the standard ΒΑΣΙΛΕΩΣ ΠΤΟΛΕΜΑΙΟΥ legend. Other attributions include Ptolemy IX and Cleopatra III. Obv: Zeus-Ammon (28 mm, Alexandria). 5. Tetradrachm of Cleopatra III and Ptolemy X (106/5 BC). Obv: portrait of Ptolemy I. Rev: Ptolemaic eagle plus ΒΑΣΙΛΕΩΣ ΠΤΟΛΕΜΑΙΟΥ, Cleopatra III's 12th regnal year (L IB), Ptolemy X's 9th regnal year (Θ) (24 mm, 14.5 gm, Alexandria or Paphos).

11. Ptolemy VI Philometor and his sister-wife Cleopatra II who ruled with him and their brother Ptolemy VIII, *c.* 170–164 BC, Temple of Sobek and Haroeris (Horus the Elder) at Kom Ombo. Difficulty of access has caused some foreshortening of the image. Cleopatra later ruled with just Ptolemy VIII (d. 116 BC) after Ptolemy VI's death, and then with Cleopatra III and Ptolemy IX in the last year of her life, disappearing by *c.* 115 BC.

12. Venal mayhem. *Left to right*: Cleopatra III, 'Wife, Queen regnant and Lady of the Two Lands', with her mother Cleopatra II, 'Sister, Queen regnant and Lady of the Two Lands', and husband-uncle Ptolemy VIII, 'King of Upper and Lower Egypt, son of Re', at Kom Ombo, west wall of the temple vestibule, *c.* 118 BC. Ptolemy VIII murdered Memphites, his son by Cleopatra II, and may have earlier murdered her son by their brother Ptolemy VI, Neos Philopator.

13. Ptolemaic gateway added to the 'Small Temple' of Amun at Medinet Habu, Thebes, which was begun under Hatshepsut of the 18th Dynasty and was then incorporated into the memorial-mortuary temple complex of Ramesses III of the 20th Dynasty. Visible cartouches on the gate are those of Ptolemy IX (who reigned variously 116–110, 109–107, 88–80 BC). The gate illustrates the Ptolemaic enthusiasm for integrating building projects into much older pharaonic tradition.

14. Ptolemy XII smites his foes in a traditional pharaonic pose on the magnificent façade of the Temple of Horus at Edu. An identical mirrored scene appeared on the other pylon. Begun in 237 BC by Ptolemy III, construction at Edfu continued until *c.* 57 BC.

15. Temple of Sobek and Haroeris at Kom Ombo, remains of the hypostyle hall. Begun by Ptolemy VI Philometor, with much work under Ptolemy XII, and continued during the Roman period. The building was never completed. Since antiquity, movement of the Nile, earthquakes, and stone robbing have reduced the temple to a semi-ruin.

16. Tetradrachms. Beyond Egypt, Alexander's name was kept alive with the Heracles silver tetradrachms struck by the Successors, and later by semi-autonomous cities and other places over which the Ptolemies constantly sought to maintain control. These gave way to regnal issues. *Left to right by rows: 1st row:* Corinth (Greece), attributed to Demetrius Poliorcetes, *c.* 310–290 BC; Phaselis (Lycia), *c.* 217–216 BC*. *2nd row:* Perge (Pamphylia), *c.* 221–188 BC*; Aspendus (Pamphylia), *c.* 191–190 BC*. *3rd row:* Rhodes, *c.* 205–190 BC; Antiochus III, 223–187 BC, Antioch(?). *4th row:* Antiochus VII Grypus, 136–135 BC, Tyre; Cleopatra VII and Mark Antony, 37–33 BC, Antioch(?) – note the similarity of their portraits. * = countermarked for use in the Seleucid kingdom. Diameters 26–32 mm.

17. Polychrome mosaic made of marble tesserae from the dining room of a wealthy house in Alexandria in the Al-Shatby quarter, second century BC. The design, including geometric forms and acanthus jars, is wholly Greek and owes little to Egyptian tradition, reflecting the city's cosmopolitan nature.

18. Ptolemaic-era anthropoid coffins. *Left*: wooden coffin of Harsinakht in traditional style but with distinctive Ptolemaic-era features (such as the large shoulders). Bought 'off the shelf' and with a crude hieratic inscription naming him inserted in a blank panel below (Kharga Oasis). *Centre*: gilded cartonnage coffin of Nedjemankh, priest of the ram god Heryshaf, at Heracleopolis Magna (*c.* 150–50 BC). *Right*: gilded wooden inner coffin of the priest Hornedjitef, made *c.* 240 BC, found at Asasif, Thebes.

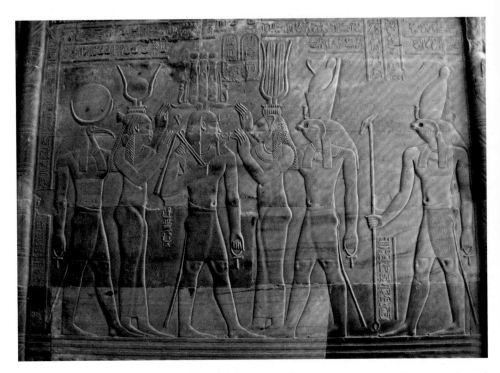

19. Ptolemy XII, wearing the triple atef (hemhem) crown, still enjoys the protection of Egypt's traditional gods right at the end of the period. From left to right: Thoth, Isis, Ptolemy XII, Sekhmet, Horus, and far right, another Horus. Temple of Sobek and Haroeris, Kom Ombo, *c.* 51–47 BC.

20. Granite-sandstone statue of Pen-Menkh, governor of Dendera, royal deputy and priest of Hathor and Horus during the reign of Cleopatra VII. The figure is a striking example of how at the very end of the Ptolemaic period traditional Egyptian and classical styles and techniques had been brought together. Slightly less than lifesize.

21. Tradition and the Ptolemies. *Left*: a superbly executed granite statue of Thutmose III (1479–1425 BC), warrior pharaoh of the 18th Dynasty, Karnak. *Right*: an anonymous Ptolemaic king, but probably Ptolemy XV Caesarion, from around 1,400 years later, also granite, thought to be from Karnak. The less accomplished Ptolemaic sculpture has emulated the traditional impassive expression and nemes headdress but introduced Hellenistic stylized realism.

22. Roman trireme warship with ram. Roman naval power, developed during the First and Second Punic Wars in the third century BC, was the decisive factor in Rome's complete dominance of the Mediterranean world in the second and first centuries BC. This culminated in the defeat of Antony and Cleopatra VII's fleet at Actium in 31 BC. From the tomb of Cartilius Poplicola (a local magistrate), Ostia, Italy, *c*. 25–20 BC.

23. Cleopatra VII and her son Caesarion (Ptolemy XV) by Caesar on the rear wall of the Temple of Hathor at Dendera, mid-30s BC. Caesarion, still a child, is depicted as an adult pharaoh and bears a Horus name. The design follows convention with Cleopatra in the subordinate role behind her son, but there was no doubt who held the power.

24. Rome in Egypt, Egypt in Rome. *Left*: relief of Augustus (centre) named here as *Autokrator Kaisaros* ('the Emperor Caesar') in hieroglyphs on the Opet temple at Karnak, completing unfinished Ptolemaic work. *Right*: obelisk from Heliopolis of Psammetichus I (Psamtik I) of the 26th Dynasty brought to Rome by Augustus and used as a sundial pointer in his *Horologium Augusti*, built in the Field of Mars in 10 BC to commemorate the twentieth anniversary of the annexation of Egypt. Now in the Piazza Montecitorio.

12

QUENCHING THE FLAME OF BOLD REBELLION

Ptolemy V Epiphanes (204–180 BC) and
Cleopatra I (193–176 BC)

Ptolemy V Epiphanes' mother Arsinoe III was murdered shortly after her brother-husband's death. Too young to rule on his own, Ptolemy V was at the mercy of Sosibius and Agathocles who lay behind the plots to maintain their own control of the crown until they fell. Thereafter, foreign relations only showed how much weaker Egypt had become. Just as Rome turned a corner in its fortunes, the Ptolemaic reign had to face the humiliation of a rebellion in the Thebaid region that lasted two decades.

SOSIBIUS AND AGATHOCLES

In 204 BC Ptolemy V Epiphanes (the 'Illustrious' or 'Manifest') was still so young when he succeeded, the assumption would have been that Arsinoe III would serve as co-ruler or regent. The king's death left his son at the mercy of his own staff and Antiochus III who now planned to seize Egypt. However, the courtiers Sosibius and Agathocles were the ones really in control.[1] There were precedents for a regency in earlier Egyptian history. None had yet occurred under the Ptolemies. Nor was one to happen on this occasion, even if that had been the plan, because Arsinoe was killed shortly after the king died.[2]

Within five days of Arsinoe's murder, Sosibius and Agathocles made their first move. The king's bodyguard, household troops, and the officers of the cavalry and infantry were called to the palace where Sosibius and Agathocles had set up a dais. The event was tightly stage-managed. Ptolemy V was simultaneously crowned as the new ruler, with the epithet Epiphanes, and a fraudulent will read out that declared his late father had made Sosibius and Agathocles the boy's guardians. The soldiers were urged to support the new reign.

Only then were the deaths of Ptolemy IV and Arsinoe III made public. That was when Sosibius and Agathocles' plans went awry. The urns supposedly containing their cremated remains were displayed, which (if true) suggests no attempt to mummify them had taken place. If foul play had been involved, cremation would have conveniently hidden the evidence. However, Arsinoe's urn allegedly only contained spices, causing even more fevered speculation about what had really happened to her, of much more concern to the people than her husband.[3]

When the penny dropped that Arsinoe had been murdered, there was much upset. This was more about the hatred of Agathocles, whose reputation was as bad as that of the dead king. He and Sosibius offered the soldiers two months' pay, instructed them to take an oath of loyalty, and ordered the people to stop mourning. According to Polybius, Agathocles had arranged for Arsinoe III to be murdered by Philammon who was then packed off to Cyrenaica to be libyarch (ruler in Libya).[4] The young Ptolemy V was placed in the care of Agathocles' mother and sister, Oenanthe and Agathocleia.

Agathocles executed his plans assiduously. It is easy to see why he and Sosibius might have killed Ptolemy IV. Diplomatic missions were sent to Rome, Philip V of Macedon, and Antiochus III. Through his envoys, Agathocles begged Antiochus to honour Ptolemy V's coronation and asked Philip to step in should Antiochus cause any trouble. Part of the reason for sending the diplomats was to remove from Egypt any high official who might start being obstructive or asking awkward questions.

They were told not to hurry back. Mercenaries were hired because Agathocles was planning a war against Antiochus. He also wanted to purge the household troops and bodyguards, and replace them with the new mercenaries who would be loyal to him first.[5]

The bumptious and over-confident Agathocles relaxed into his new-found powers. He packed out the new king's 'friends', supposed to be the monarch's trusted confidants, with dissolute cronies of his own. He slid into as much of a debauched lifestyle as that of the dead king. The description is a stock one, drawn from popular rhetorical images of the corrupt courtier who takes over from a weak ruler. Agathocles' power and influence were bitterly resented by the people.[6]

The only hope was Tlepolemus, governor of the Pelusium district. He avoided the court while Ptolemy IV was alive but returned to public duty after Ptolemy V's accession, hoping that a suitable council of advisers would govern the country. He was disappointed. Even worse, he was under threat from the disreputable men Agathocles had brought into government. Tlepolemus decided he could try and become Ptolemy V's guardian and take control. He touted for support among military officers and officials by inviting them to banquets. There, he tested them with gentle gibes about Agathocles, working up gradually to outrageous insults. Not surprisingly, news reached Agathocles, who promptly charged Tlepolemus with treachery and of plotting to bring Antiochus III in. Far from inspiring the public to turn on Tlepolemus, this had the opposite effect because it looked like everything was heading towards a showdown.[7]

Agathocles persisted in trying to entice the Macedonian troops to support him. Having no escape plan in place he plotted to get rid of more of his enemies. Events moved fast. A court bodyguard called Moeragenes was accused of some misdemeanour. Furious, he told Tlepolemus everything that was going on. For that he was arrested and taken off to be tried and tortured under the supervision of a secretary of state called Nicostratus. Nicostratus was brought a message, the contents of which are unknown, but it probably told him that the people's outrage was about to blow up in Agathocles' face. Nicostratus wisely did a runner. So did the torturers, leaving a bewildered and naked Moeragenes clutching his vitals. He hobbled off to the Macedonians, telling them to save themselves and the king. As the news broke, Alexandria erupted. Agathocles' circle panicked. Open spaces throughout the city filled up with mobs of enraged men and women, and even children. 'As the people had long been disposed to revolt and required only some man of courage to appeal to them, once the movement began it spread like wildfire.'[8] It was a long and terrifying night. Agathocles locked himself up in the palace with the king, a few loyal bodyguards, and his own family members.

At sunrise, Alexandria was still seething. A mob demanded the king be brought out. They tried to force their way in. Agathocles pleaded with the bodyguards to send a message to the Macedonians that he would step down. They refused but one of them, Aristomenes (an enthusiastic supporter of Agathocles), obliged. When Aristomenes reached the Macedonians, they nearly killed him but let him go on condition that he came back with Ptolemy V or not return at all. The Macedonians followed him to the palace and tried to burst in. Agathocles and Agathocleia begged for their lives, Agathocleia allegedly baring her breasts and insisting she had suckled the infant king. It was not the clincher she had hoped for. At that moment, Sosibius' son, also called Sosibius, intervened. He was a member of the bodyguard and asked the king to give up the names of anyone implicated in what had happened to him and his mother. Ptolemy V agreed and went with Sosibius junior. Meanwhile, Agathocles and Agathocleia bolted to their own houses, hotly pursued by the crowd.

The grisly end took place in the stadium. Agathocles was dragged in chains into the arena and stabbed to death. He escaped lightly. Next came:

Agathocleia stripped naked with her sisters and then all her relatives. Last of all they dragged Oenanthe from the Thesmophorion [sanctuary of Demeter Thesmophorus where women met during their annual autumn festival] and led her to the stadium naked on horseback. All of them were delivered into the hands of the mob, and now some began to bite them with their teeth, some to stab them and others to gouge their eyes out. Whenever one of them fell they tore the body from limb to limb until they had thus mutilated them all. For terrible is the cruelty of the Egyptians when their anger is aroused. At the same time some young girls who had been Arsinoe's close companions, hearing that Philammon, who had directed the queen's murder, had arrived from Cyrene three days before, rushed to his house and forcing an entrance killed Philammon with clubs and stones. They strangled his son who was no longer a child, dragged out his wife naked into the square, and slew her.[9]

The outcome was that Tlepolemus became regent, sharing the guardianship of Ptolemy V with Sosibius junior. Tlepolemus was too interested in good living and fame. He enjoyed handing out state funds to soldiers at court and even to visiting diplomats. This, and his inappropriate style of leadership, frustrated Sosibius junior who was ousted by Tlepolemus. By 201 BC Tlepolemus had been pushed out too. Aristomenes was made regent and guardian instead, but by then Ptolemy V was being protected by Rome.[10] Aristomenes was 'an able administrator'. For the moment the king enjoyed some popularity, but his relationship with Aristomenes was to sour.[11]

THE FIFTH SYRIAN WAR (202–195 BC)

After Ptolemy IV's death and the purge of the Agathocles faction, and presumably while Tlepolemus was still in post, an Egyptian embassy was sent to the Romans. They meekly asked them to serve as guardians for the child Ptolemy V and to help defend Egypt against Philip V and Antiochus III who had made a secret agreement. The Romans were pleased and sent their own deputation to thank Ptolemy V for Egypt's support. Now they had an excuse to go to war against Philip, seen as posing a serious threat. Their main concern was that Antiochus did not form an alliance with Philip, but the embassy gave them an opportunity to assess his intentions.[12]

Marcus Aemilius Lepidus was sent from Rome to serve as guardian for the Egyptian boy king, commemorated on the silver denarius coinage in Rome issued by his descendant of the same name in *c*. 61 or 56 BC with the legend TVTOR REG(IS), 'tutor of the king'.[13] The Romans were soon bolstered by the arrival of other embassies in 201 BC from Rhodes and Attalus I (241–197 BC) of Pergamum against whom Philip had gone to war while also seizing islands in the Aegean.[14] With the Second Punic War now over, the risk of fighting in two places simultaneously had been eliminated. The Romans could now confront Philip.

Antiochus III might have had his nose bloodied at Raphia in 217 BC but by 201 BC, older and wiser, he was back with a vengeance. In 202 BC he had taken Damascus, an event that marked the outbreak of the Fifth Syrian War. Dion, the Egyptian commander of the garrison there, was too good at his job. Antiochus concluded that a normal siege would achieve nothing. Instead, he laid on a massive Persian festival and made everyone of note contribute to its costs. That led Dion to believe he had nothing to fear because Antiochus and his men were partying. Antiochus heard that Dion and the citizens had relaxed. He immediately took a force to sneak up on the city and capture it by surprise. The tactic illustrated just how dangerous Antiochus was.[15]

Philip's progress across Thrace and Anatolia led the Romans to believe that war was inevitable. In 200 BC they sent an embassy to Philip to demand that he stop attacking Greek states and 'not to lay hands on any of Ptolemy's possessions'. They knew Philip would refuse.[16] A Roman diplomatic mission was also sent to both Alexandria and Antiochus to encourage them to settle any differences, triggered by a complaint made by Egypt to Rome that Antiochus had stolen Syria and Cilicia from them, but really to find out what Antiochus was up to.[17]

Antiochus used his handy new base at Damascus from which to advance. The Romans tried to warn him against troubling the orphaned

Ptolemy V in their care.[18] Antiochus recovered Gaza but faced resistance in the Phoenician cities that were held by Egypt. Although territory in Palestine was recaptured by Ptolemaic forces, by 198 BC Sidon fell to Antiochus who then turned to consolidating his control of Coele-Syria and Phoenicia. His next move was to take the cities of Cilicia, Lycia, and Caria and join forces with Philip.[19] Tetradrachms struck c. 220 to the 190s BC by cities such as Aspendus, Phaselis, and Perge were countermarked to validate their circulation in Seleucid-controlled territory. Among the marks used was an anchor, commemorating the same motif on a ring given in myth by Apollo to Seleucus I's mother after he had fathered her son (see plate 16).

Since Rome's immediate focus was on dealing with Philip V, Egypt now looked as if it was being abandoned to Antiochus. His power grew, largely at Egypt's expense.[20] By 197 BC Antiochus had taken control of Ephesus from Egypt, coveted by him because of its unmatched strategic position on the Ionian coast.[21] From there he could jump on into Europe. By the same year the Romans had defeated Philip at Cynoscephalae in Thessaly. Any cities in Thrace that Antiochus had taken from Egypt were restored to independence by the Romans, rather than returning them to Ptolemaic control (as the Romans had originally demanded in 198 BC).[22]

Restoring Egypt's power and influence was becoming elusive. In 197 BC a saviour of sorts appeared. Polycrates, commander in Cyprus, had managed his stewardship so well since Ptolemy IV's time that he turned up in Alexandria with a vast sum of money for the king. In 196 BC, having now reached his majority (despite being only about twelve years old), Ptolemy V had been crowned in Memphis, perhaps paid for by Polycrates' money.[23] Up until around this time, Aristomenes had continued to enjoy the trust of Ptolemy V but one day woke the king when he fell asleep during an audience of ambassadors. Ptolemy's flatterers told him that Aristomenes should have been more discreet, so 'Ptolemy sent for a cup of poison and ordered the poor man to drink it up'.[24] From thereon Ptolemy V fell increasingly under the influence of courtiers. Despite replacing Aristomenes, Polycrates later destroyed his reputation by a dissolute lifestyle in retirement. He also, much to Ptolemy V's frustration, kept the young king away from warfare.[25]

In *c.* 196 BC the Romans decided to confront Antiochus at Lysimachia (in Marmara, Thrace) and make a series of demands, ostensibly on behalf of Ptolemaic Egypt. The point, of course, was that Egypt was unable to act for itself. It was a charade. The Roman representatives demanded that Antiochus hand back the cities he had taken from Ptolemy V.[26] They also resented the fact that Antiochus had helped himself to other cities held by Philip while the latter was fighting the First Macedonian War (214–205 BC) with Rome. The reasoning was simple: Rome had gone through all the privations and expense of war and was not going to tolerate Antiochus reaping the rewards. Moreover, by entering Europe, Antiochus was effectively declaring war on Rome.[27] Antiochus retorted by saying what happened in Anatolia (which the Romans came to know as Asia Minor, referred to by this name hereafter in this book) was none of Rome's business, adding the preposterous claim that having taken some of the Ptolemaic cities there he was now able to come to an amicable agreement with Ptolemy V.[28]

A rumour emerged that Ptolemy V had died. All the participants at the negotiations abruptly broke off to decide what to do. Antiochus set sail immediately for Ephesus to prepare an invasion of Egypt while there was an interregnum. He had to abandon the plan when he learned that the rumours of Ptolemy's death had been greatly exaggerated.[29]

The peace treaty with Philip V of Macedon in 196 BC, at the end of the Second Macedonian War (200–197 BC), was modelled on Scipio Africanus' settlement with Carthage in 201 BC. The Macedonians were to be hugely restricted in their ability and entitlement to wage war outside Macedon and were obliged to pay tribute for years to come (the sources available to Livy disagreed on the amounts and time). Philip was to relinquish control of Greek cities in Europe and Asia. These cities were to become free rather than pass under the control of Rome.[30] This culminated in a proclamation at the Isthmian Games near Corinth that Greek states formerly subject to Philip would thereafter be free, administered by their own laws and with no liability to pay tribute to Rome.[31] The terms graphically illustrated how Rome could weaken the Hellenistic states, but in ways that did not look as if Rome was trying to take over. Rome's main agenda was to neutralize Antiochus. Ring-fencing Macedon was part of the preparations.

MARRIAGE

Everything changed in 195 BC. Antiochus III had bigger fish to fry because the Romans were far more important enemies than Egypt. They had the power to stop him, something beyond Egypt's capabilities. Antiochus betrothed his ten-year-old daughter Cleopatra, 'the Syrian', to Ptolemy V. In 194 BC they were married at Raphia. This first of the Cleopatras brought Coele-Syria with her as a dowry, which Antiochus had so recently captured, and would later bear her husband three children. In practice, Coele-Syria remained under Seleucid control; the dowry was a mirage. Ptolemy V never recovered the region. Two more daughters were used to secure alliances with Pergamum and Cappadocia.[32] None of this meant that Antiochus had given up on Egypt. The marriage alliance only put the matter on hold by flattering Ptolemy V.

Cleopatra I's status matched that of Berenice II, ruling as a joint divinity with her husband. At Edfu one of the inscriptions features Cleopatra's name and titles, which eventually included a carefully feminized pharaonic Horus name with some components adapted from the Horus names of other Ptolemies including her husband's.[33] Cleopatra is here a female Horus, *hwnwt-hqat* ('youthful woman ruler'), beloved by the gods, adorned by the king of Lower Egypt, and, among other divine associations with Khnum and Thoth, is possessed of 'great strength'. However, this text is secreted away on a subterranean temple wall, inaccessible to anyone except priests. Exactly what bearing this had on her public and practical status, as well as exercise of monarchical power, is less clear. Since building work at the temple was suspended from 206 to 186 BC, when a major rebellion in the Thebaid broke out (see below), the text recording Cleopatra I's titles can only have been executed after then.[34] Nonetheless, given her foreign origins, her honours were remarkable and, after her husband's death in 180 BC, she took full advantage of them. Some bronze coins may depict her (or Cleopatra II) as Isis on the obverse but, with no identifying legend, this is not certain and might apply to her regency over her son Ptolemy VI (plate 10.2).[35]

If Antiochus thought he had bought Egypt, he was wrong. By 192 BC he was at war with Rome. Fighting had developed out of attempts by both to exert influence over Greece and the Aegean, with the Romans wanting Antiochus to pull back from Asia Minor and leave it as a buffer zone. Ptolemy V and Philip V were both keen to see Antiochus put into reverse, despite Ptolemy being Antiochus' son-in-law. They sent embassies to Rome offering help, Ptolemy promising money. The Romans politely declined both, so the pair offered to send their armies instead but 'Ptolemy was excused from this'.[36]

ANTIOCHUS III THWARTED

In 192 BC Antiochus invaded Greece, only to be defeated the following year at Thermopylae by another Roman army. When the news of the battle reached Alexandria, Ptolemy and Cleopatra congratulated Rome and offered to send their army into Asia, adding that, with everything being in such a state of confusion, they were at the Romans' disposal. They were brushed off with more thanks and a going-home present for the ambassadors of 1,000 bronze asses each, which was possibly more insulting than if the Romans had ignored them.[37] Once upon a time, and not that long before, Egypt's conniving friends in Rome had pretended to defend Ptolemaic interests to gain a foothold in the politics of the region.[38]

In 190 BC a further Roman victory at Magnesia, led by Scipio Africanus and his brother Lucius, ended Antiochus III's ambitions in Greece. In 189 BC the Aetolian League, which had supported Antiochus, capitulated to Rome. The settlement once more involved tribute and hostages but also required the Aetolians to fight for Rome in any future wars.[39] Antiochus was forced to ask for terms. Under the peace of Apameia he had to pull back beyond the Taurus Mountains, pay reparations and annual tribute for twelve years, hand over prisoners of war, support Rome against its enemies, give up Hannibal who had found sanctuary with Antiochus, and reduce his armed forces. Caria and Lycia were handed over to Rhodes. Autonomous cities that had once paid tribute to Antiochus but been faithful to Rome were exempt from paying any more; those that had not been loyal to Rome now had to pay their tribute to Eumenes II of Pergamum, who also received cities in Lydia, including Ephesus which had once been such a great Ptolemaic stronghold. Chios, Smyrna, and Erythrae were given territories they had claimed.[40] Antiochus III was prohibited from having any elephants and limited to a token navy, among other restrictions. Antiochus agreed to the peace which was settled in 188 BC.[41] The terms were ignored by Antiochus IV in 170 BC (see below) but for the moment Ptolemaic Egypt was a little safer.[42]

THE THEBAN KINGS' REVOLT

In 206 BC, not long before the death of Ptolemy IV, another rebellion had broken out in the Thebaid in Upper Egypt. Although long-standing tensions in Ptolemaic society were undoubtedly part of the problem, it is less clear what provoked a rising at this point. As in 245 BC, economic hardship resulting from failed Nile floods is likely, themselves possibly the result of environmental issues including volcanic eruptions.[43]

A long building inscription dated to 90 BC from the Temple of Horus at Edfu itemizes several key events in the building's history, which began in 237 BC, including the rebellion:

> Its main gates and the double doors of its chambers were completed by year 16 of His Majesty (Ptolemy IV, 206 BC). Then trouble broke out. There was an uprising of rebels in Upper Egypt, and work on the throne seat of the gods [the temple] was suspended.[44]

Next, the text says the rebellion lasted until year 19 (186 BC) of Ptolemy V 'who put an end to the trouble completely'. The revolt had caused the work to be stopped, or the rebel leaders had ordered the labourers to down tools. Several projects also under way at Karnak were suspended.[45]

The rising was led first by a would-be king called Harwennefer, in Greek Haronnophris (reigned approximately 206/205–200 BC), and then by Ankhwennefer, in Greek Chaonnophris (reigned about 200–186 BC). Both names are linked to Osiris (also known as Onnophris), thereby suggesting that the breakaway regime was interested in restoring traditional cults to their former pre-eminence. This makes it likely that both men were priests, who therefore would have had access to temple resources to fund their regimes. Harwennefer may mean 'Horus-Onnophris', while Ankhwennefer can be translated as 'May Onnophris live'. They sound more like names adopted for the cause, choosing Osiris over Ptah whose temple at Memphis was a centrepiece of the Ptolemaic dynasty's religious legitimization. The audacious breakaway regime left lasting effects.[46]

Thebes, with its temple complex of Amun at Karnak, was an obvious focus for the aggrieved. The temple of Osiris at Abydos might even have come under the rebels' control, though that depends on the tenuous evidence of a single handwritten inscription. A graffito from the mortuary temple of Seti I there was composed in Egyptian but using Greek letters, reading 'Year 5 of pharaoh Hyrgonaphor loved by Isis and Osiris, loved by Amon-Re king of the gods, the great god' by which time the revolt had reached further north from Thebes.[47] Evidently, the fan who wrote the text preferred, or was perhaps only able, to use Greek script, though it provides a hint of what the Egyptian name of the rebel king might have sounded like: *Hurgonnafor*. The author was probably bilingual but had never learned to write Egyptian.

Working out exactly when the revolt began and ended and the chronology of possible events, including perhaps even coronation ceremonies, has been the subject of much (and largely futile) scholarly speculation.[48] Far more important is that it happened at all, transcended two reigns, and lasted as long as twenty years before the Ptolemaic regime crushed it. Since we know so little about the rebellion and nothing about who the two consecutive 'kings' were – whether prominent locals, priests adopting avatars, or fictitious figureheads – there is little further to say until the time Ptolemy V made his move. Even if the discovery of Ptolemaic documents in Thebes, dated to 199 BC, really means Ptolemy V's army had recovered control there, is impossible to say. The situation was likely so febrile that few people at the time could have known who controlled where and what, or what was going on.[49]

In 186 BC Ankhwennefer, described as 'the enemy of the gods', was defeated by the Ptolemaic general Comanus in a battle that took place near Thebes. The occasion is recorded in the Second Philae Decree, dated to the 19th regnal year of Ptolemy V (186 BC).[50] Ankhwennefer was captured, but his son, the commander of the rebel army, and the leaders of the Nubians who had joined them were killed. The inscription, allowing for some uncertainties in the reading, explained how:

> The rebel against the gods, he who had made war in Egypt, gathering insolent people from all districts on account of their crimes, they did terrible things to the governors of the nomes, they desecrated (?) the temples, they damaged (?) the divine statues, they molested (?) the priests and suppressed (?) the offerings on the altars and in the shrines. They sacked (?) the towns and their population, women and children included, committing all kinds of crimes in the time of anarchy. They stole the taxes of the nomes, they damaged the irrigation works.

Describing the insurrection this way helped legitimize the treatment of Ankhwennefer, who was executed. It also claimed he had targeted everything the Ptolemaic regime stood for, challenging its ideology and legitimacy. In crushing the rising, Ptolemy is thereby the saviour, and explicitly compared to Horus and his destruction of rebels in myth.[51] The divide in society was laid bare by another passage, which ethnically distinguished the regime and its army from the native population:

The king of Upper and Lower Egypt Ptolemy, loved by Ptah, has given many orders and showed considerable care for protecting the temples. He stationed Greek troops and soldiers of people who had come to Egypt, who obeyed his orders, being joined with him and being like people born with him. They did not allow the rebels, who had instigated war against him and against his father, to approach (?). His Majesty caused that great quantities of silver and gold came to the land to bring troops to Egypt, money from the taxes of the nomes, to protect the temples of Egypt against the impious men who violated them.

Taxation of the nomes was to be used to pay for these soldiers. Whatever grievances the rebels might have had, the crown was determined to come down even more heavily on ordinary Egyptians.

Ptolemy V took the title 'Lord of Victory' but it was an empty honour. The king and his army had had to fight on home territory for the Ptolemaic regime's survival. It was a severe blow to the crown's prestige and marked a permanent shift away from asserting legitimacy through successful foreign military campaigns against rival states.

The following year an amnesty decree was issued which softened the official approach. Only those guilty of murder and theft from temples were denied clemency. The king had no choice. Farmers were fleeing their villages, preferring to live as landless outlaws than put up with further oppression. One of the clauses told officials that no-one 'is to arrest anyone for a private debt or [private] wrongdoing, nor is any of these officials to detain, either in homes or other places, because of a private hatred, free men'.[52] The regime took no chances. Pathyris (Gebelein) and Crocodilopolis (Medinet el-Fayum) were two of the military settlements established in the region after the revolt.[53]

The instability of the reign, especially in Upper Egypt, meant that little temple building took place under Ptolemy V. Consequently, there were very few opportunities to display the king and queen, as his living consort, together on major public reliefs.[54] This denied Ptolemy V the chance to use Cleopatra I as a visible strengthening of the image of joint divine rulers.

DELTA REBELS

Bringing down the rebellion in the Delta proved to be challenging. By 197 BC rebels under 'Egyptian chiefs', who may have been in league with those in control of Thebes, held the city of Lycopolis but were besieged by Ptolemaic forces. The executions, which took place at the time of his coronation, also appear on the Rosetta Stone which says Ptolemy V 'punished them all as they deserved, at the time he came there to perform the proper ceremonies for the assumption of the crown' (Cleopatra I is unmentioned).[55] By 185 BC surviving chiefs, called 'Athinis, Pausiras, Chesufos, and Irobastos, forced by circumstances, came to Saïs to entrust themselves to the king's good faith. But Ptolemy, violating his faith, tied the men naked to carts, and, after dragging them through the streets and torturing them, put them to death.'[56]

Ptolemy used Tanis as the springboard for a campaign into the Delta. Another amnesty followed the final defeat in c. 182 BC of any Delta-based rebels, recorded in a decree at Memphis in which Cleopatra I is this time mentioned as co-ruler and Lady of the Two Lands.[57]

THE DEIFICATION OF PTOLEMY V

Under Ptolemy V the Ptolemaic kings began claiming divinity in their lifetimes on official dedications (as opposed to private, unofficial dedications). At Philae, between 186 and 180 BC, Ptolemy V and Cleopatra I appeared in a brief dedication: 'King Ptolemy and Queen Cleopatra, "the Illustrious Gods" [*Theoi Epiphaneis*], and their son Ptolemy [have dedicated this temple] to Asklepios'. The earlier Ptolemies had avoided this; it sidestepped having to enforce the claim on subject peoples who may have objected. The change in policy was perhaps an attempt to prop up the crown, in a time of lost territory and domestic rebellion, with a compensatory formula that reclaimed royal power and prestige.[58] During this period there was also greater use of honorific titles awarded to officials such as the governors of nomes and dioiketes, a practice that persisted for decades.[59] Such labels, including 'first of friends', a Greek equivalent of Egyptian titles from earlier times, were a means of encouraging loyalty.

THE END OF THE REIGN

There was one piece of good news. Whatever mischief or machinations Antiochus III might have had in mind, his ambitions were terminated while sacking a temple of Bel in Persia in 187 BC when he was abruptly blotted from life's page by an enraged mob. The following year his daughter Cleopatra I secured the Ptolemaic line by producing a son who would succeed as Ptolemy VI Philometor ('Lover of his Mother').

Aristonicus, the court eunuch and childhood friend of Ptolemy V, was packed off to Greece to hire mercenaries whom he handed over to Ptolemy V at Naucratis, who took them to Alexandria. Despite his condition Aristonicus was regarded as unusual for his interest and competence in military affairs, and his easy familiarity with soldiers.[60] In 182 BC he was described in a decree at Memphis as 'His Majesty's Beloved, the King's Confidant' when delivering gold (?) and silver to pay for the troops. In the same text Cleopatra I was labelled pharaoh, just as her husband was.[61]

Ptolemy V and Cleopatra renewed friendships in Greece. An envoy was sent to the Achaean League which dispatched its own embassy to Egypt to exchange oaths. If the sequence of events seems bewildering at this distance in time, it was no better for contemporaries. At the subsequent Achaean Assembly at Megalopolis, the Achaean delegates were confused about which Egyptian alliance they were renewing, since there had been so many.[62] They gave up and adjourned the debate though the alliance must have been ratified, whichever one it was. Egypt soon afterwards offered the Achaeans a 'squadron of quinqueremes which delighted them since they regarded it as a gift worth having'.[63]

The envoy to the Achaeans went out of his way to describe his royal master in the terminology of the great pharaonic past:

> When mention was made of the king at the banquet, the envoy was profuse in his praises of him, cited some instances of his skill and daring in the chase, and afterwards spoke of his expertness and training in horsemanship and the use of arms, the last proof he adduced of this being that he once in hunting hit a bull from horseback with a javelin.[64]

This kind of rhetoric can be found in various inscriptions from, for example, the New Kingdom which record the king's ability to kill animals in hunt and hit targets while moving. However, there is a technical change reflected in the depiction of Ptolemy IV on horseback in the Raphia Decree (see Chapter 8). In any case, the restrictions imposed by Polycrates on Ptolemy V's participation in war made it all a sham anyway.[65]

Despite the envoy's enthusiastic eulogizing of his bull-impaling master, Ptolemy V failed to impress his own followers. This was mainly because he had allegedly been planning to tap them for the funds necessary to reconquer Coele-Syria, referring to them as his 'money bags'. For this he was killed by a conspiracy involving his own generals in 180 BC.[66] Cleopatra I was left with a son too young to rule, as well as two younger children.

The reigns of Ptolemy V and Cleopatra I marked a further downturn in Egypt's fortunes. Ptolemaic power had always resembled an apparition fashioned out of bluster, diaphanous alliances, and febrile loyalties. The emergence of Rome as a world power had been so sudden and unexpected that every other state in the region was caught off guard. Egypt went from being consequential to incidental in a few decades. The eruption of the breakaway Theban state off the back of years of simmering discontent showed how fragile Ptolemaic power was, even at home.

13

HAVOC AND CONFUSION

Ptolemy VI Philometor (180–164, 163–145 BC),
Cleopatra II (175–145 BC), and Ptolemy VIII
Euergetes II (170–163 BC)

The Ptolemaic dynasty now entered a chaotic period. Porphyry described it thus: 'The elder was called Philometor and the younger, Euergetes the second. Their combined reigns totalled 61 years. We present their reigns as one due to the confusion of the period, since they were perpetually at war with each other, and one was always seizing the throne from the other.' He omitted to mention that their sister Cleopatra II reigned alongside them.[1] Although the three maintained Egypt's autonomy the brothers increasingly sought backing from Rome to support their individual causes.

On the face of it, the five- or six-year-old Ptolemy VI's assumption of the crown in 180 BC was seamless. He ruled under the supervision of his Syrian mother Cleopatra I, the first Ptolemaic female regent (not counting the possible brief tenure of Arsinoe III), except that Cleopatra was already ruler in her own right. Cleopatra had successfully overcome the potential handicap of her Syrian origins to ensure her primacy.[2] When Antiochus III died in 187 BC, he was succeeded by Cleopatra's brother Seleucus IV (187–175 BC). Cleopatra cancelled the dead Ptolemy V's plans to fight Seleucus which meant avoiding another exhausting and expensive war. In 176 BC Cleopatra I died too, leaving her ten-year-old Macedonian-Syrian son at the mercy of court factions and opportunists.

EULAEUS AND LENAEUS

The carelessness of losing both his parents was the prelude to more misfortune for Ptolemy VI. Eulaeus the eunuch, a former slave born in Coele-Syria, was already on hand because he had served as a nurse to the boy when he was smaller. Since he must therefore have been chosen by Cleopatra, it is likely he had formed part of her entourage when she married Ptolemy V. With Eulaeus came Lenaeus, a former slave from Syria, but Eulaeus was more important.[3] This double act took control of the child and ruled through him.[4] Eulaeus may have had the presumption to have an abbreviated form of his name struck on some bronze coins (plate 10.3).[5]

The young king and his sister-wife and co-ruler Cleopatra II supposedly appear on a fragmentary and undated lintel inscription in Greek from the temple of a little-known Nubian lion deity called Arensnuphis at Philae, where he was worshipped as Isis' companion. Ptolemy VI is said to be named there as a god (though that section is missing and has been restored, and so too is the name Philometor). There is a reference to the king's sister as queen (βασιλισσ[ης Κλεοπάτρς]), though her name is also lost; restoring Cleopatra II is not unreasonable but hardly conclusive and there are no Egyptian ruler titles either.[6] The text has been claimed to be evidence of Eulaeus and Lenaeus moving quickly to shore up their position, but there is unsurprisingly no reference to either of them on the inscription.[7] The text told a Greek reader nothing about the suite of Egyptian titles these rulers held, of importance when it comes to assessing the Ptolemaic women's honours. A more convincing depiction of Cleopatra II's status in Egyptian terms appears at Kom Ombo where she is clearly labelled *nbt-t3wy*, 'Lady of the Two Lands', matching Ptolemy VI next to her (see plate 11). However, the point about the real-world significance of her mother Cleopatra I's Horus name and titles when they were only displayed in such an inaccessible location applies here too (see Chapter 12).[8]

FOREIGN AFFAIRS

In 179 BC there were developments in Macedon. Philip V, greatly troubled by having had to execute his eldest son Demetrius for treason the previous year, had fallen ill and died. He was succeeded by his younger son Perseus (179–168 BC). Perseus set about assembling a grand Hellenistic alliance that could confront Rome (in the Third Macedonian War, 171–168 BC). His scheming did not start well. In 175 BC the Seleucid throne passed to Cleopatra I's brother Antiochus IV Epiphanes (175–164 BC), after his elder brother Seleucus IV was assassinated by one of his officials. Antiochus had thereby also usurped his nephew Demetrius I Soter (then a hostage in Rome). Antiochus IV, Ptolemy VI, and Eumenes of Pergamum turned Perseus down, preferring to continue supporting Rome, as a Roman deputation sent out to test the water discovered in 172 BC.[9] Only Rhodes joined Perseus, who did not give up.

Meanwhile, Eulaeus and Lenaeus 'attempted to regain Syria, which Antiochus [III] had dishonestly seized'. At least, that was the plan.[10] Next:

> When Apollonius, the son of Menestheus [Seleucus IV's governor of Coele-Syria?], was sent to Egypt for the coronation of [Ptolemy VI] Philometor as king, Antiochus [IV] learned that Philometor had become hostile to his government, and he took measures for his own security. Therefore, upon arriving at Joppa he proceeded to Jerusalem.[11]

Antiochus IV decided to pre-empt any Egyptian decision to go to war against him by doing everything he could to guarantee victory, aware that Egypt was ruled by his nephew, now aged about thirteen, and a couple of self-serving courtiers operating way above their pay grade. He next sent Apollonius in 173 BC on a mission to Rome to curry support. He had been behind with his tribute payments imposed at Apameia in 188 BC. Apollonius arrived armed with some suitable excuses. More to the point, he brought the outstanding amount in full and threw in a consignment of gold vases weighing 500 lbs (225 kg). Next, he asked that the 'friendship and alliance' between Rome and Antiochus' father (Antiochus III) be renewed, promising to offer any service Rome desired. Apollonius received the answer he wanted: the agreements were renewed, and the gifts gratefully received.[12]

Perseus pointed out to Eumenes and Antiochus that if Macedonian independence and its monarchy ended then Rome, which was picking off one place after another, would move next to Asia and then on to Syria. He cited how Rome had already taken control of some Asian cities 'in the pretence of making them free'.[13] An unconvinced Eumenes went to Rome and delivered a speech to the Senate warning of Perseus' determination to make war and the resources he had available.[14] In 171 BC the Third Macedonian War broke out with Rome which provided Antiochus IV with the chance to fight Egypt over Coele-Syria while the Romans were diverted. Eumenes did not want Perseus to win, jealous of the glory Perseus would gain.[15] Ptolemy VI sent a gift of grain to Rome to help.[16]

THE END OF EULAEUS AND LENAEUS

Eulaeus and Lenaeus prepared for a war to retake Coele-Syria. Success would legitimize their power. They also took care to offer help to Rome in the Third Macedonian War.[17] Since a delegation of Roman envoys had toured the various friendly Hellenistic states, the Romans must have known what Eulaeus and Lenaeus were up to in Ptolemy VI's name.[18] Ptolemy VI's name was not enough. To prop up their campaign even further, the self-styled regents declared that Egypt was now ruled by the trio of siblings: Ptolemy VI, Cleopatra II, and Ptolemy VIII. The co-regency was possibly marked by new coins that doubled the eagle on the reverse of the bronze coins but did not pluralize the legend (plate 10; there is some uncertainty about the attribution). If so, Cleopatra's involvement was not mentioned.

The enterprising Eulaeus and Lenaeus made a reckless promise to the Alexandrians: they would bring the war to a speedy end. As Diodorus bluntly observed, they were correct: they brought the war swiftly to a conclusion but also an end to themselves. Inexperienced, and out of their depth, they had contrived the absurd fancy that the war would go so well that they would capture not just Coele-Syria but all of Antiochus' possessions. To that end they hand-picked from the palace in Alexandria all sorts of valuables which included court clothing and jewellery. These were to be used as bribes and gifts for anyone who surrendered cities or fortresses to their triumphant army.[19]

Around this time, the war for Coele-Syria broke out (the sequence is not clear), now known as the Sixth Syrian War (170–c. 168 BC). Both Antiochus IV and Ptolemy VI sent envoys to Rome bleating their causes. Antiochus wailed that Ptolemy was about to wage a war without 'any just cause'. Ptolemy complained that Antiochus had no right to Coele-Syria which had belonged to his predecessors.[20] That they both felt the need to plead their cases in advance showed how after just three decades they believed only Rome had the force to be the supreme arbiter. Since Rome was in the throes of fighting the Third Macedonian War no attempt was made to take sides. The Egyptian envoys planned to persuade Rome to come to terms with Perseus, the purpose obviously being to free Rome up to support Egypt against Antiochus IV. In the end they kept their mouths shut after the *princeps senatus*, Marcus Aemilius Lepidus, told them not to broach the subject. Rome was bent on finishing off the Macedonian threat once and for all. Instead, it was arranged that Ptolemy VI would be written to on Antiochus' behalf and the matter left there for the moment.[21]

The plans went wrong instantly. Antiochus IV set off flagrantly equipped with a navy and elephants, neither of which he was supposed to have after Apameia, and chariots. He defeated the Egyptians at Pelusium and seized the stronghold.[22] The disaster led to the sacking of Eulaeus and Lenaeus who were replaced by Comanus and Cineas as the king's official chief advisers.[23] Antiochus spared Ptolemy VI who was, after all, his nephew and said he was only protecting his interests.[24] His subsequent actions showed that his intentions were anything but honourable and he was remembered only for setting out to exploit Ptolemy.[25]

Determined to blame Eulaeus for the fiasco, Comanus and Cineas organized a diplomatic deputation which included all the Greek missions in Alexandria. They set out to meet Antiochus and sue for peace.[26] Antiochus patiently and courteously itemized all his justifications for acting as he had. He denied there had ever been any promise to hand over Coele-Syria as a dowry for Cleopatra I. Ptolemy V had been stitched up.

According to Polybius, Eulaeus was still on hand and wielding an unhealthy influence over Ptolemy VI. Allegedly, he persuaded the young king to abandon his throne temporarily, take all his money with him, and escape to Samothrace. The real purpose was to save Eulaeus' skin.[27] This 'ignoble flight' was blamed by Diodorus on Eulaeus who had brought Ptolemy up 'amid luxury and womanish pursuits'.[28]

Meanwhile, in 168 BC, Perseus was decisively defeated by the Romans at Pydna and fled. With no friends, he eventually gave up and surrendered. He was taken to Rome and imprisoned nearby for the rest of his life. This was the first major collapse of a Hellenistic state since Alexander's death. Macedon was partitioned and ceased to be of any relevance, permanently altering the balance of power in the region. Macedon could no longer serve as a distraction to Rome which Antiochus IV had exploited to attack Egypt.

COINS OF EULAEUS?

Eulaeus may have been responsible for the abbreviation ΕΥΛ (EUL) which appears on some undated coins attributed to Ptolemy VI. If so, that would represent a radical departure from tradition and suggest that Eulaeus publicized himself as regent. However, these include bronze coins with a Zeus-Ammon obverse and on the reverse the standard legend ΒΑΣΙΛΕΩΣ ΠΤΟΛΕΜΑΙΟΥ, with ΕΥΛ (Eul-) between the legs of the eagle (see plate 10 and Appendix 4). The lotus mintmark is normally associated with Aphrodite in Cyprus. Some therefore now believe the coin was more likely struck at Paphos in Cyprus and the abbreviation probably refers to an unknown local magistrate.[29] ΕΥΛ is not found on other Ptolemaic-era coins.

TACKLING ANTIOCHUS IV

It may have been this moment of confusion that led 'the people' to declare Ptolemy VI's younger brother king as Ptolemy VIII in Alexandria (his first rule, 170–164 BC).[30] It was an easy decision to make. Ptolemy VI was allegedly 'so weakened by daily luxurious indulgence, that he not only neglected the duties of his royal station, but even, through excessive gluttony, had lost all human feeling'. He joined his brother in Alexandria from where they begged the Achaeans (unsuccessfully) for armed help.[31] They had more success with Rome (see below).

Cleopatra II continued as pharaoh of Egypt. Livy refers to her and Ptolemy VI as *regibus* ('from the rulers', using the ablative plural form of *rex*).[32] Meanwhile, Antiochus IV set out to besiege Alexandria, supposedly defending Ptolemy VI's interests against Ptolemy VIII.[33] It was obviously a pretext for pursuing his own ambitions. Ptolemy VIII and Cleopatra II's new court sent an embassy to Rome, still embroiled in the final stages of the Third Macedonian War, and tried moral blackmail: if Rome would not help then Cleopatra II and Ptolemy VIII would turn up in Rome as hostages, and then wouldn't the Romans be sorry they hadn't helped? The Romans planned to send their own deputation to Antiochus and then Ptolemy VI (?) telling them both to abstain from war and that whoever was responsible for the war continuing would be treated as neither a friend nor an ally.[34]

Antiochus failed to break into Alexandria but, without any direct intervention from Rome, was able to take control of the rest of the country. He installed Ptolemy VI in Memphis so that he could continue to pretend to support him. Antiochus withdrew to Syria, probably to build up his forces, but left a garrison at Pelusium so he could reinvade Egypt when he wanted.[35] With Antiochus IV gone by 169 BC, at least for the moment, the brothers and their sister patched up their differences and resumed joint rule, seeking help from Rome. They were, for the moment, all awarded the title Philometor ('mother-loving') and were known as the Philometores.

Antiochus IV had no intention of giving up on Egypt.[36] He had prepared for the renewed war carefully and was determined to defeat both Ptolemies, even sending a fleet to Cyprus while he marched on Egypt through Coele-Syria in early 168 BC. Ptolemy VI's envoys tried to head him off by asking him to name his terms rather than go to war. Antiochus wanted Cyprus, Pelusium, and Pelusium's hinterland.[37] But Antiochus had not anticipated the end of the Third Macedonian War coming as soon as it did, thereby freeing up the Romans. Not long after Perseus' ambitions were ended for good that summer at Pydna, the Roman commander in Delos, Popilius Laenas (and one of the proposed ambassadors to be sent to Antiochus, above), learned of the Roman victory. A delegation was immediately sent to Egypt to try and settle the war with Antiochus. The Roman delegation met Antiochus at Eleusis, about 4 miles (6.5 km) from Alexandria.[38] A famous incident followed. Popilius peremptorily:

> acted in a manner which was thought to be offensive and exceedingly arrogant. Popilius was carrying a stick cut from a vine, and with this he drew a circle round Antiochus and told him he must remain inside this circle until he gave his decision about the contents of the letter. The king was astonished at this authoritative proceeding, but, after a few moments' hesitation, said he would do all that the Romans demanded. Upon this Popilius and his suite all grasped him by the hand and greeted him warmly. The letter ordered him to put an end at once to the war with Ptolemy.[39]

A stunned Antiochus complied and pulled out of Egypt, a turn of events prophesied by a native priest of first Isis and then Thoth called 'Hor of Sebennytus', who participated in the Thoth ibis cult at Memphis. In his dream, Hor had foreseen how Alexandria would be restored to safety and that Antiochus would leave by sea in the second year of the reign (168 BC). The dream was written down in demotic on an ostracon.[40]

Popilius first had to invade Cyprus and force Antiochus' troops out. This saved Ptolemaic Egypt for the moment, achieved without hurling a single sling bolt, let alone mounting a campaign. Had Perseus not been defeated, Antiochus might not have been so amenable. The Hellenistic monarchies were gradually fading in the face of Rome. Macedon had been neutralized. Egypt remained independent but its rulers were becoming habituated to run to Rome for help. The Seleucids were reduced to realizing that they were also subject to Rome's pleasure.[41]

'PTOLEMY VII' (145 BC)

The sharp-eyed reader will notice that Ptolemy VII is unaccounted for. His identity remains a matter of dispute and it may be that he should be eliminated altogether.[42] He may have been 'Ptolemy Neos Philopator', supposedly son of Cleopatra II by her brother Ptolemy VI (see Chapter 14). His theoretical existence is partly a product of the enumeration of the Ptolemaic kings being only a modern convention. Alternatively, he may have been really Ptolemy Memphites, son of Cleopatra II and Ptolemy VIII, who was murdered by his father c. 130 BC. Arguing over the inconclusive evidence is a long-running pastime for some scholars of the period.

MORE DISTURBANCES

The contempt Ptolemy VI and his younger brother Ptolemy VIII felt for each other created an opportunity for court malcontents. Dionysius

Petoserapis ('Sky of Serapis') was supposedly one of Ptolemy VI's 'Friends' and had an unmatched military reputation. For a man of his skills, propping up a monarchy led by such inexperienced young men was frustrating. He decided to start a rumour that Ptolemy VI was hatching a plot against Ptolemy VIII.

The Alexandrians were furious when they learned the 'news' and headed for the stadium in a frenzy. They were about to set off to kill Ptolemy VI and hand sole rule to Ptolemy VIII, who was still popular. Dionysius' scheme collapsed. The 'pious and magnanimous' Ptolemy VI heard what was going on and was appalled. He called his brother to court, insisted the story was a monstrous fabrication, condemned Dionysius for putting it about, and insisted that if Ptolemy VIII still had any suspicions, then he would hand over power on the spot. Ptolemy VIII realized his elder brother was sincere so the two appeared in public at the palace, assuaging the crowd's concerns and posing as being 'in harmony'.[43]

Wisely disappearing temporarily into hiding, Dionysius sent a message to the soldiers inviting them to join him. Next, he went to Eleusis in the Fayum which was used as an assembly point for a force that ended up being 4,000-strong. There he was attacked by Ptolemy VI who killed some of the rebels while others fled. Dionysius was among them. He had to leap into the river and escape inland. Far from giving up, though, Dionysius clung on to his dream and managed to encourage a significant number of Egyptians to join him. The second part of his name suggests that he may have been an indigenous Egyptian, which would explain his popularity. His moment of fame was a worrying sign that discontent was still widespread among the ordinary Egyptians.[44]

GANGS IN THE FAYUM

Around the same time, marauding gangs of rebels roamed the Fayum. With self-serving aplomb, the Ptolemies had embraced established Egyptian religion, drawing the priesthood into the clutches of the state with gifts and endowments. Priests therefore symbolized the regime in the eyes of the aggrieved.

A temple of Ammon by the Fayum's Lake Moeris, close to Crocodilopolis, was destroyed during Antiochus IV's invasion of Egypt and later rebuilt. A papyrus of *c.* 164 BC mentions that earlier damage and restoration, but goes on: 'Afterwards when the Egyptian rebels had attacked it and not only thrown down parts of the temple but split the stonework of the shrine and carried off the door-fixtures and other doors to the number of more than 110 and also torn down some of the boarding.' The writer, whose name is lost but was one of the priests, recorded that he had started patching the building up.[45] Between 169 and 164 BC a priest's property deeds were burned by 'Egyptian rebels' (Αἰγυπτίων ἀποστατῶν, *Aigyptiōn apostatōn*) who were engaged in a 'war'. The papyrus is from Soknopaiou Nesos, another settlement near Lake Moeris in the Fayum.[46] The rebels evidently knew that legal documents proved the rights and prerogatives when it came to property. By destroying the deeds, they were attempting, symbolically at least, to deny the priest his entitlements.

These incidents are isolated, but they are recorded on a pair of fragmentary papyri whose survival is a mere matter of chance. The most likely scenario is that at the time there were frequent sporadic bouts of assaults committed by resentful Egyptians on anything or anyone associated with the state. The damage meted out to this temple of Ammon, although there may have been some exaggeration for effect, was inflicted by a motivated and well-equipped mob. These were dangerous times in the Fayum and other areas where for several decades resistance to Ptolemaic rule had become endemic.

RENEWED REBELLION

The city of Panopolis (Akhmim) lay about 82 miles (132 km) northwest of Thebes though the distance is considerably greater along the Nile Valley. Since it lay on higher ground and was more easily defended, it was a suitable stronghold for any of the disaffected Egyptians in the region. Around the same time as the itinerant rebels were roaming in the Fayum, another group gathered in the Thebaid and set themselves up in

Panopolis. They probably used this as a base from which to launch roving guerrilla-style attacks on anything associated with the hated state.

Ptolemy VI led a force down to the area and succeeded in swiftly regaining control except for Panopolis which held out. He besieged the city, 'undergoing every kind of hardship', until he recaptured it. Diodorus calls it 'yet another' rebellion. A pair of ostraca in Greek found at Saqqara belong to a class of dream-oracle texts and to this period. The various fragments of these surviving texts, which are filled with errors in grammar and syntax, include one addressed to 'King Ptolemy, King Ptolemy the Brother, and Queen Cleopatra the Sister' by a priest called Horus. There is no doubt then that it belongs to the period 170–164 BC and probably after Antiochus IV had left. The text refers to a group of Egyptians that needed to be turned back and that the king must go to the Thebaid. It is surely referring to the same rebellion as Diodorus.[47] Resistance was becoming liable to pop up without warning almost anywhere in the country.[48]

The risings had only made matters worse. Land had been abandoned and there were water shortages because irrigation had been neglected. It was typical of the Ptolemaic state that it instinctively piled on the pressure, exacerbating the problems that had led to the tension in the first place. Inflation was triggered when the government reduced the size and weight of copper coins but maintained their face value. This undermined the relationship between silver and copper coins, worsened by a shortage of silver and declining agricultural production in the face of disorder and corruption.[49] By 160 BC as many as 275 copper drachmas were needed for a single silver drachma, when less than sixty years earlier only two would have been required (see Appendix 4).[50] The effect would have been to devastate the value of savings, though an unintended consequence was that the date of papyri based on the amount paid in taxes on commodities, for example beer, can be estimated.[51]

A royal ordinance (prostagma) was issued in the names of the three monarchs in the late summer or early autumn of 165 BC to try and force farmers to return to the land.[52] Irrigation was traditionally managed on a local basis with systems dating back to much earlier times. Efficient irrigation was probably the single most important factor in successful agriculture in Egypt where rainfall can be disregarded as a source of water. The Ptolemies, like their pharaonic predecessors, had not introduced centralized management or supervision of irrigation (leading to salinization problems, see Chapter 8).[53] The new ordinance was conceived as an indirect solution. By compelling people to farm the land that had been abandoned, they believed the system of water distribution would be restored to full capacity.[54]

The new rules were enforced with characteristic attention to detail, filtering down through the hierarchy of officials until they came up against the Egyptian farming underclass. These included low-grade soldiers who metaphorically stood their ground until it was agreed that the measures would only be applied on an individual basis, rather than demand an individual take on and farm a plot of land that he was incapable of coping with.[55]

PTOLEMAEUS THE KATOCHOS

One way of escaping the obligations of the time was to seek sanctuary at a shrine as a katochos (κάτοχος) which means 'held down' or 'overpowered'. In this context it meant being subject to the control of a god, and thereby exempt from any further obligations to the state. Katochoi served the cult as workers.[56]

Ptolemaeus was a katochos whose Macedonian father Glaukias had been killed in one of the Egyptian rebellions in 164 BC.[57] From the age of about thirty he lived in the Temple of Astarte (a Near Eastern goddess), part of the Serapeum complex in Saqqara, during the febrile 160s and on into the 150s BC. He performed various duties, including recording and interpreting dreams and writing petitions for others. He also sold porridge and traded clothing and textiles to earn money.

The dislike felt by ordinary Egyptians for those of Greek origin was an ongoing problem for Ptolemaeus. He had written his own petition in 161 BC, his twelfth year at the Serapeum, recording a serious incident. A mob of armed cleaners at the shrine and other local tradesmen had turned up, bent on vandalizing the temple. It was the second time in two years they had come for Ptolemaeus.

Ptolemaeus slammed the temple door in their faces. The crowd refused to disperse and instead beat up and robbed Diphilos, another katochos with a Greek name. Ptolemaeus explained that there had been no-one available to follow up a similar episode two years earlier. The cleaners on this repeat assault had been accompanied by some of those involved in the earlier attack. They were a doctor called Harchebis, a baker named Imouthes, Mys who sold winding sheets, Psosnaus the yoke carrier, a grain merchant called Harembasnis, and a water carrier named Stotoetis, among others Ptolemaeus could not remember. Their names give them away as Egyptians. Ptolemaeus was convinced, or at least claimed, his Greek ethnicity was the reason for this motley band of assailants coming for him. But their various business interests suggest that part of the reason they targeted Ptolemacus is that his commercial activities impinged on theirs.[58]

The violence inflicted on Ptolemaeus and the effrontery of trying to break into the temple twice show how explosive the mood was. Ethnic tension between the indigenous population and the Greek ruling class was unlikely to have been isolated (see also Chapter 8 for documents from the archive of the strategos Diophanes a few decades earlier). It was becoming increasingly difficult for the Ptolemaic state to provide protection. Instead, the ruling trio of siblings were becoming embroiled in their own strife. The brotherly love, flaunted to wrongfoot Dionysius Petoserapis a few years before, gave way to dynastic breakdown during late 164 BC.

THE SERAPEUM TWINS

Ptolemaic Egypt's unique papyrus record includes documents concerned with the case of twin Egyptian girls called Thaues and Thaus (or Tages and Taous), and their probable sister Tathemis.

The documents were written by the katochos Ptolemaeus (see above). The girls' mother Nephoris had taken up with a Greek soldier called Philippos, believing she would become better off. Nephoris and her lover plotted to kill her husband Argunoutis. Philippos attacked Argunoutis who was wounded and escaped but ended up in the Nile from which he was rescued. From there he fled to his brother's house in Hieraconopolis where he died.[59] Nephoris threw her daughters out of the family home to save the cost of their marriage dowries.

The girls dashed to the Serapeum for sanctuary and asked their father's friend Ptolemaeus for help. They were given jobs acting out the roles of Isis and Nephthys in the Apis bull mourning rituals for which twins, a rare phenomenon in ancient Egypt, were essential. They fulfilled this task when the bull died in 164 BC.[60] Ptolemaeus recorded their dreams. Their new jobs entitled the girls to a grant of 'necessaries' provided by the Serapeum and the Asklepion (Temple of Asklepios).

The subsidies stopped shortly after the girls started in post. Starving, they complained to temple officials to no avail. The children wrote to Ptolemy VI and Cleopatra II three times to protest, the third occasion being when the royal couple visited the temple. The absence of Ptolemy VIII's name places their letter of complaint to around 164/163 BC when the brother-kings fell out (see below, this chapter). The twins asked Dionysus, a strategos and friend of the king, to lean on the temple supervisor Apollonius and compel him to resume the supplies, make good the past shortfall, and therefore ensure that they could fulfil their duties properly. They added that their predecessors had not been treated so badly.[61] Some of what was owing to them was made good on this occasion. Unfortunately, the record runs out. The fate of the girls is unknown.[62]

BROTHERS DIVIDED 164–163 BC

Ptolemy VIII did not kill his elder brother. Instead, he forced him out some time between early October and early December 164 BC, 'probably' at this time replacing the title Philometor with Euergetes. The first text recording his sole reign is in demotic and belongs to 7 December 164 BC.[63] From hereon he is known to history as Ptolemy VIII Euergetes II.

Ptolemy VI followed up his precipitous fall by fleeing to Rome with a eunuch and three slaves in tow.[64] When he was about 200 stades (22 miles or 35 km) from Rome he encountered the shocked future Demetrius I Soter (later to rule the Seleucid kingdom from 162 to 150 BC), his first cousin, who had been sent to Rome as a hostage by his father Seleucus IV. Demetrius, who had learned of Ptolemy's coming, greeted him with a royal costume, diadem, and a suitably gold-bedecked horse so that he could enter Rome in proper style.

The crucial point was that Ptolemy VI had reacted to his expulsion by immediately heading off to Rome. He was grateful to Demetrius but declined the offer and even asked Demetrius to remain behind. Ptolemy was downhearted but determined that the Senate see his reduced state. When the toppled king reached the city, he moved in with an Alexandrian painter. After news of his arrival reached an embarrassed Senate, the senators apologized for not sending out a quaestor (magistrate in charge of financial matters) to greet him and immediately rehoused Ptolemy in state quarters where he could receive daily gifts to restore his standard of living. They invited him to address the Senate.[65] He must have been boosted by the gestures. He later moved on to Cyprus where he was when the brothers were reconciled at the behest of the people of Alexandria who were disgusted by how Ptolemy VI had been treated.[66]

RECONCILIATION – OF SORTS

The reconciliation in the summer of 163 BC was really a division of the spoils. Ptolemy VIII was given rule of Cyrene. His twenty-three-year-old elder brother was handed what was left of the Ptolemaic kingdom which he ruled with his sister Cleopatra II who since *c.* 175 BC had been his wife. She was prominently depicted alongside him at, for example, the Temple of Horus at Edfu in cooperation with him making offerings, but not independently.[67] Ptolemy VI instructed the strategoi of the nomes to enforce an amnesty on crimes committed prior to his restoration on 17 August 163 BC.[68]

The palace staff were twitchy. By October 163 BC Ptolemy VI and Cleopatra II had moved into a palace in the Serapeum complex in Saqqara to celebrate the new year. A fortnight later, a tip-off to the chief of police stationed in the Anubeum precinct in the complex led to him taking guards round to the Temple of Astarte at the Serapeum in search of weapons. They found nothing but were obviously impressed with the valuables there. The next day a gang returned. They roughed up the katochos Ptolemaeus (see above), carried off everything that they could, leaving a seal on anything else (presumably to claim ownership), and desecrated the inner sanctum of the goddess by bursting in and wrecking it. At least two more robberies followed. An aggrieved Ptolemaeus addressed a petition directly to Ptolemy and Cleopatra but requested that, as he could not leave the temple, an intermediary be sent before them to ask for redress on his behalf. Other victims also wrote in with petitions.[69]

The Younger Ptolemy, as Ptolemy VIII styled himself, was aggrieved at only having Cyrene in the deal he had cut with his brother. Determined to have Cyprus as well, he found his brother's lack of faith in him disturbing. Granting Cyrene to Ptolemy VIII was more significant than it might at first appear; it amounted to the Ptolemaic kingdom being divided, diluting its ailing power further.[70]

RUNNING TO ROME

Ptolemy VIII headed off to Rome to bleat his cause, blaming the 'pressure of circumstances' for forcing him previously to agree to something so unfair. His ignominious adolescent wailing must have astonished the senators. Naturally they made the most of it. He implored the Senate to coerce Ptolemy VI to give Cyprus to him, insisting that even with this bonus he would still be far worse off than his older brother. Although it was pointed out in the Senate how Ptolemy VIII had become so unpopular that he was lucky to have escaped with his life and with the gift of Cyrene, Rome was no longer satisfied with simply ratifying such a deal. The Romans wanted the outcome to be their decision and in their interests. Since Egypt had the potential to be troublesome if it was ruled by an effective and determined king, the feuding brother-pharaohs had handed Rome a gift on a plate. Two Roman envoys were sent to support Ptolemy VIII and help him negotiate a handover of Cyprus, but strictly on condition that there be no war. That way, the Ptolemaic kingdom would be split and weakened, with Ptolemy VIII the Roman stooge.[71]

Roman backing did not include military support. Ptolemy VIII headed to Greece to buy up mercenaries and then moved on the southwest coast of Asia Minor. From there he intended to jump off to Cyprus. Before he left, Roman envoys caught him up with a reminder that there must be no fighting. They instructed Ptolemy VIII to abandon his plans to go to Cyprus and instead to sail to Cyrene and await further instructions. They would travel to Alexandria and tell the elder Ptolemy to comply with Rome's wishes and hand over Cyprus. Ptolemy VIII agreed and disbanded the mercenaries but went to Crete and collected another 1,000 soldiers before heading on to Cyrene.

The Roman envoys initially found Ptolemy VI a frustrating host. He refused to commit, clearly buying time. Ptolemy VIII was driven half-mad while he kicked his heels in Apis waiting for an update. Apis was a port town on the Egyptian border with Libya about 12 miles (18 km) west of Mersa Matruh. Forty days passed with no news. The Roman envoys were gradually taken with the charming Ptolemy VI and lost any sense of urgency to push him to a decision. To his fury, Ptolemy VIII then learned that Cyrene and other cities in the region had rebelled against his rule. Even worse, they were being led by his own turncoat commander Sympetesis. Sympetesis was an Egyptian, an uncomfortable reminder of how unreliable the indigenous population could be when the possibility of challenging Ptolemaic rule came along.[72]

The Cyrenaean rebels were stirred up by what they knew of Ptolemy VIII's tyrannical and arbitrary rule in Alexandria. He headed west in force to tackle the rising. After an initial success the Ptolemaic army marched on, backed up by a naval flotilla that paralleled the advance just off the coast. In the battle that followed, Ptolemy VIII was beaten though the insurrection quietened down soon afterwards. More bad news followed. One of the Roman envoys, Gnaeus Merula, reached him and told him that Ptolemy VI had refused to hand over Cyprus. Clearly, the young Ptolemaic king was not the pushover the Senate had hoped for. Ptolemy VIII, no longer distracted by fighting off Cyrenaean rebels, sent his own mission to Rome along with Merula, to turn up the heat. They were instructed to shop his brother to the Senate due to his 'greed and contempt' for Roman orders.[73]

The Senate was faced with Ptolemy VIII's mission from Cyrene and one from Alexandria. The two deputations had a fractious row in the senate house. The senators sided with Ptolemy VIII, their intention all along. The Alexandrian envoy was told to go home and inform Ptolemy VI that Rome was cutting him adrift. Legates were sent to Ptolemy VIII, then in Cyrene, to pass on the good news. Delighted, he immediately prepared another army so that he could take Cyprus.[74]

WHEN IN ROME

By *c.* 155 BC Ptolemy VI had had enough of his younger brother, or so the latter claimed. Ptolemy VIII, now a regular commuter, materialized once more in Rome to claim (and prove) that he had been the victim of an assassination attempt. He gave the Senate a colourful account of the atrocity, showed off his scars, and 'pleaded for pity'. It is impossible to know whether Ptolemy VIII was telling the truth or had had himself suitably battered by an obliging associate or slave for the purpose. He also brought a copy of his will in which he promised to leave his share of the kingdom to Rome, should he die with no suitable heir, and entrust all his affairs to the Romans.[75] He cannot really have been serious. It was a grandiose statement of his own significance, an advertisement to anyone at home who doubted what important friends he had and to warn off anyone else who fancied taking a pot shot at him.

Ptolemy VI, guilty or not, knew what his double-crossing brother was up to. He sent yet another deputation to Rome to insist on his innocence. The stream of envoys shooting back and forth was becoming farcical, the warring brothers increasingly like small children constantly running to a parent, each insisting on the other's guilt and seeking satisfaction at the other's expense.

Since the Romans had already decided they would back Ptolemy VIII, they dismissed the elder Ptolemy's ambassadors without a hearing. This time they were prepared to step in with a show of force but without any serious intention of fighting a war on behalf of the Cyrene malcontent. Five legates were appointed, each given a quinquereme warship and told to install Ptolemy VIII on Cyprus. It was as if five Iowa-class battleships had been sent to a banana republic with the US stooge on board one of them. Roman allies in Greece and Asia were invited to step in to help.[76]

In the event, Ptolemy VIII based himself at Lapethos (Lapta) on the north coast of Cyprus. From here he plotted against his brother, but Ptolemy VI defeated him. Ptolemy VI's personality, and perhaps a wariness of what might happen should Rome become more involved, prevented him from any attempt to hurt his younger sibling. Instead, he made additional grants of territory over and above the original agreement, and of grain. If this was true, it may undermine Ptolemy VIII's allegations about the assassination attempt. Ptolemy VIII seems to have been obliged, at least for the time being, to be content with holding Cyrene until his brother's death in 145 BC.[77]

THE LATTER DAYS OF PTOLEMY VI

With his brother effectively confined to Cyrene, Ptolemy VI could rule unchallenged, at least by members of his family, until 145 BC. He even offered his brother his own daughter, Cleopatra Thea, in marriage. Although she was still a child, the probable intention was to try and make sure that Ptolemy VIII would have an heir in due course. The marriage never happened. Cleopatra Thea, who became a powerful and significant figure, subsequently married the Seleucid kings Alexander Balas (150–145 BC), Demetrius II (145–138 BC, 129–126 BC), and lastly Antiochus VII (138–129 BC). Antiochus VII was killed in Parthia in 129 BC (see Chapter 14).

Ptolemy VI turned his attention to other foreign and domestic matters. Laying claim to Nubia as a territorial buffer zone and source of tribute, labour, and gold was an age-old pharaonic tradition. The Triakontaschoinos zone lay between the First and Second Cataracts of the Nile, and meant 'Land of the Thirty Schoinoi', a *schoinos* being a nominal unit of measurement along the river of about 6.5 miles (10.5 km). The northern sector was known as the Dodekaschoinos, 'Land of the Twelve Schoinoi'. By Ptolemy II's reign the tax revenue from that region was allocated to the Temple of Isis at Philae. In 157 BC Ptolemy VI renewed that privilege.[78] The renewal was a reaffirmation of Ptolemaic interests, even though the region functioned as a form of free trade zone. Ptolemy VI actively encouraged the immigration of Jews, who left Coele-Syria once it was no longer under Ptolemaic control and because of Antiochus IV's persecution. They became an increasingly important part of Ptolemaic society in Alexandria, the Delta, the Fayum, and as far south as the Thebaid, as well as serving in the army.

THE ROAD TO 145 BC

In 175 BC Antiochus IV had usurped the throne from his nephew Demetrius, then a child hostage in Rome (see above), following the death of his brother Seleucus IV. On his death in 164 BC, he was succeeded by his son Antiochus V (164–162/161 BC), still only a boy. Demetrius escaped from Italy. In 162 BC he returned to Syria where he was accepted as king and ruled as Demetrius I until 150 BC. Antiochus V was killed. In 150 BC Demetrius was ousted and killed by Alexander Balas (also known as Alexander Epiphanes), a man of questionable origin who claimed to be the son of Antiochus IV.[79] He reigned from 150 to 145 BC.

Ptolemy VI did not dispute Alexander Balas' succession. Perhaps he accepted the new king's claim, which would mean Balas was Ptolemy's cousin. Balas wrote triumphantly to Ptolemy, offering friendship and asking for Ptolemy's daughter in marriage. Appropriately enough for a family in which marriage by blood was becoming routine, Ptolemy now offered his daughter Cleopatra Thea to Balas. The two kings met at Ptolemais in Phoenicia.[80]

Given how he had seized the throne, it was inevitable that Balas' claim would be contested. Demetrius I's son, Demetrius II, was the challenger in 147 BC. This provided Ptolemy VI with an opportunity to try and recover Coele-Syria while pretending to support Balas. Once installed with his forces, though, the two fell out when one of Balas' associates tried to assassinate Ptolemy. Ptolemy transferred his support to Demetrius II, recalled his daughter Thea, and gave her to Demetrius instead.[81] For the moment there were two Seleucid kings. By 146 BC there were three. Two of Balas' ministers had given up on him but were not interested in the fifteen-year-old Demetrius II. They invited Ptolemy VI to Antioch where they handed over the Seleucid kingdom to him.

THE YEAR 146 BC AND ROME

The year 146 BC was when Rome finally destroyed Carthage in the Third Punic War, permanently ending its independent status. By 151 BC the Carthaginian liability to pay war indemnities had finished under the terms of the 201 BC peace treaty. This ended a source of income that Rome had come to depend on, and which had helped finance the Macedonian and other wars of the period. It was no surprise that the hawks in Rome wanted a new Punic war.

The Third Punic War was won by Scipio Aemilianus, a collateral descendant by adoption of Scipio Africanus. The Senate had instructed him to raze Carthage. The relative magnanimity of the peace that ended that Second Punic War was replaced with vindictiveness, the senators convincing themselves that Carthage would never be peaceful. The male population was mainly imprisoned, and its leaders held under what amounted to house arrest in Italy.[82] The region was converted into the new Roman province of Africa.

146 BC was also when Lucius Mummius, the Roman general, sacked Corinth and brought Greece into the Roman Empire. The Greek city democracies were abolished. In their place Mummius imposed government modelled on the property qualification principle used by the Romans. He banned confederations of cities such as the Achaean League. Some of these provisions were later reversed but Greece had been reduced permanently to the status of a province overseen by a Roman governor.[83]

The wars against Carthage and Greece showed now what Rome was capable of. Tinkering and interference in the affairs of other nations had been overtaken by organized, ruthless, and destructive violence that crushed opposition and resistance, followed by rapacious exploitation. The point was not lost on Ptolemaic Egypt and helps explain the obsequious but misguided greeting Ptolemy VIII gave Scipio Aemilianus and a Roman diplomatic mission just a few years later (see next chapter).

146 BC was the time identified by later Roman historians when the Roman people descended into the love of luxury for its own sake. Velleius Paterculus, writing under Tiberius (AD 14–37), was interested in how the two great Scipios had been symbolically responsible. Scipio Africanus had opened the way to Rome's world domination. Scipio Aemilianus opened the door to Rome's love of luxury and excess. Virtue had given way to corruption, or so Velleius said. He judged that the Roman state became negligent by allowing the Romans to give up on bothering with military training and readiness in favour of indolence. The money that

poured in was used to fund public monuments and luxurious private houses.[84]

The writing had been on the wall for decades. After his victory over Philip V of Macedon at Thermopylae in 191 BC, the plebeian and former tribune Manius Acilius Glabrio collected a vast quantity of booty which included 3,000 lbs (1,361 kg) of silver bullion which was shown off at his triumph in Rome.[85] Two years later he used some of his loot to buy votes when he was seeking election as censor. This disgusted the old-guard patricians of Rome who thought Glabrio was far too low-born to hold such a position. He was accused of corruption and was prosecuted. He stood down, but the case demonstrated the attractions of war and conquest to ambitious Romans. Glabrio's plans were thwarted but his case revealed how booty was the perfect way to pay for a political career and enduring prestige. Glabrio's son was allowed to build a temple of Pietas in Rome by arrangement with the Senate.[86] Posterity could see the monuments such men endowed Rome with, and their descendants could bask in inherited status.

Meanwhile, in 146 BC, 'Ptolemy entered Antioch and put on the crown of Asia. Thus, he temporarily put two crowns on his head, the crown of Egypt and that of Asia', said the Old Testament.[87] However, Ptolemy 'determined to avoid the envy of the Romans'; it was obvious to him that a king of both Egypt and Syria would be an intolerable prospect, so he urged the people of Antioch to accept Demetrius II.[88] Under the arrangement, Ptolemy held on to Coele-Syria but handed back the rest of Syria to Demetrius.

Balas, unfortunately for Ptolemy VI and Demetrius, returned in 145 BC with a new army from Cilicia and sacked Antioch. Ptolemy and Demetrius defeated him. Balas fled to Arabia, but during the fighting Ptolemy's horse was frightened by an elephant and threw the king. Left floundering on the ground with a serious head injury, he was attacked and badly wounded by Balas' men before he could be rescued. Traumatized and in a semi-coma, Ptolemy hung on for five days. On the fifth he was finally able to enjoy the sight of Balas' head, who had been caught in flight, before expiring after what Livy described as a failed attempt at trepanning.[89]

Ptolemy VI's death instantly reversed the gains of recent years. Coele-Syria remained in Seleucid control, ruled by Demetrius II who had also just been conveniently rid of Balas. Polybius, an exact contemporary, said of Ptolemy VI, 'in the opinion of some he deserved high praise and a place in history, but others think otherwise. It was true that he was gentle and good, more so than any previous king. The strongest proof of this is, that in the first place he did not put to death any of his own friends on any of the charges brought against them; and I do not believe that any other Alexandrian suffered death owing to him.'[90] Egypt now fell into the hands of Ptolemy VIII to whom fate had unexpectedly delivered his most earnest desire. He had not even needed to sail to Rome again.

14

MÉNAGE À TROIS

Cleopatra II (joint 175–131, sole 131–127, joint
124–116 BC), Ptolemy VIII Euergetes II (145–116 BC),
and Cleopatra III (joint 142–131, 127–116 BC)

Things were not yet so bad for the Ptolemies that they could not be made worse. Even by the standards of the Ptolemaic dynasty, Ptolemy VIII, Cleopatra II, and Cleopatra III's reigns stand out for the complexity of their marital arrangements and pursuit of personal ambitions. Ptolemy VIII began by marrying Cleopatra II and killing possibly his nephew before spurning her in favour of his niece, Cleopatra III. So unpopular that he was temporarily forced off his throne in favour of Cleopatra II, he fled to Cyprus with Cleopatra III and their children. A civil war ensued between the siblings which included Ptolemy VIII murdering his own son by Cleopatra II. Ptolemy VIII lasted until 116 BC, leaving only Cleopatra III and her sons, a remarkable feat of endurance.

PTOLEMY VIII'S FAMILY MATTERS

Ptolemy VI's death in 145 BC left the way open to Ptolemy VIII (plate 12), but with complications. There was the question of 'Ptolemy Neos Philopator', sometimes referred to in histories of the period as Ptolemy VII and supposedly the son of Ptolemy VI and Cleopatra II.[1] Nonetheless, the crown, and the widowed Cleopatra II, were offered to Ptolemy VIII, then in Cyrene. Why this happened is not clear, since the intention of his mother and some of the nobility was that Neos Philopator should become king.[2] The deputation sent to Cyrene must have been organized by another faction, made up of some of his previous supporters.

Ptolemy VIII counted his new reign as his 26th regnal year in a continuation of his earlier rule. In Justin's second- or even third-hand version of events, Ptolemy VI's ephemeral son Neos Philopator was in the process of being married to his mother Cleopatra II as part of consolidating his claim on the throne as 'Ptolemy VII' when his uncle had him murdered during the ceremonies. Ptolemy VIII then married his sister Cleopatra II and 'went to the couch of his sister stained with the blood of her child' before ordering his foreign troops to kill even those who had offered him the crown. This is supported by Orosius who explicitly refers to Ptolemy VIII killing his brother's son, as well as one of his own.[3] However, some now believe these sources were confusing Neos Philopator with Ptolemy VIII's own son Memphites by Cleopatra III and his grisly fate (see below). As usual, these counterarguments are a complex web of obscure evidence and inferences involving dynastic cult records and Neos Philopator's true status, bypassing the principle that the simplest explanation is more likely to be right.[4] It is obviously now impossible to be sure.

Ptolemy VIII allegedly used false accusations as a pretext to execute the wealthy and thereby help himself to their estates.[5] If he was not already, he became known as Physcon (the source word φύσκη means 'sausage') due to his corpulence.[6]

The generals Onias and Donistheus of the Jewish contingent in the army rebelled, bitterly resentful of the humiliation of Cleopatra II after the favour she and Ptolemy VI had shown them. Ptolemy VIII sent other soldiers to attack the Jews of Alexandria with elephants that were supposed to trample them. The animals had been given alcohol to steel their nerves, but they refused to crush the Jews, giving the Jews the chance to fight back and kill some of Ptolemy's followers. This is the first record of a pogrom against the Alexandrian Jews.[7]

In that 26th regnal year (145–144 BC), Ptolemy VIII tried to side-step any further objections to his rule by issuing a series of amnesty decrees. Cases would not be brought or heard, and those that had gone into hiding could return home and recover such possessions of theirs that had remained unsold. Soldiers were exempted from tax and any sums owing to the crown. The soldiers stationed in Cyprus were included in the amnesty and were awarded a salary for life.[8]

CLEOPATRA II AND CLEOPATRA III

As Ptolemy VIII's new wife, his sister Cleopatra II gritted her teeth and thought of Egypt, or more probably herself. At least this way she remained a pharaoh of Egypt, but not for long on acceptable terms. She bore her new and unwanted murderous brother-husband a son around the time the two were crowned in Memphis in *c.* 144 BC. The boy was known as Ptolemy Memphites (the other candidate for 'Ptolemy VII').

Cleopatra II had good reason to be resentful. Ptolemy VIII had a concubine called Eirene. He ordered the execution of some of his Cyrenaean henchmen who had come with him from Cyrene but criticized him for his infidelity.[9] He also took up with his niece Cleopatra III (*c.* 160/155–101 BC), Neos Philopator's sister. Within a few years he had divorced Cleopatra II, who remained a ruler, and married the young woman, known to history as Cleopatra III. Exactly when this happened is, not surprisingly, a source of some confusion but it seems to have occurred around 142–140 BC.[10] Their descendants were to include all the subsequent Ptolemaic rulers, from Ptolemy IX to Cleopatra VII and her son Caesarion.[11]

Once more there was a trio of monarchs, the king with Cleopatra the Sister (II) and Cleopatra the Wife (III) as queens regnant. It took a while before using these terms to differentiate the women was established, for example at Kom Ombo where their status and relationship to Ptolemy was exhibited (plate 12).[12]

Brother and sister despised each other. They never learned to smother their mutual hatred in the country's interests or even the regime's. The scene was set for more self-destructive plots and unpleasantness. Galaistes, a Greek prince, had been a trusted military commander under Ptolemy VI but was removed after falling out with Ptolemy VIII. Exiled to Greece, he devised a plan. He claimed that Ptolemy VI and Cleopatra II had entrusted him with the care of an unnamed son whom he would now bring back to Egypt and set on the throne with the aid of exiles. The rebellion collapsed when a loyalist general called Hierax paid off any currently unpaid soldiers, discouraging them from joining in.[13] The likelihood is that an aggrieved Cleopatra II was involved. Hierax, accomplished and popular, was the only reason Ptolemy VIII's government was holding together at all. The Egyptians were disgusted by the king's behaviour.[14]

SCIPIO AEMILIANUS VISITS EGYPT: 139 BC

In about 139 BC, a Roman diplomatic mission arrived in Alexandria. It was led by Scipio Aemilianus, victor of the Third Punic War seven years earlier. The journey was made to spy out the state of Egypt under Ptolemy VIII. Failing to understand the Romans or their true intentions, the corpulent king decided to impress his guests with a display of banqueting, the palace, and his wealth. The visitors, subscribing to the grand and self-conscious Roman traditions of abstemious dignity and restraint, were disgusted, but it was inevitable the pro-Roman Diodorus would describe them this way. Ptolemy's family arrangements go unmentioned but are unlikely to have impressed the Romans.

Scipio and his colleagues were far more impressed by Alexandria's location, wealth, and the Pharos lighthouse. They moved on to Memphis, eyeing up the fertility of the cultivable land, the large population, the cities, and the defences. It was clear to them that if only Egypt was ruled by someone capable the country could easily become the centre of a huge empire.[15] The subtext was obvious.

THE YEAR 133 BC IN ROME

Although much of Rome's territory was seized by force, some states ceded cities and land to Rome. In 133 BC Attalus III of Pergamum gave his kingdom of Asia to Rome in his will. Having no sons, Attalus decided this was the only way to prevent his domain being destroyed by factionalism and fighting after his death. Asia, 'whose luxury could corrupt Austerity herself', was so wealthy that its governance and security became almost overnight of the highest importance to Rome.[16]

Pliny, writing two centuries later, condemned the effect of the bequest on Rome. 'There was a much more devastating blow to our standards when we received Asia as a gift. Its bequest from King Attalus after his death was less to our advantage than Scipio's victory. On that day, any reservations about buying Attalus' effects in the Rome auctions vanished completely ... our community had gone from admiring foreign riches to coveting them.'[17]

Another problem had the potential to wipe out Rome's military capability. The Roman senatorial elite took over peasant farmland in Italy, thereby accumulating vast property portfolios through outright theft or pressurizing the occupants to sell. This way they created substantial estates operated by slaves. Free workers were spurned because such men were liable for military service on an unpredictable basis. Slaves offered the extra advantage of having children born into servitude, providing their masters with a self-replicating workforce, and who could be disposed of when too old to labour. This created a growing population of slaves at the expense of the free Italian families, compromising the chances of having enough Italian allies, while making a small number of senatorial families ever wealthier and more powerful.[18] Plutarch described how the 'rapacity of the rich' had 'driven out the poor', discouraging them from military service.[19]

A reforming senator called Tiberius Sempronius Gracchus was elected as a tribune of the plebs for 133 BC on a ticket warning that there would be too few eligible freeborn citizens to serve in Rome's armies as well as more risk of slave revolts (there was one ongoing in Sicily).[20] He recommended that some of Attalus' money be used to buy land and equipment for ordinary farmers.[21] Whether Gracchus' intentions were honourable or not, he came up against vested interests in the Senate who could see their lucrative estates being broken up. Gracchus and his supporters took over the Capitol, but his senatorial enemies insisted that he was breaking the law.[22] Other tribunes and the senators tried to stop his re-election. Tiberius Gracchus was surrounded in the Temple of Jupiter (where the Senate was meeting) by his bodyguards. An armed senatorial mob attacked the Gracchans. Gracchus was killed.[23] In 121 BC his reforming younger brother Gaius took his own life when faced by another senatorial mob.

These were dangerous times in Roman history which showed how high the stakes were when it came to wealth and power, which the Roman Republic and society had neither the maturity nor institutions yet to deal with. The political turmoil would last for generations. This had serious implications for Egypt where the Ptolemies needed Rome's decisive strength to prop them up. That dependency made Egypt ever more vulnerable to Roman greed and ambition.

CIVIL WAR

Although Ptolemy VIII and the two Cleopatras were depicted in documents and monuments as united rulers, by 132 BC there had been a decisive family breakdown. After the Roman fact-finding mission had left to explore other parts of the region, including Cyprus and Syria, the unpopular Ptolemy VIII grew paranoid. Terrified of plots, he withdrew to Cyprus with Cleopatra III and another son (the future

Ptolemy IX).[24] There he put together a mercenary army and went to war against his sister. The result was that in *c*. 131 BC in Alexandria Cleopatra II declared herself sole ruler in Egypt though, after Ptolemy VIII returned the following year, she maintained her own court until 127 BC. Ptolemy VIII realized that in his absence his son Ptolemy Memphites now might be made king in his place. He summoned the boy to Cyprus from Cyrene.

Meanwhile, Cleopatra II had begun a new sequence of regnal years to mark the occasion. This was followed by people pulling down Ptolemy's statues and any other images. Seeing this as a sign of Cleopatra II's popularity he 'killed the son that he had by her, and contrived to have the body, divided into portions, and arranged in a chest, presented to the mother at a feast on his birthday'. This grisly crime appalled the easily outraged Alexandrians, but this time they had good reason. The murder was a disaster for Ptolemy VIII. His limited remaining credibility was atomized when the miserable remains of the boy were put on display in an exhibition of what to expect from him, should he ever return.[25] 'The people were in a great rage against Ptolemy.'[26]

THE SUN SHINES ON THE WICKED – PTOLEMY VIII RETURNS TO EGYPT[27]

Nonetheless, by 130 BC Ptolemy VIII gambled on a return to Egypt, installing himself and Cleopatra III at Memphis. This was a more strategically advantageous base, giving him easier control of the Nile and Upper Egypt, with the bonus of cutting off Cleopatra II in Alexandria. He appointed an Egyptian called Paos to be strategos of the Thebaid. It was a significant opportunity for a man of indigenous origin and reflected the king's policy of favouring Egyptians, deliberately undermining Cleopatra II.

Paos was sent to tackle a rising at Hermonthis (Armant) about 12 miles (19 km) south of Thebes. The culprit was another royal pretender. This time it was supposedly a man called Harsiese (or Harsiesis), a contraction of 'Horus, son of Isis', a common enough

Egyptian name, transliterated into Greek as Ἁρσιῆσις. We know about him because a dismayed official called Dionysus lent Harsiese 250 talents from the state bank, not realizing what was going to happen. He was desperate to have priests help to cover up his mistake, promising to repay the money later.[28] Some scholars doubt the spectral Harsiese ever really existed, calling him a 'ghost king'.[29] A surviving letter, which does not identify Harsiese, describes the prospect of the force under Paos' command arriving in the Thebaid and is dated to the 40th year of Ptolemy VIII rather than the 2nd year of Cleopatra II. Paos seems to have been successful. Nothing else is known about the rebellion which may only have lasted for a few weeks at most, even if by 127 BC the city of Hermonthis was siding with the king.[30]

Securing the Thebaid was one thing. Taking control of Alexandria was another and was also indispensable both for practical and symbolic reasons. Whoever had Alexandria could lay claim to the Ptolemaic throne. It was inconceivable that a Ptolemaic king could do without the city's resources and strategic position.

Cleopatra II had a plan. Her daughter Cleopatra Thea had been married to the Seleucid Demetrius II Nicator during his first reign (145–139 BC) until he was captured by the Parthians. While he was in captivity the Seleucid throne passed to his brother Antiochus VII (138–129 BC). Cleopatra Thea held on to her position by marrying him. Antiochus was killed in battle by the Parthians in the winter of 130–129 BC.[31] In the meantime, Demetrius II had been released. He returned to Syria and took up with Thea again, though she hated him, and recovered his throne, ruling until 125 BC.

Currently in control of Coele-Syria, Demetrius II could do much as he pleased. Cleopatra II offered him the kingdom of Egypt in return for helping her against Ptolemy VIII and thus simultaneously ensuring her descendants would rule after him.[32] Demetrius could not resist. In 128 BC he set off for the Egyptian border immediately, forgetting about his enemies at home. While he was away, Antioch and Apameia, among other cities, rebelled against him.[33]

Inevitably, Ptolemy VIII discovered his sister's scheme and that she had darted off to Syria to join Demetrius and her daughter. Cleopatra II had taken the additional precaution of loading as much of her wealth as possible onto her ships. Ptolemy sent an Egyptian merchant's son to Syria to claim the throne, renaming him Alexander Zabinas for the purpose, on the spurious basis that he was an adoptive member of the Seleucid royal house. A consummate actor, Zabinas put on a great show of respect and mourning when the body of Antiochus VII was returned to Syria from Parthia.[34] This greatly impressed the Syrians who fell for his fake life story.

With support from Ptolemy, at Damascus in 126 BC Zabinas defeated Demetrius II whose dreams of adding Egypt to his empire evaporated. Demetrius escaped but was later killed by the governor of Tyre in or around 125 BC.[35] Demetrius was succeeded by his son Seleucus V. Within a year Seleucus' thrice-widowed mother Cleopatra Thea had killed him (apparently by shooting him with an arrow) for daring to assume the throne without her permission. She made another son, Antiochus VIII Grypus (named thus for his large nose), king but strictly as her patsy. Cleopatra Thea intended to be in charge, whatever the cost to those around her.[36] She struck coins in her name and with Antiochus VIII as joint monarchs, with her taking precedence.[37]

Ptolemy VIII had easily recovered Alexandria by 127 BC. He turned on his opponents there in a further example of what made him 'an object of hate'. This was probably when he ordered a massacre of citizens, followed up by trapping young men in a gymnasium where some were put to the sword, and others burned alive.[38] A new post, 'strategos of the city', was created so that Ptolemy could easily clamp down on any further risings in Alexandria.[39]

Alexander Zabinas, who still claimed the Seleucid throne, refused to be Ptolemy's creature and started insulting his sponsor. Ptolemy turned on Zabinas, reconciling (how he managed this goes unexplained) with Cleopatra II who by 124 BC was once more ruling in Egypt. He offered Antiochus VIII not just help, but also his probable daughter

Tryphaena ('Delicacy', a word which also had connotations of wealth and abundance, see Chapter 8), whose mother was likely Cleopatra III, in marriage. Zabinas' support evaporated and he was defeated in battle. He fled to Antioch but was killed by robbers.[40]

THE GYMNASIUM (GYMNASION)

The Gymnasium was a Greek institution introduced to Egypt in Hellenistic times and served as an integral component of the polis. Gymnasia were open only to approved members who had to be adult males, including the epheboi ('young men') in their late teens, and who swore oaths of allegiance, and paid subscriptions. Gymnasia were the equivalent of modern sports centres with a running track, exercise yard, baths, changing rooms, and facilities for preparation and practice. Other activities included recitations and lectures by visiting dignitaries.

The members could act as one in a wider social, religious, and political sense, for example in swearing loyalty to the crown as an institution rather than just the incumbent royal family. They were taught by salaried teachers who reinforced the Hellenism mindset. The gymnasium functioned as a form of higher education college intended to keep young men in order and turn out good citizens who shared common values in Greek education and culture.[41] The members were kept in order by the gymnasiarch, who also had the financial responsibility for general maintenance such as making sure oil was available for athletes and oversaw punishments for misdemeanours.[42] Gymnasia were funded by the state and private benefactions.[43] Individual gymnasia could and did apply to the court for help. In 135 BC the gymnasium at Omboi (now Kom Ombo), capital of the Ombite nome in the Thebaid, had sent one of its members to the court of Ptolemy VIII, Cleopatra II, and Cleopatra III, in search of favours. The 'truly outstanding benefits' they received, the details of which are unknown, were commemorated on an inscription.[44]

Antiochus VIII Grypus rid himself of his dangerous and turbulent mother, Cleopatra Thea. Worried that her power and influence were waning after his triumph over Alexander Zabinas, she tried to poison her son. Having already killed one child, killing another must have seemed comparatively easy. However, he forced her to drink the poison instead. With his mother thereby disposed of, he ruled in peace for eight more years before being challenged by another brother, Antiochus IX Cyzicenus.[45] In Appian's opinion Grypus 'proved himself to be worthy of such a mother', being both 'violent and tyrannical'. Given his pedigree, that can have surprised no-one.[46] Cleopatra Thea's remarkable career was not forgotten. Cleopatra VII, almost a century later, would style herself Thea Neotera, 'Thea the Younger' (see Chapter 17).

Ptolemy VIII clung on to Cyprus, but that was about all. The abandonment of Ptolemaic Aegean bases after *c.* 145 BC had simplified matters. The fall of Corinth to Rome the year before made it wise to withdraw, perhaps even on Roman instructions.[47] Egypt now had no possessions to the north, apart from Cyprus.

A SHOW OF UNITY – 118 BC

Ptolemy VIII and the two Cleopatras put on a show of unity in the aftermath of the farcical self-destructive machinations of recent years. On 28 April 118 BC a decree recorded in Greek on papyri announced that '[King] Ptolemaeus, Queen Cleopatra the Sister, and [Queen] Cleopatra the Wife proclaim an amnesty to all their subjects for errors, crimes, accusations, condemnations, and charges of all kinds up to the 9th of Pharmouthi (month) of the 52nd year, except to persons guilty of wilful murder or sacrilege'.[48] As usual in a public document, the formal Greek royal titles were used instead of the more colourful and wider-ranging traditional Egyptian titles (see Appendix 3). The 52nd regnal year given was Ptolemy VIII's, his alone appearing on the coinage.

Under the amnesty, taxes were to be remitted. Legal dues only were to be levied, not other payments. Those who had sought asylum (presumably including the katochoi) were to be left where they were and not forcibly removed. There were more orders, such as enforcing use of proper and accurate measures to prevent cultivators and others from being compelled to pay more than was legally due. Another revealing measure prohibited officials such as the strategoi from forcing people to do private work for them. Costs incurred by burying sacred animals would no longer be imposed on the population.

Such decrees served as a reaffirmation of royal power by asserting the crown's prerogative to bestow such concessions. That so many abuses existed, and there had been other amnesties before, exposed the impotence of the Ptolemaic state to maintain the kind of control it claimed to have. The potential for abuse was colossal, with so many examples of petty authority able to cream off a percentage or demand kickbacks. The problem is endemic in all states that depend on multiple tiers of bureaucracy, together with a limited ability to police at a local level. The issue would persist into the Roman period.[49]

On 28 June 116 BC, after over half a century of power unrestrained by scruple, Ptolemy VIII, 'a foul example of lustful madness', died.[50] Cleopatra II disappeared and was probably dead by 115 BC. Ptolemy VIII was an adept and manipulative statesman whose creative opportunism bridged the joyless chasms of his life. He was also a learned man, at least of sorts, once correcting Homer for using the phrase 'soft violets and celery', observing that marshwort grows alongside celery but violets do not.[51] Allegedly, he left Egypt to whichever of the two surviving sons he had had by Cleopatra III that she chose.[52] These two boys would be known to history as Ptolemy IX Philometor Soter II and Ptolemy X Alexander I (his mother's favourite). Ptolemy VIII left Cyrene and its territory to an illegitimate son called Ptolemy Apion. That decision would within two decades lead to the loss of the territory to Rome.

15

VENAL MAYHEM
Cleopatra III (116–101 BC), Ptolemy IX Philometor Soter II (116–107, 88–81 BC), and Ptolemy X Alexander I (107–88 BC)

The contortions into which the ruling house had twisted itself under Ptolemy VI and VIII continued unabated, now presided over by Cleopatra III, who was determined to rule with and through her sons Ptolemy IX and X at any price. The result was civil war, domestic rebellion, murder, and increasing intervention by Rome.

ALL IN THE FAMILY

Cleopatra III was fearsome, dominant, and ruthless. Not that any of those characteristics made her particularly unusual in the dynasty. When she ruled with her sons her name took precedence. She was the daughter of Ptolemy VI and Cleopatra II, sister of Cleopatra Thea, and niece, wife, and co-ruler with Ptolemy VIII, by whom she was mother of Ptolemy IX and X. From her were descended all the remaining rulers of the family.

Incest in the Ptolemaic royal family, involving mainly (but not only) siblings, has been a source of fascination from antiquity to modern times, and followed other attested instances in earlier Egyptian dynasties. The possibility of the higher incidence of congenital defects or susceptibility to disease affecting those born as the result of sexual relationships between those of consanguineous descent, especially when repeated over subsequent generations, is well known.[1] The potential psychological consequences are less understood outside clinical circles, partly because consanguineous marriages are relatively rare today (with the exception of some cultural communities). However, while these complications are 'likely', and may affect a significant percentage of the offspring, they are *not* inevitable.[2] Another problem is that the maternal parentage of some members of the Ptolemaic family is uncertain (for example, most of Ptolemy XII's children, including Cleopatra VII).

The potential vulnerability must be considered for Cleopatra Thea, Cleopatra III, and certain other family members. Modern studies of contemporary victims have noted significant clinical symptoms, for example 'incest victims tend to have marital difficulties, and there is an increased risk of their physically and emotionally abusing their children'.[3] There is also an 'increased generational risk', and traumatic bonding leading to abuse.[4] But these problems are in a context where incest is normally treated as taboo. In the Ptolemaic family, incest carried no such connotations.

In Ptolemy II and Arsinoe II's case it is easier to identify a religious ideology underpinning their union in which they identified themselves with the sibling deities Osiris and Isis or Zeus and Hera. Within a royal family the members can sometimes be seen as the exclusive occupants of a zone that lies between the divine and the mortal, implicitly excluding others. There were also the relatively closed circumstances of the court which restricted the association of members of the royal families with lesser beings, a factor that may have become progressively more important.[5] Holding onto wealth and land within a family was another motivation, paralleled by cousin marriages in the European Middle Ages and down to the nineteenth century for the same reason.

General books about the Ptolemies rarely consider the clinical consequences of incest, despite the repetition of the practice resulting in several key personalities being the product of incest resulting from several generations' worth of consanguineous unions. We know little about the physiology of the Ptolemies apart from how some were given to morbid obesity (which could be down to environmental and behavioural reasons), but their aberrant and dangerous behaviour was commented on in antiquity. Although some of this could be dismissed as part of the stock rhetorical depictions of tyrants, or the result of circumstances, the stories are too consistent for incest to be dismissed outright as a potential cause.

Incest is traditionally, and understandably, seen as morally degenerate. It is a short leap to explaining aberrant behaviour as an inevitable consequence, and therefore that incest was a pivotal factor in ending the Ptolemaic dynasty. We cannot measure how much, and there were many other causes. However, grandly dismissing bigoted ancient authors and 'the perspective' of some modern commentators for exaggerating the effects is probably going too far. This has become a trope in some contemporary scholarship in which modern theories, often based on weak foundations (since the necessary standard of evidence does not exist), are presented as preferential alternatives.[6] There are good reasons why most societies treat incest as abhorrent. The logical, and simplest, conclusion is that it is known to be dangerous in various ways.

CLEOPATRA III

Subscribing to the view that it was not too late to be what she might have been, Cleopatra III ruled with consummate determination following Ptolemy VIII's death in 116 BC and her mother's soon after, until her younger son Ptolemy X had her murdered in 101 BC. Until then, she dominated her family and the state with an ardent lack of self-sacrificing affection. The effect of her being on those around her was thereby incalculably destructive.

Cleopatra's standing, in her eyes at least, was enhanced by Ptolemy IX's auspicious birth. Aged twenty-six when his father died, he had come into the world on the same day as the Apis bull on 18 February 142 BC. He was thus both Horus and 'the living Apis'. This meant that Cleopatra III could, and did, portray herself as the mother of the Apis bull, even though she resented not being allowed by the Alexandrians to make her favoured younger son king instead. She also posed as a manifestation of a living Isis, mother of Horus in the form of her son, and was even described as a female Horus in her own right (in Egyptian *ḥrt*; where the addition of a 't' feminizes the name of the god) as for example Cleopatra I had been. A column from Kom Ombo is one of the few surviving inscriptions of the pair and recounts their titles.[7] In 105 BC Cleopatra III strengthened her credentials by becoming a priestess of the cult of Alexander the Great (see below), until then managed solely by men.

Positioned above other mortals and some of her female predecessors, Cleopatra III ruled as regent for her sons in an unprecedentedly dysfunctional arrangement. She lived to make life more difficult for both. Cleopatra III wished to make the younger boy king but was compelled by the people, to her annoyance, to appoint the elder one.[8] Ptolemy IX loved and was married to a sister called Cleopatra IV (by whom he may have had Berenice III). By 115 BC (and according to Justin, *before* he was made king) their mother had forced him to divorce her and, sticking with the incestuous tradition, marry a younger sister called Cleopatra V Selene. Some scholars call her only Cleopatra Selene, impacting on the enumeration of later Cleopatras; however, the evidence for the genealogy of the later Ptolemies is a much disputed minefield.[9] Cleopatra V Selene was to have a remarkable marital career as both an Egyptian and Seleucid queen before being executed in 69 BC by the Armenian king Tigranes II, the Great.[10]

Ptolemy IX acquired his own nickname, Lathyrus ('Chickpea'). Pausanias thought the fact that he was also called Philometor to be a joke, 'no king known to history having been so hated by his mother'.[11] He was to rule, if one could call it that, until 107 BC. In the meantime, his younger brother was made strategos in Cyprus (113 BC).

Cleopatra IV did not take her rejection lying down. She planned to marry Antiochus IX Cyzicenus, then fighting his half-brother Antiochus VIII Grypus. She took her own dowry in the form of Grypus' army 'whom she had induced to desert'. The plan went awry when she was besieged in Antioch by Grypus whose wife Tryphaena, despite being Cleopatra IV and V's other sister, regarded Cleopatra IV now as her enemy and wanted her killed. Despite her husband's protestation at the futility of such an action, Tryphaena went ahead and organized an assassination squad to take out Cleopatra IV. She should have listened to her husband. Antiochus VIII seized Tryphaena after a subsequent battle that he won and killed her in revenge for Cleopatra IV.[12]

In 115 BC Ptolemy IX visited Elephantine during his inconsequential first reign. He went with his mother in their shared 2nd regnal year. Her name preceded his on the Greek inscription that records the event, allegedly demonstrating the reality of his subordinate status.[13] The prominence of preceding Ptolemaic rulers made this an unsurprising development. Conversely, Cleopatra III went unmentioned on the coins which stuck doggedly to the portrait of Ptolemy I and unchanging legend 'King Ptolemy' (ΒΑΣΙΛΕΩΣ ΠΤΟΛΕΜΑΙΟΥ).

STRANGERS IN A STRANGE LAND

Three Roman visitors reached the Temple of Isis complex on the island of Philae, south of Aswan. Caius Acutius, Marcus Claudius Varus, and Sp(urius?) Varaeus were there on 26 August 116 BC and left an inscription to record their visit. Acutius said it was the first time he had been there, but it is unlikely he meant that the others had been there before. He also added his name in Greek letters. The inscription is the earliest known in Latin in Egypt and the first bilingual one in Latin and Greek. None of the men explains who they were or why they had come. They were probably seeking out commercial opportunities, though the visit to Philae may have been recreational.[14] There was nothing unusual about traders going beyond Roman-controlled territory in search of business prospects or for tourism. There is another possibility.

On 29 August 116 BC a total eclipse of the sun passed to the south through northern Sudan which they may have hoped to see.[15]

In 112 BC Lucius Memmius, a senator from an old Italian family, visited Egypt. According to a papyrus planning his visit, he disembarked at Alexandria before cruising up the Nile to the Arsinoite nome 'to see the sights'. This innocent abroad was treated with unctuous delight by his tour managers who arranged 'the special magnificence' he could enjoy at each stop.[16] There was no question of roughing it. They laid on titbits he could throw to the sacred crocodile of Petesouchus in the Fayum. His tour included a visit to the so-called 'Labyrinth', beside the temple of the Middle Kingdom pharaoh Amenemhet III, or what was left after Ptolemy II dismantled it (plate 7). Memmius was making the most of a well-established tourist industry that is still in action today, even if the hungry crocodile is long gone.

'Nilotica' (Egyptian-themed art) began to appear in Rome and Italy at this time. The existence therefore of a temple of Serapis in a busy port town like Puteoli around the same time that Memmius made his way up the Nile is unsurprising.[17] Isis also became well-established but not initially among the Roman elite. She had already been absorbed into Greek mythology as the deified Io (the priestess of Hera and mortal lover of Zeus). She was described as such by Ovid with her 'crescent horns upon her forehead' and with her associates Anubis, Bubastis, Apis, and Osiris. The latter two had been combined as Serapis.[18]

Isis was associated with rebirth and immortality because of her role in bringing her brother-husband Osiris back to life. She was regarded as a benevolent and compassionate goddess whose nurturing and maternal interest in her followers was symbolized in her caring for the infant Horus and her tears of sorrow at hardship in Egypt caused by failure of the annual inundation of the Nile which was depended on for fertility, growth, and prosperity.

Compared to the petty and vengeful classical deities of the Roman pantheon, her appeal was obvious.

In another twist, the eagle astride a thunderbolt motif on Ptolemaic coins once more found its way onto a denarius, struck in Rome by the moneyer Lucius Aurelius Cotta in 105 BC. Perhaps he had visited Egypt too. The use of a monarchical emblem might seem a strange choice for Republican Rome but was almost certainly seen by the Romans as a symbol of Jupiter Capitolinus, the divine sponsor and guarantor of Rome's destiny. More examples followed in the next fifty to sixty years.[19]

HOURLY COINING PLOTS

Cleopatra III seethed at having been forced to make her elder son king. She turned the people of Alexandria against him, painting herself as a victim. She had her most faithful eunuchs attacked and then told the Alexandrians it was all part of her son's plot against her.[20] The Alexandrians fell for the ruse. In 107 BC Ptolemy IX was pushed into exile in Cyprus and made to give up Cleopatra V Selene, further humiliating him. The younger brother was recalled to Egypt from Cyprus and became king as Ptolemy X Alexander.

Cleopatra III ensured that she and Ptolemy X posed as joint divine monarchs, taking the names Philometor Soteira and Philometor Soter, and initiating a new regnal year sequence, one of the most explicit and radical expressions of a woman of the dynasty ruling in her own right. She also possessed the Horus name *k3-nkht nb(t)-t3wy* (Ka-nakht neb(et)-tawy), 'strong bull, Lady of the Two Lands', but in a masculine format. Appropriately enough, a new type of royal Hellenistic portraiture for the new brand of Ptolemaic female pharaoh evolved. Derived from male royal sculpture, the features were heavy and fierce, the expressions grim, the steely-eyed gaze unfaltering, and the lips set and determined. Only the hairstyle and headdress make it clear the subjects were female.[21]

Cleopatra maintained her regnal year numbering throughout her reign, even once Ptolemy IX had been supplanted by his younger brother.[22] A land sale papyrus in 106 BC by three 'Persian' sisters to Psennesis, another 'Persian of the Epigone', begins with the formula 'The 11th which is also the 8th year' for Cleopatra III and Ptolemy X 'Philometores' respectively. Ptolemy X's regnal years were counted from when he became governor of Cyprus.[23] Although Cleopatra III remained unnamed on the coinage, an innovation was the appearance on the tetradrachms of her regnal years with Ptolemy X's during 106–101 BC, but with hers taking precedence (plate 10.4).[24]

In the years 107–106 and 106–105 BC Ptolemy X replaced his elder brother (who had held the post from 117 BC) as one of the two priests of the cult of Alexander in Alexandria. In an unprecedented move, Cleopatra took over the king's priesthood herself from 105–104 BC, thereby making it clear who she believed had the real power.[25]

Ptolemy X was horrified by his mother's actions.[26] Cleopatra III dispatched a military hit squad to Cyprus to eliminate Ptolemy IX. One step ahead, he escaped to Seleucia-in-Pieria, reluctant to fight a war against her. When the general in charge of the failed mission returned to Egypt, she executed him. While Ptolemy IX was there, one of his own friends, presumably put up to the task by Cleopatra III, tried to kill him. The plot was uncovered. Thereafter, the ousted king realized he could trust no-one.[27] Nevertheless, he managed to retake Cyprus and ruled there until 88 BC.

Meanwhile, the reluctant new king Ptolemy X tried to dissociate himself from his mother. He had already decided that being a ruler was far too risky a business, though she managed to persuade him to support her in the conflict to come.[28]

Cleopatra III was worried that her elder son would head to her nephew, the Seleucid king Antiochus IX Cyzicenus, to help recover his throne. Her plan was to invite her other nephew Antiochus VIII Grypus to support her, offering him Cleopatra Selene as an enticement (Cyzicenus and Grypus were half-brothers, sharing Cleopatra Thea as mother).

THE WAR OF 103–101 BC

Modern books summarizing this period generally brush over the machinations of the next few years because of their complexity. It is easy to see why. From 116 BC Cyzicenus and Grypus had been fighting a sporadic civil war which had broken out when Cyzicenus challenged his half-brother for power. By 103 BC the enervated and fragmented Seleucid kingdom had started to lose ground to a new player: the Jewish Jannaeus (or Iannaios), king of Judaea (103–76 BC), whose reign was marked by territorial conquest in the region, and extreme cruelty and barbarism. In 103 BC Jannaeus began the siege of Ptolemais (Phoenicia). The inhabitants asked Ptolemy IX for help. Although they soon changed their minds, he was already in the area. Jannaeus realized that Ptolemy was a potential threat to his own ambitions. He was right. At Asophon in Galilee that year Ptolemy defeated Jannaeus before roaming and plundering at will across Judaea. Josephus provides a graphic description of Jannaeus' soldiers killing tens of thousands of men before turning on the women and children, murdering them and boiling and eating their dismembered bodies.[29] Such atrocities are not unusual in ancient historians' accounts and their accuracy impossible to assess.

Cleopatra III realized that Ptolemy IX was now so powerful, and close to Egypt, that he presented an imminent existential threat to her.[30] Ever ready like her deceased husband Ptolemy VIII for an opportunity, she had already moved herself and her grandchildren to the comparative safety of Kos, just off the south-west coast of Asia Minor. The baggage included money, art, precious stones, and 'women's ornaments'.[31] The children concerned were Ptolemy X's son, the future but very short-lived Ptolemy XI Alexander II, and Ptolemy IX's daughter Berenice III and his illegitimate sons, the future Ptolemy XII and 'Ptolemy of Cyprus'. Cleopatra III's latest scheme was evidently to jump a generation and rule through the grandchildren.

Keen to take advantage of the Ptolemaic support for the Jews, Cleopatra III appointed two Jewish brothers as her generals, the trusted

Chelkias and Ananias, sons of the Jewish high priest Onias IV. Cleopatra did nothing without their advice.[32] She instructed Ptolemy X to attack Phoenicia with a fleet, while she led a force to besiege Ptolemais, leaving her grandchildren safely on Kos. While his mother was distracted, Ptolemy IX chanced a march into Egypt, assuming he would have an easy run because there would be no army there. He was wrong. His younger brother drove him back at the border and he had to return to Cyprus. On the plus side Chelkias had died while chasing Ptolemy IX as he made his attempt to retake Egypt.[33]

With Ptolemy IX removed, Cleopatra III could regroup. By 102 BC Ptolemais had fallen to her army. Ptolemy X tried to make up with his mother. Some of her friends said now was the time to imprison him and seize control of the region, a move that would effectively recover Coele-Syria for Egypt. Ananias disagreed. He told Cleopatra that she would make an enemy of all the Jews. She gave up the idea in favour of mutual assistance.[34] She returned to Egypt, and Jannaeus to his wars of conquest. The Seleucid kingdom was so reduced that Cleopatra III's war against her elder son had been conducted with impunity in what was supposed to have been Seleucid territory.

THE END OF CLEOPATRA III

Ptolemy X emerged from the war scarred and demoralized. One claim is that he had so despaired of his mother he even left Egypt for a while (if he had not already done so before the war) but was persuaded by her to come home.[35] He was still interested in escaping the dangers of being a royal figure. Having seen what his mother was capable of, he must have feared for his life. He finally decided Cleopatra III was a lost cause.

In 101 BC Ptolemy X had his mother killed, though how is uncertain, she 'having, indeed, well deserved so infamous an end'.[36] At Kom Ombo, the inscription commemorating the benefits awarded to the gymnasium there from Ptolemy VIII, Cleopatra II, and Cleopatra III, in 135 BC was treated to some selective *damnatio memoriae*, but probably not until 101 BC or afterwards. Ptolemy VIII's and Cleopatra III's names were both hacked out. Cleopatra II's was left untouched.[37] Cleopatra III's regnal years of course disappear from the coins. Ptolemy X had been married to an unknown woman who was the mother of his son, the future Ptolemy XI. He now married Berenice III (sometimes referred to as Cleopatra Berenice), his brother's daughter by their sister Cleopatra IV (or Cleopatra V) and thus his niece. They had an unknown daughter.

THE LATTER DAYS OF PTOLEMY X

Freed thus from his murderous and conniving mother – not a misogynistic judgement since Cleopatra III behaved no differently to her uncle-husband Ptolemy VIII – Ptolemy X continued to rule Egypt. Ptolemy X was later said to have become grossly obese, like his father, and hated.[38]

The remainder of Ptolemy X's reign was unhappy, but only a madman would have expected otherwise. In 101–100 BC the Romans passed a law against Cilician piracy in the Mediterranean. This included the instruction that the next consul to take office should 'write to the kings who reign in the island of Cyprus, in Alexandria and Egypt, Cyrene, and Syria, who have friendship and alliance with the Roman people'. The letters were to prohibit any of those places from receiving the pirates in their territory or allowing the pirates to operate or base themselves there, in the interests of cooperating with Rome for everyone's safety.[39]

It was clear what was expected by Rome of Egypt and the other nations as subordinate allies (the law included threats of penalties for non-compliance). This endemic plague of pirates, which worsened, would not be comprehensively dealt with until the Roman general Pompey's naval war against them in the mid-60s BC, but the current measures temporarily abated the problem. Meanwhile, Cilicia and Crete were made Roman provinces.

Cyrene was by then under the control of Ptolemy VIII's illegitimate son, Ptolemy Apion, to whom he had bequeathed it. By 96 BC Apion had died and in turn bequeathed Cyrene to Rome.[40] The Senate accepted the gift, but declared the cities of Cyrenaica to be *liberas*, 'independent'.[41] This exempted Rome from any immediate obligation to organize provincial management of the new territory while still being entitled to tribute. Cyrenaica was not organized as a new Roman province until *c.* 75 BC, but Rome had acquired a vast and wealthy foothold in North Africa to add to the Carthaginian lands taken in 146 BC. The Ptolemies' empire had just shrunk a little more.

YOU ONLY RULE TWICE:
THE RETURN OF PTOLEMY IX 88–80 BC

At the end of the 90s BC yet another rebellion broke out in Upper Egypt. The evidence is a papyrus that refers to trouble in the Pathyris (Gebelein, about 24 miles or 40 km south of Thebes) district in the 24th regnal year of an unnamed king.[42] This must be the trouble that festered at least until 88 BC when Platon, strategos of the Thebaid, wrote to villagers imploring them to stay loyal to the local commander Nechtyris until he arrived.[43]

Nechtyris is an Egyptian name. He was probably another native who had chosen a career in the service of the state. If so, he was now fighting against his own countrymen, based in a fort established there almost a century earlier following the Theban Revolt of 186 BC.[44] Platon also wrote to Nechtyris to encourage him to hang on until he arrived, dating this letter to the 26th regnal year of what must be Ptolemy X. Platon wrote again not long afterwards with an update that 'King Soter' (Ptolemy IX) had arrived at Memphis and appointed Hierax to lead the campaign against the revolt. The change in king was treated seamlessly by dating the second letter to Ptolemy IX's 30th regnal year.[45] The speedy updates to the regnal years suggest Theban officials were falling over themselves to stay neutral, rather than ally themselves with any rebels, unlike in 206–186 BC.[46] Ptolemy X was still around, and not forced out until 88 BC (see below).

The rebels were defeated, but not decisively enough to secure the crown's hold. Pausanias claimed that so much damage was done 'that there was nothing left in Thebes to remind them of their happiness'.[47] The rebellion marked a further downturn in Ptolemaic influence, despite the vast Ptolemaic Temple of Horus at Edfu, just 42 miles (68 km) to the south and still under construction (since 237 BC). The Pathyris fort was given up after 88 BC, but not because the regime had successfully crushed opposition.[48] Ptolemaic power was gradually falling back on its heartland in the north. Economic ruin and onerous taxation continued to whittle away the will of some villagers to carry on. By 83 BC much of the land in the Heracleopolite (now Ihnasya el-Medina) nome had been abandoned with farmers defaulting on their taxes. A surviving papyrus lists the various tax arrears owed by various districts (toparchies) within the nome, and the dates by which instalments were due to be paid.[49]

By 88 BC Ptolemy X had been expelled from Egypt, apparently in part because his pro-Jewish policy had angered the Alexandrians (he had 'assaulted them with the help of some Jews'), and fell out with his own soldiers. He was, as far as was possible, deleted from the king lists. The other reason, so Strabo claimed, was that he had stolen Alexander the Great's golden coffin and replaced it with one of glass (or alabaster). More importantly, regardless of her behaviour, the murder of Cleopatra III by her son was seen as intolerable and unnatural. His elder brother Ptolemy IX was recalled to rule Egypt in his place. He did so for seven years (there is some confusion about exactly when Ptolemy X was pushed out, see n. 49). The crisis spanned the two reigns. Ptolemy X appears to have done nothing about the rebellion before he was ousted.

Ptolemy X's luck went from bad to worse. In 88 BC he was defeated in a naval battle during an attempt to retake Egypt. He took refuge in Lycia with his family and then tried to recapture Cyprus, the place he had begun his adult career as strategos under his elder brother's first reign. During this campaign he was defeated by a force commanded by a Ptolemaic admiral called Chaereas and was killed. He left a widow, his niece Berenice III.[50] Ptolemy IX now ruled Egypt unchallenged.

Cyprus was Egypt's last meaningful overseas possession. Ptolemy X had borrowed from Rome to fund his last war. Roman ambassadors were sent to Tyre in Phoenicia to recover the cash. He had allegedly made over Egypt to the Romans in his will in return.[51] Cicero later mused on how any Roman offered the governorship of Egypt could turn down such an 'opulent kingdom' and a 'beautiful country', and worried it might encourage other Romans to emigrate there. Cicero's main fear was that a wealthy member of the Roman elite might be able to buy up so much land in Egypt that he could create a rival power base with his supporters and the resources to turn on Rome. The Romans did not pursue the will for the moment. Nor did they seek to interfere in the restoration of Ptolemy IX who ruled with his daughter Berenice III as co-regent, but this depends largely on a few documents that supposedly cite their individual but unnamed parallel regnal years.[52] However, the Athenians paid her honours along with her father which does support the theory (see below, this chapter).

ROME'S DISASTER OF 88 BC

In 88 BC Mithridates VI, king of Pontus, invaded Asia, one of Rome's wealthiest provinces, during the First Mithridatic War (89–85 BC). Like a wildfire, his army of a quarter of a million infantry and 40,000 cavalry ravaged the region, leading to at least one unlikely claim that 150,000 Romans were killed 'in a single day'.[53] Mithridates took Kos, where he captured the children of Ptolemy IX and X (they had been taken there for safety by Cleopatra III and included the future Ptolemies XI and XII). He betrothed two of them to his daughters.[54] It was forty-five years since Asia had become a Roman possession, bequeathed to Rome by its childless ruler Attalus III.

Asia was a favourite place for wealthy Romans to invest. They blithely ignored the much higher level of risk involved than lending money at home, attracted by charging ruinous interest rates (as much as 30 per cent, or even more).[55] Many found they had lost their investments and money they had lent, including to traders who were killed in the war. Mithridates even specifically targeted Roman or Italian moneylenders operating in the province and rewarded debtors who killed their creditors with remission of half their debts.[56] This had a domino effect in Rome. Bankers who had lost money in Asia were then unable to offer fresh loans in Italy or pay back those who had deposited money with them in the first place. Credit at home collapsed and along with it the repayment of loans, presumably because some of those who had invested in Asia had borrowed heavily to do so.[57]

As Rome's influence spread further, its power and wealth had become ever more exposed to instability in other regions, driven by a desire to profiteer. The prospect of loans carrying high interest rates was simply too attractive to pass over, despite the risk. The possible consequences for the financial market in Rome were ignored. Disruption in a province could seriously damage the financial interests of Romans. It could also damage Rome's phys-ical security. Defeating Mithridates was therefore a critical matter for the Roman state. It was crucial to demonstrate that men like Mithridates could be destroyed or forced to come to terms for Roman financial and economic stability. The implications for other nations in Rome's sphere of interest were obvious: for Rome, total control of their affairs was both more desirable and profitable.

SULLA

In Rome, the imperators Gaius Marius and Lucius Cornelius Sulla were squabbling over who would lead the army against Mithridates. The Roman Republic was descending further into factionalism. Marius used a corrupt tribune to engineer a law that would give him the command against Mithridates. The law was passed but the consuls, one of whom was Sulla, promptly suspended business for the day. Marius led troops into the forum. His men killed the son of the other consul, Pompeius, and apprehended Sulla who was forced to reverse the decision.

Marius had secured the command, but his tactics backfired. He sent military tribunes to take over Sulla's army at Nola in Campania.[58] That army's loyalty lay with its commanding officer, rather than the state. Sulla's soldiers murdered the tribunes and Sulla was able to march on Rome with six legions (35,000 men). Sulla had turned his soldiers into a political force, something Marius had not done. This spectacular but notorious, illegal, and outrageous breach of precedent was one of the most infamous acts of the Republic.[59] Marius started killing Sulla's supporters in Rome and even took the extraordinary step of promising freedom to slaves who would join him. Just three did. Marius fled and escaped by ship from Ostia, not even waiting for his son.[60]

Sulla's actions did nothing to restore order in Rome, though he claimed they had done so. There was no turning back. Sulla had to accept the rejection of his candidates for office; after all, since he had claimed to have set things right, he could hardly complain if a normal election went ahead. One of the consuls for 86 BC, Lucius Cornelius Cinna, tried to impeach Sulla, who ignored him and headed out to the war against Mithridates.[61] The campaign had already cost Rome dear. In 88 BC public property from unspecified sources was sold off to raise 9,000 lbs (4,082 kg) of gold to pay for it.[62] It was, of course, an investment. Victory would, as it did, repay the costs untold times over.

During Rome's first war against Mithridates Ptolemy IX was left in a quandary. He needed to keep Rome's support but was reluctant to take sides until the outcome was known. For all Rome's dominance, Mithridates had inflicted a staggering reversal in Roman fortunes. Ptolemy wined and dined Sulla's quaestor Licinius Lucullus, who had arrived on a mission to shore up support for Rome and obtain ships from Egypt and Cyrenaica. Crete came onside immediately. Cyrene was in a state of disorder after a series of tyrannies. Lucullus reformed the Cyrenaean constitution but was attacked by pirates when he headed on to Egypt, losing most of his fleet.[63] He nevertheless managed to stage an impressive entry to the port at Alexandria where he was greeted by the Egyptian fleet.

Ptolemy IX offered Lucullus money, most of which was declined, but provided him with ships to take him to Cyprus. Such was the urgency of the war that Lucullus turned down the tempting prospect of a visit to Memphis and the other great sights of Egypt, dismissing this as 'the privilege of the luxurious and leisurely sightseer'. Lucullus went on eventually to Rhodes, picking up more ships along the way from the maritime cities in Asia en route.[64] Ptolemy had successfully put on a show for Lucullus' sake but skilfully avoided any commitment while he waited to see what would happen in the Mithridatic war.

Ptolemy IX went out of his way to court the Athenians, who dedicated statues to him and Berenice.[65] Where this left him when Athens sided with Mithridates and was rewarded for this decision by Sulla sacking the city in 86 BC is unclear, like so many aspects of Ptolemaic history.[66]

While Sulla was on campaign against Mithridates, Marius returned to Rome. Next, he presided over a bloody purge of anyone and everyone he suspected of being supporters of Sulla or his enemies.[67] Sulla's house was burned down.[68] With this horror in full swing, Sulla had to return but that meant ending the war against Mithridates. In 84 BC Mithridates was persuaded to abandon his ambitions in Asia and Paphlagonia and other kingdoms and pay Rome an indemnity as well as hand over seventy warships.[69] That at least settled the problem of the threat he had posed to Roman financial interests in Asia. Sulla also received into his care the future Ptolemy XI who had escaped from Mithridates.[70] The negotiations did not stop there but the real problem was Sulla's army. The soldiers were outraged at the thought of Mithridates getting away with having ordered the massacre of Romans in Asia. Sulla convinced them that he had had no choice.[71]

A RASH AND BLOODY DEED:
THE FLEETING REIGN OF PTOLEMY XI (80 BC)

By the very end of 81 BC Ptolemy IX had died. He left his widowed daughter and co-regent Cleopatra Berenice III the sole ruler of Egypt.[72]

She was the first queen of Egypt to rule without a husband or son since the widowed Tawosret (1191–1189 BC), the last ruler of the 19th Dynasty. Ptolemy IX's death ended a bewildering saga of family trauma and strife involving himself, his parents, and his siblings and marked the start of another. Berenice III was only to rule independently for about four months into early 80 BC.[73] The reason was her stepson Ptolemy XI Alexander II who had been recalled from Rome to take up the throne. This was apparently on the direction of Sulla, now a self-appointed kingmaker, who had taken Ptolemy XI there after rescuing the boy from Mithridates and 'become closely acquainted with him'. Sulla had two motives: despite Berenice III, he regarded the Egyptian throne as vacant and 'expected to reap a large reward from a rich kingdom'.[74]

Within less than three weeks, the high-handed Ptolemy XI decided he had no wish to rule with his stepmother and cousin (though the genealogy is exceptionally confused at this point, and their exact relationship uncertain; some claim she was also his half-sister). In another twist of the self-destructive Ptolemaic saga, he murdered her. He had only a short time to reflect on his action. The irate Alexandrians, who had taken to the apparently faultless and noble-hearted Berenice III, turned on him. Armed men from the gymnasium seized and killed him after a reign of about eighteen or nineteen days.[75] Ptolemaic rule of Egypt had fifty years left to run. At the rate things were going, fifty days looked challenging.

16

THE TUNE OF FLUTES
Ptolemy XII Neos Dionysos Auletes (80–58, 55–51 BC),
Cleopatra VI (79–69 BC), and Berenice IV (58–55 BC)

Ptolemy XII ruled for several decades, including a gap of several years while he temporarily fled to Rome and was briefly replaced by his daughter Berenice IV. Regardless of how weak he might appear to have been, Ptolemy XII held on to his throne and passed it to his daughter, Cleopatra VII, and her brothers, securing a guarantee from Rome.

According to Justin, Syria and Egypt had long been accustomed to fighting with their neighbours. Now restricted in this pastime by the increasing proximity of the Romans, they exhausted themselves by fighting with each other and became the objects of derision in the eyes of those neighbours.[1]

After the death of her fifth husband Antiochus X by 88 BC, and the killing of Ptolemy XI in 80 BC, Cleopatra V Selene was left with two sons, including Antiochus XIII. They were the only remaining legitimate males of the Ptolemaic royal line. Selene optimistically went with them to Rome to claim the throne of Egypt on their behalf. After all, if Rome in the form of Sulla could make Ptolemy XI king, it was a logical step to take. She was disappointed. The Romans did nothing, having other distractions at the time.[2]

In any case, Selene's sons were not the boys the Alexandrians were looking for. The throne was taken by Ptolemy IX's illegitimate elder son who acceded as Ptolemy XII Neos Dionysos.[3] Within a year he had married Cleopatra VI Tryphaena, his probable sister or half-sister (or even cousin) and made her co-regent as 'sibling gods'. Their mother or mothers are not known.[4] Cyprus was made a separate kingdom ruled by his younger brother, inconveniently known to history as 'Ptolemy of Cyprus'. This divided up Ptolemaic territory in a way that ought to have neutralized it in the eyes of Rome, giving it a better chance of surviving as an independent state. That might have happened had the Romans not spotted the opportunity to help themselves to Cyprus just over twenty years later.

Ptolemy XII was eventually crowned in 76 BC by the high priest of Ptah, Pasherenptah (this long-lived man did not die until the 11th regnal year of Cleopatra VII). The king had appointed him when as a boy he had visited Alexandria, replacing his father who had just died (the priesthood was usually hereditary). Ptolemy XII was using royal patronage to reinforce the links between the crown and the priesthood.[5] 'I set the adornment of the serpent-crown upon the head of the king on the day that he took possession of Upper and Lower Egypt, and performed all the customary rites . . . I was the leader in all the secret offices', said Pasherenptah on his tombstone. The ceremony took place in the royal palace in Alexandria, not Memphis, breaking with tradition. The king was riding in his chariot to the Temple of Isis, but stopped close to Pasherenptah and made him his Prophet. Subsequently, Ptolemy XII visited Pasherenptah in Memphis, cruising up and down the Nile in his ship to see both sides of the city.[6] At Kom Ombo Ptolemy XII was shown in the protection of the increasingly impotent traditional gods (plate 19).

At Edfu the magnificent Temple of Horus was dedicated in 70 BC where Ptolemy was shown in a traditional pharaonic pose of smiting his imaginary enemies (plate 14). This important event was triumphantly recorded on the building inscription there (completion came around thirteen years later).[7] The temple's imposing appearance belied the state of Ptolemaic authority, just as the warlike reliefs of Ptolemy XII masked the emasculated nature of his kingship. Roman dominance of the eastern Mediterranean world meant that the endemic warfare between the Hellenistic kingdoms was being steadily stifled out of existence.

To Ptolemy XII's various names and epithets, another was added, thanks to the new king's love of playing the flute. He acquired the nickname Auletes (Αὐλητής, 'flute player'). Ptolemy XII went down in Roman lore for his 'general licentiousness' but his habit of playing the flute in public and even competing in the palace with other contestants seems to have left a more lasting impression. Roman-period sources disparaged him for it, but in Greek culture the flute formed an integral part of polite society and achievement, appearing as an attribute as far back as Homeric heroes.[8]

In 76 BC Cleopatra VI Tryphaena had been named *pr3t* (the feminized form of pharaoh) on a demotic stela, matching Ptolemy's *pr3*.[9] By 69 BC, despite her status, she had ceased to feature in written references to the royal couple; reliefs of her on the pylon at Edfu were covered over with plaster.[10]

Cleopatra VI's disappearance from court coincided with Ptolemy XII taking up with a mistress and may have been the reason for her removal.[11] It is possible that this unnamed mistress rather than Tryphaena was the mother of Cleopatra VII, who was born about this time. Strabo states that of Ptolemy XII's daughters only the eldest, Berenice IV, was legitimate.[12] The mistress's origins have been the source of pure speculation, for example that she came from an Egyptian family of the priests of Ptah but even then was likely to have had some Macedonian ancestry.[13] Either way, there is no foundation for believing Cleopatra VII's ethnicity diverged much, if at all, from her Macedonian and Syrian dynastic forebears, especially as her paternity is beyond doubt. Eleven years later, Ptolemy XII and Tryphaena's eldest daughter Berenice IV was made queen in her father's place when he was temporarily ousted. Tryphaena may have returned briefly during Berenice's reign (see below).

THE LOYAL VILLAGERS OF PSENAMOSIS

In 67 and 64 BC the village farmers of Psenamosis (Kom Tukala) near Alexandria decided to show their loyalty to the crown. A formal association of landowners in the village clubbed together to purchase land from Paris, a wealthy local man, to build a gymnasium and a hall where they could hold meetings and make sacrifices to the crown. Spotting an opportunity to promote his own loyalty with a display of competitive munificence, Paris gave them the land instead, for which of course the grateful village awarded him honours such as statues of him in the hall and gymnasium. The statues would be crowned on days when ceremonies were held. They are likely to have been in the increasingly individualized style characteristic of late Ptolemaic elite sculpture (plate 20).[14]

Paris was made priest for life and after his death an annual ceremony would be carried out at his tomb. The Greek inscription which records the arrangements is unique for a village in Ptolemaic Egypt. The worthies of Psenamosis were probably also competing with other villages in the region, where similar projects had been initiated, and emulating other examples in the major cities. The physical proximity of Psenamosis to Alexandria obviously helps explain the need felt to honour the Ptolemaic royal line this way, even at such a late date. It illustrates the formality that a modest settlement could adopt when making such gestures.[15]

Roman dominance was vested in conquest and territorial acquisition to provide ever more tribute, wealth, and opportunity, just as under the Hellenistic kingdoms. In 65 BC Marcus Licinius Crassus, then censor in Rome, 'embarked upon the dangerous and violent policy of making Egypt tributary to Rome'. He was opposed by his colleague in the office, leading them both to resign.[16] It was not the first time the issue had been raised by Crassus, according to Cicero.[17]

Ptolemy XII had his eye on the most important men in Rome. The dynamic Pompey was fresh from his success against the Cilician pirates and his victory in the Third Mithridatic War in 63 BC, as well as the defeat of Tigranes the Great of Armenia in 64 BC (who in 83 BC had effectively destroyed what was left of the Seleucid kingdom) and the annexation of Syria as a Roman province. Now Pompey received an invitation from the Egyptian king 'to suppress a sedition', but it might also have been worked up as an enticement. The sort of risings some of Ptolemy's predecessors had faced had not gone away. Pompey declined, despite the offer of gifts (which included a heavy gold crown) and money and clothing for his troops, wary of the envy he might provoke from his enemies.[18] Pompey would have been able to take Egypt for himself if he had entered with his forces but he knew that would be at the price of his political destruction at Rome.[19] More to the point, Ptolemy XII was burning cash with his expensive gifts, every one of which was paid for off the backs of Egyptian farmers.

DIODORUS AND THE CAT

The cult of the cat deity Bastet (or Bubastis) was centred on Bubastis in the Delta.[20] In about 60–59 BC, the historian Diodorus was in Egypt. He was astonished by an incident, which he witnessed, involving the accidental killing of a cat by a visiting Roman. Local people who were trying to please the Romans erupted into rage. The tension resulted from the wariness the Egyptians felt for the Romans, a general resentment of autocratic foreigners, the conflict between different religious traditions, and the affiliation local communities felt for their favoured deities. Diodorus' story is best told by himself:

> So deeply implanted also in the hearts of the common people
> is their superstitious regard for these animals [cats] and so
> unalterable are the emotions cherished by every man regarding

the honour due to them that once, at the time when Ptolemy [XII] their king had not as yet been given by the Romans the appellation of 'friend' and the people were exercising all zeal in courting the favour of the embassy from Italy which was then visiting Egypt and, in their fear, were intent upon giving no cause for complaint or war, when one of the Romans killed a cat and the multitude rushed in a crowd to his house, neither the officials sent by the king to beg the man off nor the fear of Rome which all the people felt were enough to save the man from punishment, even though his act had been an accident. And this incident we relate, not from hearsay, but we saw it with our own eyes on the occasion of the visit we made to Egypt.[21]

Some modern historians have described Diodorus as saying that the offending Roman had been killed by lynching. The passage does not, strictly speaking, say that, though it is possible.[22]

CAESAR

Ptolemy XII was pressured into transferring his affections to Julius Caesar, the rising star in Rome. Caesar's ambitions were expensive. He had borrowed extravagantly already and was interested in new sources of cash. He offered to have Ptolemy recognized as the rightful king of Egypt by himself (and Pompey, who apparently knew nothing of this), overturning the claims of Selene's children, in return for a 6,000-talent kickback.[23] Caesar fulfilled the promise 'now at last' (*aliquando*, Cicero) in 59 BC by arranging for a decree of the Senate to that effect. This left Ptolemy in hock to Caesar's protection racket for a ruinous 17.5 million drachmas.[24]

Ptolemy XII was bankrupting Egypt, but at least he had held on to the crown. He could not object when Rome in 58 BC passed a law, taking advantage of Ptolemy X's will, that enabled his younger brother's kingdom of Cyprus to be made a Roman province and any Ptolemaic royal funds there confiscated. The prospect was so enticing that a queue of enthusiastic senators lined up to govern Cyprus, which was given to a reluctant Cato the Younger, a man with a reputation for determination and self-discipline, 'the purest of all the Romans'.[25] Ptolemy, king of Cyprus, refused to concede. He tried to sail off with all the money he had accumulated, intending to sink the fleet and go down with the ships himself rather than hand it all over. Unable to bring himself to send his wealth to the bottom of the sea, he headed back to Cyprus but in 57 BC took his own life by drinking poison, realizing he was powerless.[26]

Meanwhile, Ptolemy XII had fallen out with the Alexandrians. His expensively purchased confirmation as king and 'friend and ally' by Caesar and the Senate turned out to count for nothing in the city he was trying to rule from, especially when he started extorting money to pay back his debts.[27] Ptolemy fled to Rome, very probably with his second daughter Cleopatra in tow, where Cato, whose political career had been built on his disgust at the corruption in Rome, privately told him that even if the whole of Egypt was liquidated into hard cash there would still not be enough to glut the greed and ambition of the 'chief men at Rome' whose dishonesty and rapacity he was exposing himself to. Ptolemy wobbled. Sobered by Cato's sound advice he headed back home, but his friends persuaded him to revert to his original scheme. Once more Ptolemy headed for Rome, where he was greeted by Pompey. Ptolemy's heart sank when he realized he had ignored advice that might as well have been a divine prophecy.[28]

THE BRIEF REIGN OF BERENICE IV (58–55 BC)

Ptolemy XII had made off from Egypt so fast that the Alexandrians had no idea where he was. Some assumed he was dead. Accordingly, they placed his eldest child and daughter Berenice on the throne along with her mother Cleopatra VI Tryphaena who seems to have returned from exile, when two women served as co-regents between 58 and 57 BC.[29] Within a year Tryphaena was dead.[30] Ptolemy's sons, the future

Ptolemies XIII and XIV, were too young to be considered as candidates.[31] Their other sister, Cleopatra VII, was passed over for the moment.

During her short reign the helpful Alexandrians sought out a suitable husband for Berenice. She was concerned about the Romans but made no preparations for any impending campaign. She greeted the suitors like a praying mantis. The first up was Seleucus Cybiosactes ('the Salt-Fishmonger'), a pretender who claimed to be a member of the Seleucid royal line. Berenice accepted him at first but soon discovered the Alexandrians despised him as much as she did, thanks to his 'coarseness and vulgarity'. Her solution came straight from the Ptolemaic handbook of kingship, also deployed later for troublesome consorts in Roman imperial times. She had him strangled. Cybiosactes was replaced by another pretender called Archelaus who posed as a son of Mithridates VI and had been made high priest of the city of Comana in Pontus in 63 BC by Pompey. He was to last a little longer (see below), but not much. How these two men made their way through the vetting procedure to get as far as they did is a mystery.[32]

When the Alexandrians discovered where Ptolemy XII was, they sent a deputation to wise the Romans up about his conduct. Ptolemy got wind of this and planted thugs on the routes into Rome to kill as many of the Alexandrians as possible. Others were bribed to keep their mouths shut, which even turned out to include the leader of the envoys, while Ptolemy enjoyed the protection of Pompey.[33] He was delayed by the 'discovery' (probably faked) of an oracular pronouncement in the sacred Sibylline Books that advised if a king of Egypt came seeking help, he should be offered friendship but not provided with great help or 'else you shall have both toils and dangers'. This led the Senate to vote against Ptolemy, instructing that he be escorted back home to Egypt in case by lingering in Rome he gave Pompey the opportunity to increase his power even more.[34] In 57 BC Ptolemy gave up on Rome and left for Ephesus where he killed time loitering in the great Temple of Artemis for no obvious purpose.[35]

PTOLEMY XII RETURNS

Pompey meanwhile had intervened in the East, which had been his plan all along. In an extraordinary attempt to justify his cause, various papers were 'found' distributed around the forum and the Senate house in which Ptolemy supposedly expressed his earnest wish that Pompey be his commander in Egypt.[36] Pompey proposed that Aulus Gabinius, the new proconsular governor of Syria (from 57 BC), invade Egypt and recover it for Ptolemy XII. Gabinius arrested Archelaus but let him go for two reasons, both to do with greed, making it look as if he had escaped. Firstly, Archelaus had bribed him. Secondly, if Archelaus was under arrest the invasion of Egypt would look like a walkover and Ptolemy might refuse to pay in full for the venture. In the event, Gabinius was able to invade Egypt unopposed, defeat an Egyptian force, and follow that up with two more battles, one on water and one on land.[37]

Gabinius discovered that the Alexandrians were 'completely useless' at war, for all the noise they made and their enthusiasm for causing trouble (see Chapter 7). The city gave in easily. Egypt fell into his hands and was given back to Ptolemy who on arrival executed Berenice IV, his own daughter, though that hardly made him unusual in Ptolemaic history. Archelaus was disposed of, either by execution or in battle by Gabinius. Strabo, confusingly, provides both versions in separate places. Gabinius was prosecuted in Rome for overstepping his remit as governor and was forced into exile. The killings profited Ptolemy XII little, regardless of how they happened. He only recovered his crown because a Roman army had won it back for him but died of disease in 51 BC. He left his two sons and Cleopatra VII, and their younger sister Arsinoe IV, to rule a country that was a rump of its former self.[38]

MORE ROMANS IN EGYPT

Two striking changes appeared during Ptolemy XII's second reign. Rabirius Postumus, a Roman banker of equestrian status, had supported

Gabinius' campaign, even lending money to Ptolemy. His reward was to be made dioiketes, effectively placing him in charge of Ptolemaic royal finances. Rabirius went native, to Cicero's disgust. He was going about in 'an Egyptian robe, and with having had about him other ornaments which are not worn by a Roman citizen . . . he lent money rashly to the king and trusted his fortunes and his character to the royal caprice.' Rabirius had been persuaded to take the post by the wheedling Ptolemy as the one way he might recover the money he had lent the king.[39] Whatever the reason, there was now a well-connected emigrant Roman flunky in King Ptolemy's court.

The other development was the presence of Roman soldiers in Egypt who had once served under Gabinius. In the mid-first century BC there was still no standing Roman army. That came under Augustus, a few decades later. The Roman armies of the late Republic were raised on an as-needed basis from Roman citizens as an obligation of military service to the state, but increasingly included poor men who had no other career prospects and were of various non-Italian origins. Nothing specific is known about the army of Gabinius, except that he led 20,000 soldiers into Egypt, of whom a fair number had stayed there after the war when demobbed.

These Roman ex-military residents of Egypt were joined by 'freebooters and brigands' from Syria, as well as criminals, exiles, and runaway slaves. This relic of a Roman army had become accustomed to the old military tradition of robbing the rich, extorting pay rises from the king, toppling kings who did not comply, and installing new ones. They had also settled on land grants, marrying local women, and raising families.[40]

Ptolemy XII Auletes left his kingdom in his will to his eldest son Ptolemy XIII and his eldest surviving daughter Cleopatra VII. For all the languid weakness of his rule and the increasingly vulnerable and dependent nature of Egypt, Ptolemy XII had reigned for a considerable time. Despite losing his throne temporarily, he had recovered it. More importantly, he had sacrificed his autonomy to leave his throne to his descendants with a Roman guarantee that his wishes would be honoured. This was a significant but doomed accomplishment under the circumstances.[41]

In his poem *Pharsalia*, Lucan has Cleopatra say, 'read my father's last testament, which granted me equal share of power, [and] gave me in marriage to my brother'.[42] The will also instructed that the siblings rule according to the 'custom of the Egyptians'. Cyprus was given to their younger siblings, even though it was by then in Roman hands (it would be down to Caesar in 48 BC to make sure that happened).[43] Cleopatra VII was seventeen years old. Her father recognized her capabilities.

In his will Ptolemy urged the Romans to back his children's accession. He sent a copy to Rome where the political chaos prevented any support being forthcoming. The document had to be given to Pompey for safekeeping.[44] In 53 BC Marcus Licinius Crassus, by then one of the three unofficial triumvirs in Rome, had been killed just after the Battle of Carrhae (now Harran, eastern Turkey) by the Parthians, leaving Caesar and Pompey. Rioting in Rome had delayed the consular elections until mid-summer. Caesar was still campaigning in Gaul. In 52 BC vicious feuding between the senators Clodius Pulcher and Annius Milo had led to their gangs of supporters rampaging and fighting, ending with the murder of Clodius. With Pompey set to take supreme power, in 50 BC Caesar returned and crossed the Rubicon into Italy in early January 49 BC. The Roman civil war between him and Pompey began. Egypt would provide the star member of the cast in the drama that followed.

17

PASSION AND WITCHERY

Cleopatra VII Philopator Thea Neotera (51–30 BC),[1]
Ptolemy XIII (51–47 BC), Arsinoe IV (48–47 BC), Ptolemy
XIV (47–44 BC), and Ptolemy XV (Caesarion) (44–30 BC)

In his Akhenaten, *the writer Dominic Montserrat devoted much of his discussion to the 18th Dynasty heretic king's 'cultural afterlife', like others such as Alexander the Great and, indeed, Cleopatra, and how such figures become both legacies of the past and facts of the present. Each has evolved into a mythologized artefact of the mind, culture, and personal experiences of those who write about them. Cleopatra's reign, although she is venerated for her ingenuity, intellect, and initiative, was of little benefit to Egypt. Her ambitions were determined, but also extravagant and unfulfillable.*

DUX FEMINA FACTI
('THE LEADER OF THE ENTERPRISE, A WOMAN')[2]

These words come from Vergil's *Aeneid*. He was describing the fictitious Phoenician queen of Carthage, Dido, for whom Cleopatra probably served as inspiration. The phrase perfectly sums up Cleopatra, pointedly associating the male noun *dux* with *femina*. Cleopatra's story is about her, far less Egypt, even if the country served as the setting for her drama. Our sources for her life are Roman. Having amply demonstrated her genius and effective talent in life, she received from them posthumously the tribute of moderate praise and severe criticism.

These sources, such as Dio and Plutarch, were mainly concerned with Cleopatra's personality and how she worked the Roman elite in pursuit of her dream of unchallenged rule of a reinvigorated autonomous Ptolemaic Egypt. Of life in Egypt during Cleopatra's reign we know comparatively little apart from disastrously low Nile inundations leading to famine and disease. Her token efforts to ameliorate the distress exhibited her impotence to provide a solution. In dynastic terms, the Ptolemaic story was already over. She held her crown at the pleasure of the Romans. Some books on the period regard Cleopatra as so unimportant to the wider picture of Egypt under the Ptolemies that she can go unmentioned.[3]

A legitimate phenomenon in every way, Cleopatra stands apart from her Ptolemaic forebears while at the same time being a true scion of the dynasty. She followed the Ptolemaic tradition of fearsomely assertive and uncompromising women. She presided over a kingdom that could by then only pretend to independence and self-determination. She sought a future for her rule and dynasty with foreign men to father her children, a dangerous and taboo route normally spurned by Egypt's female pharaohs because of the obvious threat to the country's autonomy.[4] She played Caesar and Antony, for both of whom she was an irresistible torment, for all they were worth and killed anyone who got in her way, even members of her own family. In the annals of human history and power, this should occasion no great surprise, especially when the stakes were so high. Octavian, who would be her nemesis, was no different. After Caesar's assassination she made Mark Antony into her creature and saw him turn to dust in her hands.

The Ptolemaic female rulers who preceded her, even the most violent and arbitrary, are usually perceived as preludes to Cleopatra VII. What we know, or think we know, about Cleopatra symbolizes the problem that plagues all studies of the ancient world. Our sources are patchy, biased, often written much later, and invariably by men. There is no doubt that some of these authors were titillated by the thought of Cleopatra and the impact she had on Caesar and Antony. Roman historians invariably belonged to a tradition in which becoming prey to the effeminating influences of women was the benchmark by which they judged the fall of a man. Cleopatra's effect on Caesar, and especially Antony, was of more interest than her role as a ruler of Egypt. Dio, who referred to her 'passion and witchery', believed that with her attributes she had 'enslaved' Antony.[5]

THE REIGN OF PTOLEMY XIII AND CLEOPATRA VII, 51–47 BC

Cleopatra VII may have been made a co-regent alongside her father in the last few years of his rule because she appears so prominently alongside (but behind) him in the crypts at Dendera.[6] Under the terms of his will she was made co-regent of Egypt in 51 BC with her brother Ptolemy XIII Theos Philopator. She reigned until 30 BC when she died by her own hand, after the defeat at Actium the previous year.

Although Cleopatra VII is usually described as a queen of Egypt today, that is to miss the point. On the rare occasions when a woman ruled Egypt in her own right, she had to adopt at least some of the attributes of a male pharaoh to do so, sometimes explicitly posing as what we would call a king. This was most obviously the case with Hatshepsut (c. 1479–1458 BC), but it also applied to Cleopatra's own dynastic female predecessors. Onnophris, an Egyptian temple official (*lesonis*), understood this. The stela he created in Cleopatra's honour in 51 BC shows her as a pharaoh, offering to Isis, with whom she was identified, in a typical example of Egyptian ambiguity. The text is in Greek, a practice Egyptians usually adopted when making public offerings to their Ptolemaic rulers.[7] Cleopatra also took a pharaonic Horus name that appears in two forms: 'Great Lady of perfection, excellent in counsel' (Weretnebetneferuakhetseh), and 'the Great One and the image of her father', the second effectively a synonym for her personal name.[8]

Like Hatshepsut and Tawosret in Egypt's remoter history, who ruled and died with no direct heirs, Cleopatra had no young son when she took the throne.[9] Although she was married to two of her brothers, unlike some of her Ptolemaic predecessors she did not have children by either (both were dead by their mid-teenage years anyway). Instead, Cleopatra produced sons later in her reign, the first of whom was Julius Caesar's son Caesarion. She did not abdicate in Caesarion's favour, or that of the boys she bore Mark Antony subsequently, even though she raised Caesarion to nominally equivalent status to her. She escaped the native posthumous vilification suffered by earlier Egyptian female kings, because there were no later Egyptian rulers to organize such a campaign. Instead, the Romans produced a torrent of bile about her.

Cleopatra VII's appeal lay not in her looks, which were not considered memorable, but in her charm and physical presence. She had remarkable intelligence and ability, a consistent theme in the Roman sources. She was said to be able to speak so many languages that she scarcely ever needed an interpreter and was able to use both charm and persuasiveness in speech. Cleopatra is often said to have been the only member of the Ptolemaic dynasty to learn Egyptian. This comes from Plutarch, but his observation is more oblique than is usually suggested. He lists several peoples she could speak to freely, among them Ethiopians, Arabs, Syrians, and Medes. He goes on to say that this was unlike the 'kings of Egypt before her' who 'had not even made an effort to learn the native language'. From this we can infer that she also knew Egyptian, but it falls short of a direct claim, and we have no means of assessing her competence in the tongue (or any of the other languages). Mithridates VI allegedly learned the languages of the twenty-two nations he controlled to save himself needing an interpreter but for some reason this is never heralded today as a remarkable achievement in the way Cleopatra's linguistic skills are.[10]

If Cleopatra did know Egyptian the obvious, but unanswerable, question is who did she learn it from? The speculative, but wholly unsubstantiated, possibilities include the anonymous mistress candidate for her mother (instead of Cleopatra VI Tryphaena) who has been claimed by some to have been at least part-Egyptian, but her identity and origins are unknown.[11]

Such descriptions as Plutarch's are vested as much in tradition as in truth, and the need to rationalize Cleopatra's life and behaviour. None of those who made such claims had known or even seen her. Nor did they know anyone who had, or anyone with whom to compare her. They were dependent on other sources which they do not identify, and which they had used selectively. This of course is true of most ancient authors but, with such a vivid and powerful personality as Cleopatra VII, unravelling the reality from the construct is virtually impossible and even more tantalizing.

Understanding the Roman historians means considering how much Cleopatra served as a historical explanation for Antony. Unable to live without the hope of her, how Antony fell under her sway was the story they were interested in. The Cleopatra of the Roman histories is in part a creation necessary for that narrative. None of this means that what we know, or think we know, about Cleopatra is wrong. But it means that dismantling Cleopatra in the record is a precarious path and full of mirrors on which modern writers and historians unknowingly project themselves as much as they seek to find her, and just as ancient historians did.

CLEOPATRA'S MAJESTY

Soon after coming to power, Cleopatra pushed her brother Ptolemy XIII out, at least temporarily. A short receipt from the Fayum refers to her as the 'queen Cleopatra, goddess Philopator'.[12] Her brother is unmentioned. By 27 October 50 BC a royal edict, on a papyrus from the Heracleopolite nome, starts with 'king and queen in command', ordering produce to be taken from Middle Egypt to Alexandria, where it seems food riots had threatened to break out. The donation to the Apis funerary rites at Memphis in 50/49 BC were in both their names.[13] Perhaps this means he had resumed his position, but Ptolemy XIII was, after all, just thirteen or so years old and his inclusion just a formality. Within a short time, he (or rather his court faction) was at war with his sister.

Ptolemy XIII's affairs were managed by a court eunuch called Potheinus, a rhetoric teacher called Theodotus of Chios, and his commander of the royal troops, an Egyptian called Achillas, 'the chief counsellors of the king among the chamberlains and tutors'.[14] They all resented the idea of being ruled by a woman, but that is according to a Roman historian.[15]

Pompey's defeat by Caesar at Pharsalus in Greece in 48 BC was a turning point in Cleopatra's fate. Pompey fled in an Egyptian rescue fleet, hoping that Ptolemy XIII would also provide him with military backing in return for his earlier support of Ptolemy XII.[16] This created a crisis for Potheinus, Theodotus, and Achillas who believed that welcoming Pompey would automatically make an enemy of Caesar, whereas killing Pompey would make Caesar a friend. They arranged for a treacherous former tribune of Pompey's called Septimius to trick Pompey as he came to shore and kill him.[17] Pompey's fate was a source of fascination to Dio. Here was one of the mightiest of Romans who had 'subdued the entire sea' but 'perished on it' and been killed 'like one of the lowest of the Egyptians'. His final comment positioned ordinary Egyptians in the Roman mindset with callous succinctness.[18]

When the news reached Caesar, he furiously set off with a small squadron ahead of his fleet and made for Alexandria where he arrived with one legion (reinforced later).[19] The Alexandrians were in uproar, believing Pompey had been betrayed to appease Caesar. Caesar waited on his ship until Ptolemy, who had come from Pelusium, sent him Pompey's head and seal ring. Appalled and distressed – an irony not lost on observers, given how Caesar had done everything possible to destroy his greatest rival – Caesar bitterly criticized Pompey's killers instead of being grateful, as they had hoped.[20]

CAESAR IN ALEXANDRIA

With vast financial obligations to his troops and political ambitions, Caesar set about extorting money from the Alexandrians and especially their temples. Caesar started arbitrating between the warring Cleopatra and Ptolemy XIII, but his preference for Cleopatra's cause agitated the people of Alexandria who worried that Caesar would hand over Egypt to her sole rule. That led to riots. Sensing her advantage, Cleopatra arranged a meeting in person. According to Dio, she was 'brilliant to look upon and to listen to, with the power to subjugate everyone'. Whatever the truth, the secret encounter at night had the desired effect. Caesar immediately called for Ptolemy and 'tried to reconcile' the pair, promoting Cleopatra's interests for his own purposes. Ptolemy was enraged and Caesar's troops had to restrain him. The Alexandrian mob stormed the palace and Caesar, who had insufficient troops, had to calm them down in person.[21]

Caesar then read out Ptolemy XII's will which stated that his children Ptolemy XIII and Cleopatra should rule jointly, and that the Roman people should be their guardians. Caesar said that as a dictator of Rome it was beholden on him to honour the will and protect the children's interests. However, he was concerned not to appear to be taking control of Egypt himself. He granted Cyprus to the younger Ptolemy and Arsinoe, even though it was a Roman province.[22]

The Potheinus faction suspected that Caesar was buying time until he could give Egypt to Cleopatra, a prospect that appalled them. They decided to set out for Alexandria. Caesar urged Achillas, Ptolemy's troop commander, to calm matters down. Instead, Achillas whipped up his troops into a fury. Caesar had to send for more of his own men from Syria and meanwhile fortified the royal palace. Achillas turned up with his men, many of whom had once fought for Gabinius, and seized most of Alexandria. The city started to go up in flames. One of the losses was possibly part of the library.[23]

Arsinoe was now made queen (Arsinoe IV, 48–47 BC) as a rival to Cleopatra at the behest of a court eunuch called Ganymede. Fearing that Potheinus would capture Ptolemy, Caesar had Potheinus killed and strengthened Ptolemy's guard. Theodotus escaped to Asia.[24] A naval battle between Ganymede's forces and Caesar's broke out, Caesar narrowly escaping with his life. A force put together by Mithridates of Pergamum, a general of Caesar's, and the Syrian legions arrived in the nick of time and the Egyptian forces were defeated. They handed over Arsinoe IV in return for Ptolemy so that peace terms could be negotiated. Caesar, believing the boy was no threat, gave them Ptolemy in the

hope the Egyptians would accept his terms. He was wrong. They immediately resumed the war but were defeated in a surprise attack. During
their flight Ptolemy XIII was killed.[25]

THE REIGN OF CLEOPATRA VII AND
PTOLEMY XIV, 47–44 BC

After nine months of strife, Caesar confirmed Cleopatra, with whom he
was now cohabiting, as ruler of Egypt and had her marry her younger
brother, Ptolemy XIV Theos Philopator.[26] This nominally restored
sibling joint rule. Both she and Caesar knew her brother was only a sop
to tradition. In her 6th regnal year (45 BC) she appears as sole ruler on a
private funerary stela.[27] More significantly, before long Cleopatra was
pregnant by Caesar. He took a voyage up the Nile with Cleopatra ('and
enjoyed himself with her') in a flotilla of 400 vessels and, allegedly, would
have continued all the way to 'Ethiopia' had his soldiers not refused to
carry on.[28] Caesar might have lingered but was soon forced to leave the
country and deal with mounting problems elsewhere.[29] Cleopatra gave
birth shortly after he left.[30] The child was named Ptolemy and Caesar,
colloquially Caesarion. He was said to resemble his father.[31] Cicero
referred to 'the queen and that Caesar(ion) [of hers]'.[32] Today Caesarion
is counted as Ptolemy XV, the last of the line.

There was never any doubt that Caesarion was Caesar's son. He
appeared and was named as such on monuments (for example at
Dendera, see below) and in private material. In one, a funerary memorial of a Memphis priest called Psen-Ptah, Cleopatra is called 'ruler' by
virtue of the hieroglyph for a crook (ḥqa) and 'Lady of the Two Lands',
as in 45 BC (see above), but here with the addition of 'and her son Kysrs
[Kaisaros]'. His name is also in a cartouche, clearly marking out his
royal status as heir and her co-ruler, but her name comes first.[33]

Few may have been able to read these hieroglyphic texts, but
Caesarion's parentage was evidently common knowledge in Egypt.
Conversely, Cleopatra's affair with Caesar was of comparatively little
importance to him, though he knew she made the Roman people

uneasy. In Rome Caesar was therefore evasive, one of his friends even pointlessly issuing a denial that Caesar was the father which only drew attention to the boy.[34] Caesarion was a time bomb for Caesar. His wife Calpurnia had borne him no children. Caesarion's existence proved it was more likely to be her who was infertile. Since Caesar had no other blood son, Caesarion was a threat to any other potential heir, especially an adopted one, as long as he lived.

Caesar took no chances. He left three legions behind in Alexandria to prop up Cleopatra and Ptolemy XIV. As Caesar's friends their popularity was seriously compromised. The Ptolemaic dynasty had never been so vulnerable. Now it needed Roman soldiers to stay in power.[35] Egypt was, if it had not been already, a *de facto* client kingdom under the protection of the Roman Empire.[36] By 44 BC four Roman legions were stationed there.[37] Caesar had to head north and tackle a rising led by Pharnaces II of Pontus, the youngest son of Mithridates VI. Caesar returned to Italy to deal with affairs there before sailing to North Africa to confront Pompey's supporters, defeating them at Thapsus in 46 BC.

Caesar's Egyptian triumph was one of a series held in Rome that same year to commemorate his successes. Arsinoe IV in chains was among the captives since she had nominally led the Egyptian army against him. The crowd was appalled by the spectacle of a queen reduced to such ignominy, even though she escaped execution.[38] Arsinoe eventually sought sanctuary at the Temple of Artemis in Ephesus. She was subsequently killed there by Mark Antony's men on Cleopatra's instructions. An extant octagonal tomb at the city has been claimed to be hers, based on the recovery of the skeleton of a girl in her late teens in an elaborate marble sarcophagus but, with no substantiating inscription, the theory has not been widely accepted.[39]

The conditions under which Cleopatra ruled Egypt might have suited her but whether they suited Egypt or the Egyptians was another matter altogether. Egypt's continued notional independence depended on whoever was in control at Rome. Caesar was not the first to recognize that any Roman taking over Egypt risked arousing fury among his enemies because it would give that person unmatched power and resources. Caesar was already lurching towards a level of monarchical power that no-one in Rome since 509 BC had enjoyed. In early 44 BC accepting the status of *dictator perpetuus* (dictator for life) would lead to Caesar's assassination. For the moment he held back. For all her skill and guile, Cleopatra had done nothing to assert her independence though ironically the fact that she had become embroiled in a personal and sexual relationship with Caesar indirectly saved Egypt for the moment from becoming a Roman province.

By the summer of 46 BC Cleopatra arrived in Rome with her brother-husband. They openly took up residence in one of Caesar's houses in the city. She wanted Caesarion confirmed as Caesar's heir. Cicero was disgusted. 'I hate the queen', he told his friend Atticus.[40] He was not the only one. Caesar's reputation plummeted, especially when he flagrantly presented Cleopatra and her brother with the honorific and formal status of 'friends and allies'.[41] In Roman culture, falling prey to a woman and being seen to do so was political and public suicide though the woman would be held largely responsible. Caesar did not care or professed not to, but he did not live long enough to face the consequences. Caesar was regarded by his enemies as a tyrant. Cleopatra's presence and visible hold over him only exacerbated the unedifying impression that he was at her feet.[42]

Accepting the position of dictator for life was the last straw for Caesar's enemies. By the time he was assassinated on 15 March 44 BC, accused of tyranny, he had not recognized Caesarion as his heir. That privilege went to his great-nephew and legal heir Gaius Octavius (more commonly known today as Octavian), son of his niece Atia, his sister's daughter. Under the terms of Caesar's will, Octavian became Gaius Julius Caesar and Caesar's adopted son. Caesarion was a conspicuous threat to Octavian who formed an alliance, the triumvirate, with Mark Antony and Lepidus and claimed to be acting under the legitimate authority of the Republic of Rome. They set out to annihilate the tyrannicides Brutus and Cassius and their supporters. Antony was a distant cousin of Caesar's, had fought with him in Gaul, and had become his political supporter in Rome.

Caesar's death was, on the face of it, a catastrophe for Cleopatra. She might understandably have given up her cause as lost. Instead, she headed home, her gloves off and bent on seizing other opportunities. It was her 8th regnal year and Ptolemy XIV's 4th and last. He was killed on her orders soon after their return.[43] Now she ruled effectively alone, following the dynastic precedents set by Berenice III and Berenice IV though her brother was replaced by Caesarion as Ptolemy XV for show (plate 21).[44] She also pursued her ambitions in a way that did not diverge from Ptolemaic tradition.[45]

The queen was only interested in having the rule of Egypt vested in herself, and at any price, though she went to great pains to integrate herself and Caesarion with traditional cults. She built a new temple, now destroyed, at Hermonthis, to showcase the pair in appropriate scenes. At the Temple of Hathor in Dendera, still under construction, Cleopatra and Caesarion were depicted on the external relief on the south wall, the boy shown as an adult king. He was additionally named as 'Caesar, living forever, beloved of Ptah and Isis' (in Egyptian, *kysrs* *'nḥ-ḏt mry-ptḥ-3st*). It is interesting, though, that one of the variants of the Horus names attributed to him appears behind him and directly below the cartouche bearing her name and reads 'The strong bull, shining like the beams of Ra and Iah' (plate 23). If so, then Cleopatra's own Horus name is absent. Despite concessions to the traditional format of a queen standing behind the king, this was only a nominal co-regency. Cleopatra 'held the power in her hands'.[46] The scene also illustrated Cleopatra's loyalty, at least for the moment, to the triumvirs' Caesarian cause.

EGYPT IN THE 40S BC

The annual inundation of the Nile always fluctuated, since it depended on the rise of the Blue Nile, itself determined by rains in Ethiopia. Anything between 21.3 and 23.3 feet (6.5–7 m) was regarded as good.

Anything below 17.5 feet (5.3 m) threatened famine. In 48 BC the flood was a catastrophic 7.3 feet (2.3 m).[47] Seneca recorded that in Cleopatra's 10th and 11th regnal years (43–42 BC) there was no inundation at all, and that this was seen as an omen of the fall of Egypt's two rulers.[48]

The consequences were famine and disease in Egypt during much of the 40s BC.[49] Royal stocks of grain were made available but not to the Jews in Alexandria, though no reason is stated.[50] The primary motive was probably to offset the chances of dangerous rioting. The second may have been that the Jews were not citizens, and that the stocks were insufficient to supply them too. Alexandria was the priority. The rest of Egypt could be left to its own devices, at least for the moment.

CLEOPATRA AND ANTONY

Cornelius Dolabella, one of Caesar's supporters (who briefly backed Caesar's assassins until Antony offered him a military command), had guaranteed Ptolemy XV's status as king. Cleopatra sent him the four legions in Egypt. En route through Palestine, the tyrannicide Cassius surrounded and took them over, ending up with twelve legions under his command.[51] That advantage was soon lost. After the Battle of Philippi in 42 BC that left Brutus and Cassius dead, the Roman world and the fate of Egypt were in the hands of the triumvirs.

By late 41 BC Antony controlled the eastern Roman Empire. He set himself up in Tarsus (now in south-central Turkey, approximately 100 miles or 160 km north-east of Cyprus). Antony summoned Cleopatra there to account for the allegations that she had helped Cassius. 'She was going to visit Antony at the very time when women have the most brilliant beauty and are at the acme of intellectual power', said Plutarch, pruriently setting the scene for Antony's fall.[52]

In 41 BC Antony was at the top of his game but was still married to his forceful wife Fulvia. They acted as if they were both consuls of Rome, an extraordinary position for a Roman woman.[53] Coins were even struck at Rome with her portrait.[54] Fulvia's powerful personality and influence over Antony were later blamed for softening him up so much that he was easy prey for Cleopatra. Distressed by Antony's affair with Cleopatra, Fulvia intervened by going to war against Octavian with the help of Antony's younger brother Lucius to divert Antony's attention from the east and Cleopatra. Octavian defeated Lucius at Perusia in early 40 BC. Fulvia fled to Greece where she died soon afterwards, dispirited by Antony's anger.

Next, the triumvirs carved up the Roman world at Brundisium (Brindisi) in Italy in the autumn of 40 BC, confirming Octavian's control of the West, Antony's of the East, and giving their makeweight colleague Lepidus provinces in north Africa. Part of the deal was to marry the newly widowed Antony to Octavian's sister Octavia. This key alliance was supposed to preserve the triumvirate's integrity, even though Antony's affair with Cleopatra was well under way.[55] In late December 40 BC she gave birth to Antony's twins, Alexander Helios and Cleopatra Selene II. With Octavian's sister humiliated, the scene was set for one of the most celebrated feuds of all time. In 39–38 BC Antony was still striking coins with his portrait and Octavia's at Athens and Ephesus.[56]

By 37 BC Octavia, mother of several of Antony's earlier children, had travelled out to Greece. She brokered a conciliatory military deal between Octavian and Antony and was sent back to Italy. It had been hoped that Antony was 'over' Cleopatra, but he went back to her as soon as he returned to the East.[57] Soon afterwards, Antony bigamously married Cleopatra (two such rites were only wrong in Roman law).[58] They believed they would be empowered and magnified by the union. Instead, they subtracted from one another, and before long each discovered what it was like to be alone.

In 36 BC Antony's campaign in Parthia ended in defeat but he regrouped. That same year a total eclipse of the sun passed across Middle Egypt on 19 May. It is unlikely to have been seen as a positive omen.[59] Cleopatra bore Antony another son, Ptolemy Philadelphus, his third child by her.

On tetradrachms and other coins issued between 37 and 33 BC, including a double-headed one with Antony issued from an uncertain

Syrian (?) mint, Cleopatra was called 'Thea Neotera' ('the young Cleopatra Thea'). This title is only known for Cleopatra on those coins, none from Alexandria, and was never used by any of her predecessors.[60] She was claiming power over Syria, emulating Ptolemy VI's daughter and her great-great-aunt, Cleopatra Thea, queen of Antiochus VII and mother of Antiochus VIII and Seleucus V. She would thus be ruler of Egypt and of Syria.

Antony and Cleopatra posed as joint Hellenistic monarchs. Antony had suffused himself in Cleopatra's world. He might have had his will, but she would have her way with him. He rearranged Rome's eastern provinces so that he had effectively created a new Ptolemaic Empire for her. In 34 BC in Alexandria, Antony 'declared Cleopatra Queen of Egypt, Cyprus, Libya, and Coele-Syria, and she was to share her throne with Caesarion . . . he proclaimed his own sons by Cleopatra Kings of Kings' (Alexander Helios and Ptolemy Philadelphus). Various provincial territories were divided up among the boys. 'Cleopatra, indeed, both then and at other times when she appeared in public, assumed a robe sacred to Isis, and was addressed as the New Isis.' By 'New Isis' a Hellenistic manifestation was meant. Cleopatra would be both a divine Egyptian queen and Hellenistic monarch as the means of leading Ptolemaic pharaonic rule into a new age.[61] This was her solution to the next stage of modernizing and adapting Egypt, absorbing rather than being absorbed by Rome. It was already too late.

Cleopatra's complex image of power was a mirage. In 33 BC an order was issued in her name that provided Antony's general Publius Canidius with a tax-free allowance of wheat exports and wine imports and to be exempt from any laws concerning land he held, all protected by the crown.[62] There were certain niceties to be observed in her relationship with her Roman friends, which meant selling Egypt even further down the river in the interests of clinging on to power.[63]

The original papyrus order, which has survived, was intended to be a manifestation of Cleopatra's ability to bestow such largesse. The word γινέσθωι (*ginesthōi*), written at the end of the order in a different hand, is believed by some to be hers, on the basis that no-one else could have had the authority to issue the command. This is an enticing possibility and has been translated as 'make this happen' but a more literal reading is '[these matters are] to come into being'. The distinction is important. The word is more a statement of intent and, without any parallels or knowledge of the normal procedures, it is impossible to say who added it. Whether that last instruction is in her hand or not, the order's purpose was to convey the impression that Canidius' privileges and their fulfilment remained in Cleopatra's gift. If she really believed she was still in charge, she was fooling herself. But perhaps the gesture pleased her for the moment. After all, the worst was yet to come.

CLEOPATRA'S COINS

Cleopatra's coinage in Egypt was not extensive but because some coins bear her portrait, they have always attracted interest. The silver tetradrachms continued to feature Ptolemy I's image, but the single silver drachm pieces carried hers and her name, as did several bronze types. The profile on these silver and bronze pieces resembles Ptolemy I's, the only difference being the hair. Although obviously Cleopatra's, they also belonged to the generic tradition of Ptolemaic coins but with a gender modification. Cleopatra made similar appearances on coins struck in Askalon, Cyprus (one showing her with Ptolemy XV Caesarion as a baby), Damascus, and Tripolis. It is only the silver tetradrachms struck for her and Antony at Antioch around 36–34 BC that bear a more realistic image. Cleopatra wears a diadem, earrings, necklace, and embroidered dress. Even so, her profile, especially the nose, bears a striking similarity to Antony's, suggesting that her face is more symbolic than realistic.[64] Regardless, the portrait does nothing to recreate the effect she is said to have had in person.

NOW, MARK ME HOW I WILL UNDO MYSELF[65]

In 32 BC Octavian and Antony's relationship reached its nadir with their factions feuding in the Senate. Some of Antony's supporters changed sides and gave Octavian the priceless intelligence that under Antony's will the whole Roman world was left to his children by Cleopatra. Octavian broke the law to read the will, but outrage at the news meant no-one in Rome was concerned with such technicalities. That was the end for Antony. Disappointment and opposition had inflamed his mind and attached him still more to his mistakes.[66]

Antony was remembered by the Romans as an enervated, effeminate, and degraded man who had fallen prey to a hated oriental female ruler and turned to dust in her hands. He was 'under her tutelage', she acting as his constant companion as they played dice, drank, and hunted together, and his admiring audience while he practised with his arms. So said Plutarch, who was plainly inspired by how Vergil depicted Aeneas falling under Dido's spell until Mercury came to him in a vision to pull him to his senses.[67]

No Mercury came for Antony. Believing that he had found his destiny in Cleopatra, he had only immersed himself in the reflex of his own inclinations and impulses. The Senate declared war on Cleopatra, not Antony, and thereby evaded the unacceptable indignity of one of their own being an enemy of the Roman Republic. The war that followed reached its climax but not its end at the naval Battle of Actium off the west coast of Greece on 2 September 31 BC (plate 22). Octavian and Agrippa's victory was no foregone conclusion. Dio called the fighting 'inconclusive', blaming Cleopatra for losing her nerve and ordering a retreat, leaving Antony and his men confused because they thought the Egyptians had fled of their own accord. Nonetheless, Antony put up sustained resistance and was only forced to back down when the Roman fleet set Antony's ships ablaze.[68]

Whatever happened and however lucky Octavian and Agrippa had been, Cleopatra fled back to Egypt. Many had died so far during her bid to cling on to power and more were to follow, but the blessing for Cleopatra was that she cared for none of them. Her only real interest was in survival, not a sustainable future. 'She slew many of the foremost men, inasmuch as they had always been displeased with her and were now elated over her disaster; and she proceeded to gather vast wealth from their estates and from various other sources both profane and sacred, sparing not even the most holy places, and also to fit out her forces and to look about for allies', said Dio.[69] The ambiguous euphemism he used for the holy places was ἀβάτων which has the sense of places 'not to be trodden' or besmirched by entering rather than a class of structure. While this may mean temples it could also mean tombs.

Antony and Cleopatra's erstwhile allies disappeared one by one. In the summer of 30 BC Octavian invaded Egypt and besieged Antony's forces which had fallen back on Alexandria. The bitter fighting and name-calling dragged on for the whole of July. Cleopatra abandoned Pelusium to Octavian and prevented the Alexandrian forces from fighting back at one point because she allegedly believed she could beguile Octavian as she had Caesar.[70] A few days into August, Octavian launched a decisive assault. Antony's forces started to desert and change sides, some allegedly egged on by Cleopatra.[71] The city fell. Antony committed suicide, fooled by Cleopatra into believing she had already taken her own life, and then realizing he had been betrayed. Before he expired, having learned she was still alive, he was carried to her tomb where she had taken refuge. He died there.[72] With Antony out of the way, the ever-optimistic Cleopatra tried and failed to play Octavian in a famous meeting.

This at least was how the Roman historians presented Cleopatra in those last days as continually manipulative, treacherous, and scheming. That way the hapless Antony could be seen as her victim and the higher-calibre Octavian above such temptations. Whatever the truth of those fast-moving events, the Battle of Alexandria had been Cleopatra's last gamble in the struggle to cling on to the Ptolemaic throne. She killed herself when she realized Octavian planned to display her as a trophy in his triumph in Rome.[73] Octavian sent his agents to murder the fleeing Caesarion, then aged seventeen. This shameful murder of a guiltless king was another instance of Octavian's precision ruthlessness that placed him on a par with several of the Ptolemies, Cleopatras, and Berenices, except that he was a more accomplished practitioner.[74] The last of the Ptolemaic kings left no legacy. Virtually nothing is known about Caesarion except that he was used as a pawn by his mother (plates 21, 23).[75]

Octavian, who could not help admiring Cleopatra, ordered the tomb completed and that she be buried with full honours alongside Antony.[76] Antony and Cleopatra's children were taken into his sister Octavia's household and disappeared from history, apart from their daughter Cleopatra Selene who became the queen of Juba II of Mauretania. Selene and Juba II's son, Ptolemy of Mauretania, died at Caligula's hands in Rome in AD 40.[77]

Cleopatra remained a notorious figure in Roman culture. The poet Horace called her a 'mad queen' attended by 'polluted followers'. He could not bring himself to name her.[78] Much later, Propertius called her 'the whore queen'.[79] She became the butt of anecdotes, whether real or invented, that associated her with decadence and profligacy. She once poured satiric scorn on a banquet of Antony's, mocking his poor show of splendour. Antony asked her how it could possibly be more magnificent. Cleopatra replied that she could spend 10 million Roman sesterces on such an occasion, proving her point by laying on a lavish, but routine, spread. Antony laughed, but next she dissolved one of her fabulously valuable pearl earrings in a bowl of vinegar and drank it.[80] Or so the story went. Yet her golden statue that stood beside that of Venus in the Forum of Caesar in Rome was still there in Appian's time under Hadrian and doubtless longer.[81] It is of course long lost, like Cleopatra's dreams.

What mattered to Egypt was that the Ptolemaic royal line had ended. Egypt was too valuable to be allowed to remain volatile and independent. It became part of Octavian's personal estate. Cleopatra's vision of a revived Ptolemaic Egypt under her rule was gone with the wind.

18

THE END OF EGYPT'S GILDED AGE

Such are the changes which a few years bring about, and so do things pass away, like a tale that is told.

Dickens, *The Old Curiosity Shop*[1]

Modern popular ancient history is obsessed with the Romans. This easily pushes the Hellenistic kingdoms into the background, yet it was the acquisition of these realms (or what was left of them) that played so huge a part in the expansion of Roman power. Although certain personalities, Alexander and Cleopatra VII being the most obvious, have maintained a high profile it is almost as if they occupied a parallel universe; until, of course, Caesar encountered Cleopatra.

One by one, those kingdoms were shrunk to provinces of the Romans who increasingly intervened in the endless wars and treachery that defined the Hellenistic monarchies. Given their perennial territorial squabbles, extravagant posturing, fragile alliances, and fighting it is easy to see why this happened.[2] 'Two or three nations rarely come together to repel a common threat. They fight individually and thus all are conquered', said Tacitus about the tribes in Britain but he could not have summed up the fate of the Hellenistic kingdoms more aptly.[3] Likewise, it is easy to understand why their populations for the most part accepted Roman rule rather than suffer any more instability and feuding. The Ptolemaic kingdom of Egypt is an essential part of understanding the Roman story while at the same time being a remarkable tale of its own. Its survival as the last Hellenistic kingdom was partly a function of its unique nature and its integrity as a state. It was also because, in Ptolemaic Egypt's later years, Rome's forbearance with a nation that had ceased to be any threat lasted longer than it had with the other Hellenistic states like the Seleucid kingdom and Macedonia.[4]

The decisive event in the creation of Egypt's Ptolemaic Gilded Age was Alexander's death. Cleopatra VII's suicide 293 years later marked the end of Egypt as an independent nation. Nonetheless, Lucan's 'shameful dynasty' had held on to power for almost three centuries, outlived the other Successor kingdoms, created a sophisticated state, and embarked on a remarkable revival of Egyptian traditions and architecture which we at least have much to be grateful for.

By 30 BC Rome had no meaningful challenge to its power. Egypt was a spoil of war. Ironically, just as the Ptolemaic ruling dynasty ceased to be, Rome came under the control of what amounted to a hereditary and despotic monarchy under Augustus, though he did everything to pretend that he had restored the Republic, which went on to exhibit much of what had befallen the Ptolemies.

Once gathered up under the umbrella of Roman power, the former Hellenistic kingdoms left a greater legacy than their rulers might once have imagined. They formed the basis of the Greek culture of the eastern Roman Empire which mutated into the Byzantine Empire, gradually shrinking to a rump until Constantinople fell to the Ottoman Turks in 1453. Meanwhile, Egypt had been lost to the Muslim Arabs in 642.

Egypt was unique in the Roman experience of empire building. Its antiquity, traditions, and structural integrity were unmatched by any other Roman province. So was its geography.[5] After Actium the Ptolemies, Arsinoes, Berenices, and Cleopatras endured as historical curiosities, the source of scandalous anecdotes, excess, and other yarns. Their monuments remained. A wealthy Alexandrian and friend of

Cleopatra's called Archibius paid Octavian 2,000 talents in return for leaving her statues in the city undamaged. Antony's were trashed, but the base of at least one has survived.[6]

Alexandria remained the effective capital of the eastern Mediterranean, even if it had lost primacy to Rome. It had played the pivotal part in the showdown between Octavian and Antony. There were other major roles for Alexandria yet to play in Roman history, such as during the Roman civil war of AD 68–69 when for a time it was Vespasian's base. Its volatile population continued to be easily roused.[7]

The Ptolemaic army was replaced by a Roman garrison. The great Temple of Luxor, with its shrine of Alexander, was eventually incorporated within a late Roman fort. Roman centurions served as local police officers. Veterans settled in village communities, and often included native Egyptians who had enlisted in Roman fleets in Italy. Most, as was common in the Roman army, were functionally literate. They brought money, found wives among local women or slaves, and became farmers or traders in honourable retirement. Egyptians, however, remained marginalized from Roman society. It was not until the reign of Septimius Severus (AD 193–211) that an Egyptian was admitted to the Roman Senate, though that was better than Britain.[8] The celebrated fertility of the Nile Valley was harnessed for the benefit of the Romans and especially those entitled to the grain dole. Grain transports embarked from Alexandria to make their way to the ports at Puteoli and Ostia, joining fleets from Sicily and other Roman breadbaskets along the way.

The Romans were adept at incorporating local social structures and government systems into the administration of new provinces. In Ptolemaic Egypt they acquired a functioning bureaucracy and infrastructure. The ordinary Egyptian could have been forgiven for not noticing much, if any, change except that Roman emperors did not rule from Egypt.[9] In any case, the process of change was gradual and not immediate, and while some benefited, others did not.[10] Augustus installed an equestrian prefect, rather than a senatorial governor. This device kept Egypt out of the hands of a senator who might act as Antony had. The closed currency system was also maintained. Roman coins struck at Alexandria according to the Ptolemaic system of denominations bore a bust of the reigning emperor, labelled ΚΑΙΣΑΡΟΣ ΑΥΤΟΚΡΑΤΟΡΟΣ ΣΕΒΑΣΤΟΣ for 'Caesar Emperor Augustus', and a far more extensive array of reverse designs. Like the Ptolemies, no attempt was made to depict them as Egyptian pharaohs other than on temple reliefs and in statues.

Ptolemaic pharaohs still conspicuously strode across the great pylon of the Temple of Horus at Edfu to smite Egypt's foes, real and imagined, in a motif later copied for the emperor Titus (AD 79–81) at Esna. Nor was he the only Roman emperor shown this way. The emperors' names were clumsily transliterated into hieroglyphs making them otherwise indistinguishable from the kings of old on reliefs. Beyond the priestly class, hieroglyphs fell into decline. Temple building endured in traditional style, often continuing Ptolemaic projects. Ptolemy VIII was responsible for most of the work at the temple of the hippopotamus goddess Opet at Karnak but most of the external decoration was completed under Augustus. He was shown there as an Egyptian pharaoh but conspicuously labelled in hieroglyphs that transliterate as AWTWKRTR and KYSWRS for *Autokrator Kaisaros*, 'The Emperor Caesar' (plate 24).

Egypt became increasingly Christian from the second century AD on, the worship of Isis and Horus for example being easily adapted into that of Mary and Jesus. The Christian monastic tradition also began in Egypt around the same time. Despite surviving evidence for Christian iconoclasm at Philae and Dendera, by the fifth century AD both had become Christian places of worship involving temporary co-existence with pagan cult activities.

Under the emperors, statues and obelisks were shipped to Rome to serve as trophies in temples and stadiums (plate 24). Two granite statues of Ptolemy II and Arsinoe II from Heliopolis were installed in the Gardens of Sallust in Rome and now reside in the Vatican Museum.[11] A huge basalt sculpture of the Nile with sixteen of his children, to indicate the number of cubits representing the ideal height of the Nile during the inundation (about 28 ft or 8.5 m), was brought to Rome by Vespasian (AD 69–79) and displayed in his Forum of Peace.[12] One of the four Vitruvian classes of domestic *oeci* (usually three-sided chambers used for dining or admiring views) was called Egyptian, and was defined as having an architrave and clerestory windows supported on columns, resembling a basilica.[13] The 'Fourth Style' of painting, best known from Pompeii, was perhaps inspired by descriptions of Ptolemy II's pavilion (see Chapter 4).[14] Many Romans were seduced by the charms of the cult of Isis, and the exotic appeal of Serapis. Roman tourists, including Germanicus and Hadrian, and their entourages, continued to arrive and gawp at the sights.[15] Hadrian famously memorialized his visit with his 'Canopus' pool at his villa in Tivoli, which was supposed to represent the Nile.[16]

Greek and Roman historians regaled their readers with Ptolemaic anecdotes, however scurrilous and usually unsubstantiated. Pliny's observations have popped up several times in this book. Ausonius, a Gallo-Roman poet of the fourth century AD, looked back over six hundred years to remind his readers of the lodestone in the Temple of Arsinoe, Ptolemy II's 'incestuous bride', at Alexandria.[17] Another century later, the Gallo-Roman bishop of Auvergne, Sidonius Apollinaris, described how Cleopatra's fleet had arrived at Actium laden with *Ptolemaide gaza*, 'the treasure of the Ptolemies', which had become a metaphor for excess.[18] Macrobius, writing in the fifth century AD, repeated the story about Cleopatra's pearl earrings.[19]

By 1776–88 Edward Gibbon could look back to 'the ruin of the Ptolemies'.[20] The Napoleonic expedition during the campaign of 1798–1801 produced magnificent drawings of Dendera, Edfu, and other places, inspiring a new era of Nilotica. As more travellers began to explore Egypt, the surviving Ptolemaic temples provoked as much wonder as the ruins of earlier buildings (plate 1).

The Ptolemies and their queens, with a few exceptions, were not celebrated for memorable achievements, but few rulers are. Had they been greater, perhaps circumstance would have been less decisive in their decline. Their early feats of war and government became besmirched with dishonour, despotism, extravagance, and infamy – a fate that has befallen so many other regimes, including that of the Romans. This has always been coloured by a fascination with the Ptolemies' faded glamour and ersatz version of ancient Egypt which echoes down to today. Nonetheless, they clung on to power for a remarkable length of time and in the face of considerable challenges. Their state-building might have been flawed, but it was highly organized and resilient. The Romans, with their indisputable talent for pragmatism, recognized this and, far from destroying Ptolemaic Egypt, preserved and rebranded it in their own image until Egypt fell to the Muslim Arabs in 642.

The Egyptian nationalist *Oracle of the Potter*, composed in the late second century BC, prophesied how the foreigners (the Macedonian Greeks, dismissed as 'belt- or girdle-wearers') would 'fall like leaves from the branch', the statues taken away would come back, Alexandria would become a place to dry fish, the Guardian Spirit would return to Memphis, and a new king would come, under whom the forsaken Nile would be replenished and the trees bear leaves.[21] That messianic king never emerged, but the ruined Ptolemies were gone, and the Romans in turn after them. Today, the old gods still watch over Egypt and the Nile from the temples embellished with their images, and this antique land is once more in charge of its own destiny.

APPENDIX 1

KEY DATES

This is a very select timeline and only intended as a basic guide. Dates in some cases are approximations.

333 BC	Alexander the Great defeats Darius III at Issus
332	Alexander enters and takes Egypt. Site of Alexandria chosen
326	Formal foundation of Alexandria?
323	Death of Alexander, his empire divided, accession of his half-brother as Philip III
	Ptolemy, son of Lagus, given Egypt
321–320	First War of the Diadochi (Successors)
317	Murder of Philip III, accession of Alexander's son, Alexander IV
315	Seleucus I flees to Ptolemy
313	Revolt in Cyrene
312	Battle of Gaza: Demetrius defeated by Ptolemy and Seleucus
312/311	Peace between Ptolemy, Cassander, Lysimachus, and Antigonus
310	Murder of Alexander IV, but his reign was continued in name until 305 BC

306	Battle of Salamis: Ptolemy beaten by Demetrius
	Demetrius and Antigonus become kings
305	Ptolemy becomes king of Egypt as Ptolemy I Soter
304	Revolt in Cyrenaica breaks out (until 300)
295	Cyprus becomes a Ptolemaic possession
285/284	Ptolemy I appoints his son Ptolemy II Philadelphus as joint monarch
282	Death of Ptolemy I, sole reign of Ptolemy II starts
280	Pharos lighthouse begun
279	Ptolemy II's queen, Arsinoe I, is banished. Ptolemy marries his sister, Arsinoe II. Ceraunus is killed in battle
274	First Syrian War (274–271) breaks out
270 (or 268)	Arsinoe II dies – her apotheosis follows
267	Chremonidean War breaks out
264	First Punic War between Rome and Carthage starts
260	Second Syrian War (260–253) starts
246	Death of Ptolemy II, accession of Ptolemy III Euergetes
	Third Syrian War (246–241) breaks out
245	Rebellion in Egypt
241	First Punic War ends with Roman victory over Carthage
238	Canopus Decree
237	Construction of the Temple of Horus at Edfu begins
227	Earthquake on Rhodes
222	Death of Ptolemy III, accession of Ptolemy IV Philopator
219	Fourth Syrian War (219–217) begins
218	Second Punic War breaks out between Rome and Carthage
217	Ptolemy IV marries his sister Arsinoe III. Revolt in Lower Egypt
	Hannibal defeats Rome at Lake Trasimene
216	Hannibal defeats Rome at Cannae
214	Rome's First Macedonian War (214–205) begins

212–211	Rome introduces its silver denarius coinage
c. 211	An exhausted, starving Rome begs Ptolemy IV for corn
210	Arsinoe bears Ptolemy IV their son Ptolemy V. Ptolemy IV falls under the control of Agathocleia and her brother Agathocles; Roman diplomatic mission in Egypt
206	Rebellion in the Thebaid: Harwennefer made king (206/205–200)
205	First Macedonian War ends inconclusively
204	Death of Ptolemy IV, accession of Ptolemy V Epiphanes. Murder of Arsinoe III; Sosibius and Agathocles rule Egypt in Ptolemy V's name
202	Fifth Syrian War (202–195)
	Battle of Zama. Rome defeats Carthage
201	Formal end of the Second Punic War
200	Second Macedonian War (200–197)
	Philip V of Macedon takes Thrace; Roman diplomatic mission in Egypt
197	Roman victory in Second Macedonian War
196	Land grants and tax remissions recorded on bilingual Rosetta Stone
	Ankhwennefer leads revolt in Thebes
195	Ptolemy V and Antiochus III make peace
194	Ptolemy V marries Cleopatra I, daughter of Antiochus III, the Great
	Rome's war against Antiochus III (192–188) breaks out
191	Philip V of Macedon defeated by Rome at Thermopylae
188	Antiochus III concedes defeat and accepts Roman terms at Apameia
187	Antiochus III killed
180	Murder of Ptolemy V, accession of Ptolemy VI Philometor under the regency of his mother Cleopatra I
176	Death of Cleopatra I, Ptolemy VI falls under the control of Eulaeus and Lenaeus

173	Roman diplomatic mission in Egypt
171	Third Macedonian War (171–168) begins
170	Sixth Syrian War (170–*c.* 168) breaks out. Eulaeus and Lenaeus defeated at Pelusium by Antiochus IV, Ptolemy VI captured. Egypt declares Ptolemy VI's younger brother king as Ptolemy VIII with their sister Cleopatra II as queen.* Rome intercedes: Ptolemy VI rules from Memphis, Ptolemy VIII in Alexandria
168	Antiochus IV withdraws. Ptolemy VI now rules Egypt, and Ptolemy VIII rules in Cyrenaica
165	Rebellion of Dionysius Petoserapis. Rebellion in the Thebaid
164	Ptolemy VII rules alone in Alexandria. Ptolemy VI in exile
163	Return of Ptolemy VI who rules with Cleopatra II. Ptolemy VIII rules in Cyrenaica but goes to Rome to plead his case which is recognized but ignored
154	Ptolemy VIII once more in Rome
149	Third Punic War (149–146 BC) between Rome and Carthage begins
146	Carthage destroyed and Corinth sacked by Rome Ptolemy VI is declared King of Egypt <u>and</u> Asia after the Seleucid kingdom is given to him
145	Ptolemy VI killed in battle in Syria. Ptolemy VIII marries his widowed sister Cleopatra II and kills her son Neos Philometer (? possibly 'Ptolemy VII'), but appoints her daughter to be joint queen as Cleopatra III
144	Ptolemy Memphites born
141–140	Ptolemy VIII spurns Cleopatra II and takes up with Cleopatra III

* The existence of a Ptolemy VII in amongst these complications is disputed.

139	Diplomatic mission led by Scipio Aemilianus to Egypt
133	Attalus III leaves Pergamum to Rome
	Tiberius Gracchus killed in Rome
132	Ptolemy VIII, highly unpopular, flees to Cyprus with Cleopatra III and their children. War between Ptolemy VIII and Cleopatra II breaks out
131	Cleopatra II's sole rule begins in Alexandria
130	Ptolemy VIII takes control of Memphis and kills his son by Cleopatra II, Ptolemy Memphites, to prevent her making him king
129	Ptolemy VIII returns to Egypt, Cleopatra II flees
124	Ptolemy VIII and Cleopatra II make peace
116	Death of Ptolemy VIII. Cleopatra III rules, the latter as regent with her son Ptolemy IX
	Cleopatra II vanishes, her fate unknown. Assumed to have died by now or *c.* 115 BC
	Ptolemy X rules in Cyprus. Roman visitors at Philae
115	Ptolemy IX obliged by his mother Cleopatra III to divorce his sister Cleopatra IV and marry his other sister Cleopatra V
114	Cleopatra IV marries Antiochus IX Cyzicenus
112	Cleopatra IV killed by Antiochus VII Grypus
	Visit to Egypt of the senator Lucius Memmius
107/106	After accusations of plotting to kill his mother, Ptolemy IX flees to Cyprus. Cleopatra III marries her son Ptolemy X. They rule as co-regents with coins bearing their separate regnal years
103	Syrian War breaks out. Cleopatra III sends her grand-children to Kos and lays siege to Ptolemais
101	Murder of Cleopatra III at the behest of Ptolemy X
91–88	Renewed revolt in the Thebaid
89	Ptolemy IX returns. Rome's First Mithridatic War (89–85) starts

87	Ptolemy X killed trying to retake Cyprus
84	Ptolemy IX seeks sanctuary in Rome with Sulla
82	Dictatorship (82–80) of Sulla in Rome begins
81	Death of Ptolemy IX
	Accession of Ptolemy IX's niece Cleopatra Berenice III as sole ruler
80	Berenice III marries her nephew Ptolemy XI
	Berenice III murdered by Ptolemy XI, killed himself by an Alexandrian mob
	Cleopatra V Selene fails to have her son Antiochus XIII made king of Egypt
	Accession of Ptolemy XII, an illegitimate son of Ptolemy IX
	Ptolemy XII marries his sister/half-sister (?) Cleopatra VI Tryphaena
76	Coronation of Ptolemy XII
73–71	Rome's Servile (Spartacus) War breaks out
70	Temple of Horus at Edfu dedicated
70/69	Birth of Cleopatra VII
67	Pompey's campaign against the Cilician pirates
59	Caesar confirms Ptolemy XII as king
58	The unpopular Ptolemy XII flees to Rome
	Accession of Ptolemy's daughter Berenice IV who rules with Cleopatra VI Tryphaena. Berenice marries a cousin descendant of the Syrian Seleucid line, Archelaus
c. 57	Temple of Horus at Edfu completed
	Death of Cleopatra VI Tryphaena
55	Berenice IV and Archelaus toppled
	Ptolemy XII returns with Roman backing and executes Berenice IV
52	Cleopatra VII co-regent with her father
51	Death of Ptolemy XII, accession of his daughter
	Cleopatra VII with her husband-brother Ptolemy XIII

APPENDIX 1

48	Arsinoe IV declares herself ruler of Egypt after escaping from Caesar
47	Arsinoe IV betrayed to Caesar by Egyptian officers. Death of Ptolemy XIII while campaigning against the Romans. Cleopatra marries her other brother, Ptolemy XIV. Cleopatra VII gives birth to Ptolemy XV Caesarion
46	Cleopatra in Rome
44	Assassination of Caesar in Rome
	Cleopatra returns to Egypt, murders Ptolemy XIV
	Ptolemy XV (Caesarion) now co-regent with Cleopatra
41	Cleopatra meets Mark Antony
	Murder of Arsinoe IV on Antony's orders at Cleopatra's behest
34	Antony declares Cleopatra Queen of Egypt, Cyprus, Libya, and Coele-Syria
32	Octavian reads out Antony's will in Rome
31	Cleopatra and Antony's forces defeated at Actium
30	Suicides of Antony and Cleopatra
	Annexation of Egypt by Octavian (later Augustus)

APPENDIX 2

FAMILY TREES

1. THE PTOLEMIES

The following family tree shows a simplified Ptolemaic line of descent. Most other family members are omitted. There is no consensus for the numbering of later Cleopatras. The genealogy of the other later Ptolemies and Cleopatras is very unclear, a problem compounded by the identical personal names, erratic use of epithets, and often a lack of information about the maternal line of descent; but all were descended from Ptolemy V and Cleopatra I. See Bennett (1997), 65, and Walker and Higgs (2001), 16, for alternatives. For female rulers' regnal years see chapter headings.

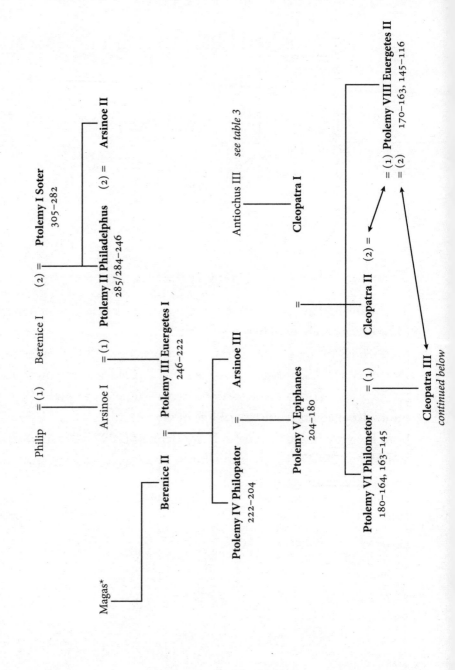

Philip =(1) Arsinoe I =(1) Ptolemy III Euergetes I
                                246–222

Magas* Berenice II

Berenice I (2) = Ptolemy I Soter
                   305–282

Ptolemy II Philadelphus (2) = Arsinoe II
285/284–246

Arsinoe III

Ptolemy IV Philopator
222–204

Ptolemy V Epiphanes
204–180

Antiochus III   see table 3

Cleopatra I

Ptolemy VI Philometor
180–164, 163–145

Cleopatra II (2) =

=(1)

Ptolemy VIII Euergetes II
170–163, 145–116

= (1)
= (2)

Cleopatra III
continued below

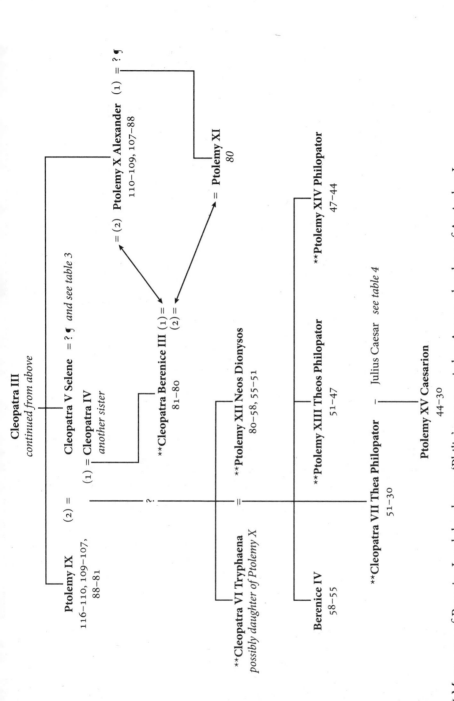

Cleopatra III
continued from above

* Magas, son of Berenice I and the obscure 'Philip', was married to Apama, daughter of Antiochus I.

** In these cases, the maternal line of descent is uncertain – the individuals may have been illegitimate. Note also that huge confusion surrounds Cleopatra V Selene and her sister Cleopatra IV – Ptolemy IX's children individually or collectively may have been by either.

*** Ptolemy VIII's **first** marriage was to his sister Cleopatra II, his **second** to his niece Cleopatra III. From this union the latter part of the royal line was descended.

¶ Possibly Cleopatra V Selene.

APPENDIX 2

2. MACEDON

The Argeads

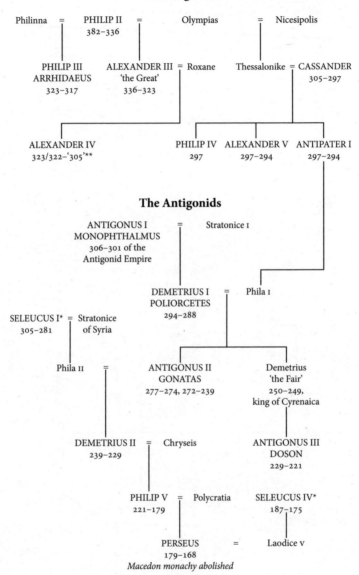

Philinna = PHILIP II = Olympias = Nicesipolis
382–336

PHILIP III   ALEXANDER III = Roxane   Thessalonike = CASSANDER
ARRHIDAEUS   'the Great'   305–297
323–317   336–323

ALEXANDER IV   PHILIP IV   ALEXANDER V   ANTIPATER I
323/322–'305'**   297   297–294   297–294

The Antigonids

ANTIGONUS I = Stratonice I
MONOPHTHALMUS
306–301 of the
Antigonid Empire

DEMETRIUS I = Phila I
POLIORCETES
294–288

SELEUCUS I* = Stratonice
305–281   of Syria

Phila II =   ANTIGONUS II   Demetrius
               GONATAS   'the Fair'
               277–274, 272–239 250–249,
                                king of Cyrenaica

DEMETRIUS II = Chryseis   ANTIGONUS III
239–229   DOSON
                            229–221

PHILIP V = Polycratia   SELEUCUS IV*
221–179   187–175

PERSEUS = Laodice V
179–168
Macedon monachy abolished

---

* See next family tree, 3. The Seleucids.
** Killed in 309 BC, but not publicly acknowledged.

3. THE SELEUCIDS

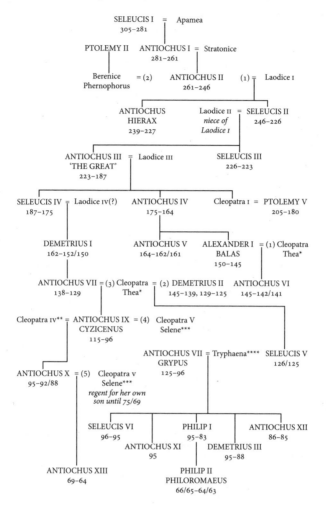

* Cleopatra Thea. Daughter of Ptolemy VI and Cleopatra II. Wife of Alexander I Balas, Demetrius II, and Antiochus VII.

** Cleopatra IV. Daughter of Ptolemy VIII and Cleopatra III. Wife of Ptolemy IX and Antiochus IX. Probably mother of Cleopatra Berenice III by Ptolemy IX. See Table 1.

*** Cleopatra V Selene. Daughter of Ptolemy VIII and Cleopatra III. Wife of Ptolemy IX, Ptolemy X, Antiochus VIII, Antiochus IX, and Antiochus X. Executed 69 BC by Tigranes II. See Table 1.

**** Tryphaena. Daughter of Ptolemy VIII and Cleopatra III. Not to be confused with Cleopatra VI Tryphaena, daughter of Ptolemy IX or X, and queen/co-regent of Ptolemy XII.

N.B. The latter part of the Seleucid Dynasty is a confused period of overlapping and rival reigns, with some detail unclear. Philip II was the end of the line.

4. THE FAMILY OF CLEOPATRA VII THEA PHILOPATOR

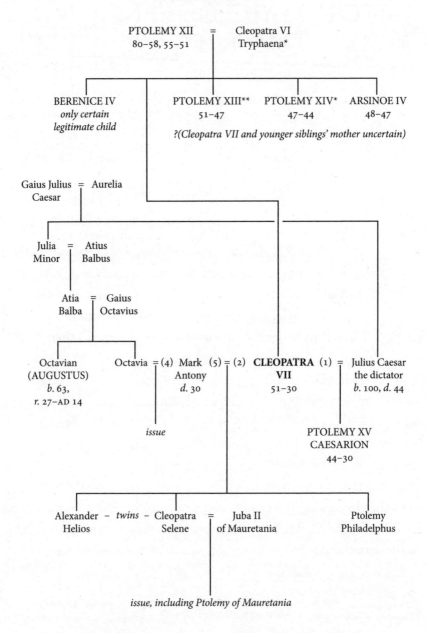

* Ptolemy XIII and IV's marriages to Cleopatra VII are ignored for this family tree.

N.B. Mark Antony's earlier marriages (1–3) are not shown.

APPENDIX 3

PTOLEMAIC QUEENS AND THEIR TITLES

The term 'queen' is a slightly unsatisfactory one in a Ptolemaic context since in Greek (and English, among other languages) 'queen' can mean queen consort *or* queen regnant. Ptolemy I's queen, Berenice I, was a queen consort. Arsinoe II, however, ruled alongside her brother-husband Ptolemy II in her own right. This was also true of certain others, sometimes ruling alone or with their husbands or sons.

Greek texts such as coin legends (see Appendix 4), petitions, edicts, and poetry tended only to refer to Ptolemaic queens as βασίλισσα (Basilissa = 'queen', a later form of βασίλεια) or variants thereof, occasionally identifying where relevant their relationship to the male incumbent, for example 'sister' (ἀδελφιῆι) or 'wife' (γυνὴ), but without specifying their royal prerogatives for which there were no Greek equivalents, thereby leaving their status ambiguous.[1] Most poets of the period avoided even βασίλισσα but Theocritus, for example, used it when referring to Arsinoe II. On the Rosetta Stone (Greek text, line 9) of 196 BC Ptolemy V's deceased mother Arsinoe III is βασίλισσης along with Ptolemy IV as βασίλεως, placing them implicitly on a par. Conversely, the Roman historian Herodian later used βασίλισσα for the Roman emperor Marcus Aurelius' empress Faustina the Younger who was a consort and did not rule (legally, no Roman woman could rule).[2] The two examples illustrate the ambivalence of the term.

The Egyptian titles for Ptolemaic women rulers, which appear generally on stelae or temple texts, were more elaborate and frequently include honours which were equivalent to those borne by the kings, such as pharaoh, *ḥq3(t)*, 'female ruler' or 'queen regnant', *nbt-t3wy* (nebet-tawy, 'Lady of the Two Lands'), and sometimes *nsw(t)-bitj* ('King/Queen of Upper and Lower Egypt') as first in Arsinoe II's case (following precedents set by much earlier female pharaohs), and even female versions of kingly Horus names (plate 12).[3] However, these Egyptian titles are usually known from very few examples, often located within temples where they would have been inaccessible to most people who could not have read (or understood) them anyway, and they vary considerably. They are also usually undated, making it impossible to know exactly how and when these honours were acquired. This raises questions about their practical significance. For example, at Kom Ombo Ptolemy VIII is explicitly 'King of Upper and Lower Egypt', but this title does not appear either by his sister Cleopatra II or wife and niece Cleopatra III (plate 12). In the absence of any Greek terminology or parallels for these titles and their hierarchy of technicalities and significance, they were ignored beyond hieroglyphic or demotic texts.

APPENDIX 4

THE COINAGE OF PTOLEMAIC EGYPT

Ptolemy I fully monetized the Egyptian economy. Coinage, though not wholly unknown in Egypt shortly before his time, was struck in large quantities in silver and bronze at Alexandria, and intermittently from Ptolemy III and Berenice II on at subsidiary mints in Ptolemaic possessions such as Paphos, Tyre, Sidon, and Joppa. Gold, apart from high-value and rare presentation pieces, played little part.

The dominant bullion coin was the silver tetradrachm (4-drachm) piece set at the 'Phoenician standard' of about 14.2 g, compared to the Attic standard of about 17 g (plate 3). Silver tetradrachms of *c.* 200–80 BC frequently bear the enigmatic mint/control mark ΠA, once thought to stand for Paphos in Cyprus but which 'had become a convention, without particular administrative significance' also used at Alexandria (plate 10).[1]

The system was closed. Arrivals in Egypt had to surrender their coin which was melted and restruck at the Egyptian standard, with a profit to the state. Other Hellenistic states and cities generally issued silver tetradrachms at the higher Attic standard used under Alexander (plate 16).

Bronze or copper subsidiary coins included the drachm and the obol (1/6 drachma). Inflation set in during the later third century BC as silver became scarce due to Egypt's wars. Eventually, as many as 450 bronze drachms were needed to match a single silver drachm but the two metals seem to have been used quite separately – bronze for everyday currency, silver for storage and as surety.[2] Harmiysis was a farmer at Kerkeosiris (Fayum) who had been robbed in 113 BC. He complained to Menches the scribe, saying that two items of women's clothing worth 8,000 drachmas in total had been stolen, along with a jar containing 1,600 drachmas in copper.[3] He was citing copper values for the clothing which was therefore worth about 9 silver drachmas or 2¼ tetradrachms. The jar consequently contained the equivalent of about 3.6 silver drachmas, or less than a single standard silver tetradrachm.

Ptolemaic coinage has little historical value. Most tetradrachms carried the portrait of Ptolemy I with no other dynastic information (indeed, no legend at all).[4] By perpetuating Ptolemy I's portrait on tetradrachms as a dominant type, the state evoked a sense of continuity and could disguise debasement (plates 3, 10). That way the standard appeared to be maintained while silently adjusting the exchange rate between gold and silver (and with bronze). Portraiture of other members of the royal house was mainly limited to special issues in gold and silver, probably issued on specific occasions for distribution to the elite and senior military figures. Regardless of their status, female rulers rarely appeared or were named on the Ptolemaic regnal coinage, Cleopatra VII being the most conspicuous exception.

Ptolemaic bronze coins usually bear the head of Zeus-Ammon on the obverse and one eagle or two standing on Zeus' thunderbolt on the reverse, motifs that symbolized kingship. Some bear an obverse portrait of Isis, though she is not labelled as such.[5] There is normally no legend.

Reverse designs rarely referred to buildings, battles, or other historical events and nor did they carry any information about state aspirations or attributes. Instead, they almost invariably carry, bronze and silver alike, generic reverses depicting the Ptolemaic eagle and the simple legend ΒΑΣΙΛΕΩΣ ΠΤΟΛΕΜΑΙΟΥ, 'King Ptolemy', and under later reigns the regnal years, including those of Cleopatra III (plates 10, 16). This legend was only occasionally supplemented by one of the identifying kingly titles, such as Philometor for Ptolemy VI or Euergetes for Ptolemy VIII.[6] Some rare instances of more distinctive coins are mentioned in the main text.[7]

The Ptolemaic closed coinage system continued in Egypt under the Romans. However, as well as the appearance of individual emperor portraits, there was a vast increase in reverse designs. Inflation led to the tetradrachm degenerating into a base metal shadow of itself by the later third century AD. Most of the bronze fractional denominations had by then been abandoned.

GLOSSARY

aroura

An earlier pharaonic unit of land measurement remaining in use under the Ptolemies and the Romans. An aroura was a square with sides of 100 cubits. At approximately 52.5 cm per cubit, an aroura was *c*. 52.5 m x 52.5 m = 2,756 m², or 0.28 of a hectare.

artaba

Unit of capacity, equivalent to *c*. 70 pints (40 litres).

chora (χώρα)

'The place wherein things happen.' Commonly used in books about Ptolemaic Egypt to refer to the country as distinct from Alexandria, without defining it.

cleruch (kleruch or klerouchos)

An 'allotment holder', but meaning in Egypt a soldier, not in active service, holding a land grant on preferential terms from the state, thus a military settler. Grant size was determined by rank. Native Egyptians, admitted to the status in 217 BC, received less.*

* Lewis (1986), 24.

Diadochi ('Successors')
Normally applied to the followers of Alexander the Great who divided up his empire between them. Also used as a title by the Ptolemies and awarded as an honorific title to soldiers.†

dioiketes
Ptolemaic minister of civil administration and finance appointed by the crown.

drachm/drachma
Silver or bronze coin. The silver version was increasingly debased, but shortage of silver also led to inflation and the bronze version becoming worth far less, hundreds of times so, than the silver coin by the second century BC. See also tetradrachm.

epigone
See Persian of the Epigone.

epistates (plural epistatai)
Local representative of the king serving in any one of a variety of supervisory roles, such as the police and the collection of taxes.

epistrategos
Governor of a large district.

Iseum
A temple of Isis.

katochos (pl. katochoi)
Men (usually) who 'secluded' themselves within the confines of a shrine where they remained indefinitely in cult service. Sometimes defined as a hermit, or one who is under the power of the cult or god].

† See, for example, the reserve soldier Dryton in 126 BC who included diadochi among his titles.

GLOSSARY

lesonis
A priest temple-official responsible for the temple's taxation obligations to the state.

nomarch
Governor in charge of a nome (q.v.). See also strategos.

nome
An administrative district, for example the Arsinoite nome in the Fayum.

obol
A bronze or copper coin, struck at six to the drachm.

oikonomos
Local official in charge of tax collection.

Persian of the Epigone
Non-active, unpaid soldier or the equivalent of a rank only used with 'Persian'. Persian (*perses*) was a pseudo-ethnicity, probably used as a taxation category with the word 'epigone' coming to mean that status. There were also those known as a 'Cyrenaean of the Epigone'.

prefect
Roman equestrian governor of certain provinces, most notably Egypt.

Serapeum (or Sarapaion)
Temple complex of the cult of Serapis.

strategos
Governor in charge of a nome (q.v.). See also nomarch.

talent
Monetary unit, approximately valued at 60,000 drachmas.

tax farmer
Tax contractor who had bid for and been awarded the concession to collect taxes at a location. He was liable for the sum the area had been

assessed for and had to collect it, for which he was paid a commission. Introduced by Ptolemy II in 263 BC, replacing payments to temples.

tetradrachm
Four-drachm silver coin. Issued throughout the period but in variable quantities and purity. The Ptolemaic tetradrachm weighed about 14.2 g, compared to the Attic version of about 17 g.

Thebaid
The region of Upper Egypt centred on Thebes (now Luxor).

NOTES

FOREWORD

1. Tetisheri was mother of Ahmose I's parents, Seqenenre Tao (*c.* 1560–1555 BC), killed in battle against the Hyksos, and his sister-queen Ahhotep I. See Breasted (1906), 15, no. 36.
2. Strabo 17.1.27 (Loeb VIII, p. 79).

INTRODUCTION

1. For an excellent collection of classical-style portraits of members of the Ptolemaic dynasty, see Walker and Higgs (2001), especially 38–75, and also Stanwick (2003) who emphasizes the importance Ptolemaic Egyptian-style portrait sculpture placed on native tradition and iconography.
2. The principal difference of course was that the Ptolemies lived in and ruled from Egypt.
3. Manning (2010), 5. The twenty-year rebellion in the Thebaid initiated by Harwennefer between *c.* 206 and 186 BC (see Chapter 12).
4. Livy 1, *praefatio* 12.
5. Lloyd (2000), 375.
6. By Ptolemaic times the normal form was πόλεμος (polemos) but the earlier, Epic Greek, form was πτόλεμος (ptolemos), creating the name Πτόλεμαιος.
7. Cole (2019).
8. Bowman and Crowther (2020), 1.
9. Rutherford (2016), 4.
10. Fox (2004), 11.
11. The evidence for Berenice IV's co-regency with her mother relies in part on regnal years for unnamed rulers on a few papyri, see Chapter 16 and Ricketts (1990).
12. Thucydides 1.1, 1.20.1; Diodorus 1.3.3–4.
13. Herodotus 2.100.

14. Diodorus 1.44.4.
15. Manetho: see Loeb, p. 211 (Appendix 1) for the (probably apocryphal) letter of Manetho to Ptolemy II. Athenaeus, *Deipnosophists* 37 (http://www.attalus.org/old/athenaeus13b.html#576).
16. Diodorus 1.4.6; Suetonius, *Claudius* 41.2.
17. Strabo 17.1.11–12. He considered Ptolemies IV, VII, and XII to be the worst.
18. Vandorpe (2014), 160.
19. Thompson (2003), 107.
20. Bowman and Crowther (2020), 8, in connection with their corpus of Ptolemaic inscriptions, say, 'coverage of the social and economic history of Hellenistic Egypt is inevitably lacunose', i.e. full of gaps.
21. George R. Martin, author of the *Game of Thrones* novels, quoted for example in the *Daily Express* (23 August 2022).

1 THE ROAD TO SIWA

1. Arrian, *A* 3.3.2.
2. Diodorus 17.45.3.
3. Diodorus 17.46.4.
4. Plutarch, *Alexander* 72.
5. Arrian describes Alexander's arrival in Egypt in the *Anabasis* 3.1ff.
6. Diodorus 17.49.1.
7. Arrian, *A* 3.1.4.
8. Arrian, *A* 3.1.5.
9. Arrian, *A* 3.2.1 ff.
10. Strabo 17.1.7.
11. Pseudo-Callisthenes 1.32.7, 'And Alexander, present in person, consecrated the city and the herōon itself on the twenty-fifth of the month Tybi' (http://www.attalus.org/translate/alexander1c.html).
12. Livy 8.24.1.
13. Vitruvius 2, *praefatio* 1–4.
14. Pseudo-Callisthenes 1.4 ff.
15. BM acc. no. EA 10 (https://www.britishmuseum.org/collection/object/Y_EA10).
16. Diodorus 16.48.6, 49.2–3.
17. Diodorus 17.51; see also Curtius Rufus 4.7.27–28.
18. Plutarch, *Alexander* 27.
19. Reported by Strabo 17.1.43, citing other authorities.
20. Arrian, *A* 3.5.1.
21. *Alexander Romance* or Pseudo-Callisthenes 1.34.
22. Arrian, *A* 3.1.4, and Hölbl (2001) 9.
23. Plutarch, *Alexander* 27–9.
24. Diodorus 17.52.7.
25. Bowman (1996), 22, just says 'there may also have been a ceremonial coronation at Memphis'. Fletcher (2008), 30–1, describes a full Egyptian coronation.
26. Plato, *Statesman* 290D.
27. For Alexander the Great's Egyptian names, see https://pharaoh.se/pharaoh/Alexander-the-Great.
28. Fox (2004), 196; Bosch-Puche (2014), 61, 82.

29. Pausanias 1.6.2.
30. Diodorus 17.108.1–3.
31. Arrian, *A* 3.5.2.
32. Arrian, *A* 7.15.5. The original source seems to have been Cleitarchus (*fl.* mid to late fourth century BC), whose history of Alexander is lost but some fragments survive. Fragment 23 appears to mention an embassy from Rome. See C. Müller's *Scriptores Rerum Alexandri Magni* (1846), 75.
33. Plutarch, *Alexander* 77.
34. Curtius Rufus 10.10.11–13. See also 9.1.34 for his dilemma about what to do with suspect source material.
35. Diodorus 18.26.3: αρωμάτων = any spice or sweet herb (https://www.perseus. tufts.edu/hopper/text?doc=Perseus%3Atext%3A2008.01.0541%3Abook%3D1 8%3Achapter%3D26%3Asection%3D3).
36. *Alexander Romance* Syriac version 22 (https://www.attalus.org/translate/alexan-der3d.html).
37. Toynbee (1996), 41–2.
38. The author noted the presence of coins of Constantius II (AD 337–61) scattered on the surface on a visit in 2004.

2 LEFT TO THE WORTHIEST

1. Arrian, *A* 3.6.6; 6.28.4.
2. Arrian, *A* 3.18.9.
3. Arrian, *A* 3.29.7.
4. For Alexander's death after heavy drinking, see Diodorus 17.117.1–2.
5. Arrian, *A* 4.8.1–9.1.
6. Arrian, *A* 4.13–14 passim.
7. Arrian, *A* 4.15.7–8.
8. Arrian, *A* 4.16.2.
9. Arrian, *A* 4.23.3–4.
10. Arrian, *A* 4.23.3–25.4.
11. Arrian, *A* 4.29.1–30.4.
12. Diodorus 17.103.4–8.
13. Arrian, *A* 6.10.2–11.2–8.
14. Arrian, *A* 7.4.4–6.
15. Diodorus 17.106.1–3; 17.108.1–3.
16. Shakespeare, *The Winter's Tale* 5.1.
17. Justin 11.10.2.
18. Curtius Rufus 10.6.1.
19. Curtius Rufus 10.10.8, and see Waterfield (2021), 94, who believes the scheme was doomed.
20. Pausanias 1.6.3.
21. Diodorus 18.21.8–9.
22. Diodorus 18.3.3 (note some texts enumerate this passage over 18.3.3–5); Curtius Rufus, 'they should have his body transported to Hammon [= Ammon, i.e. Siwa]', 10.5.4.
23. Strabo 17.1.8.
24. Aelian 12.64.

25. Pausanias 1.6.3.
26. Pausanias 1.7.1. Son of Eurydice.
27. Pausanias 1.6.3, 1.7.1; Curtius Rufus 10.10.20; Diodorus 18.28.4.
28. Diodorus 18.29.1.
29. Diodorus 18.29.7 ff, 33.1.
30. Diodorus 18.36.6.
31. Frontinus, *Stratagems* 4.7.20.
32. Diodorus 18.39.5 ff.
33. Diodorus 19.11.7. Polyperchon had been made regent of the empire in 319 BC.
34. Diodorus 19.51.5–6.
35. Plutarch, *Alexander* 70.5.
36. Diodorus 19.55.1–5.
37. Diodorus 19.56.1 ff.
38. Diorodus 19.58.1, 59.2–3, 61.5.
39. Diodorus 19.62.1.
40. Diodorus 19.79.1–3.
41. Fischer-Bovet and von Reden (2021), 2–3.
42. Diodorus 19.81.4 ff.
43. Diodorus 19.84.1 ff.
44. For example, a gold coin of Ptolemy I, struck 299–295 BC (https://numismatics. org/collection/1967.152.621, *Coins of the Ptolemaic Empire*, vol. I, Part 1, no. 103).
45. Diodorus 19.85.1.
46. Diodorus 19.86.3.
47. Diodorus 19.93.5–7.
48. Diodorus 19.105.1.
49. Diodorus 19.105.4.
50. Diodorus 20.28.1–3.
51. Translation 1878 (http://www.attalus.org/egypt/lagides.html).
52. Alexander IV's names and titles were also carved on the secondary, smaller, rock-cut temple at Speos Artemidos in Middle Egypt, but the cartouches next to the figures of the king were left empty (personal observation).
53. Diodorus 20.19.3–5.
54. Plutarch, *Demetrius* 16.
55. Diodorus 20.47.4; Thompson (2003), 108.
56. Diodorus 20.37.5.
57. Diodorus 20.73 ff.
58. Diodorus 20.75.1 ff.

3 FOUNDATION

1. *opes firmavit.* Tacitus, *Histories* 4.83–4. See also Plutarch, *On Isis and Osiris* 28.
2. Worthington (2016).
3. Murray (1970), 141.
4. Gardiner (1994), sign E23; the open mouth sign for 'r' is D21.
5. Johnson (1995), 154.
6. Curtius Rufus 4.7.31.
7. See https://pharaoh.se/late-period.

8. Personal observation.
9. For Ptolemy I's names: https://pharaoh.se/pharaoh/Ptolemy-I.
10. For example, https://www.britishmuseum.org/collection/object/G_1956-0519-1.
11. Pliny, *NH* 35.89–90.
12. The Rhodes siege comes primarily from Diodorus 20.81.1 to 20.99.4. The details of the military activity are not of relevance to Ptolemy's story and are largely omitted in this book.
13. Diodorus 20.85.4.
14. With 500 men. Diodorus 20.88.9.
15. Diodorus 20.92.3–5.
16. Diodorus 20.94.3.
17. Diodorus 20.96.1.
18. Diodorus 20.98.1–3.
19. Diodorus 20.99.2–3.
20. Diodorus 20.100.3–4.
21. Diodorus 20.106 passim.
22. Diodorus 20.113.1–2.
23. Diodorus 21.1.4–5.
24. Polybius 5.67.
25. Plutarch, *Demetrius* 31.3–5.
26. Plutarch, *Pyrrhus* 4–5.1.
27. Plutarch, *Demetrius* 31.3–4, 33.1.
28. Plutarch, *Demetrius* 33 passim.
29. Hölbl (2001), 23, for references to this. Also, Plutarch, *Demetrius* 32.4, 33.3 (loss of Cyprus).
30. *Supplementum Epigraphicam Graecum* 28.60. Text and translation available at: http://www.attalus.org/docs/seg/s28_60.html.
31. Hölbl (2001), 24.
32. Most of the contents of this paragraph are to be found in Plutarch, *Demetrius* 44 ff. and his *Pyrrhus* 10–11.
33. Arrian, *A* 7.4.6; Plutarch, *Eumenes* 1.3, calling her Apama by mistake.
34. Athenaeus, *Deipnosophists* 13.37 (http://attalus.org/old/athenaeus13b.html#576).
35. See van Oppen de Ruiter (2011) for the argument that Ptolemy married Berenice *c.* 320–315 BC.
36. Polybius 2.41.
37. Aelian 13.13.
38. Strabo 17.1.42.

4 MARRIAGE COMES BY DESTINY

1. Polybius 5.34.
2. Johstono (2020).
3. Aelian, *Various History* 3.17, 'in Egypt also, living with Ptolemy, he was chief in making laws'; Plutarch, *On Exile* 7. Also Fraser (1972), 114–15.
4. Diogenes Laertius 5.5.78.
5. Cicero, *For Rabirius Postumus* 23; Pausanias 1.7.1 (Argaeus). Justin 15.2.6 (http://www.attalus.org/translate/justin1.html#15.2); implied at Plutarch, *Demetrius* 17.1. For the possible other, see Pausanias ibid., 'a half-brother, Eurydice's son, for

treason in Cyprus', but it is unclear who this was or whether Pausanias was confused.

6. *Letter of Aristeas to Philocrates* 9, dated to the third or second century BC (https://www.attalus.org/translate/aristeas1.html), the earliest mention of the library. For Demetrius' role and why he was not credited, see Tracy (2000), especially 343–5.

7. Vitruvius 7, *praefatio* 4, 8. The story about Zoilus being executed is probably apocryphal.

8. Josephus, *Antiquities* 12.2.1, paraphrasing the *Letter of Aristeas*.

9. Tracy (2000), 343–5, 'By then Demetrius was out of favour at court; he could not, therefore, have been head of the library'; Gruen (2009), 135.

10. Diogenes Laertius 5.3.58.

11. http://www.attalus.org/docs/other/inscr_258.html.

12. https://www.attalus.org/egypt/great_mendes_stela.html. Text by S. Birch, after a German translation by Brugsch-Bey, 1875, *Records of the Past*, Series 1, Vol. 8.

13. Justin 17.2.9 (http://www.attalus.org/translate/justin2.html).

14. Justin 17.1.4.

15. Justin 17.2.4.

16. Justin 17.2.6 ff.

17. Justin 24.2–24.3 passim (http://www.attalus.org/translate/justin3.html).

18. Diodorus 22.3.1–2; Justin 24.3.5.

19. Porphyry in FGrHist 260.3.10 who incorrectly identifies Gonatas as Ceraunus' brother (http://www.instonebrewer.com/TyndaleSites/Egypt/ptolemies/meleager_fr.htm); note that Diodorus (22.4) mistakenly claims he was a brother of Ptolemy I. See Eusebius, *Chronicon* 89 (http://www.attalus.org/translate/eusebius2.html#235).

20. Livy, *Periochae* 14.6. Also, Dio 10.41 (fragments; Loeb I, p. 367); Dionysius of Halicarnassus 19.14.1, where the envoys are named: Numerius Fabius Pictor, Quintus Fabius Maximus, and Quintus Ogulnius.

21. The so-called 'Stone of Pithom' (http://www.attalus.org/docs/other/inscr_258.html).

22. The relief can be seen at: https://harvardartmuseums.org/collections/object/289668. The word for Apis bull is *ḥp*.

23. Minas (2005), 134. See also a relief from San el-Hagar where she is depicted with kingly titles. BM acc. no. EA1056 (https://www.britishmuseum.org/collection/object/Y_EA1056).

24. For example, a gold octadrachm piece, BM acc. no. 1883 320.12 (https://www.britishmuseum.org/collection/object/C_1868-0320-12).

25. Skuse (2017), 89, and van Oppen de Ruiter (2015), 23.

26. Theocritus, *Idyll* 15 (https://www.gutenberg.org/files/11533/11533-h/11533-h.htm#IDYLL_XV): 'And we'll to Ptolemy's, the sumptuous king, to see the *Adonis*. As I hear, the queen provides us something gorgeous.'

27. Pausanias 1.7.1.

28. Athenaeus 14.621.a (https://www.attalus.org/old/athenaeus14a.html).

29. Theocritus, *Idyll* 17.115.

30. Baralay (2020), 119.

31. Bowman (1996), 24.

32. Pausanias 1.7.1.

33. van Oppen de Ruiter (2010) argues for 268 BC.

34. Carney (2013), 2.

35. Stela of Mendes (http://www.attalus.org/egypt/great_mendes_stela.html).

36. For example, BM Catalogue 74 c. 290–281 BC (https://www.britishmuseum.org/collection/object/C_HPB-Unc-10).

37. Callimachus, Fragment 228 (https://www.loebclassics.com/view/callimachus-lyric_poems/1973/pb_LCL421.163.xml).

38. Pliny, NH 34.148; Ausonius, The Moselle 310 ff. (Loeb I, p. 249).

39. Pliny, NH 36.68.

40. Diodorus 1.37.5, and Agatharchides, Fragment 20 (https://www.attalus.org/translate/extracts.html#agatharchides).

41. Pliny, NH 6.168 and 170–1; see also Strabo 16.4.4, and 8. Hölbl (2001), 57, suggests is now Aqiq. Foundation of the city and elephant hunting mentioned on the Stone of Pithom. For Ptolemy II's interest in hunting elephants, see Agatharchides, Fragments 1 and 57 (https://www.attalus.org/translate/extracts.html#agatharchides).

42. OGIS 219 (Ilion 32). Antiochus I or III could be meant, but Antiochus I is generally assumed (http://www.columbia.edu/itc/classics/bagnall/3995/readings/b-d2-1b.htm). Also Jones (1993).

43. Hölbl (2001), 37, makes this claim but provides no meaningful evidence to support it.

44. In Jacobus FGrH 434.17 (http://www.attalus.org/translate/memnon1.html).

45. Pithom Stela (https://www.attalus.org/docs/other/inscr_258.html).

46. SEG 28.60 (http://www.attalus.org/docs/seg/s28_60.html). Note that Wilkinson (2010), 472, describes Ptolemy's expansion of power into 'southern and western Anatolia' as a fact.

47. At Üsümlü (4th regnal year) and Isindis, TAM 1.35 (p. 32) and 65 (p. 59) (https://archive.org/details/gri_33125010455224/mode/2up).

48. Pausanias 1.7.2.

49. Ptolemy II's Galatian trichryson/pentadrachm can be viewed here: https://en.numista.com/catalogue/pieces302901.html. Or see Johstono (2020), fig. 1b.

50. Pithom Stela (https://www.attalus.org/docs/other/inscr_258.html). Egypt here called Kemet.

51. Hölbl (2001), 40 and note 25, a reference to Babylonian astronomical diaries for 270 BC (text at: http://oracc.iaas.upenn.edu/adsd/adart1/pager, taken from Sachs and Hunger (1988), 355,–270 B, v. lines 18–19; and reached from https://www.attalus.org/bc3/year273.html#2 which cross-references to Hölbl (2001), 40). This turns out to be less than convincing. There are references to 'lamentation priests', the cost of salad, that Antiochus had camped in Transpotamia (lands west of the Euphrates), and a phrase translating as 'there was much [. . .] in the land', for which perhaps 'plague' (or 'famine' or 'misery') can be supplied but, for an era when so much of the evidence is tenuous, this is flimsy to the point of desperation.

52. Bagnall (1976), 12.

53. Pausanias 1.1.1 and repeated at 1.7.3.

54. Pausanias 3.6.4–6.

55. Frontinus, Stratagems 3.2.11; Johstono (2020), 131.

56. Polynaeus 5.18 (http://www.attalus.org/translate/polyaenus5B.html), who names the various protagonists involved but without enough precision to attribute this event to a reliable date.
57. See Skuse (2017) for a detailed discussion of the identity of 'Ptolemy the Son' in connection with the Mendes Stela of 264 BC (https://www.attalus.org/egypt/great_mendes_stela.html), concluding that he was an heir apparent. Also Tunny (2000).
58. Appian, *SW* 11.11.65.
59. Plutarch, *Moralia* 545 (also given as 'How can one praise oneself without exciting envy') 16; Athenaeus, *Deiponosophistae* 5.209e (https://penelope.uchicago.edu/Thayer/E/Roman/Texts/Athenaeus/5C*.html).
60. Plutarch, *Aradus* 2.12 (http://penelope.uchicago.edu/Thayer/E/Roman/Texts/Plutarch/Lives/Aratus*.html).
61. On a demotic ostracon found at Karnak. Bresciani (1983).
62. Athenaeus 5 (https://penelope.uchicago.edu/Thayer/E/Roman/Texts/Athenaeus/5B*.html).
63. Theocritus, *Idylls* 17.86 ff.
64. Theocritus, *Idylls* 17.86 ff. ps://penelope.uchicago.edu/Thayer/E/Roman/Texts/Athenaeus/5B*.html"https://penelope.uchicago.edu/Thayer/E/Roman/Texts/Athenaeus/5B*.html).
65. Manning (2010), 93.
66. Foertmeyer (1988) argued for the winter of 275–274 BC.
67. Keyser (2016). There is a great deal of inconclusive scholarly debate about the details of when the parade took place.
68. Josephus, *Jewish War* 7.123 ff. (for Vespasian and Titus).
69. Polybius 14.11.2–4.
70. Vandorpe 2007, 165.

5 GREAT BENEFACTORS

1. The Canopus Decree (http://attalus.org/egypt/Canopus_decree.html).
2. Polybius, Fragment 73 (Loeb VI, p. 541).
3. The marriage is referred to and dated in P. Cair. Zen. 2.59521 https://papyri.info/ddbdp/p.cair.zen;2;59251.
4. Appian, *SW* 11.11.65–66; Justin 27.1 passim, 27.3.4 (http://www.attalus.org/translate/justin4.html).
5. For example, BM acc. no. 1987.0649.281 (https://www.britishmuseum.org/collection/object/C_1987-0649-281).
6. Catullus 66.
7. Bennett (2005), 91. For the Callimachus text, see https://dcc.dickinson.edu/callimachus-aetia/book-3/victory-berenice; she is identified only by euphemism. Berenice was the daughter of Magas and Apama II.
8. Clayman (2014), 4.
9. Llewellyn-Jones and Winder (2016).
10. Hölbl (2001), 85.
11. Adulis Inscription: *OGIS* 54 (https://www.attalus.org/docs/ogis/s54.html); for Esna, see Budge (1902), 216. For the death of Seleucus II, see Jerome, *Commentary*

on the Book of Daniel, Chapter 11, verse 10 (https://www.tertullian.org/fathers/jerome_daniel_02_text.htm).

12. Jerome, *Commentary on the Book of Daniel*, Chapter 11, verses 7–9 (https://www.tertullian.org/fathers/jerome_daniel_02_text.htm).
13. Justin 27.1.9 (http://attalus.org/translate/justin4.html#27.1).
14. Yale University research. Manning et al. (2017) (https://www.nature.com/articles/s41467-017-00957-y).
15. Justin 27.2 passim (http://www.attalus.org/translate/justin4.html).
16. Plutarch, *Aratus* 24.4, 41.3.
17. Frontinus, *Stratagems* 2.6.5.
18. Polybius 2.46ff.
19. Pausanias 1.5.5, 10.10.1.
20. Plutarch, *Cleomenes* 22.4–10.
21. Polybius 2.63.1.
22. Polybius 2.65–69; Plutarch, *Cleomenes* 29–32.
23. Plutarch, *Cleomenes* 32.
24. Jerome, *Commentary on the Book of Daniel*, Chapter 11, verses 7–9 (https://www.tertullian.org/fathers/jerome_daniel_02_text.htm).
25. For example, Graeco-Roman Museum, Alexandria, acc. no. P.10035, or BM acc. no. 1895, 1030.1 (https://www.britishmuseum.org/collection/object/G_1895-1030-1).
26. Thompson (2020). See also Heinz and van der Wilt (2019).
27. Text at: http://attalus.org/egypt/canopus_decree.html.
28. Hölbl (2001), 49, says that the title may have been in use from 243 BC.
29. Pfeiffer and Klinkott (2021), 236–7, 238–9, 241.
30. Stela of Canopus (http://attalus.org/egypt/Canopus_decree.html).
31. See https://www.artic.edu/artworks/5782/octadrachm-coin-portraying-king-ptolemy-iii-euergetes at the Art Institute, Chicago, acc. no. 1922.4935.
32. Johnson (1999) and (2002).
33. Polybius 5.88–89.
34. Polybius 5.88.

6 THE SHAPE OF THINGS TO COME

1. Callimachus, Fragment 384. See Loeb, Callimachus, *Minor Epic and Elegiac Poems*, 230–1.
2. Polybius 5.35.7.
3. Philammon also murdered Arsinoe III, see Polybius 15.33.11.
4. Polybius 5.34.10, 35.6, and 14.12.1–4.
5. Justin 29.1.4 (http://www.attalus.org/translate/justin4.html) claimed Ptolemy IV killed both his parents, probably linked to the tradition mentioned by Zenobius 3.94; see second paragraph below, this chapter.
6. Polybius 5.34.3–4.
7. Polybius 5.34–39 passim is the source for all these events.
8. Polybius 15.25.1, 12.
9. Zenobius, *Proverbia* 3.94 (https://www.attalus.org/translate/extracts.html). Hölbl (2001), 128, cites Zenobius but not the allegations against Ptolemy IV therein or

his decision to build the family tomb out of guilt (hence the proverb 'well-disposed [is] the slayer').

10. Polybius 5.34.10, 35.6.
11. Polybius 14.11.5; Justin 30.1.7.
12. For example, on a scarab from Tell el-Daba (TD 8622: https://pnm.uni-mainz. de/3/inscription/9501#41505).
13. Athenaeus, *Deipnosophists* 7.2 (https://topostext.org/people/13586).
14. Athenaeus, *Deipnosophists* 5.37; Plutarch, *Demetrius* 43.4.
15. Polybius 5.59–61.
16. Polybius 5.59.61, 40.1–3 (in that order).
17. Polybius 5.61–2.
18. Polybius 5.64; Fischer-Bovet and Clarysse (2012), 26–35.
19. Johstono (2020), 245.
20. Polybius 5.65.
21. Polybius 5.66–7.
22. Polybius 5.70.
23. Casson (1993), 89.
24. Polybius 5.81. At 5.83 Polybius says Arsinoe was there.
25. Polybius 5.83.
26. Goudriaan (1992), 78: Dio 55.24.7 on pseudo-ethnicity in the Roman army. Fischer-Bovet (2014), 133, 177 ff., 186, and see 193 for the idea that a *persus te epigone* might have become a rank of sorts.
27. *SP* II, no. 270 (217 BC), P. Enteux. 48 (https://papyri.info/ddbdp/p.enteux;;48). For the 'modestly well off' owning 15–30 arourae, see Bowman (1996), 101.
28. Charles (2007) considers the reliability of Polybius' reference to the elephants.
29. Polybius 5.85.
30. Polybius 5.86.
31. Raphia Decree, Memphis (https://www.attalus.org/docs/other/inscr_259.html).
32. Polybius 5.87.
33. Livy 23.10 passim.
34. Polybius 5.100.9.
35. Polybius 7.2.2; Livy 24.26.1.
36. See Derow (2003) for Roman interventions in the region.
37. Polybius 11.6.1–3.
38. Polybius 9.11a.
39. Livy 27.4.10. Livy refers to Arsinoe III as Cleopatra, probably because it had become a generic name taken by Ptolemaic female rulers. Given its literal meaning this is unsurprising.
40. Diogenes Laertius 7.177 (anecdote), 185 (invitation).
41. Aelian, *Various Histories* 13.22. The anecdote dates to the early third century AD. There is no other attestation of the building and its features.
42. de la Bédoyère (2022), 192, 229, 362–5.
43. Quack (2017).
44. For an example, see Museum of Fine Arts, Boston, acc. no. 35.195 (https://collections.mfa.org/objects/3167).
45. Svoronos (1904–8), 1124. Landvatter (2012) discusses the specific issue of these coins. The issue is rare now.
46. Faucher and Lorber (2010), 50.

47. Polybius 5.107.1–3.
48. Polybius 14.12.4
49. Goudriaan (1998), 112, in reference to Document no. 109 (BGU 1215); Préaux (1936), 530.
50. Rosetta Stone, *OGIS* 90 (http://www.attalus.org/egypt/rosettastone.html).
51. Polybius 15.20.1.
52. Polybius 15.20.2–3.

7 A TOWN LIKE ALEX

1. Schuster (1999).
2. Rosetta Stone, *OGIS* 90 (http://www.attalus.org/egypt/rosettastone.html).
3. Mao (2001).
4. See Cole (2022) for elite households and their fittings.
5. British Museum (2016); Stanley and Toscano (2009).
6. Strabo 17.1.42.
7. Snape (2014) provides an excellent overview of cities in ancient Egypt.
8. Fischer-Bovet and von Reden (2021), 24–5.
9. Manning (2010), 139; Ades and Glaeser (1995), 216, note 15; Diodorus 17.52.6.
10. Glaukias (d. 164 BC), a cleruch of Macedonian ancestry, may have visited Alexandria only once even though he lived not far from Memphis. Lewis (1986), 74.
11. Fischer-Bovet (2014), 240–1.
12. For example, P. Tebt. 1.5, 'where Egyptians make an agreement with Greeks by contracts written in Greek' (116 BC, available at: https://papyri.info/ddbdp/p.tebt;1;5).
13. Strabo 17.1.7; Scheidel (2001), 67 (typhus), 79 (malaria).
14. Grant (1982), 151–6.
15. Erskine (1995); Fischer-Bovet and von Reden (2021), 24.
16. Bagnall (2002), 348.
17. Rösler (2009), 433.
18. Tracy (2000), 343–5; *Letter of Aristeas to Philocrates* 9 (https://www.attalus.org/translate/aristeas1.html).
19. Aulus Gellius, *Attic Nights* 7.17.3.
20. Caesar, *Civil Wars* 3.111.
21. Dio 42.3.8.2.
22. Plutarch, *Antony* 55.
23. Suetonius, *Claudius* 42.2.
24. Philo, *Embassy to Gaius* 20.132 (http://www.earlychristianwritings.com/yonge/book40.html).
25. Josephus, *JA* 12.1 (https://penelope.uchicago.edu/josephus/ant-12.html).
26. Josephus, *JA* 13.7.2 (https://penelope.uchicago.edu/josephus/ant-14.html).
27. Hölbl (2001), 190.
28. Baralay (2020), 118.
29. Pliny, *NH* 36.18.
30. Pliny, *NH* 36.83; Lucian, *How to Write History* 62. This sort of retrospective nickname or pseudonym for individuals with special reputations was not unusual in antiquity.

31. Zientek (2017), 146.
32. Josephus, *Jewish War* 4.10.5. The exact length of a stade is unknown.
33. Plutarch, *Alexander* 76; Arrian, *A* 7.26.2.
34. Plutarch, *Moralia* 28 (http://penelope.uchicago.edu/Thayer/e/roman/texts/plutarch/moralia/isis_and_osiris*/b.html). Another version was given by Tacitus, *Histories* 4.84.
35. Pausanias 1.18.4.
36. McKenzie et al. (2004).
37. Thompson (2020), 112.
38. Quotes from Ammianus Marcellinus 22.16.12, writing in the AD 380s. The temple may already have been closed to worship by then.
39. Savvopoulos (2020), 82.
40. *CPI* 9 TM 6083, in Savvopoulos (2020), 83.
41. *CIL* 10.1781 (Puteoli).
42. McKenzie et al. (2004), 98.
43. Herodian 4.8.6–7; *Historia Augusta* (Severus) 17.4.
44. McKenzie et al. (2004), 107, 113.
45. Savvopoulos (2020), 84.

8 THE YOKE OF GOVERNMENT

1. O'Neil (2006).
2. Polybius 15.26.
3. Manning (2004), 764.
4. Bowman (2006), 210, who suggests that Ptolemy II was the principal agent in this.
5. Thutmose III appears to be riding a horse on a crude steatite plaque, but this is exceptional. Metropolitan Museum of Art, New York, acc. no. 05.3.263 (https://www.metmuseum.org/art/collection/search/548708); see also Schulman (1957).
6. For the Raphia scene: https://www.attalus.org/docs/other/inscr_259.html.
7. von den Hoff (2021), especially, 165, 169, and 187–9.
8. Manning (2004), 764.
9. Turner (1984), 120; Manning (2010), 181, 183. See also P. Tebt. 1.5 from 116 BC (https://papyri.info/ddbdp/p.tebt;1;5) where a royal decree sets out the way courts heard cases involving contracts between Greeks and Egyptians.
10. Aelian 14.43. Aelian said it did not matter which Ptolemy and Berenice he was writing about. The story may well have been apocryphal but was rooted in the reality of Ptolemaic power (https://penelope.uchicago.edu/aelian/varhist12.xhtml#chap54).
11. Fischer-Bovet (2014), 170; Monson (2012), 47.
12. Manning (2010), 50.
13. Bingen (2007), 240–55.
14. Westermann (1929), 60–1; Fischer-Bovet (2014), 251–2.
15. Dryton's will (https://papyri.info/ddbdp/p.grenf;1;21) can be found in *SP* I, no. 83, pp. 239–43, and Lewis (1986), 100–1.
16. Manning (2010), 5–6; Butzer (1976), 37, 47; Bingen (2007), 83–93.
17. Honigman (2022).
18. Monson (2012), 53–4, 67–9.

19. Strabo 17.1.13; 'last and most indolent', Gibbon (1776–88), chapter 4, part 6, ignoring Cleopatra's brothers and son Caesarion.
20. For the royal oil monopoly under Ptolemy II see P. Rev. Laws (https://papyri.info/ddbdp/p.rev;;2nded and *SP* II, no. 203).
21. Turner (1984), 139–40.
22. P. Hal. 1 lines 124ff. (https://papyri.info/ddbdp/p.hal;;1, *SP* II.201), first paragraph, dated to *c.* 250 BC.
23. P. Rev. Laws columns 38–56 (https://papyri.info/ddbdp/p.rev;;2nded, *SP* II.203).
24. P. Cair. Zen. 59341 (https://papyri.info/ddbdp/p.cair.zen;3;59341, *SP* II.267). Calynda (now lost) is mentioned by Herodotus at 1.172.
25. Skeat (1966).
26. Clarysse and Thompson (2006), vol. 2, 62.
27. P. Cair. Zen. 4.5973a (https://papyri.info/ddbdp/p.cair.zen;4;59734).
28. Monson (2012), 87.
29. Turner (1984), 120–1.
30. B&D no. 86, pp. 147–8. For the original Greek, see https://papyri.info/ddbdp/p.hib;1;110.
31. Clarysse and Thompson (2006), vol. 2, 66.
32. Manning (2010), 128–9.
33. Ibid., 142–3.
34. P. Tebt. 703 (https://papyri.info/ddbdp/p.tebt;3.1;703 and *SP* II, no. 204).
35. For the pigeons, see Vandorpe and Vanopré (2020); for the vineyard, see Thomas (2012).
36. Monson (2012), 7.
37. Bauschatz (2007), 36.
38. Manning (2010), 117–19.
39. P. Tebt. 1.39 (https://papyri.info/ddbdp/p.tebt;1;39 and *SP* II.276), 114 BC.
40. Turner (1984), 130.
41. Clarysse (2002), 101–2 (https://www.researchgate.net/publication/250975606_Three_Ptolemaic_Papyri_on_Prisoners).
42. La'da (1994), 8.
43. For the archive of Diophanes, see Lewis (1986), 56–68, including both those referred to here (the Tetosiris petition can also be found here: https://papyri.info/ddbdp/p.enteux;;86; the Heracleides petition: http://www.attalus.org/docs/select2/p269A.html and https://papyri.info/ddbdp/p.enteux;;79).
44. P. Coll. Youtie 1.16 (https://papyri.info/ddbdp/p.coll.youtie;1;16).
45. Bauschatz (2007), 27. The papyri can be found in the Papyrus Hib. series starting at: https://papyri.info/ddbdp/p.hib;1;51.
46. P. Cairo Zenon 2.59245 (https://papyri.info/ddbdp/p.cair.zen;2;59245).
47. P. Tebt. 1.68 and 1.75n (https://papyri.info/ddbdp/p.tebt;1;68 and https://papyri.info/ddbdp/p.tebt;1;75).
48. Knopf (2023). For an instance of 'declarations on oath ... for the protection of the annual crops', see P. Tebt. 27, ll. 30–35 (https://papyri.info/ddbdp/p.tebt;1;27).
49. Bresciani (1983); Bowman (1996), 57.
50. Clarysse and Thompson (2006), vol. 2, 62, 66.
51. P. Tebt. 703 (https://papyri.info/ddbdp/p.tebt;3.1;703 and *SP* II, no. 204).
52. P. Tebt. 10 (https://papyri.info/ddbdp/p.tebt;1;10 and *SP* II.339), 119 BC.

53. P. Hamb. 24 (https://papyri.info/ddbdp/p.hamb;1;24 and *SP* II.349), 222 BC. On banks in Ptolemaic Egypt, see Muhs (2018).
54. P. Hib. 1.98 (https://papyri.info/ddbdp/p.hib;1;98 and *SP* II.365), 252 BC.
55. P. Grenf. 2.23 (https://papyri.info/ddbdp/p.grenf;2;23a and *SP* I.27), 107 BC.
56. Schreiber et al. (2013), 205.
57. Lewis (1986), 155.
58. Nifosi (2022).
59. Baralay (2020), 123.
60. Manning (2010), 146–8.
61. Boswinkel and Pestman (1982); Lewis (1986), 124–39; Manning (2003), 55.

9 TEMPLES OF THE PTOLEMIES

1. Manning (2010), 131, 134.
2. Thompson (2003), 112.
3. Vandorpe (2007), 166.
4. See Manning (2010), 82–3, 128, for a discussion of this and further references.
5. Clarysse (2020b), 166.
6. Fischer-Bovet (2014), 342.
7. Fraser and Rumpf (1952).
8. Wilkinson (2000), 111.
9. *SP* I.100 (https://papyri.info/ddbdp/upz;1;70).
10. Dogaer (2021).
11. Parsons (2007), 103.
12. Fischer-Bovet (2020), 134 (for Lichas); ibid. (2014), 267–8.
13. Fischer-Bovet (2020), 155, dating the Ombite nome text to 174–164 BC citing Trismegistos 6327 (*CPI* 407) as a reference where it is dated 160–145 BC (https://www.trismegistos.org/text/6327); ibid. (2014), 342–3.
14. Fischer-Bovet (2014), 342–3, and 335–49.
15. Moyer (2011), 15–16; Fischer-Bovet (2014), 335; Fischer-Bovet (2015), 44.
16. Hornblower (2020), 217.
17. Paganini (2020), 193–202. Such associations also set up altars or dedications in other locations.
18. Lanciers (2014).
19. Petrie (1902); Hölbl (2001), 160–1, cites various other examples of Ptolemy IV's temple works.
20. For Ptolemaic texts from this temple, see http://www.attalus.org/egypt/medinet_habu.html and for a photographic record, see https://www.osirisnet.net/monument/kasr_agouz/e_kasr_agouz_01.htm.
21. Russman (2005), 23, 27 (n. 3).
22. Minas (2005), 129–33, 137–8.
23. Ibid., 140–1.
24. Dodson (2019), 32, fig. 32 illustrates the remnants of the Ramesside pylon.
25. Kemp (1989), 100.
26. Connor (2022), 151.
27. See the building text inscription (translation) at https://www.attalus.org/egypt/horus_edfu.html.

28. Watterson (1979). The full passage, shown here in partial transliteration, which cannot replicate the alliteration, reads, 'Your altars are enriched with thousands of offerings that you may eat of them, oh winged beetle. Meats are upon them that you may smell their odour. Your enemies are fallen upon their execution blocks as you hasten to your shrine.'
29. Stele of Harmachis, Memphis, now in the Louvre, Paris, acc. no. IMM 4146 (https://collections.louvre.fr/en/ark:/53355/cl010075032). For the text, see http://attalus.org/egypt/apis_bulls.html and scroll down to entry H.

10 MUMMIES, GRAVES, AND GRIEVING

1. *Ptolemaeorum manes seriemque pudendam pyramides claudant indignaque Mausolea*, Lucan 8.692–9; Fraser (1972), vol. 2, 35, note 83. Also, Dodson (2016), 124–5.
2. Dio 51.8.6, 10.7 (reference to superstructure); Plutarch, *Antony* 74.1 (προσῳκοδόμησε τῷ ναῷ τῆς Ἴσιδος), 76.2; Fraser (1972), vol. 2, 34, note 82.
3. Shakespeare, *Hamlet* 5.1.
4. Two of the more recent publications are Erskine (2002) and Saunders (2006).
5. Pausanias 1.6.4.
6. Strabo 17.1.8; see also Fraser (1972), vol. 1, 15–16.
7. Zenobius, *Proverbia* 3.94, using Didynus of Alexandria and Lucillus of Tarrha in Crete, Ptolemy IV 'was so troubled in his dreams by her death that in the middle of the city he built a memorial to her, which is now called the Tomb (Sema); and he placed the remains of her and all his ancestors in there, along with Alexander the Great; and on the sea-shore they constructed a shrine to her, which they called the shrine of Berenice who saves.'
8. Strabo 17.1.8.
9. https://www.britishmuseum.org/collection/object/Y_EA10.
10. Lucan, *Pharsalia* 10.1–52.
11. Suetonius, *Augustus* 18; Dio 51.16.5. Samuel Pepys (*Diary* 23 Feb. 1669) kissed the body of Henry V's queen, Katherine of Valois (d. 1437), then displayed in Westminster Abbey. By 1742 the bones were still 'firmly united, and thinly clothed with flesh, like scrapings of tanned leather'. See the R. Latham and W. Matthews edition of *The Diary of Samuel Pepys*, Bell & Sons, London, vol. IX, 1668–9, p. 457 and n. 1.
12. Suetonius, *Caligula* 52. Suetonius is ambiguous (*repetitum e conditorio eius*) about whether Caligula took the breastplate in person, or whether it was acquired for him.
13. Herodian 4.8.9.
14. Ammianus Marcellinus 26.10.15–19.
15. Naunton (2018), 199 ff., covers Alexander's tomb in more detail.
16. Suetonius, *Augustus* 18.1.
17. For example, 'Archaeologists Seeking Cleopatra's Tomb Uncovered a "Geometric Miracle" Tunnel', in *Science Alert* (May 2023) (https://www.sciencealert.com/archaeologists-seeking-cleopatras-tomb-uncovered-a-geometric-miracle-tunnel), and 'Will We Ever Find Cleopatra's Tomb?', in *Discover* magazine (June 2023) (https://www.discovermagazine.com/the-sciences/will-we-ever-find-cleopatras-tomb).

18. Cannata (2020) provides a recent survey of this massive subject.
19. BM acc. no. EA23 (https://www.britishmuseum.org/collection/object/Y_EA23).
20. P. Hamb. 74 (https://papyri.info/ddbdp/p.hamb;1;74 and *SP* I.78), dated to AD 173–4.
21. Cannata (2020), 510.
22. BM acc. no. EA52949: https://www.britishmuseum.org/collection/object/Y_EA52949 (plate 18).
23. Riggs (2002), 93.
24. Hornung (1999), 151–2.
25. Dodson and Ikram (2008), 293–4. Video tours of the tomb are available, for example on YouTube.
26. Lembke (2012), 209–10.
27. Unpublished by 2024, but widely reported in the press.
28. Landvatter (2013), 242.
29. Ramose's tomb (TT55) can be explored here: https://www.osirisnet.net/tombes/nobles/ramose55/e_ramose55_01.htm.
30. For the inner coffin, see BM acc. no. EA6678 (https://www.britishmuseum.org/collection/object/Y_EA6678). For the outer (EA6677) (https://www.britishmuseum.org/collection/object/Y_EA6677). For the mummy itself in its cartonnage (EA6679) (https://www.britishmuseum.org/collection/object/Y_EA6679). See also Walker and Bierbrier (1997), 29–30.
31. See example G at http://www.attalus.org/egypt/burial.html (taken from Muhs et al. (2021), no. 2).
32. Dogaer (2018) provides a useful summary of Osoroeris the choachyte. See also Pestman (1993), but more recently Cannata (2020), especially 31–6.
33. Schreiber et al. (2013), 187 ff.
34. Budka and Mekis (2017). See also: https://ankhhorproject.wordpress.com/2019/02/24/some-aspects-of-the-re-use-of-coffins-in-ptolemaic-thebes/.
35. See Riggs (2010), who goes into more detail; also Cannata (2020), 208.
36. Hornblower (2020), 225.

11 WAR OF THE WORLDS

1. Polybius 1.10–11.
2. *RRC* 23/1, Sear (2000), no. 599. Sometimes described as a 'double-litra' but the denomination is uncertain.
3. Polybius 1.20–21.
4. Polybius 1.22.
5. Polybius 1.26.
6. Polybius 1.29.
7. Polybius 1.32.
8. Polybius 1.35.
9. Polybius 1.36–37.
10. Fraser (1972) I.152 ff. Strabo 2.1.40 for Timosthenes at the western end of the Mediterranean.
11. Appian, *Of Sicily* 5.1. Loeb I, p. 127. See Livy, summary of Book 14 (Loeb IV, p. 551), for Ptolemy II's alliance with Rome. The Loeb edition attributes this to 252 BC but without any clear basis for doing so.

12. Polybius 1.59–60.
13. Polybius 1.63.
14. Eutropius 3.1. Hölbl (2001), 54, says the embassy 'appeared in Alexandria'. This is assumed. Eutropius says nothing about Alexandria.
15. Livy 21.1.
16. Livy 20 (summary).
17. Polybius 9.11a.
18. For example, *RRC* 44/2 (211–208 BC), a gold 60-*as* piece, equivalent to six of the new silver denarii (at the time worth ten bronze asses each). Other multiples of a similar design appeared. See https://numismatics.org/crro/id/rrc-44.2, also Kay (2014), 16.
19. Livy 29.25.6–7.
20. Appian, *SW* 11.5.22 (Loeb II, p. 145).
21. Polybius 15.18–19.
22. Livy 28.38.14 and Polybius 16.23.7.
23. Livy 30.45.3.
24. Eckstein (2008), 4–5.

12 QUENCHING THE FLAME OF BOLD REBELLION

1. Justin 30.2, 31.1.1 (https://www.attalus.org/translate/justin4.html#30.2) for Sosibius and Agathocles.
2. Polybius 15.25.12.
3. Polybius 15.25.3–9.
4. Polybius 15.25.12.
5. Polybius 15.25.10–19.
6. Polybius 15.25.20–24.
7. Polybius 15.25.25–37.
8. Polybius 15.29.3.
9. Polybius 15.33.6–11.
10. Polybius 16.21–22.
11. Diodorus 28.14, on Aristomenes.
12. Polybius 16.27.5; Livy 31.2.3–4; Appian, *SW* 11.1.2.
13. Justin 30.3.2–8, 31.1 (https://www.attalus.org/translate/justin4.html#30.3). For the Lepidus coin, see Sear (2000), no. 373 and *RRC* 419/2.
14. For the Egyptian embassy to Rome, see Justin 30.2.8; for the 201 BC embassies, see Livy 31.2.1.
15. Polyaenus, *Stratagems* 4.16 (https://www.attalus.org/translate/polyaenus4B.html).
16. Polybius 16.34.3.
17. Appian, *SW* 11.1.2 (mistakenly referring to Ptolemy V as Philopator; Loeb II, pp. 107–9).
18. Justin 31.1.2–3.
19. Livy 33.19.8–11. See plate 10.
20. Appian, *SW* 11.1.2.
21. Polybius 18.40.1; Livy 33.38.1.
22. Polybius 18.1.14.
23. Recorded on the Rosetta Stone (Greek text at: http://www.attalus.org/egypt/rosettastone.html).

24. Diodorus Siculus 28.14; Plutarch, *Moralia* 71c–d (https://www.gutenberg.org/files/23639/23639-h/23639-h.htm).
25. Polybius 22.17.6.
26. Polybius 18.49–50.
27. Livy 33.39.4–7.
28. Livy 33.40.1–3, 18.51.
29. Livy 33.41.1ff.; Appian, *SW* 11.1.4.
30. Livy, 33.30.
31. Livy, 33.33.
32. Appian, *SW* 11.1.5 (Loeb II, p. 113); Livy 35.13.4.
33. Rochemonteix (1892–7), vol. 1, 517 de soubassement, section 2, rh column, lines 1–2 (https://books.google.co.uk/books?id=zWZZOik1BZEC&printsec=frontcover&dq=rochemonteix+temple+d%27edfou&hl=en&newbks=1&newbks_redir=0&sa=X&redir_esc=y#v=onepage&q=rochemonteix%20temple%20d'edfou&f=false), and see Hölbl (2001), 167.
34. For the inscription recording this at Edfu, see https://www.attalus.org/egypt/horus_edfu.html. Cleopatra I is unmentioned.
35. For example, Svoronos (1904–8), 1384. An alternative is Cleopatra II. Reverse carries the standard ΒΑΣΙΛΕΩΣ ΠΤΟΛΕΜΑΙΟΥ (King Ptolemy).
36. Livy 36.4.1–2.
37. Livy 37.3.9–11. The *as* was the basic unit of Roman bronze currency, tariffed at the time at ten to the silver denarius.
38. Shakespeare, *Antony and Cleopatra* 1.2.277.
39. Polybius 21.32.
40. Polybius 21.45.8.
41. Livy 37.45, 55, 38.38.
42. Polybius 21.42 passim but especially 21.42.12–14.
43. Manning et al. (2017) (https://www.nature.com/articles/s41467-017-00957-y).
44. *Ancient Egyptian Texts* 8.13 (https://www.attalus.org/egypt/horus_edfu.html).
45. Porter and Moss (1972), vol. 2, 225; Blyth (2006).
46. Hölbl (2001), 155; Thompson (2003), 115.
47. Graffito in Pestman et al. (1977) 13, no. 44.
48. Pestman (1965) is a good example of this inconclusive pursuit.
49. Ibid., 167.
50. *Translations of Hellenistic Inscriptions* 260 (https://www.attalus.org/docs/other/inscr_260.html).
51. Pfeiffer and Klinkott (2021), 243–4.
52. P. Koeln. 7.313 (https://papyri.info/ddbdp/p.koeln;7;313).
53. Manning (2003), 87.
54. Minas-Nerpel (2011), 61.
55. http://www.attalus.org/egypt/rosettastone.html, sections 25D–30D.
56. Polybius 22.17.1–5.
57. Cairo RT 2/3/25/7 (https://www.attalus.org/docs/other/inscr_262.html). The text depends on much restoration.
58. *OGIS* 98. Johnson (2002).
59. Lanciers (2020).
60. Polybius 22.17.6, and 22.

61. Nespoulous-Phalippou (2015), 121 ff., and especially 127. For Cleopatra's titles, see p. 53, bottom line.
62. Polybius 22.7.1, 9.1 ff.
63. Polybius 24.6.
64. Polybius (whose father was one of the envoys sent to Ptolemy) 22.3.8.
65. Polybius 22.17.6.
66. Diodorus 29.29.

13 HAVOC AND CONFUSION

1. Eusebius, *Chronicon* 58, citing Porphyry as his source.
2. Wong (1995) argues that Cleopatra recognized her potential vulnerability as a Syrian and had worked assiduously to ensure she was unassailable.
3. Polybius 28.22.1–5, referring to later events, only mentions Eulaeus in connection with important decisions.
4. Jerome citing Porphyry, FGrHist 260 F49a (https://www.attalus.org/translate/daniel.html); Diodorus 30.15.1.
5. For example, Svoronos (1904–8), 1396.
6. Bérnand (1969), no. 11, p. 118.
7. Hölbl (2001), 143, makes this claim. However, the inscription is undated and some of the names are missing, restored only by elimination.
8. See also another Kom Ombo relief showing Cleopatra II and III with the *nb-t3wy* title and also the *ḥq3* crook symbol of kingship: https://upload.wikimedia.org/wikipedia/commons/5/54/Cleopatra_Kom_Ombo.JPG.
9. Livy 42.26.8.
10. Jerome citing Porphyry, FGrHist 260 F49a (https://www.attalus.org/translate/daniel.html).
11. 2 *Maccabees* 4.21; Polybius 31.13.3. Hölbl (2001), 143, interprets this as Antiochus IV 'immediately . . . positioned troops in the border area between Syria and Palestine'. Antiochus may well have done, but the source does not say that. The identity of Apollonius is uncertain.
12. Livy 42.6.12.
13. Livy 44.24.1–7.
14. Livy 42.11 passim.
15. Livy 44.25.1–4.
16. B&D no. 48, p. 89.
17. Livy 42.29.7.
18. Livy 42.26.7.
19. Diodorus 30.15–16.
20. Diodorus 30.2.
21. Polybius 28.1.8–9, 18.
22. I *Maccabees* 1.17.
23. Polybius 28.19.1.
24. Jerome citing Porphyry, FGrHist 260 F49a (https://www.attalus.org/translate/daniel.html).
25. Diodorus 30.18.2; Polybius 30.26.9.
26. Polybius 28.19.
27. Polybius 28.21.1.

28. Diodorus 30.17.
29. Svoronos (1904–8), 1401 (Alexandria). Svoronos believed that Eulaeus was represented and that the coin was struck at Alexandria, not Paphos. That such divergent views can be held only serves to prove how uncertain study of Ptolemaic coinage is.
30. Polybius 28.23.4.
31. Justin 34.2.7–8 (http://www.attalus.org/translate/justin5.html); and Polybius 29.25.7.
32. Livy 44.19.5, 12.
33. Polybius 29.23.4; Livy 44.19.8 for Antiochus' claims of protecting Ptolemy VI.
34. Livy 44.19.10–14.
35. Livy 45.11.1; Antiochus' control of Egypt was a matter of concern to Rome, Polybius 29.2.1; Hölbl (2001), 146, suggests Antiochus had difficulties in Syria and Palestine but cites no evidence to suggest that there were any, merely that Antiochus passed through them.
36. Polybius 29.26.1.
37. Livy 45.11.8–11.
38. Livy 45.12.3.
39. Polybius 29.27.4–7; Justin 34.3.1–4.
40. Bowman (1996), 31. See also Ray (1976) for Hor's complete archive. Other dreams of Hor's can be found at: https://www.attalus.org/egypt/hor_dreams.html.
41. Polybius 29.27.10–13.
42. Huss (2001), 597 ff.; Nadig (2020).
43. Bowman (1996), 26.
44. Diodorus 31.15a.
45. P. Tebt. 3.1 781 (https://papyri.info/ddbdp/p.tebt;3.1;781).
46. P. Amh. 2.30 (https://papyri.info/ddbdp/p.amh;2;30).
47. Skeat and Turner (1968), specifically Text E, p. 204.
48. Diodorus 31.17b.
49. Faucher and Lorber (2010), 53.
50. Segre (1942), 175.
51. Clarysse and Lanciers (1989).
52. P. Genova 3.92 (https://papyri.info/ddbdp/sb;16;12821).
53. See Lewis (1986), 37–45, for the engineer Kleon and the vast amount of logistical effort poured into maintaining irrigation works under normal circumstances.
54. Manning (2010), 39–40, 44.
55. Hölbl (2001), 182.
56. *SP* I.97.
57. B&D no. 172, p. 280. See also Lewis (1986), 69–87, for a detailed survey of Ptolemaeus' texts.
58. Thompson (1988), 229–30; B&D no. 138, pp. 232–3; Goudriaan (1992), 75.
59. Thompson (1988), 234.
60. Ibid., 235 ff., covers this whole episode in detail.
61. For the petition to Ptolemy VI and Cleopatra II, see P. UPZ 1.42 (https://papyri.info/ddbdp/upz;1;42 and https://www.attalus.org/docs/select2/p271C.html), and Thompson (1988), 239–40. For some of the dreams, see Thompson (1987), 115.

62. *SP* I.100 (https://papyri.info/ddbdp/upz;1;70).

63. Lanciers (1988), 410–13, 420, 'probably' (*wohl*), 433 (https://archive.org/details/pap-cong-18-2/page/n215/mode/2up).

64. Diodorus 31.18.1–4.

65. Valerius Maximus 5.1.1f.

66. Diodorus 31.17c.

67. Minas-Nerpel (2011), 61.

68. P. UPZ 1.111 (https://papyri.info/ddbdp/upz;1;111) to the strategos at Memphis.

69. Thompson (1988), 215–16.

70. Thompson (2003), 118.

71. Poybius 31.10 passim.

72. Polybius 31.17.1–8.

73. Polybius 31.17.9–16, 19.1–4.

74. Polybius 31.20.1–5.

75. For the will of Ptolemy VIII, see B&D no. 51, pp. 92–3.

76. Polybius 33.11.1–6. There are of course only four Iowa-class battleships (the fifth and sixth being cancelled).

77. Diodorus 31.33; Polybius 39.7, or 39.18 (depending on the source text used). Book 39 of Polybius only survives in fragments, creating some confusion. He also calls Ptolemy VI at this point 'King of Syria', referring to the title he was given by Antioch on his last war in Syria. See: http://www.perseus.tufts.edu/hopper/text?doc=Plb.+39.18&fromdoc=Perseus%3Atext%3A1999.01.0234#note1.

78. In the Dodekaschoinos Stela, still at the Temple of Isis. Török (2009), 400–4.

79. I *Maccabees* 10.48.

80. I *Maccabees* 10.54–8; Josephus, *JA* 13.4.1.

81. Diodorus 32.9c; Josephus, *JA* 13.4.6–7.

82. Zonaras, *Epitome* 9.30 (fragments of Dio 21 in the Loeb II, p. 399).

83. The story comes from Dio 21.31, 72 (Loeb II, pp. 399ff.), and Pausanias 7.16.

84. Velleius Paterculus 2.1.1–2.

85. Livy 37.5.4 (booty); 37.46.3 (triumph).

86. Livy 37.57.10–15, 58.1 (censor election); 40.34.5 and *CIL* 1.626 (temple).

87. I *Maccabees* 11.10.

88. Josephus, *JA* 13.4.7.

89. Josephus, *JA* 13.4.8; Livy, *Periochae* 52.

90. Polybius 39.7 (https://penelope.uchicago.edu/Thayer/E/Roman/Texts/Polybius/39*.html) or 39.18, depending on the edition used.

14 MÉNAGE À TROIS

1. This is Dodson and Hilton's (2010, 280), 'Ptolemy D'.

2. Justin 38.8.2.

3. Justin 38.8.5; Orosius, *Against the Pagans* 5.10.6 (thought to be based on a lost book of Livy).

4. Neos Philopator, Memphites, and the various sources, ancient and modern, are discussed here: https://www.instonebrewer.com/TyndaleSites/Egypt/ptolemies/memphites_fr.htm. See Chauveau (2001) for a re-evaluation. Hölbl (2001), 194, and Fletcher (2008), 59, are among those who accept Justin's version.

5. Diodorus 33.6, 6a, 12.

6. Strabo 17.1.11; Matheson (2018). A familiar accusation levied against despots of the ancient world.
7. Josephus, *Against Apion* 2.5.
8. *SEG* 37.1372 (http://www.attalus.org/docs/seg/s37_1372.html, and see also https://www.trismegistos.org/tm/detail.php?tm=6054).
9. Diodorus 33.13.
10. Justin 38.8.5; Livy, *Periochae* 59; Lanciers (2019a).
11. Dodson and Hilton (2010), 268–9.
12. Lenzo (2015) discusses a stela (BM acc. no. EA 612) with the two Cleopatras and Ptolemy VIII where the women are given the same name and no other distinguishing label. For the stela, see https://www.britishmuseum.org/collection/object/Y_EA612.
13. Fischer-Bovet (2014), 102; Diodorus 33.20 (https://www.attalus.org/translate/diodorus33.html).
14. Diodorus 33.22–23.
15. Diodorus 33.28b.
16. Valerius Maximus 9.1.5.
17. Pliny, *NH* 33. 147–50. 'Scipio' is Lucius Cornelius Scipio Asiaticus, brother of Africanus.
18. Appian, *CW* 1.7–8; Plutarch, *Cato the Elder* 4.3–5.1.
19. Plutarch, *Tiberius Gracchus* 8.1–3, 9.4.
20. Scullard (1982), 1; Diodorus 34/35.2 (passim; https://www.attalus.org/translate/diodorus34.html).
21. Plutarch, *Gracchus* 14.1–2.
22. Appian, *CW* 1.14; re-election was not illegal but had not occurred for two centuries and under very different circumstances, Scullard (1982), 27.
23. Appian, *CW* 1.15–16. Plutarch, *Gracchus* 19.5 says the senators' attendants had brought weapons.
24. Justin 38.11.
25. Diodorus 34/35; Valerius Maximus 9.1 ext. 5. Justin 38.8.11–15. See earlier in this and the previous chapter for whether Memphites was the same person as Neos Philopator/Ptolemy VII.
26. Diodorus 34/35.14.
27. 'The sun . . .', quote from Seneca, *On Benefits* 4.26.1.
28. For the document in Greek, see https://papyri.info/ddbdp/upz;2;199; for the original publication, see P. UPZ I.199 (https://archive.org/details/urkundenderptole0002wilc/page/218/mode/2up); for a discussion of the meaning of the text, see Skarsouli (2020), 52; see also Thompson (1988), 152 for further references.
29. Vandorpe (2014), 166.
30. M&W vol. I, no. 10, pp. 17–18: https://archive.org/details/grundzgeundchr12wilc/page/18/mode/2up.
31. Justin 38.10.10.
32. Justin 39.1.2.
33. Justin 39.1.3.
34. Justin 39.1.6.
35. Justin 39.1.4–8.
36. Justin 39.1.8–10; Appian, *SW* 11.11.69.

37. For example, *Handbook of Syrian Coins* (HSC) by O. Hoover (2009), Lancaster PA, no. 1192 with the legend ΒΑΣΙΛΙΣΣΗΣ ΚΛΕΟΠΑΤΡΑΣ ΚΑΙ ΒΑΣΙΛΕΩΣ ΑΝΤΙΟΧΟΥ ('Queen Cleopatra and King Antiochus'), *c.* 125–121 BC.
38. Valerius Maximus 9.2. ext. 5.
39. The post, held by a man called Antaios, was previously believed to apply to the Arsinoite nome. See Lanciers (2019b).
40. Justin 39.2 passim.
41. Grant (1982), 136–7; Paganini (2021).
42. B&D, p. 131.
43. See Chapter 16 for the initiative by the farmers of Psenamosis.
44. Rossini (2022).
45. Justin 39.2.7–10.
46. Appian, *SW* 11.11.69.
47. 'Enfin, dès le règne d'Évergète II, les dernières possessions extérieures en Crète, à Théra et à Arsinoé-Méthana furent évacuées; il ne resta que Chypre et c'est à la stratégie de ce territoire qu'on joignit dorénavant la navarchie.' Van 't Dack (1973), 75.
48. Amnesty 118 BC. The text survives on fragments of papyri. See https://www.attalus.org/egypt/ptolemy_viii_decrees.html. For the Freek and another translation, see https://papyri.info/ddbdp/p.tebt;1;5.
49. de la Bédoyère (2020), 274–80.
50. Valerius Maximus 9.1 ext. 5.
51. Homer, *Odes* 5.72; Athenaeus, *Deipnosophistae* 2, p. 267, where 'Ptolemy II [sic] Euergetes' is erroneously given. See also Thompson (2009).
52. Justin 39.3.1.

15 VENAL MAYHEM

1. This is known in some modern communities where repeated cousin marriage is securely attested, resulting in a congenital abnormality incidence of 6.5 per cent, compared to 2.5 per cent in the general population (https://borninbradford.nhs.uk/research/publications/cousin-marriage-and-congenital-anomalies-in-a-multi-ethnic-birth-cohort/). A recent decline in the practice has followed improved awareness of the problems.
2. Ager (2005), 11.
3. Galinas, D.J. (1983), 'Persisting Negative Effects of Incest', *Psychiatry*, vol. 46 (November 1983), 312–32 (https://www.tandfonline.com/doi/abs/10.1080/00332747.1983.11024207).
4. Kluft, R. (2011), 'Ramifications of Incest', *Psychiatric Times*, vol. 27, no. 12 (https://www.psychiatrictimes.com/view/ramifications-incest).
5. Ager (2005), 18.
6. Ager (2006), 179, and see also Carney (1987).
7. Abdelhalim (2020) (file:///C:/Users/guyde/Downloads/THE_COLUMN_OF_CLEOPATRA_III_AND_PTOLEMY.pdf).
8. Justin 39.3.2.
9. See for example Dodson and Hilton (2010), 277, but some of the genealogical detail is challenged (inevitably) by some scholars; see Bennett (1997). It is impos-

sible in a book of this scale even to start becoming involved in dismantling the evidence. Nor would it lead to any useful conclusion.

10. Strabo 16.2.3.
11. Pausanias 1.9.1.
12. Justin 39.3.3–12.
13. *OGIS* 168. See: https://www.attalus.org/docs/ogis/s168.html. Strictly speaking, Cleopatra III's name is not legible in almost every instance. The reading therefore relies on restoring the name, though Ptolemy IX's name is preceded by another which can only be hers. Cleopatra the Sister also appears. Hölbl (2001), 206, says it is clear Ptolemy IX travelled on his own. This contradiction is an inevitable consequence of damaged texts.
14. Beness and Hillard (2003); *CIL* 1.2937a (Philae).
15. Due to Egypt's unsynchronized calendars, it is not easily possible to calibrate the given date of the inscription with the absolute date of the eclipse, but the Roman visitors might have ventured far enough to see it, or at least enjoyed a considerable partial eclipse: https://eclipse.gsfc.nasa.gov/5MCSEmap/-0199--0100/-115-08-29.gif (astronomical date is 29 August 115 BC which corrects to the calendrical 116 BC).
16. *SP* II, no. 416, p. 567.
17. *CIL* 10.1781 (Puteoli).
18. Ovid, *Metamorphoses* 1.747, 9.687 ff.
19. *RRC* 314/1b, Sear (2000), no. 191. Others include *RRC* 409/1, Sear (2000), no. 349 (Marcus Plaetorius Cestianus), for 67 BC.
20. Pausanias 1.9.2.
21. Walker and Higgs (2001), 60, no. 26. See: https://www.bridgemanimages.com/en/noartistknown/title/notechnique/asset/923844.
22. See for example B&D no. 169, pp. 276–7, in 106 BC.
23. *SP* I.27, giving 107 BC but it must be 106 BC.
24. For example, 106/105 BC with the regnal years L IB/Θ denoting Cleopatra III's 12th year and Ptolemy X's 9th. Svoronos (1904–8), 1727.
25. Clarysse and van der Veken (1983), 174b–184a (Ptolemy IX), 184b, 185 (Ptolemy X), 186 (Cleopatra III) (https://archive.org/details/eponymouspriests0024clar/page/36/mode/2up).
26. Shakespeare, *Cymbeline* 2.1.
27. Justin 39.4.1–2; Diodorus 34.39a.
28. Justin 39.4.3, who telescopes events in a misleading way.
29. Josephus, *JA* 13.12.6.
30. Josephus, *JA* 13.13.1.
31. Appian, *MW* 12.4.23; by 63 BC Pompey had collected some of what was left which had been given by the people of Kos to Mithridates VI. Ibid., 12.115.
32. Josephus, *JA* 13.10.4.
33. Josephus, *JA* 13.13.1.
34. Josephus, *JA* 13.13.2.
35. Hölbl (2001), 210.
36. Justin 39.4.6 lists the victims of Cleopatra III but was confused about her daughters; also, Pausanias 1.9.2.
37. Rossini (2022).

38. Athenaeus 73G, citing Poseidonios' lost history (https://www.attalus.org/old/athenaeus12c.html#550).
39. Johnson, A.C., Coleman-Norton, P.R., and Bourne, F.C. (1961), *Ancient Roman Statutes*, University of Texas Press, Austin, pp. 60–1, n. 56.
40. Justin 39.5.2.
41. Livy, *Periochae* 70; Tacitus, *Annals* 14.18.2.
42. The papyrus is P. Louvre AF 13854 (https://collections.louvre.fr/en/ark:/53355/cl010429504). Spiegelberg (1930) concluded that the most likely era is that of Ptolemy IX and X. See also de Cenival et al. (2018).
43. BM papyrus 465 (https://www.bl.uk/manuscripts/FullDisplay.aspx?ref=Papyrus_465).
44. Manning (2003), 87.
45. B&D no. 58, p. 106.
46. Honigman and Veïsse (2021), 323.
47. Pausanias 1.9.3.
48. Manning (2003), 37, for the giving up of Pathyris; *OGIS* 194 (vol. I, 275–9). (https://archive.org/details/orientisgraeciin01ditt/page/274/mode/2up).
49. Manning (2003), 47. Papyrus text (BGU 14.2370) at: https://papyri.info/ddbdp/bgu;14;2370. See also Salmenkivi (2012).
50. Porphyry, FGrHist 260 F2.9 on Ptolemy X and the Jews, accessed here via Eusebius: https://www.attalus.org/translate/eusebius1.html; Pausanias 1.9.5; Justin 39.5; Strabo 17.1.8. Note that Pausanias implies the expulsion of Ptolemy X took place immediately after the killing of Cleopatra III in 101 BC and that Ptolemy IX returned then.
51. Cicero, *Agrarian Law* speech 1.1, speech 2.41–2.
52. Cleopatra Berenice III, 'the daughter of the elder brother and wife of the younger brother, who took over control of the kingdom after the death of her father' (see below, this chapter). Porphyry via Eusebius at http://www.attalus.org/translate/eusebius1.html#165 (FGrHist 260 F 2.10–11).
53. Appian, *MW* 12.3.17; Dio 31.101; Plutarch, *Sulla* 24.4 (150,000 'in a single day'); Valerius Maximus 9.2. ext. 3 ('80,000 Roman citizens').
54. Appian, *CW* 1.102; Appian, *MW* 12.16.111.
55. Kay (2014), 161.
56. Appian, *MW* 12.4.22.
57. Cicero, *On the Imperium of Gnaeus Pompeius* or *In Favour of the Manilian Law* 19.
58. Plutarch, *Sulla* 8.3.
59. Plutarch, *Marius* 35.4.
60. Plutarch, *Marius* 35.5–6.
61. Plutarch, *Sulla* 10.4.
62. Appian, *MW* 12.4.22.
63. Plutarch, *Lucullus* 2.4.
64. Plutarch, *Lucullus* 2.2–3.2.
65. Pausanias 1.9.3.
66. Habicht (1992), 86.
67. Plutarch, *Marius* 43.4–6.
68. Plutarch, *Sulla* 22.1.
69. Plutarch, *Sulla* 23.5.
70. Appian, *MW* 12.4.23.

71. Plutarch, *Sulla* 23.5, 24.4–25.1.
72. See: https://www.ignstonebrewer.com/TyndaleSites/Egypt/ptolemies/berenice_iii_ fr.htm. Also, Porphyry FGrHist 260 F 2.10–11 via Eusebius (http://www.attalus. org/translate/eusebius1.html#165).
73. Bennett (2002) discusses the evidence for the co-regency and sequence of events (for example P. Grenf. 2 38: https://papyri.info/ddbdp/p.grenf;2;38/), but the arguments and conclusion are impenetrable.
74. Appian, *CW* 1.102.
75. Appian, *CW* 1.102. Appian does not mention the murder of Berenice. That can be found in Porphyry via Eusebius at http://www.attalus.org/translate/eusebius1. html#165 (FGrHist 260 F 2.10–11) where she is called Cleopatra for Cleopatra Berenice, and her relationship outlined.

16 THE TUNE OF FLUTES

1. Justin 39.5.4.
2. Cicero, *Against Verres* 2.4.61.
3. See Pausanias 1.9.3 (who said Berenice III was Ptolemy IX's only legitimate child); Ager (2005), 7.
4. Cleopatra VI Tryphaena is named as queen with Ptolemy XII ('sibling gods') on an ostracon of January 79 BC from Ombos, O.Joach. 1 (https://papyri.info/ ddbdp/o.joach;;1/). Porphyry believed she was Ptolemy XII's daughter, via Eusebius at http://www.attalus.org/translate/eusebius1.html#165 (FGrHist 260 F 2.10–11).
5. BM acc. no. EA 886 (https://www.britishmuseum.org/collection/object/Y_ EA886). Sometimes now called Psenptah. Full translation in Bevan (1927), 347–8. See also Thompson (1988), 138–9.
6. Potter (2021) provides an interesting example of a priestly dynasty of the period.
7. *Ancient Egyptian Texts* 8.13 (https://www.attalus.org/egypt/horus_edfu.html).
8. Strabo 17.1.11 (see Loeb VIII, pp. 43–5); Athenaeus 1.16B for Homeric flute-playing heroes, and 1.184D–E on esteemed schools where flute-playing was taught.
9. Reymond (1981), 127, no. 1, but note that he translates this term as 'queen' (p. 131), thereby missing the point that she held joint status with her husband.
10. Quaegebeur (1989).
11. Dodson and Hilton (2010), 277.
12. Strabo 17.1.11, but Bennett (1997), 60, believes Strabo 'causes difficulties', preferring his own take on the evidence and suggesting that all Ptolemy XII's children were by Cleopatra VI. This sort of contradiction is typical of studies of the period.
13. Roller (2010), 15, 'Cleopatra VII, then, was perhaps three-quarters Macedonian and one-quarter Egyptian', with 'perhaps' being the operative word. There is no evidence to support the contention.
14. For example, BM acc. no. EA 55252: https://www.britishmuseum.org/collection/ object/Y_EA55252. See also Cafici (2014).
15. Paganini (2021), 186–8. For the full text in Greek and translation, see: https:// philipharland.com/greco-roman-associations/decree-honoring-a-donor-to-a-

synod-of-farmers/. Psenamosis means something like 'bread of Ahmose ("moon born")'.

16. Plutarch, *Crassus* 13.1.

17. Cicero, *On the King of Alexandria* (https://www.attalus.org/translate/bobiensia.html#alex).

18. Appian, *MW* 17.114; Josephus, *JA* 14.3.1. The claim by Hölbl (2001), 224, that Ptolemy supplied 8,000 cavalry for Pompey's campaign in Judaea in 63 BC (Pliny, *NH* 33.136) does not bear up. At best the reference is ambiguous and seems only to have been an observation of Ptolemy's wealth at that time since it goes straight on to describe a feast for 1,000 guests with 1,000 golden goblets renewed at each course.

19. Plutarch, *Caesar* 11.3–4.

20. Herodotus 2.137–8.

21. Diodorus 1.83.8–9.

22. Hölbl (2001), 225, claims the Roman was 'slaughtered'. If that had been the case, then one might have expected Diodorus to say so.

23. Suetonius, *Caesar* 54.3.

24. Caesar, *Civil Wars* 3.107; Plutarch, *Caesar* 48.8; Cicero, *Letters to Atticus* 2.16.2.

25. Livy, *Periochae* 104; Plutarch, *Cato the Younger* 34.2–7.

26. Valerius Maximus 9.4. ext. 1; Dio 29.22.2–3; Plutarch, *Cato the Younger* 35.1, 36.1. For clarity: Ptolemy, king of Cyprus, was Ptolemy XII's younger brother.

27. Dio 39.12.1.

28. Plutarch, *Cato the Younger* 35.2–5. For Cleopatra (VII) in Rome with her father, see Goodchaux (2001), 131.

29. Documentary evidence for the titles and status of Cleopatra VI and Berenice IV is very limited. See Ricketts (1990), and a papyrus from Oxyrhynchus (P. Oxy. 55.3777; https://papyri.info/ddbdp/p.oxy;55;3777) in which Berenice is described as βασιλευούσης, 'ruling'.

30. Porphyry (FGrHist 260 F 2.10–11) via Eusebius (http://www.attalus.org/translate/eusebius1.html#165), but he was confused and believed Berenice IV and Cleopatra VI Tryphaena were sisters. See Hölbl (2001), 252, note 24; Dio 39.13.1.

31. Strabo 17.1.11 (Loeb VIII, p. 45).

32. Dio 39.57; Strabo 17.1.11 (Loeb VIII, p. 45). There are examples of the disposing of troublesome Roman consorts, for example Agrippina the Younger's alleged murder of her husband Claudius in AD 54, or Nero's brutal killing of his empress Poppaea in 65. See also Ricketts (1990), 59, who rejects the idea that Archelaus was ever a co-regent.

33. Dio 39.13.1–14.4.

34. Dio 39.15.1–16.2.

35. Dio 39.16.3.

36. Plutarch, *Pompey* 49.6.

37. Dio 39.57.3–58.1.

38. Strabo 17.1.11 (Loeb VIII, 45) says Ptolemy XII killed Archelaus when he executed Berenice but at 12.3.34 (vol. V, 437) says Archelaus was killed in battle by Gabinius, who was fighting *for* Ptolemy.

39. Cicero, *For Rabirius Postumus* 25.

40. Caesar, *CW* 3.110.

41. Siani-Davies (1997), especially 339–40.
42. Lucan, *Pharsalia* 10.92–99.
43. Dio 42.35.4; Caesar, *CW* 3.106.
44. Caesar, *CW* 3.108–9.

17 PASSION AND WITCHERY

1. This title is only known from coins. See later, this chapter.
2. Vergil, *Aeneid* 1.364.
3. Thompson (1988) and Manning (2010) are just two examples, among others.
4. When Tutankhamun's widow Ankhesenamun sought a Hittite prince for her husband, he was killed probably by a palace conspiracy. She disappeared, her fate still unknown. An elderly courtier, Ay, became pharaoh instead. See de la Bédoyère (2022), 333–54.
5. For 'passion and witchery', see Dio 49.34.1.
6. Minas (2005), 150.
7. Clarysse (2020a), 39, fig. 4.3, Louvre acc. no. E27113 (https://commons.wiki-media.org/wiki/File:Cleopatra_Isis_Louvre_E27113.jpg); Savvopoulos (2020), 92. See also: http://www.attalus.org/docs/other/inscr_3.html.
8. Most conveniently accessed in hieroglyph form here: https://pharaoh.se/pharaoh/Cleopatra-VII.
9. Roth (2005), 12.
10. Plutarch, *Antony* 27; for Mithridates VI, see Valerius Maximus 8.7. ext. 16.
11. Roller (2010), 15.
12. 'βασιλίσσης Κλεοπάτρας θεᾶς Φιλοπάτωρ', Fayum 3.205 (https://epigraphy.packhum.org/text/216121).
13. 'βασιλέως καὶ βασιλίσσης προσταξάντων'. C.Ord.Ptol.73 (https://papyri.info/ddbdp/bgu;8;1730). For the Apis stela, see Chapter 9, penultimate paragraph and note.
14. Plutarch, *Pompey* 77.2; ibid., *Caesar* 48.5; Caesar, *CW* 3.108.
15. Dio 42.3.4, 36.3.
16. Dio 42.2.6.
17. Plutarch, *Pompey* 77–80.
18. Dio 42.3.1–4.5, 5.2–5.
19. Caesar, *CW* 3.106.
20. Dio 42.8; Plutarch, *Pompey* 80.5.
21. Dio 42.9.1; 42.34.1–35.4; Caesar, *CW* 3.109 ff.
22. Dio 42.35.5–6.
23. Dio 42.36.1–38.4
24. Plutarch, *Pompey* 80.5–6. Potheinus' death, Caesar, *CW* 3.112. Theodotus was later killed by Cassius. Appian, *CW* 2.90. There is some confusion about what happened to Achillas. Dio 42.40.1 says Arsinoe killed Achillas, Plutarch that it was Caesar.
25. Dio 42.39.1–43.4; Plutarch, *Caesar* 49.9, just says he 'disappeared'.
26. It has been argued that Cleopatra may have tried to elevate her younger brother in 50 BC and displace Ptolemy XIII then. See Ricketts (1979).
27. Reymond (1981), 170, 176. Cleopatra has the feminized *ḥq3t* crook ruler symbol and the unfeminized title 'Lord of the Two Lands', using the formula *nb-xpr-xpr*

where a pair of scarabs represent the Two Lands of Egypt instead of the earlier horizontal bars in Middle Egyptian.

28. Suetonius, *Caesar* 52.1; Appian, *CW* 2.90.
29. Dio 44.1–45.1.
30. Suetonius, *Caesar* 52.10.
31. Plutarch, *Caesar* 49.10; Suetonius, *Caesar* 52.1.
32. Cicero, *Letters to Atticus* 14.20.2.
33. Reymond (1981), 143, line 5, and 149.
34. Suetonius, *Caesar* 52.2.
35. 'Caesar' (Hirtius), *Alexandrine War* 33.
36. Suetonius, *Caesar* 76.3.
37. Cicero, *Letters to his Friends* 12.11.1, *quattuorque legiones quas A. Allienus ex Aegypto eduxit traditas ab eo mihi esse scito* ('rest assured the four legions which Aulus Allienus led from Egypt have been handed over to me').
38. Dio 43.19.3.
39. Josephus, *JA* 15.4.1; Beard, M. 'The skeleton of Cleopatra's sister? Steady on', *Times Literary Supplement* (16 March 2009).
40. *reginam odi*, 'I hate the queen'. Cicero, *Letters to Atticus* 15.15.20.
41. Dio 43.27.3.
42. Cicero, *Letters to Atticus* 14.8.1.
43. Porphyry via Eusebius (http://www.attalus.org/translate/eusebius1.html#159).
44. Bingen (2007), 44–56.
45. Goodchaux (2001). For the reliefs, see for example https://iiif-prod.nypl.org/index.php?id=44080&t=v.
46. Translated from Minas (2005), 151.
47. Pliny, *NH* 5.58.
48. Seneca, *Natural Questions* 2.4.15, who adds that an unspecified 'earlier period' of nine years without inundations had occurred (https://archive.org/details/physicalsciencei00seneiala/page/172/mode/2up).
49. Appian 4.61, 108; Monson (2012), 4–5.
50. Josephus, *Against Apion* 2.5.
51. Appian 3.68, effectively repeated at 4.59; Cicero, *Letters to his Friends* 12.11.1.
52. Plutarch, *Antony* 25.3.
53. Dio 48.4.1.
54. Sear (2000), nos. 1516–17, 42–41 BC.
55. Plutarch, *Antony* 31.2.
56. Sear (2000), nos. 1511–1513, 39–38 BC.
57. Plutarch, *Antony* 35–36.
58. He wrote to Octavian to that effect. Suetonius, *Augustus* 69.2; Seneca, *Suasoria* 1.6 refers to the bigamous marriage.
59. 19 May 36 BC (adjusted from astronomical year 35 BC; astronomical dates count a year 0), see https://eclipse.gsfc.nasa.gov/5MCSEmap/-0099-0000/-35-05-19.gif and https://www.eclipsewise.com/solar/SEprime/-0099--0000/SE-0035May19Tprime.html. Alexandria was outside the path of totality.
60. Cleopatra is named thus on coins issued in her name and on one with Antony. See Buttrey (1954) who suggests that it is a proclamation of her status as a Seleucid monarch. For the coin see Walker and Higgs (2001), 234, who reference

Buttrey, and https://www.artic.edu/artworks/194522/tetradrachm-coin-portraying-queen-cleopatra-vii.

61. Plutarch, *Antony* 54.
62. van Minnen (2000). Illustrated and described by Walker and Higgs (2001), 180, no. 188.
63. Line adapted from Admiral Roland's in *Where Eagles Dare* by Alistair MacLean (1967).
64. *RPC* I 4094.
65. Shakespeare, *Richard II* 4.1.
66. Plutarch, *Antony* 58.3; Dio 50.3.4–4.1; and thanks to Alexander Hamilton (1774) for the phrasing borrowed here.
67. Plutarch, *Antony* 29.1; Vergil, *Aeneid* 4.554–570.
68. Plutarch, *Antony* 68.1; Dio 50.31 ff.
69. Dio 51.5.5.
70. Dio 51.9.6.
71. Plutarch, *Antony* 76.
72. Dio 51.10.6; Plutarch, *Antony* 77.
73. Dio 51.11–13.
74. Antony had confirmed Caesarion's paternity to the boy: Dio 50.3.5.
75. Gray-Fow (2014), 65. It is of course theoretically possible that Caesarion escaped Octavian's assassins; if so, he had the wit to disappear without trace.
76. Plutarch, *Antony* 86.4.
77. Strabo 17.3.7; Pliny, *NH* 5.11; for a life of Cleopatra Selene, see Draycott (2022).
78. Horace, *Odes* 1.37.
79. Propertius 3.11.39.
80. Pliny, *NH* 9.119–21. The other earring was divided in two and used to adorn the ears of Venus in the Pantheon in Rome. Repeated by Macrobius at 3.17.14–17.
81. Appian, *CW* 2.102.

18 THE END OF EGYPT'S GILDED AGE

1. Charles Dickens, *The Old Curiosity Shop*, chapter 73.
2. 'One could say the Romans freed the Greeks right into the Roman Empire', Anson (2023), 4. The beginning of the paragraph is borrowed from Byron's *Childe Harold's Pilgrimage* (1812–18) 4.12.
3. *Rarus duabus tribusve civitatibus ad propulsandum commune periculum conventus. Ita singuli pugnant, universi vicuntur*, Tacitus, *Agricola* 12.2.
4. Alston (1995), 10.
5. Millar (1981), 182–95, provides a succinct, if now dated, summary of how Ptolemaic Egypt was absorbed into the Roman province of Egypt.
6. Plutarch, *Antony* 86.5. For a statue base of Antony from Alexandria, see Walker and Higgs (2001), 232, no. 213.
7. Strabo 17.1.53.
8. Dio 77.5.5.
9. Cole (2019).
10. Monson (2012), 3–4.

11. Vatican Museums acc. no. 22682 (https://m.museivaticani.va/content/museivati-cani-mobile/en/collezioni/musei/museo-gregoriano-egizio/sala-v--statuario/gruppo-con-tolomeo-ii.html).
12. Pliny, *NH* 36.58. The statue is lost but a copy survives in the Vatican Museums, acc. no. 2300 (https://catalogo.museivaticani.va/index.php/Detail/objects/MV.2300.0.0?lang=en_US).
13. Vitruvius 6.3.8–9.
14. Clarke (1991), 67.
15. Tacitus, *Annals* 2.61.1 (Germanicus); *Historia Augusta* (Hadrian) 14.5, Dio 69.11 (passim).
16. Alfano's essay in Walker and Higgs (2001) is a useful survey of Nilotica in Roman Italy.
17. Ausonius, *The Moselle* 310 ff. (Loeb I, 249).
18. Sidonius, *Poems* 5.457 ff.
19. Macrobius 3.17.14–17.
20. Gibbon (1776–88), chapter 52.
21. *Oracle of the Potter*, cited by Bowman (1996), 31. Some of the text is also available at: https://www.attalus.org/egypt/potters_oracle.html.

APPENDIX 3

1. These are taken from the amnesty decree of 118 BC, P. Tebt. 1.5 (https://papyri.info/ddbdp/p.tebt;1;5).
2. Theocritus, *Idylls* 15.24 ἀκούω χρῆμα καλόν τι κοσμεῖν τὰν βασίλισσαν, 'I am told the Queen is giving a fine show', and see Parsons (2011), 151; Herodian 1.7.4 for Faustina the Younger as βασίλισσα. For the Rosetta Stone, see https://digitalcollections.nypl.org/items/510d47e2-6f38-a3d9-e040-e00a18064a99.
3. See for example Wong (1995), 58–9.

APPENDIX 4

1. Watson (2014), 17; quote from Iossif and Lorber (2021), 222.
2. Segre (1942), 174; Lewis (1986), 17, estimates the ratio at 500:1. But Faucher and Lorber (2010), 54, are sceptical about the ability to measure these ratios and their impact.
3. P. Tebt. 1.46 (https://papyri.info/ddbdp/p.tebt;1;46; also in Lewis (1986), 121).
4. 'It was by no means the norm for Ptolemaic kings after Ptolemy I to place their portraits on their [silver] coins. The portrait of Ptolemy I remained the standard design': Walker and Higgs (2001), 85.
5. Faucher and Lorber (2010), 36 and throughout, discuss the problems with dating the Ptolemaic bronze coins. To the layman the subject is impenetrable and, frankly, many solutions to attribution are rather less than convincing while having minimal significance for the history of the period.
6. For example, Svoronos (1904–8), 1486 (Ptolemy VI), 1649 (Ptolemy VIII).
7. See Lorber (2016) for a detailed survey of Ptolemaic coinage.

FURTHER READING

ABBREVIATIONS

A	Arrian, *Anabasis of Alexander*
AJN	*American Journal of Numismatics*
AncSoc	*Ancient Society*
B&D	Bagnall, R.S., and Derow, P. (2003) (see Books and articles below)
BASP	*Bulletin of the American Society of Papyrologists*
BGU	Ägyptische Urkunden aus den Staatlichen Museen Berlin, Griechische Urkunden, I–XIV, 1895–
BM	British Museum
CIL	*Corpus Inscriptionum Latinarum*
CNG	Classical Numismatic Group (http://www.cngcoins.com)
CPI	Corpus of Ptolemaic Inscriptions (http://cpi.csad.ox.ac.uk/inscriptions/)
CUP	Cambridge University Press
CW	Civil Wars (Caesar and Appian)
FGrHist	Jacoby (1923–58) (but mainly derived here from http://attalus.org/egypt/index.html; see individual notes for links and below under Websites)
Hist: ZfAG	*Historia: Zeitschrift für Alte Geschichte*
JA	*Jewish Antiquities* (Josephus)
JEA	*Journal of Egyptian Archaeology*
JNES	*Journal of Near Eastern Studies*
M&W	Mitteis, L., and Wilcken, U. (1963) (see Books and articles below)
MW	Mithridatic Wars (Appian)
NH	*Natural History* (Pliny the Elder)
OGIS	*Orientis Graeci Inscriptiones Selectae* (Dittenberger, W., 1903)
OUP	Oxford University Press
P.	Papyrus (followed by various identifying suffixes)
RPC	*Roman Provincial Coinage* (https://rpc.ashmus.ox.ac.uk/)

FURTHER READING

RRC   *Roman Republican Coinage* (Crawford, M.H., 1974)

SEG   *Supplementum Epigraphicum Graecum*

SP   *Select Papyri*, Loeb series vols I and II

SW   *Syrian Wars* (Appian)

T&H   Thames & Hudson

TAM   *Tituli Asiae Minoris*, by Österreichische Akademie der Wissenschaften (Vindobonae 1901) (https://archive.org/details/gri_33125010455224)

ZPE   *Zeitschrift für Papyrologie und Epigraphik*

1. WEBSITES

Many websites are featured in the notes. These now provide an unmatched opportunity to access many useful texts, hitherto only readable in hard copy in inaccessible or exclusive libraries.

N.B. These websites were correct at the time of going to press. Over time it is likely that some will change or be removed altogether.

The Ptolemaic Dynasty: a very useful site with genealogical details and family trees: https://www.instonebrewer.com/TyndaleSites/Egypt/ptolemies/genealogy.htm

The Pharaoh.se site provides all Egyptian rulers' names in hieroglyphs with transliterations and translations. The Ptolemies can be found here: https://pharaoh.se/late-period

Attalus, a site packed with texts (including Porphyry) from the period: http://attalus.org/index.html, especially: http://attalus.org/egypt/index.html

Papyri: https://www.attalus.org/docs/index.html

Coinage: these sites provide images and descriptions of Ptolemaic coinage:
    http://ptolemybronze.com/
    http://www.ptolemaic.net/
    https://numismatics.org/pco/

Corpus of Ptolemaic Inscriptions: http://cpi.csad.ox.ac.uk/inscriptions/

Egyptian Royal Genealogy: Chris Bennett's epic website: https://www.instonebrewer.com/TyndaleSites/Egypt/index.htm and https://www.instonebrewer.com/TyndaleSites/Egypt/ptolemies/genealogy.htm covers the complex subject of Ptolemaic genealogy in spectacular detail with links to almost every possible piece of evidence, but obviously reflects its author's views.

Internet Archive, an invaluable repository of electronic versions of many obscure texts. Free to use: https://archive.org/. Fraser (1972, see below) is, for example, available in full.

Papyri: this site has a vast database of papyri texts though only some are translated:
    https://papyri.info/
    also: https://www.trismegistos.org/

Ptolemaic coinage:
    http://ptolemybronze.com/
    http://www.ptolemaic.net/

Tertullian, other texts (including Justin) at https://www.tertullian.org/fathers/index.htm

FURTHER READING

2. ANCIENT SOURCES

The written sources for Alexander and the immediate aftermath are most easily found in modern paperback translations, and in the Loeb series which provides the Greek or Latin original text with an English translation. Thereafter, the Ptolemies pop up in the works of, for example, Appian, Diodorus Siculus, Livy, Polybius, and Strabo. Many of these can be found on:

Lacus Curtius. A priceless collection of Greek and Roman source texts online, for example:

Diodorus Siculus: http://penelope.uchicago.edu/Thayer/E/Roman/Texts/Diodorus_Siculus/home.html

Polybius: http://penelope.uchicago.edu/Thayer/E/Roman/Texts/Polybius/home.html

An internet search of this site for other ancient authors' names and Lacus Curtius will show up many more.

Perseus Tufts. Another site with numerous classical texts: https://www.perseus.tufts.edu/hopper/ – enter the source required in the search box.

For more obscure texts, such as Justin and Porphyry:

Justin: https://www.attalus.org/info/justinus.html

Porphyry via Eusebius: https://www.attalus.org/translate/eusebius1.html and https://www.tertullian.org/fathers/eusebius_chronicon_02_text.htm

Porphyry via Jerome: https://www.attalus.org/translate/daniel.html

3. BOOKS AND ARTICLES

The literature on Ptolemaic Egypt is vast. The titles listed here were the most useful for the purposes of writing this book, with more recent scholarship prioritized.

Abdelhalim, A. (2020), 'The Column of Cleopatra III and Ptolemy IX from Kom Ombo in the Gem', *Shedet*, vol. 7, no. 7, Faculty of Archaeology, Fayoum University

Ades, A.F., and Glaeser, E.L. (1995), 'Trade and Circuses: Explaining Urban Giants', in *Quarterly Journal of Economics*, vol. 110, no. 1 (Feb.), 195–227

Ager, S. (2005), 'Familiarity Breeds: Incest and the Ptolemaic Dynasty', *Journal of Hellenic Studies*, vol. 125, 1–34

Ager, S. (2006), 'The Power of Excess: Royal Incest and the Ptolemaic Dynasty', *Anthropologica*, vol. 48, no. 2, 165–86

Alfano, C. (2001), 'Egyptian Influences in Italy', in Walker and Higgs (2001), 276–89

Alston, R. (1995), *Soldier and Society in Roman Egypt*, Routledge, London

Anson, E.M. (2023), *Ptolemy I Soter: Themes and Issues*, Bloomsbury, London

Bagnall, R.S. (1976), *The Administration of Ptolemaic Possessions outside Egypt*, Brill, Leiden

Bagnall, R.S. (2002), 'Alexandria: Library of Dreams', *Proceedings of the American Philosophical Society*, vol. 146, no. 4 (Dec.), 348–62

Bagnall, R.S., and Derow, P. (2003), *The Hellenistic Period: Historical Sources in Translation*, Blackwell Sourcebooks in Ancient History no. 7, Oxford

Baralay, S. (2020), 'Hellenistic Sacred Dedications: The View from Egypt', in Bowman and Crowther (2020), 114–26

Bauschatz, J. (2007), 'The Strong Arm of the Law? Police Corruption in Ptolemaic Egypt', *Classical Journal*, vol. 103, no. 1 (Oct.–Nov.), 13–39

Beness, J.J., and Hillard, T. (2003), 'The First Romans at Philae', *ZPE*, Bd. 144, 203–7

Bennett, C. (1997), 'Cleopatra Tryphaena and the Genealogy of the Later Ptolemies', *AncSoc*, vol. 28, 39–66

Bennett, C. (2002), 'The Chronology of Berenice III', *ZPE*, Bd. 139, 143–8

Bennett, C. (2005), 'Arsinoe and Berenice at the Olympics', *ZPE*, Bd. 154, 91–6

Bérnand, A. (1969), *Les Inscriptions grecques (et latines) de Philae*, Vol. I Époque Ptolémaïque, Centre Nationale de la Recherche Scientifique, Paris

Bevan, E. (1927), *A History of Egypt under the Ptolemaic Dynasty*, Methuen, London

Bilde, P., Engberg-Pedersen, T., and Zahle, J. (eds) (1992), *Ethnicity in Hellenistic Egypt*, Studies in Hellenistic Civilization III, Aarhus University Press, Aarhus

Bingen, J. (2007), *Hellenistic Egypt: Monarchy, Society, Economy, Culture. Edited with an Introduction by Roger S. Bagnall*, University of California Press, Berkeley

Blyth, E. (2006), *Karnak: The Evolution of a Temple*, Routledge, New York

Bosch-Puche, F. (2014), 'Alexander the Great's Egyptian Names in the Barque Shrine at Luxor Temple', in Grieb, V., Nawotka, K., and Wojciechowska, A. (2014), *Alexander the Great and Egypt: History, Art, Tradition*, Wrocław/Breslau, 18/19 Nov. 2011, Harrassowitz Verlag, Wiesbaden

Boswinkel, E., and Pestman, P.W. (1982), *Les archives privées de Dionysius, fils de Kephalas*, Papyrologica Lugduno-Batava, vol. 22, *Textes grecs et démotiques*, Brill, Leiden

Bowman, A.K. (2nd edition 1996), *Egypt after the Pharaohs*, British Museum Press, London

Bowman, A.K. (2006), 'Recolonising Egypt', in Wiseman, T.P. (ed.), *Classics in Progress: Essays on Ancient Greece and Rome*, British Academy Centenary Monographs, OUP, Oxford (online edn, British Academy Scholarship Online, 31 Jan. 2012 (https://doi.org/10.5871/bacad/9780197263235.003.0008)

Bowman, A., and Crowther, C. (eds) (2020), *The Epigraphy of Ptolemaic Egypt. Oxford Studies in Ancient Documents*, OUP, Oxford and New York

Boys-Stones, G., Graziosi, B., and Vasunia, P. (eds) (2009), *The Oxford Handbook of Hellenistic Studies*, OUP, Oxford

Breasted, J.H. (1906), *Ancient Records of Egypt: Historical Documents*, vol. II, University of Chicago Press, Chicago

Bresciani, E. (1983), 'Registrazione Catastale e Idiologia Politica nell'Egitto Tolemaico. A Complemente di "la Spedizione di Tolemeo II in Siria in un Ostrakon Demotico Inedito di Karnak"', *Egitto e Vicino Oriente*, vol. 6, 15–31

British Museum (2016), *Sunken Cities: Egypt's Lost Worlds*, The BP Exhibition, British Museum with T&H, London

Budge, E.A. Wallis (1902), *Egypt under the Saites, Persians, and Ptolemies*, Kegan Paul et alia, London

Budka, J., and Mekis, T. (2017), 'The Family of Wah-ib-Re I (TT 414) from Thebes', *Ägypten & Levante*, vol. 27, 219–40

Buttrey, T. (1954), 'Thea Neotera on Coins of Antony and Cleopatra', *Museum Notes (American Numismatic Society)*, vol. 6, 95–109

Butzer, K.W. (1976), *Early Hydraulic Civilization in Egypt: A Study in Cultural Ecology*, University of Chicago Press, Chicago

Cafici, G. (2014), 'Looking at the Egyptian Elite: Sculptural Production of the Ptolemaic Period', *Egitto e Vicino Oriente*, vol. 37, 111–21

Cannata, M. (2020), *Three Hundred Years of Death: The Egyptian Funerary Industry in the Ptolemaic Period*, Brill, Leiden

Carney, E.D. (1987), 'The Reappearance of Royal Sibling Marriage in Ptolemaic Egypt', *Parola del Passato*, vol. 42, 420–39

Carney, E.D. (2013), *Arsinoë of Egypt and Macedon*, OUP, Oxford

Casson, L. (1993), 'A Petrie Papyrus and the Battle of Raphia', *BASP*, vol. 30, no. 3/4, 87–92

Charles, M. (2007), 'Elephants at Raphia: Reinterpreting Polybius 5.84–5', *Classical Quarterly*, new series, vol. 57, no. 1 (May), 306–11

Chauveau, M. (2001), 'Encore Ptolémée "VII" et le dieu Neos Philopatôr!', *Revue d'Égyptologie*, vol. 51, 257–61

Clarke, J.R. (1991), *The Houses of Roman Italy, 100 BC–AD 250: Ritual, Space, and Decoration*, University of California Press, Berkeley and Los Angeles

Clarysse, W. (2002), 'Three Ptolemaic Papyri on Prisoners', in *Archiv für Papyrusforschung und verwandte Gebiete*, vol. 48, no. 1 (Jan.), 98–106

Clarysse, W. (2020a), 'Greek Texts on Egyptian Monuments', in Bowman and Crowther (2020), 35–58

Clarysse, W. (2020b), 'Inscriptions and Papyri: Two Intersecting Worlds', in Bowman and Crowther (2020), 159–78

Clarysse, W., and Lanciers, E. (1989), 'Currency and the Dating of Greek and Demotic Papyri from the Ptolemaic Period', *AncSoc*, vol. 20, 117–32

Clarysse, W., and Thompson, D.J. (2006), *Counting the People in Hellenistic Egypt*, 2 volumes, Cambridge Classical Studies, CUP, Cambridge

Clarysse, W., and van der Veken, G. (1983), *The Eponymous Priests of Ptolemaic Egypt (P.L. Bat. 24): Chronological Lists of the Priests of Alexandria and Ptolemais with a Study of the Demotic Transcriptions of their Names*, Brill, Leiden

Clayman, D.L. (2014), *Berenice II and the Golden Age of Ptolemaic Egypt*, OUP, Oxford

Clayton, P. (1994), *Chronicle of the Pharaohs*, T&H, London

Cole, E. (2019), 'Negotiating Elite Identity through Linguistic Display in Ptolemaic and Early Roman Egypt', *AncSoc*, vol. 49, 231–58

Cole, S.E. (2022), 'Negotiating Identity through the Architecture and Interior Decoration of Elite Households in Ptolemaic Egypt', *Arts*, vol. 11, no. 1 (https://doi.org/10.3390/arts11010003)

Connor, A. (2022), *Confiscation or Coexistence: Egyptian Temples in the Age of Augustus*, New Texts from Ancient Cultures, University of Michigan Press, Ann Arbor

Crawford, M.H. (1974), *Roman Republican Coinage*, CUP, Cambridge

de Cenival, F., Devauchelle, D., and Pezin, P. (2018), 'Les "révoltés" d'Hermonthis (Pap. Louvre AF 13584 R°)', in van Heel et al. (2018), 233–48

de la Bédoyère, G. (2020), *Gladius: Living, Fighting and Dying in the Roman Army*, Little, Brown, London

de la Bédoyère, G. (2022), *Pharaohs of the Sun: How Egypt's Despots and Dreamers Drove the Rose and Fall of Tutankhamun's Egypt*, Little, Brown, London

Derow, P. (2003), 'The Arrival of Rome: From the Illyrian Wars to the Fall of Macedon', in Erskine (ed.) (2003), 51–70

Dittenberger, W. (1903), *Orientis Graeci Inscriptiones Selectae*, vols I–II, Lipsiae S. Hirzel, Leipzig

Dodson, A. (2016), *The Royal Tombs of Ancient Egypt*, Pen & Sword, Barnsley

Dodson, A. (2019), *Rameses III, King of Egypt: His Reign and Afterlife*, American University in Cairo Press, Cairo

Dodson, A. (2020), *Nefertiti, Queen and Pharaoh of Egypt: Her Life and Afterlife*, American University in Cairo Press, Cairo

Dodson, A., and Hilton. D. (2010), *The Complete Royal Families of Ancient Egypt*, T&H, London (original edition 2004)

Dodson, A., and Ikram, S. (1998), *The Mummy in Ancient Egypt: Equipping the Dead for Eternity*, T&H, London

Dodson, A., and Ikram, S. (2008), *The Tomb in Ancient Egypt: Royal and Private Sepulchres from the Early Dynastic Period to the Romans*, T&H, London

Dogaer, L. (2018), 'Osoroeris son of Horos, mortuary priest (choachyte)', *Leuven Homepage of Papyrus Collections*, ArchID 50. Version 1 (2018) (https://www.trismegistos.org/arch/archives/pdf/50.pdf)

Dogaer, N. (2021), 'Beer for the Gods and Coin for the Priests: Temple Involvement in the Beer Industry in Hellenistic Egypt', *AncSoc*, vol. 51, 81–100

Draycott, J. (2022), *Cleopatra's Daughter: Egyptian Princess, Roman Prisoner, African Queen*, Head of Zeus, London

Eckstein, A.M. (2008), *Rome Enters the Greek East: From Anarchy to Hierarchy in the Hellenistic Mediterranean 230–170 BC*, Wiley, Chichester

Erskine, A. (1995), 'Culture and Power in Ptolemaic Egypt: The Museum and Library of Alexandria', *Greece & Rome*, vol. 42, no. 1 (Apr.), 38–48

Erskine, A. (2002), 'Life after Death: Alexandria and the Body of Alexander', *Greece & Rome*, vol. 49, no. 2 (Oct.), 163–79

Erskine, A. (ed.) (2003), *A Companion to the Hellenistic World*, Blackwell, Oxford

Faucher, T., and Lorber, C. (2010), 'Bronze Coinage of Ptolemaic Egypt in the Second Century BC', *AJN* (1989–), vol. 22, 35–80

Fischer-Bovet, C. (2014), *Army and Society in Ptolemaic Egypt*, CUP, Cambridge

Fischer-Bovet, C. (2015), 'Social Unrest and Ethnic Coexistence in Ptolemaic Egypt and the Seleucid Empire', *Past & Present*, no. 229 (Nov.), 3–45

Fischer-Bovet, C. (2020), *Soldiers in the Epigraphy of Ptolemaic Egypt*, in Bowman and Crowther (2020), 127–58

Fischer-Bovet, C., and Clarysse, W. (2012), 'A Military Reform before the Battle of Raphia?', *Archiv für Papyrusforschung und verwandte Gebiete*, vol. 58, no. 1, 26–35

Fischer-Bovet, C., and von Reden, S. (2021), *Comparing the Ptolemaic and Seleucid Empires: Integration, Communication, and Resistance*, CUP, Cambridge

Fletcher, J. (2008), *Cleopatra the Great*, Hodder & Stoughton, London

Foertmeyer, V. (1988), 'The Dating of the Pompe of Ptolemy II Philadelphus', *Hist: ZfAG*, Bd. 37, H. 1 (1988), 90–104

Fox, R.L. (2004), *Alexander the Great*, Penguin, London

Fraser, P.M. (1972), *Ptolemaic Alexandria*, vols I–III, Clarendon Press, Oxford

Fraser, P.M., and Rumpf, A. (1952), 'Two Ptolemaic Dedications', *JEA*, vol. 38 (Dec.), 65–74

Gardiner, A. (1994), *Egyptian Grammar: Being an Introduction to the Study of Hieroglyphs* (3rd edition), Griffith Institute, Ashmolean Museum, Oxford

Gibbon, E. (1776–88), *History of the Decline and Fall of the Roman Empire* (numerous editions)

Goodchaux, G.W. (2001), 'Cleopatra's Subtle Religious Strategy', in Walker and Higgs (2001), 128–41

Goudriaan, K. (1992), 'Ethnical Strategies in Graeco-Roman Egypt', in Bilde et al. (1992), 74–99

Goudriaan, K. (1998), *Ethnicity in Ptolemaic Egypt*, Brill, Leiden

Grainger, J.D. (2022), *The Ptolemies, Rise of a Dynasty: Ptolemaic Egypt 330–246 BC*, Pen & Sword, Barnsley

Grant, D. (2017), *In Search of the Lost Testament of Alexander the Great*, Matador, Kibworth Beauchamp

Grant, D. (2021), *The Last Will and Testament of Alexander the Great: The Truth Behind the Death that Changed the Graeco-Persian World Forever*, Pen & Sword, Barnsley

Grant, M. (1982), *From Alexander to Cleopatra*, Weidenfield & Nicolson, London

Gray-Fow, M. (2014), 'What to do with Caesarion', *Greece & Rome*, Second Series, vol. 61, no. 1 (Apr.), 38–67

Gruen, E. (2009), 'Hebraism and Hellenism', in Boys-Stones et al. (2009), 129–39

Habicht, C. (1992), 'Athens and the Ptolemies', *Classical Antiquity*, vol. 11, no. 1 (Apr.), 68–90

Heinz, S.S., and van der Wilt, V.M. (2019), 'Defining the Foundation Deposit in the Late and Ptolemaic Periods', *JEA*, vol. 105, no. 2 (Dec.), 227–42

Hölbl, G. (2001), *A History of the Ptolemaic Empire*, Routledge, Abingdon

Honigman, S. (2022), 'Migration Patterns from Palestine to Egypt in Ptolemaic Times', *AncSoc*, vol. 52, 171–205

Honigman, S., and Veïsse, A-E. (2021), 'Regional Revolts in the Seleucid and Ptolemaic Empires', in Fischer-Bovet and von Reden (2021), 301–28

Hornblower, S. (2020), 'The Corpus of Ptolemaic Inscriptions: The Metrical Texts', in Bowman and Crowther (2020), 208–25

Hornung, E. (1999), *The Ancient Egyptian Books of the Afterlife*, Cornell University Press, Ithaca

Huss, W. (2001), *Ägypten in hellenistischer Zeit. 332–30 v. Chr.*, C.H. Beck, Munich

Iossif, P.P., and Lorber, C. (2021), 'Monetary Policies, Coin Production, and Currency Supply', in Fischer-Bovet and von Reden (2021), 191–230

Jacoby, F. (1923–58), *Die Fragmente der griechischen Historiker*, I–III, Brill, Leiden (and later editions)

Johnson, C.G. (1995), 'Ptolemy V and the Rosetta Decree: The Egyptianization of the Ptolemaic Kingship', *AncSoc*, vol. 26, 145–55

Johnson, C.G. (1999), 'The Divinization of the Ptolemies and the Gold Octadrachms Honoring Ptolemy III', *Phoenix*, vol. 53, no. 1/2 (Spring–Summer), 50–6

Johnson, C.G. (2002), '"Ogis" 98 and the Divinization of the Ptolemies', *Hist: ZfAG*, Bd. 51, H. 1 (1st Qtr), 112–16

Johstono, P. (2020), *The Army of Ptolemaic Egypt 323 to 204 BC: An Institutional and Operational History*, Pen & Sword, Barnsley

Jones, P. (1993), 'The Decree of Ilion in Honor of a King Antiochus', *Greek, Roman, and Byzantine Studies*, vol. 34, no. 1, 73–92

Kay, P. (2014), *Rome's Economic Revolution*, OUP, Oxford

Kemp, B.J. (1989), *Ancient Egypt: Anatomy of a Civilization*, Routledge, London

Knopf, F. (2023), 'Ptolemaic Royal Decrees between Strong and Weak Statehood: Two Ordinances of Ptolemy II on Livestock and Slaves in the Southern Levant', in Krüger et al. (2023), 107–32

Krüger, D., Mohamad-Klotzbach, C., and Pfeilschifter, R. (eds) (2023), *Local Self-Governance in Antiquity and in the Global South: Theoretical and Empirical Insights from an Interdisciplinary Perspective*, De Gruyter, Berlin

La'da, C.A. (1994), 'Ethnicity, Occupation and ax-status in Ptolemaic Egypt', *Egitto e Vicino Oriente*, vol. 17, ACTA DEMOTICA: Acts of Fifth International Conference for Demotists: Pisa, 4–8 September 1993, 183–9

Lanciers, E. (1988) 'Die Alleinherrschaft des Ptolemaeus VIII. im Jahr 164/63 v. Chr. und der Name Euergetes', in Mandilaras, B.G. et al. (eds), *Proceedings of the XVIII International Congress of Papyrology*, Athens, 25–31 May 1986, vol. II, 405–33

Lanciers, E. (2014), 'The Shrines of Hathor and Amenhotep in Western Thebes in the Ptolemaic Period', *AncSoc*, vol. 44, 105–25

Lanciers, E. (2019a), 'Cleopatra III's Marriage with Ptolemy VIII and the Start of her Queenship: Notes on some Greek and Demotic Sources', *ZPE*, Bd. 210, 194–200

Lanciers, E. (2019b), 'Antaios, a Ptolemaic "Strategos" of Alexandria', *BASP*, vol. 56, 225–31

Lanciers, E. (2020), 'The Evolution of the Court Titles of the Ptolemaic Dioiketes in the Second Century', *AncSoc*, vol. 50, 99–128

Landvatter, T. (2012), 'The Serapis and Isis Coinage of Ptolemy IV', *AJN*, vol. 24, 61–90

Landvatter, T. (2013), 'Burial Practices and Ritual Landscapes at Ptolemaic Abydos: The 2011 and 2012 Seasons of the Abydos Middle Cemetery Project', *Near Eastern Archaeology*, vol. 76, no. 4 (Dec.), 235–45

Lembke, K. (2012), 'City of the Dead: Tuna el-Gebel', in Riggs (ed.) (2012), 205–22

Lenzo, G. (2015), 'A Xoite Stela of Ptolemy VIII Euergetes II with Cleopatra II and Cleopatra III', *JEA*, vol. 101 (2015), 217–37

Lewis, N. (1986), *Greeks in Ptolemaic Egypt*, OUP, Oxford

Llewellyn-Jones, L., and Winder, S. (2016), 'The Hathoric Model of Queenship in Early Ptolemaic Egypt: The Case of Berenike's Lock', in Rutherford (2016), 139–62

Lloyd, A.B. (2000), 'The Late Period (664–332 BC)', in Shaw (2000), 369–94

Lloyd, A.B (ed.) (2014), *A Companion to Ancient Egypt*, Blackwell Companions to the Ancient World, Wiley-Blackwell, Chichester

Lorber, C. (2012), 'Dating the Portrait Coinage of Ptolemy I', *AJN*, vol. 24, 33–44

Lorber, C. (2016), 'The Coinage of the Ptolemies', in Metcalf (2016), 211–34

Manning, J.G. (2003), *Land and Power in Ptolemaic Egypt: The Structure of Land Tenure*, CUP, Cambridge

Manning, J.G. (2004), 'Property Rights and Contracting in Ptolemaic Egypt', *Journal of Institutional and Theoretical Economics (JITE) / Zeitschrift für die gesamte Staatswissenschaft*, vol. 160, no. 4 (Dec.), 758–64

Manning, J.G. (2010), *The Last Pharaohs: Egypt under the Ptolemies, 305–30 BC*, Princeton University Press, Princeton

Manning, J.G., Ludlow, F., Stine, A.R., Boos, W.R., Sigl, M., and Marlon, J.R. (2017), 'Volcanic Suppression of Nile Summer Flooding Triggers Revolt and Constrains Interstate Conflict in Ancient Egypt', *Nature Communications*, no. 8, article number: 900 (doi: 10.1038/s41467-017-00957-y)

Mao, Y. (2001), 'A Technical Examination of Three Ptolemaic Faience Vessels', *Journal of the Walters Art Museum*, vol. 59, *Focus on the Collections*, 17–22

Matheson, S.B. (2018), 'Ptolemy VIII Returns to Yale', *Yale University Art Gallery Bulletin*, Recent Acquisitions, 80–7

McKenzie, J.S., Gibson, S., and Reyes, A.T. (2004), 'Reconstructing the Serapeum in Alexandria from the Archaeological Evidence', *Journal of Roman Studies*, vol. 94, 73–121

Merriam, A.C. (1886), 'Egyptian Antiquities. I. Two Ptolemaic Inscriptions; II. Mummy Tablets', *American Journal of Archaeology and of the History of the Fine Arts*, vol. 2, no. 2 (Apr.–Jun.), 149–54

Metcalf, W. (ed.) (2016), *The Oxford Handbook of Greek and Roman Coinage*, OUP, Oxford

Millar, F. (1981), *The Roman Empire and Its Neighbours*, Duckworth, London

Minas, M. (2005), 'Macht und Ohnmacht: Die Repräsentation ptolemäischer Königinnen in ägyptischen Tempeln', in *Archiv für Papyrusforschung und verwandte Gebiete*, vol. 51, 127–54

Minas-Nerpel, M. (2011), 'Cleopatra II and III: The Queens of Ptolemy VI and VIII as Guarantors of Kingship and Royal Power', in Jördens, A., and Quack, J.F. (eds), *Ägypten zwischen innerem Zwist und äußerem Druck: Die Zeit Ptolemaeus' VI. bis VIII*. Internationales Symposion Heidelberg, 16–19 September 2007 (Philippika 45), Wiesbaden, 58–76

Mitteis, L., and Wilcken, U. (1963), *Grundzüge und Chrestomathie der Papyruskunde*, G. Olms, Hildesheim

Monson, A. (2012), *From the Ptolemies to the Romans: Political and Economic Change in Egypt*, CUP, Cambridge

Montserrat, D. (2000), *Akhenaten*, Routledge, London

Moyer, I.S. (2011), 'Court, "Chora", and Late Ptolemaic Egypt', *American Journal of Philology*, vol. 132, no. 1 (Spring), *Classical Courts and Courtiers*, 15–44

Muhs, B. (2018), 'The Institutional Models for Ptolemaic Royal Banks and Granaries', *AncSoc*, vol. 48, 83–101

Muhs, B.P., Scalf, F.D., and Jay, J.E. (2021), *The Archive of Thotsutmis, Son of Panouphis, Early Ptolemaic Ostraca from Deir El Bahari (O. Edgerton)*, Oriental Institute Publications (Institute for the Study of Ancient Cultures), Chicago

Murray, O. (1970), 'Hecataeus of Abdera and Pharaonic Kingship', *JEA*, vol. 56 (Aug.), 141–71

Nadig, P. (2020), 'Ptolemy VII Neos Philopator', *Encyclopaedia of Ancient History*, Wiley Online Library (https://doi.org/10.1002/9781444338386.wbeah07093.pub2)

Naunton, C. (2018), *Searching for the Lost Tombs of Egypt*, T&H, London

Nespoulous-Phalippou, A. (2015), *Le Décret de Memphis (182 a.C.)*, Édition commentée des stèles Caire RT 2/3/25/7 et JE 44901, Université Paul-Valéry, Montpellier

Nifosi, A. (2022), 'The Throw of Isis-Aphrodite: A Rare Decorated Knucklebone from the Metropolitan Museum of New York', *JEA*, vol. 102, 177–89

O'Neil, J.L. (2006), 'Places and Origin of the Officials of Ptolemaic Egypt', *Hist: ZfAG*, Bd. 55, H. 1, 16–25

Paganini, M.C.D. (2020), 'Epigraphic Habits of Private Associations in the Ptolemaic *Chora*', in Bowman and Crowther (2020), 127–58

Paganini, M.C.D. (2021), *Gymnasia and Greek Identity in Ptolemaic Egypt*, OUP, Oxford

Parsons, P. (2007), *City of the Sharp-Nosed Fish: Greek Lives in Roman Egypt*, Weidenfield & Nicolson, London

Parsons, P. (2011), 'Callimachus and his *Koinaï*', in Acosta-Hughes, B., Lehnus, L., and Stephens, S. (2011), *Brill's Companion to Callimachus*, Brill's Companions to Classical Studies, Brill, Leiden and Boston, 134–52

Pestman, P.W. (1965), 'Harmachis et Anchmachis, deux rois indigènes du temps des Ptolémées', *Chronique d'Égypte*, vol. 40, 157–70

Pestman, P.W. (1993), *The Archive of the Theban Choachytes (Second Century B.C.): A Survey of the Demotic and Greek Papyri Contained in the Archive*, Studia Demotica 2, Peeters, Leuven

Pestman, P.W., Quaegebeur, J., and Vos, R.L. (1977), *Recueil de textes démotiques et bilingues*, Brill, Leiden

Petrie, W.M.F. (1902), 'A Foundation-Deposit Inscription from Abydos', *Journal of Hellenic Studies*, vol. 22, 377

Pfeiffer, S., and Klinkott, H. (2021), 'Legitimizing the Foreign King in the Ptolemaic and Seleucid Empires: The Role of Local Elites and Priests (8A The Egyptian Priests and the Ptolemaic King)', in Fischer-Bovet and von Reden (2021), 235–45

Pincock, R. (2012), 'Are There Denominational Indicators on Ptolemaic Bronze Coins?', *Numismatic Chronicle*, vol. 172, 35–46

Porter, B., and Moss, R.L.B. (1960–), *Topographical Bibliography of Ancient Egyptian Hieroglyphic Texts, Reliefs, and Paintings*, Second Edition, Revised and Augmented, 3 vols, Clarendon Press, Oxford

Potter, D.M. (2021), 'The Statue of a Sistrum-Player in Montrose and Her Position in an Early Ptolemaic Theban Priestly Family', *JEA*, vol. 7, issue 1–2, 249–63

Préaux, C. (1936), 'Esquisse d'une histoire des révolutions égyptiennes sous les Lagides', *Chronique d'Égypte*, vol. 11, 522–52

Quack, J.F. (2017), 'The So-Called Demotic Chronicle', *Originalveröffentlichung*, in Lawson Younger, K., Jr (ed.), *The Context of Scripture 4, Supplements*, Leiden, Boston, 27–32 (https://doi.org/10.11588/propylaeumdok.00005331)

Quaegebeur, J. (1989), 'Une scène historique méconnu au grand temple d'Edfou', in Criscuolo, I., and Geraci, G. (eds) (1989), *Egitto e storia antica dall'Ellenismo all'età araba. Bilancio di un confronto*, Bologna, 462–72

Ray, J.D. (1976), *The Archive of Hor*, Egypt Exploration Society, London

Reymond, I. (1981), *From the Records of a Priestly Family from Memphis*, vol. I, Ägyptologische Abhandlungen, Bd. 38, Otto Harrassowitz, Wiesbaden

Ricketts, C. (1979), 'A Chronological Problem in the Reign of Cleopatra VII', *BASP*, vol. 16, no. 3, 213–17

Ricketts, C. (1990), 'A Dual Queenship in the Reign of Berenice IV', *BASP*, vol. 27, no. 1/4, 49–60

Riggs, C. (2002), 'Facing the Dead: Recent Research on the Funerary Art of Ptolemaic and Roman Egypt', *American Journal of Archaeology*, vol. 106, no. 1 (Jan.), 85–101

Riggs, C. (2010), 'Funerary Rituals (Ptolemaic and Roman Periods), *UCLA Encyclopaedia of Egyptology* (https://escholarship.org/content/qt1n10x347/qt1n10x347.pdf)

Riggs, C. (ed.) (2012), *The Oxford Handbook of Roman Egypt*, OUP, Oxford

Rochemonteix, Marquis de (1892–7), *Le temple d'Edfou*, vol. 1, Chassinat, Paris

Roehrig, C. (ed.) (2005), *Hatshepsut: From Queen to Pharaoh*, Metropolitan Museum of Art, New York, Yale University Press, New Haven

Roller, D.W. (2010), *Cleopatra: A Biography*, OUP, Oxford

Rösler, W. (2009), 'Books and Literacy', in Boys-Stones et al. (2009), 432–41

Rossini, A. (2022), 'Letters from Ptolemy VIII, Cleopatra II, and Cleopatra III Concerning the Gymnasium of Omboi', *Axon*, vol. 62 (Dec.), 113–52

Roth, A.M. (2005), 'Models of Authority: Hatshepsut's Predecessors in Power', in Roehrig (2005), 9–14

Ruffle, J., Gaballa, G.A., and Kitchen, K.A. (eds) (1979), *Glimpses of Ancient Egypt: Studies in Honour of F.W. Fairman*, Aris and Phillips, Warminster

Russman, E.R. (2005), 'Art in Transition: The Rise of the Eighteenth Dynasty and the Emergence of the Thutmoside Style in Sculpture and Relief', in Roehrig (2005), 23–7

Rutherford, I. (2016), 'Introduction: Interaction and Translation between Greek Literature and Egypt', in Rutherford, I. (2016) (ed.), *Greco-Egyptian Interactions: Literature, Translation, and Culture 500 BCE–300 CE*, OUP, Oxford

Sachs, A.J., and Hunger, H. (1988), *Astronomical Diaries and Related Texts from Babylonia*, vol. I (Diaries from 652–261 BC), Verlag der Österreichischen Akademie der Wissenschaften, Vienna

Salmenkivi, E. (2012), 'Herakleopolite meridarchs in the first century BC?', *Accueil*, vol. 30

Saunders, N. (2006), *Alexander's Tomb: Two Thousand Years in Search of the Lost Conqueror*, Basic Books, New York

Savvopoulos, K. (2020), 'Religious Life in Ptolemaic Alexandria under the Royal Aegis: An Overview of the Epigraphic Evidence', in Bowman and Crowther (2020), 76–93

Scheidel, W. (2001), *Death on the Nile: Disease and the Demography of Roman Egypt*, Brill, Leiden

Schreiber, G., Vasáros, Z., and Almásy, A. (2013), 'Ptolemaic and Roman Burials from Theban Tomb 400', *Mitteilungen des Deutschen Archäologischen Instituts Kairo*, vol. 69 (2013), Abbildungen, 187–226

Schulman, A.R. (1957), 'Egyptian Representations of Horsemen and Riding in the New Kingdom', *JNES*, vol. 16, no. 4, 263–71

Schuster, A. (1999), 'Mapping Alexandria's Royal Quarters', *Archaeology*, vol. 52, no. 2 (Mar./Apr.), 44–6

Scullard, H.H. (1982), *From the Gracchi to Nero*, Routledge, London

Sear, D.R. (1978), *Greek Coins and Their Values. Volume 2: Asia and Africa*, Spink, London

Sear, D.R. (2000), *Roman Coins and Their Values. Volume 1: The Republic and the Twelve Caesars 280 BC–AD 96*, Spink, London

Segre, A. (1942), 'The Ptolemaic Copper Inflation *c.* 230–140 BC', *American Journal of Philology*, vol. 63, no. 2, 174–92

Seton-Williams, M.V. (1978), *Ptolemaic Temples*, Waterloo Printing, London

Shaw, I. (ed.) (2000), *The Oxford History of Ancient Egypt*, OUP, Oxford

Siani-Davies, M. (1997), 'Ptolemy XII Auletes and the Romans', *Hist: ZfAG*, Bd. 46, H. 3 (3rd Qtr), 306–40

Skarsouli, E. (2020), 'Some Remarks on the Use of ευλαβέομαι and φοβέομαι in Greek Documentary Papyri and in Literary Texts', Spudasmata, vol. 188, *Writing Order and Emotion: Affect and the Structures of Power in Greek and Latin Authors*, 47–64

FURTHER READING

Skeat, T.C. (1966), 'A Fragment on the Ptolemaic Perfume Monopoly (P. Lond. Inv. 2859A)', *JEA*, vol. 52 (Dec.), 179–80

Skeat, T.C., and Turner, E.G. (1968), 'An Oracle of Hermes Trismegistos at Saqqâra', *JEA*, vol. 54 (Aug.), 199–208

Skuse, M. (2017), 'Coregency in the Reign of Ptolemy II', *JEA*, vol. 103, no. 1 (June), 89–101

Snape, S. (2014), *The Complete Cities of Ancient Egypt*, T&H, London

Spiegelberg, W. (1930), 'Eine neue Erwähnung eines Aufstandes in Oberägypten in der Ptolemäerzeit', *Zeitschrift für ägyptische Sprache und Altertumskunde*, vol. 65, 53–7, Taf. 5

Stanley, J.-D., and Toscano, M.A. (2009), 'Ancient Archaeological Sites Buried and Submerged Along Egypt's Nile Delta Coast: Gauges of Holocene Delta Margin Subsidence', *Journal of Coastal Research*, vol. 25, no. 1 (Jan.), 158–70

Stanwick, P. (2003), *Portraits of the Ptolemies: Greek Kings as Egyptian Pharaohs*, University of Texas Press, Austin

Svoronos, J. (1904–8), Τα Νομισματα του Κρατους των Πτολεμαιων (*The Coins of the Ptolemaic Kings*), Sakellarios, Athens

Taylor, J.H. (2001), *Death and the Afterlife in Ancient Egypt*, British Museum, London

Thomas, S.E. (2012), 'Two Wooden Tablet Receipts for the Ptolemaic Vineyard Tax (Apomoira): T Norwich 1921.37.51.1 and 1921.37.51.2', *ZPE*, Bd. 193, 209–18

Thompson, D.J. (1987), 'Ptolemaeus and the "Lighthouse": Greek Culture in the Memphite Serapeum', *Proceedings of the Cambridge Philological Society*, New Series, no. 33 (213), 105–21

Thompson, D.J. (1988), *Memphis under the Ptolemies*, Princeton University Press, Princeton

Thompson, D.J. (2003), 'The Ptolemies and Egypt', in Erskine (2003), 105–20

Thompson, D.J. (2009), 'Ptolemy VIII', *Classical Review*, New Series, vol. 59, no. 1 (Apr.), 203–5, reviewing *Zwischen König und Karikatur. Das Bild Ptolemaeus' VIII*, in Nadig, P., *Spannungsfeld der Überlieferung*

Thompson, D.J. (2020), 'Foundation Deposits from Third Century BC Egypt', in Bowman and Crowther (2020), 94–113

Tomlinson, R.A. (2007), 'From Houses to Tenements: Domestic Architecture in Hellenistic Alexandria', British School at Athens Studies, vol. 15, *Building Communities: House, Settlement and Society in the Aegean and Beyond*, 307–11

Török, L. (2009), *Between Two Worlds: The Frontier Region Between Ancient Nubia and Egypt, 3700 BC–AD 500*, Brill, Leiden and New York

Toynbee, J.M.C. (1996), *Death and Burial in the Roman World*, Johns Hopkins University Press, Baltimore (reprint of Cornell University Press edition, 1971)

Tracy, S.V. (2000), 'Demetrius of Phalerum: Who Was He and Who Was He Not?', in Fortenbaugh, W.W., and Schütrumpf, E. (eds), *Demetrius of Phalerum*, Rutgers University Studies in Classical Humanities, vol. IX, New Brunswick, 331–45

Tunny, J. (2000), 'Ptolemy "The Son" Reconsidered: Are There Too Many Ptolemies?', *ZPE*, Bd. 131, 83–92

Turner, E.G. (1984), 'Ptolemaic Egypt', *Cambridge Ancient History*, vol. VII, part 1, CUP, Cambridge, chapter 5

Tyldesley, J. (2006), *Chronicle of the Queens of Egypt: From Early Dynastic Times to the Death of Cleopatra*, T&H, London

Uggetti, L. (2018), *Les archives bilingues de Totoès et de Tatéhathyris*, doctoral thesis, PSL Research University

van Heel, K.D., Hoogendijk, F.A.J., and Martin, C.J. (2018), *Hieratic, Demotic and Greek Studies and Text Editions. Of Making Many Books There Is No End: Festschrift in Honour of Sven P. Vleeming* (P.L. Bat. 34), Brill, Leiden

van Minnen, P. (2000), 'An Official Act of Cleopatra (with a Subscription in her own Hand)', *AncSoc*, vol. 30, 29–34

van Oppen de Ruiter, B.F. (2010), 'The Death of Arsinoe II Philadelphus: The Evidence Reconsidered', *ZPE*, Bd. 174, 139–50

va Oppen de Ruiter, B.F. (2011), 'The Marriage of Ptolemy I and Berenice I', *AncSoc*, vol. 41, 83–92

van Oppen de Ruiter, B.F. (2015), *Berenice II Euergetis: Essays in Early Hellenistic Queenship*, Palgrave Macmillan, New York

Van 't Dack, E. (1973), 'Les commandants de place lagides à Théra', *AncSoc*, vol. 4, 71–90

Vandorpe, K. (2007), 'Agriculture, Temples and Tax Law in Ptolemaic Egypt', in Moreno García, J.C. (ed.), *L'agriculture institutionnelle en Égypte ancienne: État de la question et perspectives interdisciplinaires*, Villeneuve d'Ascq, 165–71

Vandorpe, K. (2014), 'The Ptolemaic Period', in Lloyd (2014), 159–79

Vandorpe, K., and Vanopré, L. (2020), 'Private and Commercial Pigeon Breeding Taxed: Ptolemaic Levies on Pigeon Houses and their Revenues', *AncSoc*, vol. 50, 41–64

von den Hoff, R. (2021), 'The Visual Representation of Ptolemaic and Seleucid Kings: A Comparative Approach to Portrait Concepts', in Fischer-Bovet and von Reden (2021), 164–90

Walker, S., and Bierbrier, M. (1997), *Ancient Faces: Mummy Portraits from Roman Egypt*, British Museum Press, London

Walker, S., and Higgs, P. (eds) (2001), *Cleopatra of Egypt: From History to Myth*, British Museum Press, London

Waterfield, R. (2021), *The Making of a King: Antigonus Gonatas of Macedon and the Greeks*, OUP, Oxford

Watson, P. (2014), *A Brief Introduction to Egyptian Coins and Currency*, AuthorHouse, Bloomington

Watterson, B. (1979), 'The Use of Alliteration in Ptolemaic [Egyptian]', in Ruffle et al. (1979), 167–9

Westermann, W.L. (1929), *Upon Slavery in Ptolemaic Egypt*, Columbia University Press, New York

Wilkinson, R.H. (2000), *The Complete Temples of Ancient Egypt*, T&H, London

Wilkinson, T. (2010), *The Rise and Fall of Ancient Egypt*, Bloomsbury, London

Wong, J.K.W. (1995), *Cleopatra I: The First Ptolemaic Female Regent, Her Predecessors, Policies, and Precedents*, Master of Arts thesis, University of British Columbia

Worthington, I. (2016), 'Ptolemy I as Soter: The Silence of Epigraphy and the Case for Egypt', *ZPE*, Bd. 198, 128–30

Zientek, L. (2017), 'The Pharos of Alexandria: A Man-Made "Mountain" in Lucan's Bellum Civile', *Illinois Classical Studies*, vol. 42, no. 1 (Spring), 141–61

ACKNOWLEDGEMENTS

Many thanks to Heather McCallum at Yale who enthusiastically took on this book; her colleagues, Rachael Lonsdale, Katie Urquhart, and Lucy Buchan, for seeing the book through to press; copy-editor Robert Sargant; and the anonymous academic readers for their invaluable suggestions. My very patient friend Norah Cooper laboured through the first and later drafts picking out my grammatical and spelling mistakes, as well as pointing out passages that needed clarification. Chris Dickinson of the Ancient Egyptian Society of Western Australia generously read a whole early draft, making several important observations for which I am very grateful. Professor Joann Fletcher kindly fielded my questions about various topics, including Ptolemaic burial practices. Dr Bill Manley enlightened me with his reading of Cleopatra I's titles at Edfu, as well as offering general encouragement. As ever, my wife Rosemary has endured yet another of my book projects, being prepared to participate in a research tour of Middle Egypt as well as other visits to the Nile Valley and museums.

INDEX

Note that for place names the modern name has been prioritized where those places are most familiarly known by that form today, such as Edfu and Kom Ombo. In other instances, the ancient name is given, with the modern equivalent (if there is one) in parentheses.

INDEX

ethnicity 100, 102, 115, 126, 136, 140, 147, 189, 207, 251, 304, *see also* pseudo-ethnicity
Euclid, mathematician 117
Euergetes, Ptolemy III and Berenice II's title 86, 91
Eulaeus 195–9, 287, plate 10
Eumenes II of Pergamum 187, 196–7
Eunostus (western harbour of Alexandria) 114, 116
Eurydice, daughter of Antipater and wife of Ptolemy, son of Lagus 59–60, 64
Eurydice II, *see* Adea Eurydice II
Eurylochus of Magnesia, military commander of Agathocles and Sosibius 100
Eusebius, historian 10

family trees of: Antigonids 294; Argaeads 294; Cleopatra VII 296; Ptolemies 291–3, 6; Seleucids 295
famine 3, 128, 261, 271
favouritism, shown to Greeks with tax exemptions 132
Fayum, oasis 4, 72, 101–2, 114, 129, 131, 134–6, 139, 144–7, 159, 190, 203–4, 214, 236, 264, 300, 304
fertilizer, pigeon's droppings used for 133
festivals 143, 145; Antiochus III 182; Arsinoe II 72; Demeter Thesmophorus 181; Dionysus 98; Edfu 153–4; Kom Ombo 154; Kypranda 131; Ptolemaieia 80; Ptolemy III and Berenice II 91, 92; Ptolemy IV 104; Scipio Africanus 175
Flagon-Bearing celebration, cult of Dionysus 98
floods, *see* inundation
forts 39, 242–3, 280
foundation deposits, of temples 90–1, 122
Four Sons of Horus 160
Frontinus, Sextus Julius, Roman senator 39, 77
Fulvia, wife of Antony 271–2

Gabinius, Aulus, governor of Syria 257–8, 266

Galaistes, Ptolemaic commander 222
Galaton, painter 106
Gauls, Galatian 68, 75, 87, 100; Insubrian 174
Gaza xvi, xvii, 3, 16–17, 42, 102–3, 183, 284
Germanicus, Roman general nephew of Tiberius 282
Gibbon, Edward 282
gift estates 131
gold mines 73
gooseherds, temple benefactors 147
Gracchus, Tiberius Sempronius, Roman reforming tribune 224, 288
grain and granaries 55, 91, 141, 144, 173, 197, 207, 213, 271, 280
Greece xii, 4, 7, 23, 40, 46, 58, 68, 72, 76, 85, 88–9, 96, 105, 114, 146, 192, 211, 213, 216, 222, 265, 272, 275, 286
Greek language, used in Ptolemaic Egypt 52, 69, 131, 140–1, 147, 160, 229, 235, 252, 262, 273–4, 297
gymnasia 115, 227–8, 240, 248, 252

Hadrian, Roman emperor 277, 282
Halicarnassus 46, 75
Hannibal, Carthaginian general 3, 94, 102, 104–5, 172, 175, 187, 285–6
Hapmen, his sarcophagus copied from that of Thutmose III 159
harbours, of Alexandria 114
Harmatelia, Brahmin city besieged by Alexander 32
Haroeris (Great Horus) 146, 154, plates 11, 16
Harpocrates (Horus the Child) 91
Harpoon nome 76
Harsiese (or Harsiesis, 'Horus, son of Isis'), Egyptian rebel leader 225–6
Harsinakht, coffin of 160, plate 18
Harsomptus, child of Horus and Hathor, worshipped at Edfu 151
Harwennefer (Greek: Haronnophris), Egyptian rebel king 144, 188, 206
Hathor 69, 71, 86, 97, 146–51, 153–4, 162, 270, *see also* Dendera
Hatshepsut, of the 18th Dynasty 69, 148, 262